W9-CPY-288

The Sociology of Education in Canada

SECOND EDITION

Critical Perspectives

Terry Wotherspoon

OXFORD
UNIVERSITY PRESS

1904 ❈ 2004

100 YEARS OF
CANADIAN PUBLISHING

OXFORD
UNIVERSITY PRESS

70 Wynford Drive, Don Mills, Ontario M3C 1J9
www.oup.com/ca

Oxford University Press is a department of the University of Oxford.
It furthers the University's objective of excellence in research, scholarship,
and education by publishing worldwide in

Oxford New York
Auckland Bangkok Buenos Aires Cape Town Chennai
Dar es Salaam Delhi Hong Kong Istanbul Karachi Kolkata
Kuala Lumpur Madrid Melbourne Mexico City Mumbai Nairobi
São Paulo Shanghai Taipei Tokyo Toronto

Oxford is a trade mark of Oxford University Press
in the UK and in certain other countries

Published in Canada
by Oxford University Press

National Library of Canada Cataloguing in Publication
Wotherspoon, Terry
   The sociology of education in Canada : critical perspectives /
Terry Wotherspoon. -- 2nd ed.
Includes bibliographical references and index.
ISBN 0-19-541903-0

1. Educational sociology--Canada. I. Title.

LC191.8.C2W67 2004   306.43'0971   C2003-907332-7

Cover design: Brett Miller
Cover image: Super Stock

1 2 3 4 - 07 06 05 04
This book is printed on permanent (acid-free) paper ∞.
Printed in Canada

Contents

List of Figures, Tables, and Boxes

Boxes

Preface

Developments that occur within and to education have a powerful impact on nearly everyone. Many of our formative experiences occur in preschool, kindergarten, and school. Increasingly larger numbers of Canadians are augmenting their elementary and secondary schooling by taking post-secondary, adult, and continuing education programs and by pursuing a wide range of alternative learning opportunities. Lifelong learning, marked by innovation, adaptability, and the capacity to manage vast amounts of information, is widely touted as the key to success in a globally competitive environment. Public scrutiny over education has produced varying answers to questions about what kinds of education we should promote, who should pay for it and who should control it, who should have access to it, and how it should be recognized.

Canadian education has undergone many promising developments, along with some disappointments, in the short period since the first edition of this book appeared. Education is regarded more seriously as the stakes associated with it rise, criticized heavily on some fronts and praised on others. Educational options have expanded dramatically even as some educational alternatives have been cut back. The benefits that can be derived from forms of learning that are inclusive, fun, and engaging are being rediscovered at the same time that learners are being subjected to more testing, scrutiny, procedures, and expectations that often generate frustration and stress. In the process, though, much educational debate is moving from entrenched positions based on uncritical acceptance of presumed truths to serious efforts to understand the strengths and limitations associated with various options and their consequences. There is an emerging impetus to engage in decision-making based on empirical findings from educational research, signified especially in the form of several major collaborative initiatives among researchers, policy bodies, and diverse educational communities.

This book argues that debates over educational futures must be informed by both awareness of how institutionalized forms of education have emerged historically and analysis of the practices and experiences that make contemporary education a complex and often contradictory endeavour. The book has been written with the recognition that much of my life has revolved around formal education, first as a student at various levels of study, later as a high school and junior high school teacher, and then as a university faculty member. Education and educational change remain challenging focal points for ongoing analysis due to their complexity and their significance for individuals and their societies.

My own observations, insights, and predispositions have been shaped directly and indirectly by many of the educators, students, colleagues, and communities that I have encountered over several years. I acknowledge, in particular, the contributions of several people whose efforts and support have been especially important in the writing and production of this book. My nascent efforts to understand and appreciate the nuances associated with educational matters have been broadened considerably by members of numerous research consortia and educational bodies that I have been fortunate to be associated with in Saskatchewan, across Canada, and elsewhere. My colleagues and students in the Department of Sociology at the University of Saskatchewan have provided a supportive environment to encourage ongoing debate, discussion, and scholarship. Jason Doherty and Beverly LaPointe provided extensive assistance in the preparation of the manuscript and supporting materials. Several other current or recent graduate students, including Joanne Butler, Kevin Shearer, and Darlene Lanceley, have provided useful commentary on the manuscript along with fresh insights into educational issues.

Megan Mueller provided the initial encouragement and support to guide the book to its new edition, nurtured to its final stages by Phyllis Wilson and Richard Tallman. I appreciate also the efforts of other persons at or associated with Oxford University Press Canada, and the manuscript reviewers, for providing direction and support.

This book is dedicated to Rachel and Nicole, whose futures rely heavily upon healthy educational environments.

1

The Sociological Analysis of Education

Introduction

Education is a vital part of our social existence. Whether it occurs in formal settings or in less formal ways, education helps to shape our personalities as well as our life choices and chances. In many respects, all of our experiences are educative in the sense that we continually engage in a process of self-development as we modify and recreate the world through our everyday activities. Education can be so highly integrated into our social environment that we give little thought to its nature and purposes. In Canada and throughout the world, education has come to take on greater significance as an essential component in an emerging information society that places a premium on knowledge and learning.

This chapter outlines the main themes that emerge through a critical examination of education, especially considered within sociological perspectives. Following a brief introduction to the discipline of sociology and the core questions and frameworks associated with sociological understandings, the chapter identifies four critical approaches to the analysis of education—critical pedagogy, feminist pedagogy, anti-racism education, and political economy—that inform the analysis employed throughout the book.

The Sociological Understanding of Educational Problems

Usually when we think of education, we identify it with formal institutions—schools, colleges, universities, and other structured institutional or learning processes. Viewed in these concrete terms, education tends to be associated

Box 1.1 Sociological interest in the growth and social significance of education

The growing significance of education for Canadians is illustrated in the figure below, which demonstrates how, over the past half-century, the share of the population with university degrees has overtaken that portion of the population with less than a grade 9 education. Sociologists have offered numerous interpretations of this educational growth, and have also examined its significance for society as a whole and for different subgroups within the population.

Proportions of the Canadian Population 15 Years and Over with University Degrees and Less Than Grade Nine

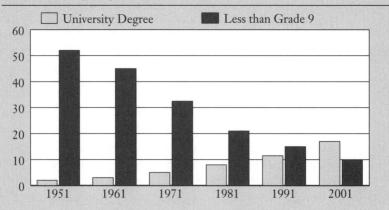

Sources: Data from Guppy and Davies (1998: 19) and Statistics Canada (2003i). This is an updated version based on a figure in Clarke (2000: 7).

with teachers, texts, and tests; knowledge, skills, and values; credentials, opportunities, and rewards; and policy, budget, and public representation. Consider the following questions:

- How and why has formal schooling come to be associated with education?
- Why are children and youth expected to attend schools for at least 10 years—and often much longer?
- Why do some people fail or drop out of school while others achieve success through post-secondary education?
- Why do most school classrooms have a readily identifiable character that distinguishes them from other social settings?
- Which social groups are served by educational institutions, and with what outcomes?
- How does teaching compare with other types of work?

- Why is Canadian education financed mostly by governments, and primarily by local, provincial, and territorial governments?
- What do people really learn at school, and how important is it for jobs and life outside of school?
- What impact do social, economic, and technological changes have on educational processes and achievement levels?
- Who decides what is in the curriculum and how is the curriculum translated into educational practice?

Each of these questions can be answered in many different ways. Canadians hold diverse opinions about many of them, as expressed in the high degree of controversy that has accompanied contemporary educational issues. Some answers involve historical facts or information that can be gathered through simple observation. Responses to other questions require more detailed data collected statistically, through interviews, or by other methodologies. Nearly all questions are subject to competing interpretations.

Sociology is a discipline or field of inquiry that provides particular frameworks through which we can make sense of questions like those outlined above as well as of the diverse responses that they generate. Sociologists are interested in education because it is so central to human social experience, to our direct and indirect relations with other people. Education, in its various guises, conveys important insights about particular kinds of societies and the people within them. The analysis of educational structures, practices, and outcomes can help us to understand, for example, what kinds of values, beliefs, and ideologies prevail in a given society, how people come to learn about and become organized within their social structures, and how open and democratic that society is.

The purpose of this book is to analyze Canadian educational practices, structures, and problems from a critical sociological framework. In many cases, international examples are employed to highlight the broader context within which Canadian education is situated. Emphasis within the book is on formal education or schooling, as opposed to other types of education, since it is in its institutional forms that education has become most highly integrated into wider social, economic, and political organization. Reference is made to a variety of sociological studies and perspectives developed within and beyond Canada to provide the reader with a sense of how distinct research traditions have been employed to understand schooling. However, the book's primary orientation is critical in nature so as to reveal how education in Canada has been from the outset a complex, contested, and contradictory endeavour. The book is not intended as a manual or an exhaustive history that details all aspects of our education systems. Instead, it employs analytical tools derived from sociology and related disciplines in an effort to answer questions about why education has developed as it has and how educational issues are interconnected with fundamental characteristics of social organization and social life. The remainder of this chapter examines the issues and approaches central to sociological analysis. The chapter concludes with a brief discussion of how these insights can be applied to educational questions in such a way as to provide a framework for the remaining chapters in this book.

Sociology and Its Relation To Other Disciplines

Sociology is the investigation of the relationships between individuals and society. It examines how social structures (relatively enduring patterns of social organization) and social practices (ongoing social activity) both shape and are shaped by human beings. It is a scientific discipline in the sense that it is based on research and theories that attempt, in a systematic and organized manner, to describe and explain important features of social reality. Sociologists analyze such institutions as schools, families, economic and political organizations, religion, the mass media, and the criminal justice system, as well as interpersonal relations, small groups, informal social practices, and much broader and sometimes less visible social forces, such as power and control.

In its scope and methods, sociology overlaps with and draws on several other disciplines and fields of inquiry. Sociology—or particular subfields of the discipline—can share much in common with such other social sciences as economics, political science, psychology, and anthropology, as well as with studies in the humanities such as history and philosophy, and with interdisciplinary studies in such areas as Native studies, women's studies, environmental studies, and regional studies. Some sociological work is influenced by and influences other fields of inquiry, including geography, biology, medicine, demography, and administrative studies.

Despite its complementarity with various academic disciplines, sociology developed from the vision of eighteenth- and nineteenth-century intellectuals, who wanted to construct a distinct science of society modelled after physics, biology, and other natural sciences. In common with closely related social sciences like psychology and economics, many of the tools that sociologists employ to examine the social world involve principles of research methodology and theory construction shared with scientists who study the natural world. However, the studies of the social and natural worlds differ in crucial ways. Social reality, complex and dynamic in nature, is not governed strictly by law-like regularities and it is not readily amenable to definitive statements about cause and effect that are the objective of much scientific inquiry. Social structures and practices are constantly being reshaped and reinterpreted by human activity. Moreover, the sociological investigator, as part of the social world being studied, may have an impact on social actions and how they are understood. Social research involves an ethical dimension that raises questions about what kinds of research activities are socially acceptable and what their consequences are for social life. These problems are shared by other sciences, since all scientific activity involves to some extent human interpretation, phenomena that are subject to change, and ethical questions, but they are much more evident within or central to sociology and other human sciences than in the scientific investigation of non-social phenomena.

With this wide array of influences, it might seem unusual that a discipline like sociology should exist, since most questions like the ones listed earlier can be investigated through one or more of the other disciplines. Two somewhat opposing points can be made in response to this concern. First, it is true that boundaries between disciplines are somewhat flexible, so that it may seem that the only clear distinction between areas is evident in the field by which people identify themselves (e.g., psychologists, educational administrators, and sociologists may all use similar methods to conduct research into the question of why some students drop out of school). The second point, however, involves the recognition that each discipline is constituted around core questions that can clearly be distinguished from one another. In the example noted above, the psychologist may be most interested in identifying the personality characteristics of school dropouts in comparison with students who stay in school; the researcher in educational administration may be most concerned with identifying ways to keep students in school longer; and the sociologist may be most interested in determining how characteristics of school organization contribute to the dropout phenomenon. The distinguishing characteristics of sociology are discussed below.

The Nature of Sociological Inquiry

Sociology, like most social sciences, emerged relatively recently compared to the humanities and physical sciences. A prolonged period of social, economic, and political upheaval in Europe, particularly during and after the mid-eighteenth century, fostered an interest in sustained inquiry into the nature of society and its relationship to the individual. The rapid advancement of the Industrial Revolution, combined with new social and political arrangements, led to serious questioning about the nature and consequences of social change. People's life experiences were altered amid challenges to existing social conventions and institutions. Among the transformations was a growing emphasis on democracy and individual rights as opposed to more traditional, hierarchical bases of social order. Out of these circumstances emerged both intellectual and pragmatic concerns to understand the conditions that produced social change, to assess the impact of the changes taking place, and to consider the possibilities and prospects for future social transformation. 'Sociology', a term first used by the French writer Auguste Comte in the nineteenth century to signify the need for a scientific study of society, was developed in order to study these issues by examining the relative impact of social stability and social change on people's lives.

Although the thematic focus and methodological substance of sociology have taken on different forms since Comte's time, many of the issues that concerned early sociologists remain at the core of the discipline. These issues are defined through responses to several fundamental questions that arise from analysis of the relations between individuals and society. Jenks (1998: 3) emphasizes the central focus of sociology, in these regards, as sensitivity to how practical social problems or issues can be understood in relation to a moral vision of a 'good society':

> All through our discipline's formative period sociologists selected their problems from the agenda of the day and treated them not simply as practical issues but also as moral issues, that is, as issues of value. . . . In the context of our society at the end of the twentieth century it is less and less easy to think about values that are shared or beliefs that are common. Sociology has adapted to this problem, in part, by beginning to find ways of addressing the personal experience of a whole range of different groups within the world of today. Now, even though we may not have abandoned our visions of the 'good society', as sociologists living in the present we tend to be concerned with more specific contexts.

Among the central questions that have given rise and remain fundamental to sociological inquiry and debate are the following:

1. At which level—individual or social—should analysis begin?
2. To what extent are individuals the products or the producers of social structures?
3. Is social life characterized more by social stability and consensus or by social conflict?
4. Should the study of society be concerned with the search for observable facts and laws (positivism) or by human interpretations of the world?

Individual versus Society

All sociological analysis is concerned at some level with relations among individuals and societies. Sociologists do not study individuals in isolation from one another, but focus instead on how people interact with each other either directly (at a face-to-face level) or indirectly (through internalized rules and expectations, the products of human activity, consciousness of others, and institutionalized patterns of behaviour). Different forms of sociological analysis emerge around questions about which factor or set of factors is regarded as most important.

The debate concerning the relations between individuals and society can be illustrated with reference to two key sociological theorists, Émile Durkheim and Max Weber, whose works were instrumental in establishing sociology as a viable academic discipline in the late nineteenth and early twentieth centuries. Durkheim defined sociology as the study of 'social facts', referring to features of society (such as rates of marriage or death, religion, law, and economic systems) that existed in their own right and had an influence on individuals' thoughts and actions. Society, in these terms, can be studied as if it is a real thing because it is present before we are born and after we die, and it affects the lives and character of each human being. Weber, by contrast, defined sociology as the 'interpretive understanding of social action', by which he meant that the discipline should emphasize how people's social decisions and behaviours are guided by interpretation or meaning. Unlike Durkheim, Weber argued that society has no independent existence outside of people's thoughts, motives, and actions (although human actions and creations have a powerful impact on our choices and actions). Posed in simpler terms, Durkheim represents a version of sociology in which the study of relations between individuals and society begins with society, while Weber's analysis begins with individuals and proceeds from there to study social relations. Contemporary sociologists continue to look to these starting points, or some intermediate position, as the basis for analyses.

Human Agency versus Structural Determination

An important question that accompanies the investigation of how individuals are interrelated with society concerns the role that free choice plays in our lives. Although we tend to think of ourselves as unique individuals, we must also recognize that our thoughts, personalities, and actions are heavily influenced by our social background and surroundings. Sociologists do not always agree about the extent to which individuals are shaped by social factors, and vice versa. One view, that of human agency, asserts that human beings are active 'agents' whose behaviour and thoughts make society possible. People are seen to be relatively free to make sense of the world in such a way as to make decisions that guide their lives and conduct. The world, according to this approach, is socially constructed—our language, cultures, and institutions are created, maintained, and changed through human activity.

A contrasting, structuralist, view emphasizes that people are social products. Social structures, or relatively enduring patterns within society and social life, give rise to our personalities and thoughts, to the choices we face, and to the courses we take in our lives. When we are born, existing social structures determine limitations and opportunities dependent on such factors as gender, race, the wealth and status of our parents, and so on. Our freedom, in other words, tends to be highly constrained by social rules and expectations.

Most sociologists and other social thinkers take a position somewhere between the two extremes of individual agency and structural determination. As Karl Marx (1963: 15) observed, people 'make their own history, but they do not make it just as they please; they do not make it under circumstances chosen by themselves, but under circumstances directly encountered, given and transmitted from the past.' A more contemporary sociologist, Anthony Giddens (1987: 11), has expressed the same point through what he calls 'the "double involvement" of individuals and institutions', in which 'we create society at the same time as we are created by it.' In other words, whatever their starting points, most sociologists agree that society is something more than a collection of individuals such that it must be studied with sensitivity to the reciprocal impact of human beings and social structures on each other.

Stability versus Conflict

As noted earlier, sociology emerged through systematic efforts to understand significant social changes occurring in conjunction with the Industrial Revolution and social upheaval. Some early social commentators feared that the changes were destructive of a social order that could never be retrieved while others welcomed the changes as a mark of progress and hope for the future. These dual concerns, of a search for social stability and a desire for social change and improvement, remain central to the discipline.

Sociologists continue to address these issues from different stances. Some sociologists, following the tradition of Auguste Comte, have attempted to uncover laws governing social order and conditions for social change. Their assumption is that stable social order, supported by consensus about fundamental values, is the normal state of a society. The development of sociology as a science, in these terms, is to identify factors that foster social harmony as opposed to those that are socially harmful or destructive. Excessive conflict and social change that proceeds too rapidly are deemed to threaten the long-term survival of a society. A contrasting approach to social analysis depicts conflict and struggle as normal features of societies. Societies, particularly if they are relatively complex in nature, are likely to contain a diversity of different collectivities and subgroups, each with specific needs and interests. Although overt conflict is not always present or apparent, social change is driven by the demands and actions of social groups to have their interests represented and their needs met. The task of sociology, in this view, is to identify and analyze the social circumstances that give rise to each set of interests.

Positivism versus Interpretative Analysis

There are different ways of looking at the world as well as of determining what should be looked at. The task of social science, for some sociologists, is to replicate, as much as possible, the rigorous approaches associated with physics, chemistry, and other scientific disciplines. The goal of science, understood this way, is to formulate laws and statements about regular patterns of cause and effect in the social world, and to specify the conditions under which these causal relations will occur. This approach, known as positivism, emphasizes that science must concern itself with phenomena that can be readily identified and measured. Like many scientists who study the natural world, these sociologists assume that the social world has a definite structure of reality that can be observed, classified, and controlled as we gain objective knowledge about each of its parts.

Other sociologists, by contrast, contend that positivism's claims to uncover objective knowledge about laws that regulate society are false. They argue that all human knowledge, including scientific observation, is based on particular interpretations of reality. Social reality, moreover, is continually being shaped and reshaped because it is based on human actions. For interpretative sociologists, therefore, the proper task of science is to identify the social bases and meanings attached to particular phenomena, and to explore how those meanings are related to people's social actions. This assessment, expressed in its most radical form within some postmodernist orientations, suggests that any scientific quest for universal truths or general laws is necessarily misguided because it does not take into account the diverse meanings and viewpoints that are characteristic of human life. Other interpretative sociology does not reject the possibility of science, but cautions that we must be aware of the limitations associated with science and the claims or authority that it carries with it.

Sociological Perspectives

Sociologists, like anyone else who investigates nature or society, must make decisions about what they study and how they study it. They require guidelines to help them focus their observations and make sense of what they see. In their most general form, these guidelines are provided in the form of what are called sociological perspectives, or ways of looking at the social world. Perspectives point to what is important, based on particular assumptions about social reality and how to study it.

Sociology, it should be emphasized, is not unique in offering perspectives to its practitioners. All sciences rely on specific assumptions that lead to different ways of conducting scientific investigation. In medical research, for example, some researchers emphasize the factors that cause a certain disorder so that appropriate cures or remedies can be prescribed, while others adopt a more holistic orientation that examines health in the context of a wide range of environmental conditions, which themselves must be modified before effective healing can take place. In physics, the study of quantifiable characteristics of matter is contrasted with the analysis of unobservable, changing forces. In all disciplines, perspectives identify ways to address these kinds of issues in a systematic manner.

It should be emphasized that sociologists share some common goals regardless of the perspectives they adopt. All theory is an attempt to enhance our ability to understand aspects of the social and natural worlds, and all research is conducted as part of an effort to provide us with information that tells us something about what those worlds are like. Scientific inquiry is unified by a search for knowledge and understanding, even though there are differences over how that search should be conducted, what the ultimate aim of that search should be, and what should be done with the information generated.

Sociological perspectives are aligned around questions governed by debates outlined in the preceding sections. Although there are different ways of labelling and organizing them, it is generally agreed that there are at least

three major sociological perspectives, identified here as structural functionalism, interpretative sociology, and critical sociology.

Structural Functionalism

Structural functionalist analysis examines social institutions and other elements of society in relation to the social system as a whole. It is sometimes
known as the order perspective because it is concerned with the maintenance
of social stability. As the name suggests, structural functionalism examines
phenomena by asking questions about what functions they serve and how
they contribute to the orderly operation of the social system. Formal education, for example, serves the social order by transmitting vital knowledge and
social aptitudes to successive generations and by sorting and selecting people
for entry into roles or positions required by the social system.

Structural functionalist analysis commonly employs an organic analogy in
which societies are compared to living organisms. Each part of the social system, like each feature of the organism, has specific roles to play to keep the
organism alive and functioning properly. Some functions are more crucial
than others to the unit's overall health and existence, but with increasing specialization, as the unit becomes more complex in nature, the system's survival
requires each element to be integrated with the others in a unified way.
Sociological analysis, as with the analysis of organic structures, proceeds to
describe these interrelationships and to identify the conditions required for
social stability. The long-term survival of society, according to this analysis,
requires that elements (whether individuals or institutional processes) that do
not fit with the whole, or are not functioning properly, must be eliminated
or modified, analogous to the Western medical treatment of a diseased body.

Although the perspective is highly abstract through its concern with general features of social systems, research conducted by structural functionalists tends to be positivistic in nature. It seeks to outline regular relationships
among phenomena through measurement of specific social dimensions, such
as degrees of socio-economic inequality, pupil dropout rates, or racial cate-
gorizations. In their assumptions that the social world has a definite, observable structure that can be made known through scientific investigation, structural functionalists often attempt to give sociology the status of a more
established natural science like physics or biology.

Structural functionalism has been highly influential in the development
of sociological theory and research. Its major contributions have been to
demonstrate the impact of social structures on social groups and individuals
and to point out how various components of societies are interrelated.
Nonetheless, the limitations of structural functionalism are evident in a critical examination of many of its central assumptions and procedures.

A first major criticism is most apparent to sociologists who adopt an interpretative orientation to social analysis. Structural functionalism, in its concern to 'map out' the social system and its constituent structures, ignores
much of the richness of everyday life. It is frequently open to the charge that

it portrays society in such a mechanistic way that it has no place for the activities and realities of living human beings, who in fact are the producers (or agents) of society and social change.

Critical sociologists have pointed to a second main limitation of structural functionalism: its emphasis on social order and consensus tends to undermine or draw attention away from struggles or tensions that operate within society. Many conflicts are more than merely transitional in nature; indeed, significant social divisions may be built into the structure of a given society. Therefore, inequalities and power struggles may be a normal rather than an abnormal occurrence. Social order, when it is evident, may itself be the consequence of political force rather than an indicator of widespread agreement about social goals. The use of coercion to achieve social stability is most obvious in societies ruled by totalitarian regimes, but it is a regular feature of life even in democratic societies. Taken together, these major criticisms sometimes portray structural functionalism as an approach limited by its attempts to impose order and control arbitrarily onto social circumstances rather than to subject them to sustained analytical inquiry.

Interpretative Analysis
Sociologists who work within interpretative traditions portray the social world as produced and interpreted by human activity. As the name of one important branch of interpretative sociology—symbolic interactionism—denotes, the main focal points for social analysis are social interactions and social symbols. People develop and share meanings with one another as they engage in social activity and attempt to make sense of their activity within a social context.

Interpretative sociology, in contrast with structural functionalism, is concerned with the analysis of social processes rather than social structures. Structures serve as guidelines for interaction that comes into being, and can be changed or modified through social activities. Individuals act, comprehend, and have motives; social structures do not. The world, viewed this way, is seen to be 'socially constructed' because the nature and meaning of social reality has no existence independent of our relations with other people, either at a face-to-face level or through the language, beliefs, knowledge, and modes of communication created and shared by people.

Because sociology and other scientific investigations are forms of social activity, scientific data and observations, like other social products, must be understood in terms of how they are processed by the human mind. Science, therefore, is subject to varying interpretations, as are other forms of social interaction. These insights do not mean that it is impossible to conduct scientific inquiry into the social world. Rather, our understanding of science (whether we are studying society or the natural world) must take into account the importance of human values and interpretations in shaping the world and how we see it.

Interpretative analysis is sometimes called microsociology because it is concerned with patterns of interaction at an everyday, interpersonal level, as opposed to the broader, macrosociological orientation of structural functionalism and much critical sociology. While it may seem that the individualistic starting point is not sociological because it does not focus on social structures, it is important to recognize that interpretative analysis studies individuals as participants in social interaction and shared meaning rather than as isolated units. The task of sociology, presented this way, is to help people develop a clear awareness of their own identities and subjectivity, their relations with others, and their place within society.

Interpretative sociology makes a valuable contribution to sociological analysis by showing the importance of our interactions with other people. It highlights the significance of everyday encounters and situations, and emphasizes how meanings are created and shared through social interaction. As opposed to structural forms of analysis that emphasize society at more abstract levels, it places active human beings at the core of sociological inquiry.

Despite its insights, interpretative sociology often fails to provide a comprehensive analysis of social life. The tendency within this approach to focus on immediate social settings is more oriented to description than to explanation. This ahistorical emphasis makes it relatively unable to explain problems such as how it is possible for enduring social inequalities to persist or how broad social positions and expectations may change. In the analysis of education, for example, an emphasis on interactions within the classroom is often unconnected with social structures and practices that shape the organization of the classroom, the curriculum, and the forces that condition the opportunities and experiences of the educational participants. Similarly, an acknowledgement that particular social circumstances and definitions are socially constructed does not necessarily indicate whose definitions are employed or what barriers stand in the way of attempts to introduce new definitions and social constructions.

Critical Sociology

Critical sociology is characterized frequently as an alternative to the traditional variants of sociology represented by structural functionalism and interpretative analysis. Critical analysis, as the term suggests, engages in a critique of social structures and practices by probing beyond descriptions of the status quo. The social world, as opposed to something neutral or mutually beneficial to all its members, is characterized by fundamental structural inequalities constituted in part by oppression by dominant groups over subordinate social groups. Critical sociology, in this regard, is committed to social change as well as to social analysis. This does not mean that the approach is unscientific. Instead, in common with interpretative approaches, it argues that science is a necessary human activity uncovering aspects of social reality that tend to be hidden from us in our everyday lives.

These characteristics can be illustrated with reference to two main branches of critical analysis, Marxism and feminism. Marxist analysis emphasizes that class, defined according to ownership and control of productive resources, is the fundamental basis of social inequality and oppression. Feminist analysis sees patriarchy, or male domination of personal and institutional life, as the primary basis of social differentiation. From different starting points, both Marxist and feminist approaches share the view that extensive analysis is required to uncover the dynamics and roots of social oppression and structured inequalities. Both theoretical stances also share a common commitment to changing repressive social conditions, although each contains varying assessments of the nature of, and strategies to advance, social change.

Despite this common ground, there are important differences among particular forms of critical analysis. Even general orientations to analysis such as Marxism and feminism contain sharply divergent approaches. Whereas radical feminism and orthodox Marxism, for example, disagree fundamentally about the origins of social oppression and how best to conduct social research, Marxist feminism and socialist feminism argue that the two approaches can be highly compatible.

Critical educational theories have been subject to recent challenges both internally and externally. Within critical analysis, proponents of various positions have often dismissed or ignored possibilities for shared insights such as an exploration of how factors like class, gender, and race interact with one another or an assessment of strategies for effective educational and social change. External pressures, including the backlash against feminism, the dissolution of Marxist regimes and loss of political support for socialist ideals, and debates over political correctness, have also posed questions about how applicable some critical theories are to a changing global order.

Several researchers, drawing on interpretative analysis as well as insights developed within other disciplines, have argued that no single approach is sufficient to provide an adequate understanding either of education or, more broadly, of human life in general (Davies, 1995; Kanpol, 1992). Postmodern thought, in particular, has emerged as a theoretical alternative suggesting that contemporary social life and personal experiences are so multi-dimensional and fragmented that no unified theory or set of ideas can adequately explain social reality. Despite these challenges, however, critical educational perspectives are able to demonstrate their resiliency when they identify issues and present analytical tools that not only advance our understanding of social problems but also seek to find effective solutions to them.

Emerging Directions in the Critical Analysis of Education

This book adopts a critical stance towards the analysis of education, in particular drawing on four interrelated forms of critical analysis that have influenced recent thinking about educational matters: critical pedagogy, feminist pedagogy, anti-racism education, and political economy. They will be outlined briefly here, discussed more fully in Chapter 2, and integrated into the analysis employed in subsequent chapters.

Critical Pedagogy

Critical pedagogy is influenced by several critical traditions and motivated by the desire to integrate educational theory and educational practice. Like Marxism and feminism, its advocates emphasize the deeply rooted power imbalances and social inequalities that infuse schooling structures and processes. In common with interpretative and postmodern analysis, critical pedagogy also stresses the symbolic importance of knowledge, language, and social action within educational practices. Education has both cultural and economic significance as a mechanism that gives shape and meaning to people's life experiences, thereby reinforcing the privileges of advantaged groups relative to powerless segments of society. Educational practices, according to critical pedagogy, must be restructured to represent the voices and experiences of all social groups, not just those who have sufficient resources and power to advance their own interests.

Feminist Pedagogy

Feminist pedagogy, like critical pedagogy, challenges the common view that education is a neutral endeavour, and commits itself to transform the education system as a consequence of the critique it offers. Feminist pedagogy argues that educational theory and practice must take into account the differential experiences, life chances, and ways of knowing that prevail for men and women in society. As teachers, mothers, and students, women tend to be excluded from key roles in educational decision-making and research, which thereby serves both to reflect and to perpetuate their socio-economic subordination relative to men. As a basis for achieving the true function of education, which is the empowerment of human beings, feminist pedagogy seeks to sensitize educators, students, and researchers to the ways in which gender structures men's and women's lives.

Anti-Racism Education

Educational approaches informed by anti-racism emphasize the powerful social impact of inequalities and ideologies based on race. Anti-racism education aligns itself with critical and feminist pedagogies in its quest to empower marginalized persons, while it shares with political economy a critique of material circumstances that produce fundamental social inequalities. Educational institutions and the knowledge and practices associated with them are implicated in the production and legitimation of racial discrimination and other forms of racism. However, schooling and post-secondary education can play a crucial role in working to address these problems.

Political Economy

Political economy stresses the interrelationships that prevail among the various segments of society, including the economic, political, and social realms. Like other approaches, there are various strands within political economy, ranging from traditional and liberal thought to orthodox Marxist perspectives. This book is informed by recent developments in critical political economy that examine the interplay among class, race, gender, and other central factors that shape and are shaped by people's life experiences. This approach argues that in order to make sense of social reality, we must examine how people collectively produce and reproduce both the material and symbolic conditions of their social existence. Education, viewed this way, has importance as a site in which people's personalities and life options take shape through interaction among the characteristics and experiences they bring with them into educational settings, the structures and practices that constitute education on an ongoing basis, and the linkages between education and the socioeconomic context within which it operates. More recent political economic analysis, informed by practices associated with globalization, has shifted its focus from education in specific national or regional settings in order to understand linkages with comparative and international dimensions of education.

Conclusion

The sociology of education, parallel to the educational realities it seeks to investigate and explain, is a multi-faceted endeavour. One must maintain sufficient scope and diversity in the analysis of education in order to capture the richness of education in its various forms. At the same time, because educational research and theory can be used to guide policy and practice, we must ensure that our understanding of educational matters develops in a comprehensive way, based as much as possible on complete and accurate information that is sensitive to its potential impact on people's lives.

The task to develop a socially meaningful understanding of education is especially daunting at a time when education faces serious challenges often considered to be of crisis proportions. Canada's growing integration into new global economic and political alignments is forcing a reassessment of how education should best be employed for competitive advantage. Educational reform and reorganization are further promoted through strategies to reduce government deficits, streamline government operations, and respond to issues related to regional diversity and national unity. Public outcries over what are characterized as declining educational standards, intolerable illiteracy and school dropout rates, lack of discipline and respect for authority, increasing crime rates among young offenders, and lack of moral guidance and focus among youth have drawn attention to the limitations of existing educational bureaucracies and to desires for accountability and choice in schooling. Changing gender relations, new patterns of immigration, and prospects for self-determination among First Nations have forced educational institutions to be increasingly responsive to issues of representation, cultural diversity, and equity. Shifting arrangements and tensions related to work, income, and family life have carried over into schooling, creating pressures for increased flexibility and demands for new educational supports and services at the same time that budgets for public education and social services are being reduced.

In the chapters that follow, historical and contemporary dimensions of Canadian education, its structure and participants, and the challenges facing it are examined through critical sociological inquiry. Each chapter highlights a theme of particular importance within the sociology of education. Chapter 2 provides an overview of major theoretical approaches and issues, contrasting traditional perspectives with more recent critical analysis. Chapter 3 is concerned with the organization and history of Canadian education, showing how divergent objectives and contestation have shaped educational policies and practices. Chapter 4 examines classroom interaction and educational practices, revealing how day-to-day educational activities reflect the tension between the need to produce distinct educational outcomes and less clearly delineated elements of human social development. Chapter 5 explores the nature and development of teaching, analyzing how teachers' work is subject to many of the same forces, such as control by external managers and demands for increased productivity, as other occupations—at the same time as its orientations to educational and social processes lend it a unique professional character. Chapter 6 addresses the relationship between education and work, highlighting in particular the notion that, contrary to persistent demands that schooling and work training should be more closely linked, the nature and purposes of formal education also are determined by other competing priorities. Chapter 7 highlights the ways in which education contributes to both socio-economic opportunity and the reproduction of structured inequalities among various segments of the population. Chapter 8, finally, shows how contemporary debates over such issues as educational finance, accountability and choice, technological change, and special educational needs reveal the importance of education to fundamental social and political choices and directions.

Annotated Further Readings

Michael W. Apple, *Power, Meaning, and Identity: Essays in Critical Educational Studies.* New York: Peter Lang Publishing, 1999. This collection of papers by one of the most influential critical analysts of education in North America offers perspectives on issues, practices, and developments central to education systems.

George J. Sefa Dei, Irma Marcia James, Leeno Luke Karumanchery, Sonia James-Wilson, and Jasmin Zine, *Removing the Margins: The Challenges and Possibilities of Inclusive Schooling.* Toronto: Canadian Scholars' Press, 2000. Drawing upon varied accounts and experiences with Canadian schooling, the authors outline a framework for the creation of inclusive educational practices that focus on how educational success must be oriented to the needs of students from diverse social and cultural backgrounds.

Lorna Erwin and David MacLennan, eds, *Sociology of Education in Canada: Critical Perspectives on Theory, Research and Practice.* Toronto: Copp Clark Longman, 1994. This collection brings together sociological analyses of contemporary educational issues and reforms, including the application of emergent theoretical perspectives, dimensions of educational inequality, curriculum reform, post-secondary education, and transitions among education and work.

A.H. Halsey, Hugh Lauder, Phillip Brown, and Amy Stuart Wells, eds, *Education: Culture, Economy, Society.* Oxford: Oxford University Press, 1997. This is one of the most comprehensive collections to analyze contemporary education systems from a variety of perspectives, with contributions from leading researchers representing diverse disciplinary and national contexts.

Chris Jenks, ed., *Core Sociological Dichotomies.* London: Sage, 1998. The contributors to this edited collection provide an introduction to sociology through an overview of the central debates and themes the discipline is concerned with, including structure/agency, fact/value, local/global, race/ethnicity, and numerous others.

Key Terms

Agency Recognition that human beings act on the basis of various degrees of choice and free will.

Anti-racism education An approach to educational theory and practice oriented to identifying and changing attitudes, policies, and practices that discriminate on the basis of race.

Critical pedagogy An approach oriented to progressive educational change by linking educational practices and experiences with social critique and a vision of educational alternatives.

Education The process by which human beings learn and develop capacities through understanding of their social and natural environments, which takes place in both formal and informal settings.

Feminist pedagogy An approach to educational analysis grounded in a critique of gender inequalities in education and the factors that give rise to them, and committed to practices to change those inequalities.

Interpretative analysis An approach to understanding social life that emphasizes the role played by meanings and intersubjective relationships in social activity.

Political economy An approach that emphasizes the interrelationships among social, economic, and political factors in social life; critical political economy examines the causes and consequences of deep-rooted forms of social and economic inequality.

Positivism A philosophic approach that emphasizes sensory experience as the basis for all knowledge, applied as a scientific framework that seeks to derive and test laws based on empirical evidence from systematic observation and measurement.

Schooling Education systems and processes organized through formal educational institutions.

Social structure Elements of social life that are relatively patterned, interconnected, and enduring, often understood with reference to the rules and boundaries associated with different forms of social action.

Sociology An academic discipline concerned with the nature and organization of societies and the relationships that exist among individuals and societies.

Study Questions

1. What is education? How does education differ from schooling and training?
2. Why is it important to examine education from different disciplines and perspectives?
3. What distinct contributions can a sociological analysis make to an understanding of education?
4. How important are educational credentials to social participation and advancement in contemporary societies? To what extent can, or should, factors other than formal education be used to assess a person's employment prospects?
5. What major social and economic forces need to be taken into account for an adequate understanding of education?

2

Sociological Theories of Education

Introduction

Theories exist to help people explain how and why particular phenomena occur as they do. They are employed as tools that enable us to make sense of the world, and are systematically developed from existing knowledge and tested against empirical evidence.

Sociological theories of education have arisen to explain everything from why some people fail and others succeed to problems of educational finance and everyday classroom interaction. It is sometimes difficult to categorize and assess the importance of sociological theories of education. Because particular groups, including educational administrators, governments, educational participants, and researchers in several academic disciplines, conduct educational research for different reasons, theories of education often are either absent from research or else are highly diversified and scattered in nature. As Parelius and Parelius (1987: 15) warn in response to the proliferation of educational research findings that are not unified into any theoretical perspectives, 'A glut of discrete findings, with no organizing framework, can be as useless as the untested speculations of the "armchair" theorist.'

With reference to the central sociological questions discussed in Chapter 1, this chapter examines representative theories of education within each of the three main theoretical perspectives, identified as structural functionalism, interpretative sociology, and critical analysis. The discussion of sociological theories of education in this chapter illustrates significant issues and models of analysis that characterize each approach, rather than being exhaustive and comprehensive in nature, and culminates by considering guidelines for an adequate understanding of educational problems.

Structural Functionalism and Liberal Theory

The earliest influential sociological theories of education emerged within structural functionalist analysis. In the late nineteenth and early twentieth centuries, French sociologist Émile Durkheim, one of the first writers to develop an explicitly sociological framework, made the examination of education systems a central part of his analysis of society. The crucial problem that guided Durkheim's sociological inquiry is one that lies at the heart of structural functionalism—'Why does the individual, while becoming more autonomous, depend more upon society?' (Durkheim, 1933: 37). Durkheim's concern arose from the observation that it was necessary to discover some basis of cohesion or solidarity that keeps societies from disintegrating amid an increase in individualism, individual rights, and self-interest. Durkheim stressed education's importance as an integrative mechanism that would bind people together and help them develop consciousness of their relationship with the wider society. He emphasized that societies, like individuals, have unique characteristics that set them apart from others. The purpose of formal education is to provide each individual with the knowledge and capabilities that are essential for meaningful participation in particular societal contexts. Education, understood in this way:

> is the influence exercised by adult generations on those that are not yet ready for social life. Its object is to arouse and to develop in the child a certain number of physical, intellectual, and moral states which are demanded of [him or her] by both the political society as a whole and the special milieu for which [he or she] is specifically destined. (Durkheim, 1956: 71)

For Durkheim, the task of sociology with respect to education and other social facts is, therefore, to uncover and specify the 'normal' characteristics for any given society in order to ensure closer integration between the individual and society and among all members of that society. Durkheim's writings on education have received less attention than other aspects of his work among sociologists. Nonetheless, recurrent themes in his work, such as a concern to preserve social solidarity, have gained recent prominence as social policy-makers turn to educational solutions to problems associated with social diversity and cohesion.

Durkheim's assumption—that a core set of social factors is general and shared widely within a society—is a defining feature of structural functionalist and liberal analysis. The work of Talcott Parsons, probably more fully than that of any writer since Durkheim, represents the functionalist view that central social institutions like the education system are responsible for inculcating common social values. For Parsons, as for Durkheim, the task of schools is more complex than simply to transmit knowledge and values to students.

Rather, such knowledge and values are to be internalized by individuals as part of their personalities. The properly 'schooled' person is one who knows intuitively and can act productively on the expectations, rules, and behaviours that accompany and give shape to social life.

Parsons (1959) conveys the most central assumptions and propositions of structural functionalist analysis in his article 'The School Class as a Social System: Some of its Functions in American Society'. As the article's title suggests, Parsons portrays schools as social systems that reflect and serve in the interests of the wider society. Within industrial democracies, schools exist to channel individuals from the emotional, person-centred demands of home and family life to the more formalized, competitive, and achievement-oriented world of work and public life. In the primary grades, for instance, school subjects are not rigidly divided like they are in high school. Rather, emphasis is on learning fundamental social and intellectual skills without comprehensive testing, and pupils are taught by one teacher (usually a woman, to provide continuity from the mother figure in the home environment). In progressively higher grades, however, there is greater emphasis on competitiveness, merit-based performance, and instruction by several teachers, primarily men, akin to the structure and division of labour that prevail in the workplace (Parsons, 1959: 314–15). Schools, in these regards, have two primary functions—allocation and socialization—that contribute to the maintenance of the social system. First, schooling, through the mechanisms of grading, granting credentials, and more informal selection processes, sorts individuals to fill distinct positions in the social hierarchy. Second, schooling contributes to individual personality formation by inculcating the dispositions necessary for successful participation in general social life as well as those that are suited for the specific social roles and experiences that accompany each person's expected social position.

Structural functionalist analysis, as illustrated clearly in the work of both Durkheim and Parsons, offers a particular perspective on the question of schools' role in social reproduction. Structural functionalists view social reproduction, the process by which social order and continuity are maintained from generation to generation, as consensual and harmonious in nature. Much like in a natural ecosystem, the normal state of society is portrayed as one in which each element (including individuals and institutions) plays a specific part that combines and is interdependent with others in such a way that the vitality of the whole system is maintained. Because all members of an organization or society have a stake in the system, there is an emphasis on mutual respect and common goals. While tensions and conflict may emerge, a successful social organization is seen as one that is able to develop mechanisms to manage conflict and change and reduce the possibility that they may cause damage to the social or institutional system.

Some structural functionalist writers carry these notions further by highlighting what they call the hidden curriculum. Whereas the formal curriculum conveys the social expectations attached to learning and educational

Box 2.1 A functionalist perspective on the sociology of education

Talcott Parsons (1959: 277–8) has presented one of the most influential structural functionalist accounts of education in his discussion of the socialization and allocative functions of schooling:

> Our main interest, then, is in a dual problem: first of how the school class functions to internalize in its pupils both the commitments and capacities for successful performance of their future adult roles, and second of how it functions to allocate these human resources within the role-structure of the adult society. The primary ways in which these two problems are interrelated will provide our main points of reference.
>
> First, from the functional point of view the school class can be treated as an agency of socialization. That is to say, it is an agency through which individual personalities are trained to be motivationally and technically adequate to the performance of adult roles. It is not the sole such agency; the family, informal 'peer groups', churches, and sundry voluntary organizations all play a part, as does actual on-the-job training. But, in the period extending from entry into first grade until entry into the labor force or marriage, the school class may be regarded as the focal socializing agency.
>
> The socialization function may be summed up as the development in individuals of the commitments and capacities which are essential prerequisites of their future role-performance. Commitments may be broken down in turn into two components: commitment to the implementation of the broad values of society, and commitment to the performance of a specific type of role within the structure of society. Thus a person in a relatively humble occupation may be a 'solid citizen' in the sense of commitment to honest work in that occupation, without an intensive and sophisticated concern with the implementation of society's higher-level values. Or conversely, someone else might object to the anchorage of the feminine role in marriage and the family on the grounds that such anchorage keeps society's total talent resources from being distributed equitably to business, government, and so on. Capacities can also be broken down into two components, the first being competence or the skill to perform the tasks involved in the individual's roles, and the second being 'role-responsibility' or the capacity to live up to other people's expectations of the interpersonal behavior appropriate to these roles. Thus a mechanic as well as a doctor needs to have not only the basic 'skills of his trade', but also the ability to behave responsibly toward those people with whom he is brought into contact in his work.

Box 2.1 (continued)

While on the one hand, the school class may be regarded as a primary agency by which these different components of commitments and capacities are generated, on the other hand, it is, from the point of view of the society, an agency of 'manpower' allocation. It is well known that in American society there is a very high, and probably increasing, correlation between one's status level in the society and one's level of educational attainment. Both social status and educational level are obviously related to the occupational status which is attained. Now, as a result of the general process of both educational and occupational upgrading, completion of high school is increasingly coming to be the norm for minimum satisfactory educational attainment, and the most significant line for future occupational status has come to be drawn between members of an age-cohort who do and do not go to college.

outcomes, the hidden curriculum refers to the more informal or less explicitly defined characteristics that, nonetheless, are regular features of the schooling process. School-based learning consists of much more than simply the content of lessons, textbooks, and rules that students are presented with. Important knowledge and skills are also conveyed by daily participation, extended over several years, within the social context of schooling. Students learn values of conformity, competitiveness, deferred gratification, obedience to authority, and adjustment to success and failure through their experiences in classrooms and other school settings (see, especially, Dreeben, 1968; Jackson, 1968).

It is useful to consider here a central assumption of structural functionalist analysis, the presupposition that social stratification and inequality are necessary structural features of advanced societies. The reproduction of society involves an assumed hierarchy of positions that must be filled with suitably qualified and motivated people. This requirement gives rise to the specified functions of schooling, including the tasks of sorting and socializing individuals and contributing to common values. As long as the social system appears to be operating smoothly, with no threats to the system's breakdown, few questions are raised about the kinds of values and inequalities being fostered or about which groups, if any, are their main beneficiaries.

An important implication of the assumptions about consensus and stratification in structural functionalist theory is that attention is drawn to the identification of mechanisms that will assure that the social reproduction process operates effectively and efficiently. In the late 1950s and 1960s, theoretical consideration of the link between schooling and socio-economic needs was enhanced by policy concerns to produce a scientifically and technically sophisticated workforce. Rapid expansion of industrial production and mass-marketed goods and services were stimulated by a combination of factors, including military production in World War II and the subsequent Cold War, the creation of new household consumer products, and relatively high wages and stable labour markets. In North America, the 'space race' between the Soviet Union and the United States served as a symbolic rallying point around which new workforce requirements, driven by science and technological knowledge, were to be implemented. At the same time, the promise of social and economic security enhanced the cultivation of home and family ties, signified by rising birth rates associated with the post-war 'baby boom' and new expectations about domestic life and leisure-time activities. Schooling figured prominently in these transitions. Educational expansion was fuelled by increases in school-age populations along with demands for a more highly educated labour force and a scientifically grounded curriculum to train the experts required by the new economy.

These changes were the focus of three interrelated strands of structural functionalist and liberal analysis (Karabel and Halsey, 1977, offer a good extended discussion of these theories). The first two, technological functionalism and human capital theory, offered an optimistic assessment of the role of education in social and individual advancement. The third, status attainment research, posed research findings that have led to considerable debate over the degree and nature of social inequality in relation to education.

Technological functionalism emphasizes the ways in which educational requirements are driven by changing technologies. Social progress, defined in terms of the advancement of technical and scientific expertise, is seen to require an increasingly qualified and specialized population. Consistent with Parsons's analysis and the general functionalist theory of stratification, technological functionalism views formal educational requirements, first, as a means to disseminate socially important knowledge and skills and, second, as a mechanism to ensure the social placement of individuals on the basis of merit. The theory contends that technological change accounts for the massive expansion of public education in the twentieth century, both in the sense that increasing numbers of people are achieving higher levels of education and that curricula are becoming increasingly more sophisticated and demanding (Clark, 1962). Educational advancement, from this perspective, is necessary to keep pace with technological change as well as to stimulate further development (Bell, 1973).

Human capital theory offers a similar analysis, placing emphasis on the importance of the returns from education to society as a whole. Education, within human capital theory, is viewed as an investment in human resources. Economic development in advanced industrial and post-industrial societies requires not only highly developed material resources, but also sufficiently skilled and motivated individuals. A society's ability to compete successfully in a highly advanced economic environment depends on the extent to which it is able to produce trained, innovative personnel who can contribute to scientific and technological development.

There is much more than theoretical significance to human capital theory. Under the guise of human capital theory, governments implemented massive programs to develop scientific and technical education. Curricula were reorganized to emphasize mathematics and sciences in elementary and secondary schools, new community colleges and technical institutes were built across Canada and the United States, and government expenditures on post-secondary education increased substantially. The influence of human capital theory remains very much alive through contemporary reforms and ideologies that emphasize competitiveness, human resource development, and the need to match skills with jobs. Business and government leaders draw on such arguments to promote programs to retrain workers, for example, or initiatives to increase productivity in the workplace. Human capital also figures prominently in discussions of the emergence of a new economy that is based on learning and knowledge related to rapid developments in information and communications technology.

Status attainment research is oriented to the quantitative measurement of socio-economic inequalities. As postulated in structural functionalist and liberal theory, advanced industrial societies are characterized by increasing formal opportunities for social advancement, especially those determined by credentials accomplished through schooling, as opposed to more informal mechanisms of sponsorship and restricted mobility that supposedly prevail in non-industrialized nations. A stratified but meritocratic social order, in which individuals achieve jobs and rewards on the basis of merit or competence, is deemed essential for a society whose welfare and progress depend on the skills, technical expertise, and commitment of its members. Status attainment research emerged as a means to provide empirical evidence that would test the strength of linkages among background characteristics (like gender, race, and socio-economic status), formal education, and other life chances.

The research findings consistently demonstrate the pervasive nature of social inequality, but are surrounded by conflicting interpretations. Blau and Duncan (1967), for example, suggest that their data offer support for the Parsonian thesis that education has come to replace family background as the primary determinant of occupational placement in the United States. However, other high-profile empirical analyses, notably the Coleman Report (Coleman et al., 1966) and the work of Jencks et al. (1972), attribute the origins of social inequality more to the home and other non-school sites than to schooling. Coleman (1968), though, argues that it is crucial to distinguish between equality of results and equality of opportunity. Schools cannot compensate for social disparities on their own, but they can make an impact by providing enriched learning conditions that give all students the chance to compete for access to desired social positions. British research such as that reported by Floud, Halsey, and Martin (1956) and the Plowden Report (Central Advisory Council for Education, 1967) offers a similar assessment of the relationship between schooling and social inequality, emphasizing, consistent with human capital theory, that talent and social possibilities are wasted when individuals are handicapped by their social backgrounds. In an influential Canadian study, Porter (1965) provides a functionalist analysis of education's contribution to social mobility, but adds the important proviso that domination by elites, selected through social factors such as class, ethnicity, and religious affiliation, places limits on the opportunity structure.

It is noteworthy that the studies cited above, conducted primarily between the mid-1950s and the late 1960s, reflect an optimistic faith in education's ability to promote social progress and democratic opportunities. While the optimism is sometimes tempered with warnings that social reforms may be required to fulfill schooling's promise, very little in these studies challenges the prevailing liberal and functionalist assumptions that inequality is socially necessary. What becomes crucially important is that social stratification must be seen to be based on open and fair selection mechanisms. The major point of debate concerns the degree to which schools could or could not contribute to the equalization of opportunities. It is perhaps not surprising, therefore, that status attainment research, like human capital theory, frequently has been cited to justify social policies and reforms that affect practices both within and outside of education systems. The Coleman Report, for instance, commissioned by the United States government, was employed as a tool in the federal War on Poverty to provide visible initiatives for the social and economic advancement of inner-city blacks and other racial minorities. Canada, the United Kingdom, Australia, and other advanced industrial nations all have employed educational attainment research both as part of the rhetoric and as an active component in labour market development strategies.

Another influential strand of liberal analysis, *educational progressivism*, offers a critique of existing social arrangements, but retains faith in the ability of schools to improve those conditions. Originating within the nineteenth-century progressive movement that promoted a humanistic vision of social change guided by the state, educational progressivism contributed most strongly to a restructuring of educational thought and practice in the post-World War I period. John Dewey, the best-known advocate of educational progressivism, was influenced by Marx as well as by liberal theory, and was also an associate of G.H. Mead and other interpretative sociologists at the University of Chicago. Like Marx, Dewey (1966) was critical of a growing uniformity of life within industrial capitalism and advocated the creation of more meaningful connections between school and practical experience. However, reflecting his liberal orientations, Dewey promoted schooling as a mechanism that would ameliorate such pressing social problems as poverty, crime, ethnic antagonism, and social dislocation caused by rapid urbanization, industrialization, and economic change. Dewey sought to replace the adherence to routine and orientation to future rewards in traditional education with child-centred educational practices. He contended that schools should act autonomously from the industrial system and its inherent dangers in order to foster individual growth and social responsibility.

Dewey's progressive, humanistic philosophy seemingly was at odds with some of the major educational reforms derived from industry early in the twentieth century. Influential administrative reformers like Ellwood Cubberly, J.F. Bobbitt, and R.W. Tyler advanced the implementation of rational models of educational management and curriculum construction based on the application of scientific principles to school organization and practice. These approaches, in stark contrast to the liberal emphasis on human development, portrayed education as an endeavour that should be planned and operated as an efficient business enterprise. There was, however, an affinity between the scientific management of schooling and the progressive vision of a better society produced through the intervention of state authorities and scientific expertise. The convergence of these orientations contributed to growing emphasis in the 1920s and 1930s on such innovations as psychological testing of student intelligence and aptitudes, systematic curriculum planning, increased demarcation of school subjects and grade levels, especially at the high school level, bureaucratic school administrative structures, and streaming of pupils by programs and ability.

Progressivism re-emerged as an influential force in educational practice and theory in the 1960s and 1970s. Educational reforms such as 'open' classrooms, curricula and teaching styles that emphasized pupil choice and participation, sensitivity to learners' backgrounds and values, and awareness of the relevance of schooling to everyday life signified a supposed shift from traditional to progressive educational philosophies in an era characterized by widespread challenges to authority and prevailing social structures. Some critics, labelled by Carnoy and Levin (1975: 16–17) as critical progressives, condemned the schools for perpetuating rather than eradicating the problems of mass society, 'arguing that far from being an instrument of social progress, education was actually deadening—much more oriented to producing failure than to developing creative, critical minds that could be the basis for a more humanistic, democratic society.'

The titles of significant studies from this period—*How Children Fail* (Holt, 1964), *Death at an Early Age: The Destruction of the Hearts and Minds of Negro Children in the Boston Public Schools* (Kozol, 1967), and *De-Schooling Society* (Illich, 1970)—convey the message that schools foster, at best, boredom and restricted opportunities for success or, worse, dehumanization and habituation into destructive routines. Unlike the more optimistic assessment of the possibilities that schooling contains for a democratic society, as advanced by educational progressivism, the critical progressive stance emphasizes that schools, at least as they are currently structured and operated, require much more than superficial changes before they can begin to fulfill their promise. Nonetheless, in common with other liberal approaches, analysis of the root causes of educational problems is ultimately given less prominence than a preoccupation with individual bases of success, failure, and opportunities.

The theories that have been examined in this section have pointed to the real and potential contributions made by formal education to social and economic development. With a few exceptions, they portray education as a progressive force that can expand opportunities for individuals as well as for whole societies. The key to a successful education system is the establishment of mechanisms that will ensure a proper 'fit' between individuals' social background, on the one hand, and the demands of the social system, on the other.

Structural functionalism is rarely employed as an explicit theoretical orientation in current educational research, in part because of some of the problems outlined below, as well as the impact that newer theoretical frameworks have had on the field. However, structural functionalism is highly significant for its formative impact on the development of the sociology of education. It has drawn attention to crucial questions about the relationship between education and other spheres of social life as well as to the role that persistent social inequalities play in advanced societies. Liberal analyses of education, by contrast, have remained popular among both academic researchers and policy-makers due to their generally optimistic assessment about prospects for expanding individual opportunity and social productivity. Several writers, though, have suggested that Durkheim's educational analysis warrants rehabilitation as societies look for solutions to challenges posed by social diversity, moral uncertainty, changing relations between individualism and community, and issues of citizenship in a global context (Walford and Pickering, 1998).

Despite their influence, there are several important limitations to structural functionalist and liberal theories of education. In particular, the theoretical model tends to offer a description of an ideal state of affairs rather than an explanation of social reality. As will be documented later, much substantial evidence runs contrary to, or at least makes questionable, the assumption of a meritocratic social structure in which educational achievement and individual effort, and not one's social origins, account for social success or failure. Even when there is a clear relationship between educational achievement and social status or occupational attainment, it is necessary to consider whether schooling reinforces or eradicates social inequalities already in existence. The impact of such factors as wealth, control and restructuring of jobs, and intrinsic rewards such as personal satisfaction with particular jobs or life situations is often not considered in the measuring of social and educational inequality. While inequality is a complex, changing phenomenon, it is also reproduced in both overt and subtle ways. Opportunities for social advancement may be restricted even if we assume that there is an open, fair, and meritorious process by which individuals are allocated to social positions. Functionalist and liberal analyses tend to overestimate the extent to which social reforms can contribute to social change, in the process ignoring or minimizing the significance of more deeply embedded power relations. By the late 1960s, the contradiction between promised socio-economic opportunities and people's life experiences resulted in a rethinking of liberal assumptions among many educational participants and analysts. Growing consciousness of the subordination of women and racial minorities, the emergence of the student protest movement, and the persistence of poverty produced a fertile environment in which alternative perspectives in academic research could flourish.

Interpretative Analysis of Schooling

Interpretative analysis has tended to focus on two features of schooling: (1) the meaning and nature of school practices for educational participants; and (2) the importance of language, knowledge, curricula, and other symbolic aspects of schooling. Learning and interaction with others are viewed as social processes, not simply as aspects of social positions and structures as they are portrayed within structural functionalist analysis. Interpretative sociologists argue that society and social outcomes are not fixed; rather, they are created, recreated, and modified continuously by human activity. Schooling, in this view, is a site of perpetual adjustment as participants attempt to decipher and share meanings with one another and, in the process, shape their personalities and lives. As expressed by Karl Mannheim (1936: 156):

> Modern education from its inception is a living struggle, a replica, on a small scale of the conflicting purposes and tendencies which rage in society at large. Accordingly, the educated [person is] . . . determined in a variety of ways.

In common with other approaches examined in this book, there are diverse roots and strands to the interpretative analysis of schooling.

Max Weber, whose work is at least as influential as that of his contemporary, Émile Durkheim, stressed the importance of education and educational credentials to the rationalization of society. Rationalization, for Weber, is a process that involves science, technical knowledge, and other elements related to systematic planning for the achievement of predetermined objectives. Rationality is perhaps most strongly apparent in bureaucratic organizations governed, at least in a formal sense, by written rules and procedures, a hierarchy of authority, impartial treatment of clients, and hiring and career advancement of officials based on formal credentials. In this context, formal education has special significance as a bureaucratic site in which training is systematically organized to provide individuals with necessary social attributes and legitimate credentials. While this analysis parallels that of functionalism in important respects, Weber is especially concerned with the ways in which credentials are used by officials and other interest groups to advance their own positions (see, e.g., Gerth and Mills, 1946: 240–4, 416ff.). Despite the overwhelming tendency towards control and predictability in modern life, in other words, Weber maintains that the processes by which these outcomes are sought or resisted are of utmost importance. Weber's work has given rise to later studies in both critical analysis and interpretative sociology.

Box 2.2 An interpretative perspective on the sociology of education

Interpretative analysis emphasizes the meanings and interactions within schools and other social settings, highlighting their implications for social actors themselves, as presented here by Martin (1976: 154–5):

There are two reasons why this study has significance for the practical aspects of teacher-pupil interactions. First, it reveals that teachers frequently categorize pupils as either non-negotiable, intermittently negotiable, or continuously negotiable. Second, it isolates the strategies teachers and pupils use to negotiate with each other.

Teachers should ask themselves whether, intentionally or unintentionally, they categorize pupils on a negotiation continuum. If so, according to what criteria? Which of the following criteria are used and what weight is given to each: performance, other teachers' definitions, demeanour and congeniality, clothing and appearance? Is the classifying of pupils simply a self-fulfilling prophecy in which the expectation of finding certain types of pupils is met, if for no other reason than that the expectation is there?

Related to the issue of categorizing pupils is the question of the permanence of a category for a given pupil. Do pupils move from one category to another? If so, under what conditions does the move take place? The answers to these questions, as communicated in teacher-pupil interactions, will be obvious indicators of the nature of the teaching being done in a given situation. For example, the significance of having pupils participate in the decision-making process of the interactions in learning situations, rather than attempting to impose a social order developed by the teachers, has been seen in a variety of situations. It is often advantageous for individuals to have a knowledge of the strategies to be employed by each other in a given interaction. More specifically, it is to the teachers' advantage to be able to predict the strategies pupils are most likely to employ in the school setting. Conversely, pupils would find it to their advantage to know the strategies a teacher is likely to use in his interactions with them. In fact, learning the subtleties of interaction is one of the basic processes of socialization. It follows that isolating the strategies most often used by certain categories of actors when interacting with each other has far-reaching practical application to the socialization of individuals in general, and of individuals who are becoming members of certain formal organizations in particular; hence the practical value of isolating the strategies employed by pupils and teachers when interacting with each other.

One such approach, known as neo-Weberian analysis, employs Max Weber's theories of bureaucracy and power to analyze contemporary schooling. C. Wright Mills (1951, 1956), who adopts elements of both Marxian and Weberian analysis in his scathing social critique, argues that the process of rationalization has contributed to the rise of a mass society in which our lives are governed by a power elite of business, political, and military leaders. Formal education, particularly within private schools and colleges, is an important mechanism through which access to elite positions can be controlled and elite solidarity fostered. Schooling and training practices facilitate rational processes of planning and management so as to produce a cadre of technical experts.

Further neo-Weberian critique of the role of education in advanced industrial society is offered by Randall Collins (1971), who disputes the technological functionalist argument that increased technical requirements for skilled labour are responsible for the expansion of the public education system. Collins argues that the link between schooling and jobs is often marginal, and, in fact, that the skill requirements for many jobs have not increased. Rather, the increase in the levels of formal education required for entry into particular occupations is a consequence of competition among status groups. The major purpose of schooling, therefore, is to provide credentials and offer legitimacy to particular status cultures within the social and occupational structures. Murphy (1994), employing international and Canadian examples, extends Collins's analysis by showing that Weber's theory enables us to assess how credentials are used in different ways by both dominant and subordinate groups in various struggles over status and cultural resources. Teachers' associations, for instance, may rely on the credentials of their members as a way of distinguishing teachers from laypersons wanting to become involved in educational matters, but they may also seek support or alliances with political parties and other organized groups to protect their own interests against more powerful forces.

The interpretative analysis of schooling and other social institutions rose to prominence through a branch of investigation that came to be called the Chicago School of sociology. This approach, which continues to have a strong influence within the discipline, was most active in the 1920s through the work of sociologists at the University of Chicago, who used their dynamic city, with its changing mix of industry, urban development, and social composition, as a living laboratory. The Chicago School stressed the interdependent nature of the personality, or self, and social interaction. W.I. Thomas's notion of 'the definition of the situation', which highlights the powerful role that perceptions and shared meanings play in guiding social action, and C.H. Cooley's concept of 'the looking-glass self', which alerts us to the process by which our behaviour and identity are shaped by our awareness of the reactions of others, illustrate the interpretative aspects of this approach. George Herbert Mead's analysis of the dynamic, interactive nature of personality formation contributed to the development of both symbolic interactionist sociology and social psychology. For Mead, as recognized by later developmental psychologists, education is part of an ongoing process of human development in which the individual learns and shares social meanings with other people (Ritzer, 2000: 403–8).

One of the earliest, most complete analyses of schooling within the Chicago School tradition is Willard Waller's *The Sociology of Teaching*, originally published in 1932. Waller (1965: 6) examines the school as a 'social organism' constituted through 'a unity of interacting personalities'. His analysis moves directly into the classroom and other school sites, providing rich examples of the complex social relations that link together pupils, teachers, administrators, parents, and other educational participants within a distinct school culture. School and social structures are viewed as maps to guide these interactions, but Waller emphasizes that schooling remains a fluid process marked by changing, sometimes conflicting, definitions of the situation.

The interpretative tradition of classroom research was extended by Becker (1952, 1953), who employed detailed interviews to explore how teachers define and act on their roles and circumstances. Becker's analysis points to the process by which teachers' expectations contribute to the social construction of different categories of students, thereby affecting students' educational experiences and chances of school success. A substantial body of later research elaborates how particular definitions of the situation held by educators result in self-fulfilling prophecies. Teachers create and apply particular labels to children and their parents (as well as to other individuals, and vice versa), based on common-sense assumptions, background information, and observations from encounters. This labelling influences subsequent educational and social career paths. Rosenthal and Jacobson (1968), in a frequently cited study of children in a San Francisco elementary school, demonstrate that teachers' presuppositions about pupils' learning potentials, even if false, tended to have more impact on student performance than did actual ability. Research by Cicourel and Kitsuse (1963) and Rist (1970) in the United States, Hargreaves (1967) and Lacey (1970) in the United Kingdom, and Stebbins (1975) in Canada, among many others, supports the finding that self-fulfilling prophecies operate as powerful influences on educational outcomes, but this research emphasizes much more fully than do Rosenthal and Jacobson the complex interactions that take place within schools.

Many research findings within the interpretative tradition ultimately support functionalist and critical analyses of social reproduction that show social outcomes of schooling as highly predictable in nature. However, interpretative analysis emphasizes that schooling cannot properly be viewed as a 'black box' that produces preselected results; instead, the most compelling interest lies with what happens inside the school (Karabel and Halsey, 1977: 60). Other classroom studies, including Canadian research by Martin (1976) and Stebbins (1971, 1975), portray schooling as a site within which complex processes of negotiation and decision-making are undertaken by all participants. Albas and Albas (1993), for instance, through observation of students' behaviour in examinations in a western Canadian university, demonstrate that students employ a wide range of actions to avoid being labelled as cheaters. Interpretive analysis, by probing into the sometimes devious ways that people engage with one another and their social surroundings, often conveys a strong sense of cynicism, expressed clearly in a chapter in which Howard Becker (1996) reflects upon many of his earlier influential studies, entitled 'Schooling is a Lousy Place to Learn Anything In'.

A conscious effort to question both school practices and the structure of knowledge and curricula emerged within what came to be known in the early 1970s as *the 'new' sociology of education*. Critical of previous conventional sociological and educational analysis that took for granted what happens in schools, the new sociology of education sought explicitly to expose the power relations embedded within educational practices (Gorbutt, 1972; Young, 1971). While this approach drew inspiration from emergent critical sociological analyses, its orientation to research problems and methodologies was primarily interpretative. However, as Karabel and Halsey (1977: 47–8) observe, the new sociology of education was predominantly a British phenomenon that paid little heed to previous, mostly North American, classroom research, such as the studies referred to above.

The strength of the new sociology of education is its ability not only to bring the schooling process to the centre of educational research, but also to challenge many of the prevailing assumptions about the content of schooling. Knowledge and how it is presented in the curriculum and delivered in the classroom are not absolute categories. Rather, they are socially constructed, given meaning and importance through the social contexts in which they appear. Consequently, much of the research in the new sociology of education, like other forms of interpretative analysis, is devoted to providing detailed descriptions and outlines of the significance of everyday occurrences, such as patterns of joking and teasing in the classroom or the hidden meanings contained within school textbooks. Whereas other forms of analysis tend to overlook or trivialize day-to-day activities, interpretative sociology brings these to the forefront as crucial components of social life.

While offering detailed insight into such crucial features of schooling as classroom processes, interpersonal interactions, and the curriculum, interpretative sociology is often limited by its failure to link what happens in schools with the world beyond schooling. Attention to the intricacies of everyday processes tends to leave unanswered historical questions about change and how things got that way in the first place. Moreover, there is a tendency to ignore the impact of broader social structures, opportunities, and decision-making processes on educational practices and outcomes. Negotiation between teachers and pupils for grades or teachers' contributions to students' self-esteem may influence students' career choices, for instance, but these choices cannot be understood without reference to such factors as labour markets, families, and other socio-economic determinants. Ultimately, like much structural functionalist analysis, interpretative sociology makes its strongest contribution in the description of social life but falls short in its explanatory powers.

Critical Analysis

The various strands in the critical analysis of schooling are unified by their concern to find the underlying causes of educational inequalities and change. Critical analysis, like the other approaches to the sociology of education, has a long history, but in North America, at least, it has really only achieved a position of some prominence in the past two to three decades. Critical analysis stresses that the education system has largely failed in its promise to promote a more egalitarian society. Moreover, this failure is not an accidental by-product that can be corrected by simple reforms. Instead, schooling, in content and process, contributes to the subordination of substantial segments of the population. The meritocratic and democratic visions promoted by liberal and functionalist analysis are criticized as ideologies that serve the interests of dominant social groups. The ways in which these issues are analyzed through three major critical approaches—political economy influenced by Marxism, feminism, and critical pedagogy—are discussed below.

Marxist educational theory shares with neo-Weberian analysis the assessment that education systems within capitalist societies are unable to fulfill their democratic potential because of the profound influence of dominant social forces. Marxism, however, attributes the root causes of social inequality to structures of class and economic production rather than to competition between status groups.

While Karl Marx wrote very little on formal education, his method and theories to analyze capitalist society offer a foundation for critical analysis, known as historical materialism, that is absent in other approaches. Marx's analysis begins with the premise that all societies emerge around the ways in which people meet their basic survival needs. As human beings we develop socially, distinct from other species, by virtue of our ability to labour. Labour, for Marx, refers in a broad sense to conscious activity devoted to the fulfillment of specific human needs. Marx's social critique emphasizes how our labour comes to be alienated through processes by which others gain control over our labouring activity and the products that we generate through it. Alienation is most extreme in capitalist society, which is distinguished from other types of societies and modes of production by the ways that capitalists are able to control and organize work to maximize profit.

Although most of Marx's analysis focuses on the structural mechanisms that drive the capitalist system and produce social class antagonisms, Marx also comments on the contradictory nature of schooling. Like other institutions within capitalism, the education system constrains human potential that is otherwise necessary for social progress. Schooling, when it is integrated with work and other crucial social activities, provides opportunities through which people can develop both critical consciousness and meaningful skills in such areas as literacy and vocational practice. Organized to serve capitalist priorities of profit and labour market discipline, however, schools fall far short of their potential, becoming more like 'sausage factories' than places for human fulfillment. Schooling, under capitalism, is a vehicle for the production of a compliant workforce, providing just enough knowledge to ensure a supply of workers ready for monotonous jobs while advancing ideologies that serve capitalist interests (see, e.g., Marx, 1977: 613–15; Wotherspoon, 1984: 211). Despite the deadening effects of work and other social practices within capitalism, however, Marx's theory emphasizes possibilities for the revolutionary transformation of society. Public schooling, Marx contends, would remain an essential part of communist society, although, by linking work and education, its aim would be to foster personal and social development rather than to serve the bourgeois order (Marx and Engels, 1965: 55, 60).

Marx's work, by virtue of its political orientation, has had a major impact on educational practice. Literacy campaigns and revolutionary movements inspired at least in part by Marx and incorporating interpretations of his work adapted to fit particular circumstances have contributed to various kinds of educational reform in many parts of the world. The student protest movement that emerged in Western Europe and North America in the late 1960s also created a receptive atmosphere for Marxist analysis in the social sciences. Schooling began to be portrayed as an 'ideological state apparatus' (Althusser, 1971) or a form of cultural imperialism (Carnoy, 1974) that contributes ideologically and materially to the perpetuation of fundamentally unequal class relations.

Insights offered by Harry Braverman (1974) exemplify the emergent Marxist critique of work and other social conditions under advanced capitalist society. In common with neo-Weberian analysis advanced by writers like Collins, Braverman challenges the popular liberal assessment that technological change has created enhanced skill requirements and more meaningful white-collar work opportunities. However, Braverman (whose analysis will be elaborated in more detail in subsequent chapters) contends that capitalist control over work involves managerial strategies that produce increasing degradation and deskilling within virtually all occupations. Education, despite its apparent contribution to individual and social development, serves primarily to prepare students, in a highly co-ordinated way, for adjustment to the routines of a world dominated by monopoly capital.

Probably the most influential neo-Marxist study of schooling to appear in the wake of the 1960s challenges to political orthodoxy has been *Schooling in Capitalist America* by Samuel Bowles and Herbert Gintis, published in 1976. Bowles and Gintis make explicit the connections between the capitalist economy and schooling only noted in passing by Braverman, beginning with a critique of the failure of liberal educational reform to deliver on its promise of a more egalitarian and democratic society. They contest, as well, conservative arguments that attribute educational inequality to inherent differences in intelligence and ability. Bowles and Gintis argue, rather, that educational reform can do little in itself to alleviate social inequality insofar as inequality is rooted in the class structure of capitalist society. They identify a 'correspondence principle' that operates between educational reform and economic change. They argue that capitalism, in common with totalitarian political systems, restricts democratic participation in order to maintain material and ideological conditions to generate profit and ensure a productive labour force.

According to Bowles and Gintis, formal education in the United States has undergone three major historical changes that correspond to changes in the capitalist economy. Initially, the rise of mass public schooling accompanied the need in the mid- to late nineteenth century for a disciplined wage labour force. During the second transition, between 1890 and 1930, progressive educational reforms converged with the growing concentration of corporate capital and a diversified workforce to produce a bureaucratic education system based on standardization, testing, and systematic control. The third phase involved correspondence between the rapid expansion of post-secondary education and the post-World War II growth of professional and white-collar occupations needed to co-ordinate labour and capital under intensified control by state and corporate agencies. Educational change frequently is marked by struggle because, as Bowles and Gintis (1976: 235) argue, 'Conflicts in the educational sphere often reflect muted or open conflicts in the economic sphere.' However, formal education serves primarily to facilitate the transformation of capitalist development in such a way as to maintain social order.

Bowles and Gintis's analysis has advanced the understanding of educational structures and practices by demonstrating that schooling, at least indirectly, is a central part of the logic that drives capitalist development and reproduces systematic social inequalities. Their work also provides a historical account, lacking in most previous studies, of forces that have contributed to the formation and growth of contemporary educational institutions.

Despite the acuity of their critique of both traditional educational theories and schooling processes in capitalist societies, the insights offered by Bowles and Gintis have sufficiently strong parallels with structural functionalist analysis that some writers (e.g., Carnoy and Levin, 1985: 21–2) consider their work to be 'critical functionalist' in nature. Among both traditional and critical analyses, in other words, there is general agreement that schools contribute to social, ideological, and labour force reproduction. Yet, there is considerable debate over what kinds of reproduction occur, how fair the system is, and who benefits from it. On either side of the debate, there is a tendency to understate the complexities characteristic of educational realities.

Livingstone (1994: 65–7) summarizes three major problems with the correspondence principle advanced by Bowles and Gintis: (1) a failure to recognize that different forms of knowledge, and not exclusively capitalist knowledge, exist and are produced within educational settings; (2) the accumulation

Box 2.3 A neo-Marxist perspective on the sociology of education

Herbert Gintis and Samuel Bowles (1980: 52–3) outline the correspondence principle that links schooling with the economy:

A main proposition in *Schooling in Capitalist America* held that a major objective of capital, in its interventions into the formation and evolution of the educational system, was precisely the preparation of students to be future workers on the various levels in the hierarchy of capitalist production. Given the quite significant success of capital directly and indirectly structuring schools and in the face of the undemocratic nature of economic life, schools could not fulfill their egalitarian and developmental objectives. We concluded that the only means toward the achievement of progressive educational reform is the democratisation of economic life, allowing for a democratic and emancipatory school system which does not conflict with the formation of adults capable of effective participation in the system of production.

We also argued specifically that the current relationship between education and economy is ensured not through the content of education but its form: the social relations of the educational encounter. Education prepares students to be workers through a correspondence between the social relations of production and the social relations of education. Like the division of labour in the capitalist enterprise, the educational system is a finely graded hierarchy of authority and control in which competition rather than co-operation governs the relations among participants, and an external reward system—wages in the case of the economy and grades in the case of schools—holds sway. This correspondence principle explains why the schools cannot at the same time promote full personal development and social equality, while integrating students into society. The hierarchical order of the school system, admirably geared towards preparing students for their future positions in the hierarchy of production, limits the development of those personal capacities involving the exercise of reciprocal and mutual democratic participation and reinforces social inequality by legitimating the assignment of students to inherently unequal 'slots' in the social hierarchy.

The correspondence principle, we believe, makes four positive contributions to progressive educational strategy. First, its explanatory value is great. Despite the considerable scepticism which greeted publication of our book, critics have made little headway in overturning our major empirical conclusions. Indeed the one major subsequent statistical investigation of sources of educational and economic success—Christopher Jencks et al.'s *Who Gets Ahead?*—

Box 2.3 continued

dramatically confirms our own findings. Second, in an era where the failures of liberal school reform have become increasingly evident to policy-makers and the public, the correspondence principle shows a positive alternative. Egalitarian and humanistic education are not unattainable due to some inherent defect in human nature or advanced industrial society, but to the undemocratic nature of participation in economic life. Educational reform requires at the same time economic transformation towards democratic socialism. Third, our formulation rectifies an earlier pre-occupation of both liberal and Marxian analysis with the overt content of schooling. By focussing upon the experience of schooling, the correspondence principle provides a consistent analytical framework for understanding the school as an arena of structured social interaction. Fourth, our formulation of the correspondence principle contributes to a more positive understanding of the goals of socialist transition. In older critiques of capitalist society, almost unique stress was laid on the private ownership of means of production. At least as far as educational reform is concerned, we have been able to show that not ownership, but control is central to social inequities. Merely passing from private to social ownership without challenging in any substantial way the social relations of economic life, can have no impact on the egalitarian and humanistic goals of progressive educational reform. The correspondence principle then represents a powerful antidote to the authoritarian tendencies all too often found in an otherwise progressive social movement.

Reprinted with the permission of Falmer Press.

of historical evidence suggesting that the correspondence between schools and economic change is, at best, incomplete and not necessarily determined by capitalist production relations; and (3) a failure to develop a complete explanation of education that goes beyond relatively simple statements about its functions. Bowles and Gintis, in response to criticisms of their work, have commented that more attention needs to be paid to the contradictions that characterize education and other social relations in advanced capitalism (see, e.g., Gintis and Bowles, 1980). Their work, despite its limitations, has remained a significant reference point for critical analysis of schooling because of the crucial questions it raises about how education contributes to social reproduction.

Within much subsequent educational analysis informed by Marxism, there has been a tendency either to take for granted the existence of a correspondence principle or else to elaborate the mechanisms through which schools are linked to state and economic structures. These trends are apparent in critical analysis from a Canadian political economy tradition oriented to explaining the development of Canada's resource-based economy, the Canadian class structure, the social and economic impact of Canada's dependence on European and American capital, and subsequent attempts to delineate the emergence of one or more distinct Canadian nations. A preoccupation with historical preconditions and patterns of economic development has often left schooling as an unproblematic or absent force in such literature. In Wallace Clement's (1974) influential analysis of *The Canadian Corporate Elite*, for instance, education is mentioned only in passing as a device for conveying class-based privilege from one generation to the next, while a generally thorough, more recent review of the 'new' political economy literature in Canada (Clement and Williams, 1989) includes chapters that cover such themes as immigration, law, and communications, but virtually no attention is paid to education.

There is, however, a substantial body of political economic analysis of Canadian education. Two important books published in the 1970s highlighted a growing literature of critical analysis that emphasized how schooling was integrated with the corporate order under capitalism. *The Politics of the Canadian Public School*, edited by George Martell (1974), documents in a manner that continues to be highly relevant several issues of importance to Canadian education, including the reinforcement of class inequalities, the infusion of corporate values and profit-making strategies into the curriculum, and the political mobilization of teachers' movements. *Reading, Writing, and Riches: Education and the Socio-Economic Order in North America*, edited by Randle Nelsen and David Nock (1978), extends this analysis, detailing such additional issues as corporate control over post-secondary education and the subordination of Native peoples.

These books, along with analysis presented by Lockhart (1979), Schecter (1977), Livingstone (1983, 1985), Wotherspoon (1987), and others, have revealed the extent to which the Canadian education system has been infused with class-based ideologies and practices. However, preoccupation with economic reproduction within Marxist and political economy frameworks has often tended to overgeneralize the powers that capitalism, capitalists, and dominant economic forces have in shaping social life, and thereby to undermine education's capacity to change and be changed through interaction among educators, students, community members, and other social forces. Gaskell (1992: 22) observes that 'Critical theory and Marxist theory, despite their impact on scholarship, made few inroads with educational practitioners, who were frequently the targets of the critique, or with policy-makers, who were told there was not much to be done anyway within the framework of a capitalist economy.' Ironically, some Marxist analysis can also be criticized for its commitment to social change, in which the impression is created that, with proper revolutionary consciousness and effective political agents, radical social transformation appears to be inevitable (Davies, 1995: 1465–6).

Growing recognition of the dual nature of education, as a force that can foster critical sensitivity and empower people to take control over aspects of their lives as well as one that contributes to subordination and disempowerment, forced educators and educational researchers to develop more sophisticated educational critiques. Analysis came to focus not only on what is wrong with schooling, which has commonly been the main theme of orthodox Marxism and political economy, but also how education might facilitate individual and social transformation. Political economic analysis is often integrated with insights derived from other critical theories, including feminism and anti-racism, as well as statistical, historical, and comparative research, to produce richer critiques of contemporary educational issues and to suggest alternative visions (Livingstone, 1999; Sears, 2003; Taylor, 2001; Torres and Mitchell, 1998).

Theories of *cultural reproduction* offer possibilities to link detailed examination of specific educational practices, akin to interpretative studies, with processes that contribute to the maintenance of social structures. This approach is heavily influenced by the work of Pierre Bourdieu (1986) in France, Paul Willis (1977) and Basil Bernstein (1977) in Britain, and Michael Apple (1979, 1982) in the United States.

Bourdieu agrees with the Marxist position that education contributes to the perpetuation of class inequalities and other dimensions of unequal social structures. However, he is more concerned with social practices that affect how these inequalities can be variously reproduced or altered. Capital exists in the form of social and cultural assets as well as being an economic factor. Power and prestige convey definite advantages to members of privileged social groups, which in turn can be transmitted across generations, but these are only effective to the extent that they can be converted from potential to real benefits. For Bourdieu, a person's family background and social circumstances contribute to 'dispositions' or understandings that influence their options and actions in relation to specific types of social situations (which he terms 'fields' of interaction). Schools and other educational institutions are infused with class-based assumptions and expectations related to such things as rules of conduct, manners of expression, and background knowledge, giving some people a competitive advantage over others in their understanding and application. However, education, as it gains significance as a mechanism to grant credentials and provide legitimate access to social and economic opportunities, also becomes a site through which various social groups struggle for position and advantage. Bourdieu and Passeron (1979: 77), echoing neo-Weberian analysis of credential inflation, observe that, 'When class fractions who previously made little use of the school system enter the race for academic qualifications, the effect is to force the groups whose reproduction was mainly or exclusively achieved through education to step up their investments so as to maintain the relative scarcity of their qualifications and, consequently, their position in the class structure.' The framework introduced by Bourdieu has been adopted by several writers, including Andres Bellamy (1993) with respect to British Columbia students, in order to understand how students' social backgrounds and schooling experiences affect the educational and occupational pathways that they subsequently follow.

Willis, through extensive observations and interviews, traced a group of boys in a working-class town in the United Kingdom from their secondary schooling into their early post-school working lives. Willis demonstrates that, while economic reproduction occurs in predictable fashion in the sense that the boys are destined for occupational futures consistent with their class backgrounds, there is a complex interplay among the social and cultural factors that produce those outcomes. Jobs and social positions are not mechanically predetermined but develop through specific choices and experiences that arise, in part, through life in schools. The working-class 'lads' Willis observes engage in forms of resistance and rebellion to schooling that range from mocking school authority to verbal abuse, theft, and vandalism because they see in the middle-class standards of schools little that is of interest or relevance to their lives. By withdrawing from the mainstream of school life, the lads select a path leading to short-term work that at first offers excitement and independence but eventually results in low-paying jobs with few prospects for meaningful working lives. Willis argues that these choices reveal what he calls 'partial penetrations'. In other words, students are able to see through or penetrate weaknesses in the dominant meritocratic ideology because their experience contradicts the official argument that school success and hard work lead to social success. However, their insights are only partial in the sense that the options they choose lead them to a life of deadening routine that reinforces rather than transforms social inequalities.

Michael Apple's analysis of schooling proceeds from the recognition that schools contribute actively to the production, as well as the reproduction, of cultural practices and social structures. Apple, like Willis, accepts the Marxist argument that schools contribute to social control and the maintenance of structured inequalities, but he argues—consistent with the new sociology of education—that schools also create and process knowledge. Schools do more than simply transmit knowledge and ascribe places for individuals in society. Within schooling, ideas and understandings about the world and our place in the world are shaped by the actions of educational participants, which in turn are circumscribed by power relations and political economic structures.

The work of Apple and Willis has helped to advance what has come to be known as *resistance theory*. Resistance theory, unlike the more one-dimensional accounts of social reproduction that tend to be conveyed by structural functionalist and orthodox Marxist analysis, portrays schooling as a contested endeavour. Students do not blindly and automatically move from schooling into preordained social positions. Rather, their active participation in schooling involves diverse responses that range from enthusiastic acceptance to blatant rejection of the curriculum, of the manner in which it is transmitted, and of other aspects of the schooling process. Moreover, there are significant variations in how curricula and educational practices are presented to and experienced by various categories of students as distinguished by such factors as gender, race, ethnicity, and age. Boys and girls, for instance, are often taught differently and bring with them distinct frames of reference through which they subsequently interpret the curriculum. Resistance theory, in more general terms, brings to the forefront the dynamic elements of educational practices without losing sight of the social, economic, and political contexts within which schooling operates.

Feminist theory has also advanced considerably our ability to understand education, in particular its divergent forms and interests. Feminist analysis has a long history that only recently has been reformulated into systematic academic and political discourse. Critiques of schooling that we would now characterize as feminist were prevalent, for instance, in eighteenth-century arguments that access to education was a fundamental right for women as well as for men; nineteenth-century debates over whether boys and girls should take the same classes as one another, whether women should be admitted into universities, and struggles by women teachers to gain recognition for their work and to improve their working conditions; and later efforts to incorporate subjects and knowledge pertinent to girls' and women's lives into the curriculum. Despite these historical roots, the emergence of a distinct feminist analysis of schooling can be traced to the rising consciousness in the late 1960s and early 1970s of gender inequalities in education as well as in other spheres of social, economic, and domestic activity (Gaskell et al., 1989).

There are several forms of feminist analysis, unified by recognition of women's disadvantage and lack of privilege relative to men and of the need for social action to redress women's oppression. Most early feminist analyses of schooling focused on questions about sexism in the classroom and curricula and unequal distributions of men and women in different positions within the education system (Kenway and Modra, 1992: 140–8). These concerns are most characteristic of liberal feminism, which proposes reforms to alleviate sex bias and create more equitable gender representation in socially important positions. In schools, for example, employment equity measures are commonly identified as a response needed to compensate for the fact that, while women teachers outnumber men at nearly all levels of schooling up to the senior grades, most educational administrators are male. Liberal feminists advocate change, but argue that gender equity can be attained through modifications within existing social, educational, and economic arrangements.

Other feminists contend that effective change requires a more fundamental restructuring of social practices and structures. It is not sufficient simply to ensure equitable numbers of women and men in socially important positions, or that textbooks contain language and examples that apply to girls' and women's as well as to boys' and men's lives. Radical feminism has pointed out that patriarchy, or the systematic devaluation and oppression of women, is embedded within all forms of social organization. Language, science, politics, the economy, and other spheres of activity are organized around ways of knowing and doing that take male experience as the norm. Women's experience, by contrast, is undermined and relegated to the margins of what is considered to be socially important. Women—and spheres of life such as the domestic and sexual realms that give particular shape and meaning to their lives—are frequently absent as subjects and objects of study. In the sociology of education, for instance, feminist analysts have criticized classroom studies, such as Willis's, for ignoring the central role that gender plays in the construction of student school experience and school outcomes (see Weiler, 1988: 41–2).

Socialist feminism, like radical feminism, views liberal reforms as insufficient to overcome gender inequalities, but emphasizes social differences among, as well as between, men and women. Women's subordination must be understood in terms not only of gender but also of class (as well as race and other important aspects of social experience). The way in which gender influences people varies insofar as our lives are shaped by the distinct positions we occupy within society, including the opportunities we have for access to power and other crucial resources.

Feminist pedagogy has emerged as a way to unify women's common concerns, moving beyond specific labels towards clearer articulation of strategies to address practical problems (Luke and Gore, 1992). Feminists argue that the incorporation of women and their experiences into research is an important part of the wider process within which women are to make sense of and reclaim their lives. This involves the recognition of issues that are meaningful in an everyday context but commonly absent from curricula and public discussion, such as domestic violence, public safety concerns, competing family and career demands, and personal encounters with sexism. Women's voices, often emerging through accounts of their own experiences, become an important device to identify, clarify, and seek positive solutions to social problems (Brookes, 1992). In this way, possibilities are created to realize the potential education holds to be truly liberating and progressive.

Recent feminist scholarship, often in conjunction with critical pedagogy, new political economy, and post-structuralist and postmodernist critique, has attempted to develop a vision of social justice that proceeds from an understanding of the multiple causes of oppression (Arnot and Weiler, 1993; Kenway and Willis, 1998). Increasing recognition is also given to analysis that links personal or biographical experiences with wider structures of power and inequality. Gaskell (1992), for example, details how changes in schooling, labour markets, and socialization processes are intertwined with life choices and chances to produce different educational and vocational career patterns for girls and boys and for women and men. Feminism, in this regard, ensures that questions about gender remain central to the analysis and equitable reconstruction of social life.

Anti-racism education shares many of the concerns central to feminism and other critical analysis, including a commitment to social change guided by social analysis, with a more explicit focus on differential and unequal treatment based on race. Racism is perpetuated through social practices and structures that subordinate racial minorities, including the language used to

Box 2.4 A feminist perspective on the sociology of education

Kathleen Weiler (1988: 59–63) outlines the central characteristics of a feminist methodology that allow us to develop a political commitment to change through an analysis and validation of women's material and subjective experiences:

Before turning to the specific nature of this study, I want to discuss in more detail the characteristics of the feminist methodology I have employed.

First, feminists have argued that it is necessary for women to ground our research from the beginning in a recognition of our oppression as women in male-dominated society. This entails identifying and articulating both objective oppression in practices and relationships and the male blindness to women's experience, the tendency of what Mary O'Brien calls 'male stream thought' to assume that 'man' implies humanity and vice versa (O'Brien, 1983). Feminists go beyond a cataloguing of oppressive practices and sexist assumptions in dominant male thought to examine our own consciousness. . . .

The central emphasis on women's subjective experience leads to the second characteristic of much feminist research: the importance given to lived experience and the significance of everyday life. The connection here is obvious. Since women have so often been relegated to the private, domestic arena, their actions in everyday life define them in a way that is not the case for men, who are accustomed to defining themselves in the public arena and who exist as actors in a world of abstract thought and concrete public action. . . .

I am arguing then that an emphasis on the everyday experiences of women and the need for the researcher to locate herself in terms of her own subjectivity is fundamental to a feminist methodology. Moreover, a different kind of relationship is called for between knower and known, researcher and the object of research. . . . One of the major goals of feminist research is for both women as researchers and women as the objects of research to come to understand and explore their own consciousness and material conditions of existence through dialogue.

This leads me to the last characteristic of feminist research, which is its political commitment. The overt recognition of the feminist researcher's own subjective position, the identification of the feminist researcher with the object of her research, and the recognition of the deeply political nature of everyday life, lead feminist researchers to a commitment to changing the existing social order. Feminist theory and methodology is grounded on a commitment to

Box 2.4 continued

praxis. This political commitment reflects the essential materialist theory of knowledge that underlies feminist research. That is, for feminists, the ultimate test of knowledge is not whether it is 'true' according to an abstract criterion, but whether or not it leads to progressive change. In this sense, feminist research simply follows Marx's famous dictum that the point is not to understand the world, but to change it.

categorize and describe people from various racial and cultural backgrounds. Anti-racism analysis extends beyond the simple categorization of people on the basis of racial characteristics in order to highlight the diverse ways in which people's lives are affected by intersecting forms of oppression based on class, gender, race, and other social characteristics. Some commentators argue that racism, more than any other factor, has limited the life chances for specific groups, such as African-American students (Ogbu, 1994) or Aboriginal people in Canada (Monture-Angus, 1995). The approach more generally has three main concerns—to expose the ways in which racism, both in itself and in conjunction with other types of oppression, contributes to the suppression of opportunities for specific racialized groups; to examine the impact of racism; and to develop strategies to counter racially based subordination. Schooling is a primary focal point in anti-racism theory. Educators and the educational contexts that they work in have a significant impact on issues and practices associated with racial difference and inequality. Education contains the potential, alternatively, to critique and modify, or to ignore and reinforce, unequal racial identities and associated practices (Dei, 1996; Dei and Calliste, 2000).

Critical pedagogy is a related form of analysis that has emerged in an attempt to link educational theory with practice. This is not unique insofar as all critical theory, including Marxism, feminism, and other critical approaches, is unified by the researcher's commitment to try to change the world, rather than to act as an external observer who is studying it in an apparently detached and objective manner. A frequent limitation of the critical theories of education discussed to this point, though, has been their tendency to have little application to real educational settings. Educational participants who have been informed by critical analysis may develop a heightened awareness of their place within schooling as they attempt to rectify problems associated with social and educational disadvantage. However, a tendency in much critical analysis to focus on powerful oppressive forces often produces a sense of futility that things cannot be changed. Critical pedagogy aims to overcome the gap between understanding educational reproduction and taking action to provide social and educational transformation.

Box 2.5 A critical pedagogy perspective on the sociology of education

Henry Giroux (1989: 146–9) has been influential in the development of critical pedagogy, which is concerned with linking people's lived experiences with an analysis of social structures and power relations in order to work towards social transformation through the empowerment of both teachers and students:

In order to develop a critical pedagogy as a form of cultural politics, it is imperative that modes of analysis be developed that do not assume that lived experiences can be inferred automatically from structural determinations: that is to say, the complexity of human behavior cannot be reduced to merely identifying the determinants, whether they be economic modes of production or systems of textual signification, in which such behavior is shaped and against which it constitutes itself. The way in which individuals and groups both mediate and inhabit the cultural forms presented by such structural forces is in itself a form of production and needs to be made problematic through related but different modes of analyses. In order to develop this point, I want to briefly present the nature and pedagogical implications of what I call the 'discourse of student experience'.

Central to this view is the need to develop an analysis of how teachers and students give meaning to their lives through the complex historical, cultural, and political forms they both embody and produce. This suggests the need for incorporating into a critical theory of schooling an analysis of those social practices that both organize systems of inequality and that assign meaning to individuals through the self- and social representations that define the dominant categories for ordering social life in any given society. Developing a theory of schooling as a form of cultural politics means analyzing how social power organizes the basic categories of class, race, gender, and ethnicity as a set of ideologies and practices that constitute specific configurations of power and politics. . . .

The discourse of student experience supports a view of pedagogy and empowerment that allows students to draw upon their own experiences and cultural resources and that also enables them to play a self-consciously active role as producers of knowledge within the teaching and learning process. This is a pedagogy in which students get the knowledge and skills that allow them to ascertain how the multiple interests that constitute their individual and collective voices are implicated, produced, affirmed, or marginalized within the

Box 2.5 continued

texts, institutional practices, and social structures that both shape and give meaning to their lives. Such a pedagogical practice would draw attention to the processes through which knowledge is produced within the ongoing relations in which teachers, students, and texts and knowledge interact. Within these relations teachers and students produce knowledge through their own particular readings of the codes that structure and give meaning to texts.

The type of pedagogy for which I am arguing is not concerned simply with creating classroom knowledge produced through individual oppositional readings of a text, but also with a recognition of the importance of understanding the various ways in which teachers and students produce different forms of knowledge through the complex patterns of exchange they have in their interactions with each other over what constitutes dialogue, meaning, and learning itself. In other words, pedagogy itself represents an act of production. For example, both teachers and students produce knowledge in their interaction with a text by attempting to understand and reproduce the codes and assumptions that inform an author's particular writing; knowledge is also produced in an interpretive practice that reads texts as part of a wider set of cultural and historical experiences and thus produces knowledge that goes beyond the said, stated, and obvious. . . .

A pedagogy of student experience must also be linked to the notion of learning for empowerment: that is, curriculum practices must be developed that draw upon student experience as both a narrative for agency and a referent for critique. This suggests curriculum policies and modes of pedagogy that both confirm and critically engage the knowledge and experience through which students authorize their own voices and social identities. In effect, it suggests taking seriously, as an aspect of learning, the knowledge and experiences that constitute the individual and collective voices by which students identify and give meaning to themselves and others.

Reprinted from *Critical Pedagogy, the State, and Cultural Struggle* by Henry Giroux and Peter McLaren, eds, by permission of the State University of New York Press.

Education, as presented within critical pedagogy, contributes to the perpetuation of knowledge and power structures that foster the oppression of subordinate groups by dominant groups, but it also contains possibilities to empower persons in subordinated positions to change their lives and the social contexts within which they live. In this sense, while critical pedagogy, as a label, is relatively new, it builds on recognition of numerous historical examples of struggles in which oppressed groups have sought to use education as a means to gain control over their lives—from colonized peoples in Asia, Africa, and Latin America to inner-city ghetto residents and First Nations peoples in North America.

Critical pedagogy begins with a dialectical and dynamic understanding of the relationship between theory and action that locates research, like all human activity, within changing relations of domination, subordination, and resistance (see, e.g., Freire, 1985; Giroux, 1983, 1988; Livingstone, 1987: 7–9; McLaren, 1998: 171ff.). Giroux and McLaren (1989: xxi) emphasize that critical pedagogy involves a 'language of protest' and a 'critical theory of education' directed towards the task of 'constructing a new vision of the future'. The analysis offsets its portrayals of the despair of everyday life and the social structures that contribute to poverty, dehumanization, and hopelessness with the promise of hope and prospects for meaningful change.

More than most other approaches within the sociology of education, critical pedagogy is grounded in the actions of classroom practitioners. Theory is oriented to address their concerns directly by enabling them to comprehend their own educational realities in relation to wider struggles for liberation. This has sometimes proven to be problematic, in part because the language and philosophical discourse employed within critical pedagogy are posed in terms that have little meaning for all but a few students and educators. While writers like Paulo Freire and Peter McLaren are careful to integrate their analysis with everyday educational experience, there is a tendency in much critical pedagogy to become overly abstract and removed from sociocultural realities. This is especially true of critical pedagogy that draws heavily on postmodernist critiques of conventional theory and practice.

To educators who have become cynical about recurrent waves of fashionable educational ideologies and prescriptions for change, the idealistic and Utopian visions of radical educational reform can be readily dismissed as irrelevant to immediate classroom problems. Nonetheless, critical pedagogy has forced educators and analysts to clarify the nature and significance of educational practices while they maintain awareness of the social contexts that shape educational possibilities and limitations.

Guidelines for Research and Analysis in the Sociology of Education

This chapter has presented an overview of several influential and representative theories within the sociological analysis of education. These theories represent diverse approaches that offer distinct ways of defining research problems, collecting and analyzing data, and explaining educational phenomena. Each of the approaches offers important insights into educational practices and structures. We have observed, as well, that several factors must be taken into consideration to assess the adequacy of any particular theory or approach. What assumptions do we make about the world and how we study it? Does our interest lie, for example, with an explanation of what happens inside classrooms or are we more concerned with social, economic, and political structures (such as questions about educational finance, policy-making, and social inequality) that operate beyond the classroom? Is our focus on current issues or historical developments? On educational practices or the outcomes of schooling? On formal or informal aspects of the curriculum? On factors that give rise to educational stability or on educational change and conflict?

Differing theoretical perspectives and approaches to scientific understanding lend themselves to distinct ways of asking and investigating sociological questions. We must recognize that no single theory can address all of these questions adequately. Increasingly, educational analysis has emphasized the paradox that, while certain problems are more amenable than others to particular theoretical questions and research methods, there is sometimes more common ground between differing perspectives than is often supposed. These considerations do not mean, however, that all theories are equally valid or that we can simply 'pick and choose' an approach in an attempt to investigate social or educational phenomena. Rather, we must be aware of guidelines to ensure that our analysis is systematic and provides an accurate account of the realities we are trying to understand.

It is useful, in this regard, to identify several aspects of educational realities we have considered so far that must be taken into account if we are to develop an adequate sociological understanding of education. These include the following:

- We must recognize education as a broad set of practices that is not restricted to specific institutional forms like schools, colleges, and universities. Education takes place both formally and informally in all aspects of our lives. Educational practices have both intended and unintended consequences.
- Formal education is a contradictory endeavour. It can contribute to enhanced social and economic opportunities, individual self-awareness, and greater understanding of our place in the world, but it can also lead to oppression, subordination, and restricted socio-economic opportunities.
- We must be able to understand, and link together, what happens inside schools as well as the organization and operation of the education system as a whole. The analysis of education, in turn, must be integrated with an understanding of wider social processes and structures and strategies for transformation.
- We must be aware of the historical factors that have given rise to educational systems and processes of educational change.
- Formal education involves the production and dissemination of knowledge and skills of various forms. We must be aware of how these

processes are selective and, therefore, not representative of all social interests.

- We must be sensitive to how the needs and actions of educational practitioners, including students, teachers, administrators, and policy-makers, can both inform and be informed by educational analysis and research. It is important, in this regard, to recognize that none of these groups is homogeneous; rather, they reflect varied experiences characterized by gender, race, ethnicity, class, and other important social characteristics.

Conclusion

This chapter has emphasized the importance of theory as a tool to guide our understanding of education and its connections with other social phenomena. Illustrative theories have been presented from three main sociological frameworks—structural functionalism, interpretative analysis, and critical approaches—to highlight the diversity of questions and explanations drawn on by sociologists. The chapter has concluded with a series of issues that need to be taken into account in order to arrive at a comprehensive understanding of education, with the recognition that any single study or theory cannot encompass all of these concerns.

The chapters that follow—informed especially by the insights of critical theories of education—address these issues. Critical analysis enables us to move beyond the surface of educational activities to examine the underlying causes and consequences of educational practice. Through this analysis, ultimately, our aim is not only to understand the contradictory nature of education but to work towards a plan of action that allows us to make progressive changes in educational practices and outcomes.

Annotated Further Readings

Samuel Bowles and Herbert Gintis, *Schooling in Capitalist America: Educational Reform and the Contradictions of Economic Life*. New York: Basic Books, 1976. This highly influential book emphasizes that, in contrast to prevailing assumptions about education's contributions to social opportunity and equality, educational reform has maintained social inequality by contributing to ideologies and labour market requirements driven by the dynamics of a capitalist economy.

Émile Durkheim, *Education and Sociology*. New York: Free Press, 1956. This book, bringing together English translations of several of Durkheim's papers, is a classic work that makes the case for, and outlines the foundational elements of, the sociological analysis of education.

Roxana Ng, Pat Staton, and Joyce Scane, eds, *Anti-Racism, Feminism, and Critical Approaches to Education*. Westport, Conn.: Bergin and Garvey, 1995. Writers from Canada and the United States examine linkages among various critical perspectives to educational issues, including anti-racism education, feminist pedagogy, and critical pedagogy.

Carlos Alberto Torres and Theodore R. Mitchell, eds, *Sociology of Education: Emerging Perspectives*. Albany: State University of New York Press, 1998. Contributions to this book examine theoretical developments in the sociology of education and the significance of different forms of educational reform and inequality in comparative perspective.

Willard Waller, *The Sociology of Teaching*. New York: John Wiley and Sons, 1965. Although originally written and published in the 1930s, this book offers significant insights into school organization and daily interactions that remain fundamental to many educational practices.

Paul Willis, *Learning to Labor: How Working Class Kids Get Working Class Jobs*. New York: Columbia University Press, 1977. This influential British study examines the complex mechanisms whereby rebellion by working-class youth against school practices and educational authority are channelled into relatively predictable labour market outcomes.

Key Terms

Correspondence principle The view that presents educational reforms and outcomes as consequences of economic requirements, labour market needs, and inequalities within a capitalist economy.

Cultural capital The resources that people possess for economic and social success include not only wealth and economic assets, but also knowledge and understandings about social expectations, dominant values, and other pertinent information that institutions use in their ongoing operations.

Cultural reproduction Recognition that, while education contributes to ongoing social inequalities, it does so through cultural and social practices as well as economic requirements.

Human capital theory A theoretical approach, with frequent policy applications, that emphasizes education, skill development, and other learning processes as investments that enhance capacities and opportunities among individuals, thereby contributing to general economic growth.

Pedagogy Processes associated with the organization and practice of teaching. The term refers more generally to various kinds of interactions (and how these are understood and organized) in teaching-learning situations.

Resistance theory Analysis that highlights children, youth, and other students as active participants who can oppose and shape their education and social futures rather than as passive institutional clients.

Self-fulfilling prophecy The notion that the assumptions and expectations that teachers and other service workers hold about students can influence students' lives and futures.

Structural functionalism A theoretical perspective that explains social phenomena with reference to their mutual influence on one another, especially through the social needs they fulfill and the contributions they make to social order.

Symbolic interactionism A theoretical perspective that emphasizes the importance of language, meaning, and use of symbols in our development of self-awareness and, through our relations with others, as the basis of societies.

Technological functionalism A perspective that emphasizes industrial and technological development as the basis for educational expansion and emerging knowledge requirements.

Study Questions

1. Why are there several distinct theoretical frameworks within the sociological analysis of education, rather than a single approach?
2. Which approach to sociological analysis offers the most comprehensive explanation of educational practices and developments in Canada? Justify your answer.
3. Discuss the relationship between theory and practice in education. To what extent, and with what consequences, can theory and practice exist without informing one another?
4. Discuss which set of factors—those related to what happens inside educational institutions, or those brought in from outside educational institutions—has the strongest impact on educational outcomes. How well are these factors accounted for in the main sociological theories of education?
5. In what ways do educational institutions mirror other major institutions in contemporary societies? How, by contrast, can educational institutions be considered as distinct from other institutions? Discuss the impact of these similarities and differences on the development of a theoretical understanding of education.

3

Historical and Organizational Dimensions of Canadian Education

Introduction

The Canadian education system, as a whole, is one of the largest enterprises within Canadian society. In 2000–1, about $66.5 billion were spent on education in Canada, constituting just over 7 per cent of the gross domestic product (the total value of goods and services produced in the nation). Nearly 6.5 million Canadians are enrolled full-time in elementary, secondary, and post-secondary education programs, and close to 400,000 more are enrolled in part-time programs (Statistics Canada, 2003d: 53–4). Education also employs substantial numbers of people in teaching, administrative, and support positions. The 2001 census identifies 581,545 Canadians as teachers and professors while, overall, there are over one million persons employed in teaching and related occupations, representing 6.4 per cent of the total labour force (Statistics Canada, 2003c).

Canadians, like people in other industrially developed nations, have come to accept formal education as a normal part of their childhood and youth experience. It has become, for many people, a central feature of ongoing development throughout the life course. In many ways, current educational realities stand in marked contrast to the situation a century ago, when most people had very little, if any, formal schooling. Those few individuals who graduated from high school often became teachers or, on rare occasions, continued into post-secondary studies so that they could gain entry into select professional fields or round out their intellectual development for social and political reasons. The dramatic expansion of public education in just over a century, from a localized and voluntary pursuit to a highly formalized bureaucracy accompanied by an increasingly large selection of alternatives, is largely taken for granted, as is the fact that almost entire populations participate in schooling and rely on formal educational credentials for career and social advancement. Nonetheless, in common with contemporary public policy discussions about how schooling should be organized and financed, and what kinds of reforms are required to maintain relevant and competitive educational programming, the expansion of public education and efforts to modify or standardize the educational base were topics of heated public debate in the late nineteenth and early twentieth centuries.

This chapter begins with a discussion of historical factors that have shaped educational growth and transformation in Canada. The last part of the chapter provides an overview of the structure, size, and scope of contemporary Canadian education systems. Throughout the chapter, particular emphasis is placed on the contested nature of educational reform and on the changing role of state involvement in the organization, financing, and delivery of educational services.

The Historical Development of Education in Canada

The story of education in Canada, like other institutional histories, involves much more than a straightforward description of key events. Many different histories of Canadian education have been written, while others have yet to be recorded. It is common for educational histories to describe important events and milestones, such as the establishment of schools and universities or the passage of legislation concerning education. Other histories concentrate on influential individuals, such as Bishop Laval in New France, J.W. Dawson in Nova Scotia, Joseph-François Perrault and Jean-Baptiste Meilleur in Lower Canada, Egerton Ryerson and John Millar in Upper Canada, Frederick Haultain and David James Goggin in the Prairies, and John Jessop in British Columbia, whose visions and leadership contributed to the advancement of a stable education system in Canada (see, e.g., Wilson et al., 1970; Titley and Miller, 1982). Still other commentators have begun to reconstruct our educational heritage through social histories that take into account the experiences of less well-known students, teachers, parents, and other educational participants (see, e.g., Axelrod, 1997; Houston and Prentice, 1988; Johnston, 1988).

From a critical sociological standpoint, it is important, in acknowledging different ways in which the story can be told, to focus not strictly on what happened but, more crucially, on why things happened as they did and how they are significant for the analysis of social life. Individuals, historical events, and life circumstances must be understood with reference to the social context in which they emerged. Educational practices and changes take shape through the intentions and actions of particular historical actors who, in turn, influence and are influenced by other actors, organizations, and structures. What results is a complex layering of forces. While it is important to acknowledge that these are likely to convey different meanings to each person involved in the system or in efforts to understand it, critical sociological analysis proceeds also from an interest in identifying the regular patterns and underlying relationships that have contributed to those practices and experiences. Therefore, the brief historical overview that follows will emphasize some of the most significant features of the education system rather than a detailed description of events.

Early Forms of Formal Education in Canada

The school system as we know it is a relatively recent development, not a natural or inevitable feature of social life. It has been produced and modified within particular social circumstances, often subject to serious contestation over its direction or resistance to its presence and forms. Schooling, by nature, is oriented to change. Implicit within the aims of formal education are the objectives to produce new knowledge, transform individual personalities, and modify or improve social conditions. While there may be little disagreement, at least at a general level, that these are worthy objectives, the demands for educational changes frequently originate within groups or forces that have distinct social agendas or interests, however much these may be challenged and modified by other factors.

Education was a central part of life in what came to be Canada long before there were any formal schools. Early education was distinguished by its incorporation into the daily life practices of First Nations people. Education was crucial for the fulfillment of material needs and cultural survival. According to Kirkness and Bowman (1992: 5), 'It was an education in which the community and the natural environment were the classroom, and the land was seen as the mother of the people. Members of the community were the teachers, and each adult was responsible for ensuring that each child learned how to live a good life.' The integration of education with everyday life suggests a highly informal system of socialization. There is evidence, however, that many First Nations had sophisticated forms of social organization more than 15 centuries ago (Sewid-Smith, 1991: 19–20). While oral traditions such as storytelling were central to learning, complex systems of knowledge were systematically transmitted among generations, sometimes with the aid of visual symbols. First Nations each had their own distinctive bodies of traditional or indigenous knowledge, supported by social practices to preserve and transmit core beliefs, values, and competencies. Many of these were endangered through subsequent efforts by European colonizers to undermine or deny such knowledge (Battiste, 2000; Royal Commission on Aboriginal Peoples, 1996a: 526–7).

The First Nations pattern of 'organic' educational practices suited to the practical needs of family, clan, or community has characterized education among many other groups in Canadian society. This has been the case most commonly for children living in regions with no established educational facilities, such as families of early European settlers, Hudson's Bay Company officials, and homesteaders on the Prairies. On some occasions, family or community members attempt to resist, or even assert control over, education despite the ready accessibility of formal educational services. Situations of this kind are most likely to arise when members of minority groups, such as those based on ethnicity or religion, dispute central features of the dominant school system, when parents assert their right to educate the children themselves, or when parents see schooling as interfering with competing demands on their children's time for work, care of family members, or other responsibilities.

The earliest formal schooling in Canada was established by missionaries and religious orders. It was oriented primarily to the replacement of indigenous lifestyles and knowledge with European concepts of morality and consciousness. However benevolent the intentions of religious authorities may have been, denominational education was promoted zealously in the belief that Europeans were morally and intellectually superior to the Native people. Later, myths of the illiterate or noble savage served both to undermine and romanticize Aboriginal life. The representation of Aboriginal peoples as uncivilized or less than full persons enabled colonizing forces to attack traditions they characterized as naive or backward.

These early educational efforts had varying degrees of success. In some cases they were rejected, while in others they were embraced by Aboriginal people. Jaenen (1986), for instance, identifies four distinct phases in the education of Aboriginal people in New France, ranging from missionary education of children and families in the mission field beginning in the seventeenth century to nineteenth-century boarding schools. Changing educational practices reflected colonial desires to devise new strategies to accomplish educational objectives, particularly those oriented to the assimilation of First Nations peoples into European-based life conditions.

Education figured prominently in the fragmentation of First Nations societies. The impact of education was destructive both in content and in form. Not only were Native children taught that their traditional ways were inferior and unacceptable, but the routines and spatial organization of schools often contributed even more strongly to the separation of children from their families and communities. Assimilation was to be accomplished at the cost of breaking down existing social relationships. Schooling was particularly destructive when it attempted to transplant European cultural and educational forms to replace stable indigenous patterns that were attuned to the demands of life in North America. At the same time, Native people were not given opportunities to participate fully and equally in the new social order (Jaenen, 1986: 60). Boarding and residential schools, introduced as official policy by the federal government in the 1870s, acted as 'total institutions' in which children were taken from their parents so as to be removed from 'regressive' influences. Children were subject to harsh disciplinary measures for such offences as speaking in their Native language, and often they were unable to associate with other family members except for brief periods each year.

Box 3.1 Life in a residential school

Recent stories of separation from family, abuse, destruction of cultural traditions, and social breakdown have highlighted the traumatic effect of residential schools on Aboriginal people and their communities. In these excerpts told by residential school survivors (Jaine, 1993: 83–4, 91–2), the freedom of traditional First Nations education is contrasted with the regimentation that prevailed in residential schools:

Lois Guss

Normally, in a Native family, a child is allowed to learn by trial and error, with love and support being freely given. My experiences in residential school were a sharp contrast to this. There, our natural curiosity was impeded by the outlook of nuns, who had no experience in life and no experience as a parent. Even the natural curiosity of the opposite sex was discouraged and one was made to feel ashamed for even having such curiosities.

There were very few times you could enjoy life as it was so regimented. There was no freedom of thought or expression allowed. Everyone had to conform to a rigid set of standard rules: pray, learn, pray, obey, pray, eat, pray. Up at 6:30 a.m., Mass at 7:00 a.m., breakfast at 8:00 a.m., class at 9:00 a.m., lunch at 12:00 noon, class at 1:00 p.m., sewing and mending at 4:00 p.m., supper at 6:00 p.m., bed at 9:00 p.m. The next day it started again.

Even our bodily functions were regimented; there were certain times to go to the washroom, and castor oil was administered once a year. We had a bath once a week, and laundry duty every Saturday. We attended church once a day and twice on Sunday. On Sundays we had a few hours of free time but we were unaccustomed to such freedom, so we usually looked to an older student to organize our activities.

A Typical Day at St Henri,
as told by Alphonse Little Poplar, No. 22

The wake-up bell came early—6 a.m. First we had to go to the chapel for Mass so we could receive Absolution before Communion. Then we had breakfast, watery porridge with sugar already stirred in, no milk, and a slab of bread with no grease. Sometimes they would give us peanut butter for the bread. On those days a nun would go around the table with a pail of peanut butter and give each boy a glob of peanut butter on their bread.

Then we went out to do the chores: milk the cows, feed the pigs, get the firewood.

At 9 a.m. we were off to school for classes. In school we did some reading and things like that. Then we would have recess and then

Box 3.1 continued

break for noon. Dinner was usually soup and one piece of bread with no grease. Sometimes the soup had a sliver of meat and a potato in it. Those were the good days. We would have berries for dessert when they were in season.

We could never help ourselves to anything when we were eating meals. Everything was served by the nuns. There were no seconds. They fed us the way animals were fed, like slopping the pigs. There was an active blackmarket of stolen food ran by those students lucky enough to work in the kitchen. The students would trade between themselves. Sometimes we would fight over food, we would get so hungry.

After dinner it was classes, recess, and then classes again till 4 p.m. After school we would get a dry bun and any food we could steal, beg, buy, or barter.

Then came chores or play, depending on whose turn it was. If it was chores we had to feed the pigs again, milk the cows, weed the garden, or do the dishes. If it was our turn to play, we did what we could with what we had. We would make our own footballs—a leather bag stuffed with old rags, we made our own sleighs in the winter. We didn't have very much. There was a swing. We didn't have a rink until years later but we could watch the white kids skate.

At 5:30 we had supper which was stew, real thin stew, and bread. Again, everything was served. The slab of bread was put on a plate and then the stew put on it. There were no seconds. Then came clean up, and after clean up there was a short period of play and then we went to bed at seven.

Oh yes, the prayers. There were prayers every time we turned around. We prayed when we got up, when we started a meal, when we finished a meal, when we went to play, when we went to bed. We sure prayed a lot. I guess they must have thought we needed a lot of praying.

We went to bed in the early evening when the sun was still high. I would lie by my window and watch the white children play ball. How I wished I could be there playing with them.

Missionaries and other individuals who were privately contracted also provided early schooling for children of British and French origin in Canada. These schools were intended primarily to keep alive connections with established European traditions or to train individuals for specific purposes. Examples of the latter include the provision of training for religious orders, political elites, and teachers. Among the general population, education tended to be sporadic, oriented to the cultivation of loyalty to religious or political orders rather than to anything more than the most basic formal lessons (see, e.g., Titley, 1982).

The origins of schooling have to be understood in the context of the general social structure. The initial development of Canada by European and, subsequently, North American interests was motivated primarily by territorial or commercial concerns. Resource-based industries such as the fur trade, gold extraction, logging, and fishing were highly volatile, and priority was given to measures that would ensure that adequate supplies of labour and access to resources were available. Moreover, with a few exceptions, such as colonial officials, merchants, and service suppliers who were in a position to settle and raise families, most of the labour force consisted of men who were single or geographically mobile. Because many regions had no children other than those who performed domestic chores or engaged in paid labour, and the relatively privileged groups could arrange to have their children tutored privately or sent to schools elsewhere, there were few demands for a general system of public schooling until the late eighteenth and early nineteenth centuries.

The Development of a Public School System

Increased immigration and settlement of families, the influx of United Empire Loyalists from the United States, and political and economic threats to Canadian lands and resources gave rise to new demands for a system of free public schooling. Whereas schooling under denominational and colonial control fostered loyalties to traditional sources (Church, class, and old-country ties), the most ardent proponents of a common public school system sought the development of distinctly Canadian identities. Schooling for the general population was to be secular—to overcome the particular intentions of denominational authorities; open to all pupils—to ensure that the entire population had a common education; and suited to the cultivation of social and political bonds within Canada. Education was a significant factor in struggles to break ties with the colonial powers of Britain and France and to preserve Canadian autonomy against American influence. In some instances, such as among Loyalist emigrants from the United States, parents agitated for schooling in order to extend opportunities they had previously experienced. In many other cases, however, the strongest advocates for public schooling were politicians, business people, educated professionals, and educators themselves who sought the establishment of stable communities (Curtis, 1988; Prentice, 1977).

Schooling offered several advantages to the school promoters. The presence of a school in a community signified a commitment to future planning and growth. Like the Church in medieval and colonial times, the school became a symbol of order and authority, with the advantage that secular public schooling was premised upon opportunities for democratic input that were absent under colonial and religious control. The provision of educational services could be used to attract relatively ambitious and prosperous settlers and their families. The curriculum, while facilitating basic literacy among the population, could also be used to cultivate new attitudes and allegiances necessary for the growth of a stable social order.

The factors that contributed to the development of public school systems in Canada reveal the dual objectives of formal education. First, schooling provides formal learning opportunities through the curriculum. Fundamental skills and knowledge are made available to all learners, and people are given a chance to encounter new ideas and challenges. At the same time, however, formal education also contributes to moral regulation and the reshaping of people's identities. In both structure and content, schooling is centrally involved in the process of disciplining the individual through emphasis on rules and habits rather than on lessons alone (Corrigan et al., 1987; Curtis, 1988). Political reformers recognized that schooling could be an important contributing factor to the process of Canadian nation-building. This process involved, in part, the shaping of individual subjects committed to the Canadian state and its institutions and values. School facilities were among the first and most prominent structures in many communities in recognition of education's importance in state formation and community-building.

The regularization of education as part of an established state apparatus was not problem-free. Educational promoters faced three main obstacles in their quest to construct a solid educational system. First, it was necessary to raise money to build schools, hire qualified teachers, and operate school programs. Funds for education had to be raised against competing priorities such as economic development and the construction of roads and other services. Current debates over the extent to which governments should be responsible for educational finance need to be understood in the context of a history of a long, contested, public discourse concerning the proper role of the state in the provision of public services. Second, educational promoters had to mobilize support for public schooling in the face of considerable opposition or indifference from various sources, including religious denominations, supporters of private schools, and community members who saw schooling as an intrusion into private life. Records reveal that just over half of the children in Canada attended schools regularly by the early part of the twentieth century. As late as 1910–11, when over 1.3 million students were enrolled in schools in Canada—which was a substantial proportion of the 1.5 million children in the 5- to 15-year-old age group—the average daily attendance rates remained below two-thirds of those children registered (Dominion Bureau of Statistics, 1924: 157; Leacy, 1983: W67–8). Attendance patterns tended to reflect regional differences in socio-economic circumstances as well as families' material conditions and class backgrounds. There were wide variations in children's school attendance, depending on family means, periodic illness, and local economic conditions such as irregular wages among labourers and shifting labour and employment patterns for children at home, on farms, and in industry (Davey, 1978; Gaffield, 1982). A third problem that

Box 3.2 Teachers' duties, 1875

This excerpt from the 1875 rules and regulations for public schools in British Columbia (1875: 47) not only spells out teachers' duties, but, more importantly, it indicates the significance of discipline, habit, morality, cleanliness, and order in the operation of schools:

It shall be the duty of every teacher of a Public School—

1. To teach diligently and faithfully all the branches required to be taught in the school, according to the terms of his engagement with the Trustees, and according to the rules and regulations adopted by the Board of Education:
2. To keep daily, weekly, and monthly registers of the school:
3. To maintain proper order and discipline in his school, according to the authorized forms and regulations:
4. To keep a visitors' book (which the Trustees shall provide) and enter therein the visits made to his school, and to present such book to such visitor, and to request him to make therein any remarks suggested by his visit:
5. At all times when desired by them, to give to Trustees and visitors access to the registers and visitors' book appertaining to the school, and upon his leaving the school to deliver up the same to the order of the Trustees:
6. To have at the end of each half-year public examinations of his school, of which he shall give due notice to the Trustees of the school, and, through his pupils, to their parents and guardians:
7. To furnish to the Superintendent of Education, when desired, any information which it may be in his power to give respecting anything connected with the operation of his school, or in anywise affecting its interests or character:
8. To classify the pupils according to their respective abilities:
9. To observe and impress upon the minds of the pupils, the great rule of regularity and order,—A TIME AND PLACE FOR EVERYTHING, AND EVERYTHING IN ITS PROPER TIME AND PLACE:
10. To promote, both by precept and example, CLEANLINESS, NEATNESS, and DECENCY. To personally inspect the children every morning, to see that they have their hands and faces washed, their hair combed, and clothes clean. The school apartments, too, should be swept and dusted every evening:
11. To pay the strictest attention to the morals and general conduct of the pupils; to omit no opportunity of inculcating the principles of TRUTH and HONESTY; the duties of respect to superiors, and obedience to all persons placed in authority over them:

Box 3.2 continued

12. To evince a regard for the improvement and general welfare of the pupils; to treat them with kindness, combined with firmness; and to aim at governing them by their affections and reason rather than harshness and severity:

13. To cultivate kindly and affectionate feelings among the pupils; to discountenance quarrelling, cruelty to animals, and every approach to vice:

14. To practice such discipline in school as would be exercised by a judicious parent in the family, avoiding corporal punishment, except when it shall appear to him to be imperatively necessary; and then a record of the offence and the punishment shall be made in the school register for the inspection of trustees and visitors:

15. No teacher shall compel the services of pupils for his own private benefit or convenience:

16. For gross misconduct, or a violent or wilful opposition to authority, the teacher may suspend a pupil from attending school, forthwith informing the parent or guardian of the fact, and the reason of it; but no pupil shall be expelled without the authority of the trustees:

17. When the example of any pupil is very hurtful, and reformation appears hopeless, it shall be the duty of the teacher, with the approbation of the trustees, to expel such pupil from the school; but any pupil under public censure, who shall express to the teacher his regret for such a course of conduct, as openly and explicitly as the case may require, shall, with the approbation of the trustees and teacher, be re-admitted to the school.

plagued early school development was the shortage of a steady supply of trained teachers. Teachers had to have adequate preparation to teach the curriculum, but, more crucially, they had an important role to play in the promotion of schooling. As school employees, they also needed to be loyal to the cause of educational goals as capable representatives in the service of the state (Wotherspoon, 1993).

These problems left many schools in jeopardy, particularly in the poorer and less established regions of the country. Lack of public support and revenue for schooling led to substandard school facilities and low wages for teachers, which in turn made it difficult for some municipalities to attract pupils and suitable teachers. An illustrative case occurred in Victoria when teachers left their jobs for two years, beginning in 1870, after they had not been paid their full wages. The strike action was precipitated by a lack of funds following the refusal of the school board to enforce collection of an educational tax of $2 per resident (Wotherspoon, 1993: 88–9). Until well into the twentieth century, the option of closing down or being left to operate with little or no funding plagued schools across the country.

In the struggle of schooling to survive, educational ideals continually gave way to the demands of harsher realities. An illustration appears in the relationship between educational authorities' objectives and the practices that eventually emerged in the development of the teaching force. Nineteenth-century educational promoters repeatedly stressed that the advancement of education, and within it the occupational status of teaching, depended on a corps of male teachers of high moral character and strong educational background. However, faced with limited resources, school boards tended to hire the cheapest, most readily available teachers, most of whom were young women whose formal qualifications fell far short of desired standards (Prentice, 1977: 108–9; Wotherspoon, 1993: 93). While critics were tempted to blame the worst educational problems on the young women who entered the classroom, it was in fact often the zeal and resourcefulness of these teachers and supportive community members, rather than any higher educational motives, that enabled schooling to flourish (Shack, 1973). Ironically, when schooling became successful in attracting large numbers of students, there was an even greater reliance on hastily prepared teachers to ensure that all schools could be staffed.

The advancement of education was also accomplished through a growing array of formal regulations. Most jurisdictions, by the late nineteenth century, introduced rules governing everything from textbooks to school behaviour, often in the form of legislation to ensure compulsory attendance, regular taxation, and other matters, as part of an effort to regularize schooling. Strict adherence to daily attendance records and specific classroom routines enabled school authorities to monitor teachers and pupils carefully, while provisions for school finance helped to secure educational stability. Classroom life could be a deadening process of enforced order with rituals of repetition to memorize information (Axelrod, 1997: 57–8). In combination, these measures were important because they represented standards and practices that distinguished schooling from everyday life. Formal education became a central element in the expansion of state rule.

The growth of schooling was enhanced by the advocacy of social reformers who portrayed schools as critical tools in the state's crusade against social disorganization. Formal education gained central importance during significant developments in the late nineteenth and early twentieth centuries that altered North American social and institutional life: new industries and technologies, urban growth, the promotion of settlement in the West, and massive immigration transformed earlier patterns. Public optimism about the future was mixed with uncertainty about new challenges. Unemployment, displacement from work, crime, poverty, unwelcome intrusions by 'foreigners', family breakdown, and generally declining moral standards loomed as supposed threats to the social order. Many reform movements seeking social intervention into private life grew from and played upon these fears. Some of these interests were driven by concern that rapid changes were undermining the social order and leading to declining standards of living. Others, motivated by concern for the welfare of families and individuals disadvantaged by social changes, called for state and civic authorities to provide more social support. They viewed the school as an institution that could mould a new society by rising above parochial interests (Moscovitch and Drover, 1987). Numerous groups—government officials, churches and religious orders, employers, workers' associations, community leaders, and many others—despite motivations and aims that could be highly divergent from one another, and often with substantial variations from one jurisdiction to the next, influenced the shape and direction that formal schooling eventually would take at the centre of public life (Charland, 2000). Schooling was a central part of increasing public interventions into private life. In the late nineteenth and early twentieth centuries, the state or authorities acting on behalf of the state gained new powers to act as legal guardians for individuals who were deemed socially unfit or problematic in some way. The Juvenile Delinquents Act, enacted in 1908, enabled the state to provide 'assistance' to young offenders who were portrayed as 'misdirected and misguided'. Similarly, during the 1890s, provincial governments authorized teachers to act *in loco parentis*, effectively granting them parental responsibilities for the time that children were at school. Other reforms, demanded by such groups as charitable and welfare organizations and mental and public health movements, were based on the designation of particular groups as problematic or incapable of supporting themselves, thereby warranting the personal and professional services of official agents.

The arguments employed by social reformers emphasized the need for state intervention in the absence of proper guidance by parents (Sutherland, 1976). The following plea, written in the late 1860s by school officials in Prince Edward Island for compulsory attendance legislation to counteract the 'evils of irregular attendance', is typical of the justifications of the need for public education and other mechanisms to ensure compliance with state rule: 'If then, from the poverty, the cupidity, or the apathy of parents, the education of their children be neglected, it is surely the duty of the State to interpose its authority in their behalf, by means of a compulsory law' (cited in Prentice and Houston, 1975: 165). This kind of appeal blamed individual children and their parents for ignorance or neglect, leading to social problems that demanded a social solution by the state, which was posed as the protector of the public or common interest. In this case, compulsory schooling was a mechanism to keep children off the streets, teaching them in the process rules of discipline, proper conduct, and perhaps even useful skills and knowledge.

Industry, Science, and the Bureaucratic Organization of Schooling

While the historical evidence indicates that schools were not established simply to meet employers' demands to produce a compliant industrial work-force, industry doubtless affected the rise of public schooling in significant ways. Educational administrators sought to ensure the success of schooling by making the education system relevant—and perceived as useful—to life in industrial societies. They emphasized that students had to be trained to adapt to a changing world and to come out of schools with skills and knowledge that would contribute to their gainful employment. This was more often a matter of sensitivity by school authorities to external forces than a conse-quence of direct intervention into schooling by business and industry offi-cials. The financial and organizational viability of schooling depended on successful efforts by school officials to cultivate the support of business lead-ers, parents, and other public interests.

Educational officials also looked to industry for models to govern cur-riculum and school organization. The physical arrangement of the classroom, with its rows of desks under the watchful gaze of the teacher, the division of the school day into distinct periods or blocks of time, an early emphasis on memory work and rote exercises, and concern for punctuality, proper man-ners, and good habits were derived from military and religious training, but they were also highly amenable to a factory system of industrial production. Modern industry, moreover, provided models of organizational and class-room management oriented to educational efficiency. Scientific management, a strategy by which employers could assert control over industrial produc-tion processes by dividing tasks into their simplest, cheapest operations, was promoted by many educational administrators as a most effective method of lesson planning. Curricula were to be organized and planned systematically, not left to guesswork and reliance on teaching methods that were used sim-ply because they seemed to work in the classroom (Wotherspoon, 1995a).

Educational reform has been driven by more than an industrial logic, however. Schools have at their core a social and interpersonal dimension that cannot be reduced to work preparation and other economic prerogatives. Complex and contradictory dynamics leave the goals, structures, practices, and outcomes of schooling open to contestation.

The interplay of contradictory forces in educational development can be illustrated with reference to the role that educational progressivism played in school reform. In the early twentieth century, many educators advocated a philosophy of educational progressivism based on faith in the twin virtues of science and humanism. Educational progressives viewed schools as institu-tions that contributed to the realization of social progress by allowing stu-dents to develop their full human potentials. Families, schools, and other agencies that treated child development as a matter of routine acceptance of tradition or factory-like regulation were dangerous because they did not allow room for creativity and positive growth. Individuals needed to be given options to pursue their interests and opportunities to enhance their personal qualities. Progressivism advocated the incorporation within schooling of sub-jects that allowed for artistic and interpersonal development rather than strict academic courses. Teachers, in turn, had to have specialized training, in part to learn the scientific principles on which pedagogy and human development were grounded. In the process, a series of educational reforms emerged. These reforms were driven simultaneously by objectives for a more democratic and humanistic learning environment and by a desire for the creation of 'an educational system which was highly centralized, bureaucratic, autocratic, geared to the development of a meritocracy of intelligence, and designed to lead and direct an adequately socialized majority' (Mann, 1980: 115).

As the school system became governed increasingly by principles of rational organization derived from business and industry, there was a contradictory significance for the development both of schooling and of teaching as a professional occupation. Increasingly specialized training, grounded in science, gave teaching a degree of expertise that could advance its status as a professional occupation. By World War II, schools in most regions of Canada had become centrally organized as bureaucratic structures within larger school units. The average school size in Canada increased from 66 pupils per school in the mid-1920s to 156 in 1960 and 350 in 1970 (Manzer, 1994: 131). There were several advantages to the amalgamation of smaller schools and school districts into larger units. Many smaller schools were not financially viable, and although each school was required to provide a range of basic programs and services, it was often not possible for many schools to offer complete programs or attend to diverse educational needs. Larger schools offered better prospects for stable educational services accompanied by more extensive facilities, more complete educational programs, and a variety of curricular and extracurricular choices. It became possible for school districts to offer teachers better pay and job security and, particularly in the senior grades, to provide conditions in which teachers would be better able to teach in their areas of specialization.

Both community input and teacher professionalism, however, faced direct and indirect constraints that limited their influence on educational practice. Teachers were subordinated within an educational bureaucracy, subject to the supervision of educational administrators and guided by regulations set by officials outside the occupation. Indirect control over teaching was extended by the development of scientific curricula and central planning, which tended to move educational decision-making over many crucial issues, such as selection of textbooks and the organization of curricula, from the classroom to sources outside the school (Popkewitz, 1991). In the process, the treatment of educational matters as technical problems also minimized opportunities for meaningful community involvement in the education system. Experts, claiming legitimacy through training and knowledge related to principles of educational management, child development, curriculum planning, and pedagogy, assumed authority over a growing domain of issues beyond the reach of most public participants.

Educational Expansion in the Post-World War II Period

The role of schooling in society, paralleling debates over educational purposes, increased in complexity throughout the twentieth century. Educational practices expanded in two general ways. First, an increasing array of educational institutions, programs, and curricula emerged, incorporating a broad range of courses and subject areas not previously taught. Second, growing numbers of people enrolled in educational programs and remained in them for longer periods of time. The result has been massive increases in enrolments and educational attainments since the end of World War II. At the same time, significant changes occurred in the nature and quality of schooling. For the most part, classrooms were better equipped, teachers were better qualified, and curricular offerings were more diverse than ever before.

Formal education also gained an increasingly central place in social and economic life beyond the schools. In its formative years, schooling was concerned with habit formation and citizen development. As industrialization expanded, greater emphasis was placed on the contributions that schooling could make to training individuals and preparing them for entry into the labour force. By the mid-twentieth century, formal education gained increasing recognition as a credentialling mechanism. The attainment of educational certification became a mark of entry into specific occupations and jobs as well as a requirement for advanced education and training. As new employment opportunities were created in a context of rising industrial productivity, mass distribution of consumer goods and services, and the expansion of employment in human services through the growth of the state sector, there was a high correlation between educational achievement and the attainment of stable jobs with good wages and working conditions. Social reformers also looked to schools as sites where people could be taught to develop interests that would enable them to use their leisure time and meet the diverse demands of advanced liberal democracies more fruitfully.

By the 1960s, formal education appeared to be well-positioned to fulfill its promise to contribute to a more equitable social order. Educational expansion, combined with favourable social and economic circumstances, suggested that all persons, regardless of social background, had potential opportunities for social and economic advancement.

Although there was considerable reason to be optimistic, heightened emphasis on the value of schooling prompted a reassessment of educational realities suggesting that education could not always deliver what it promised. Beginning in the late 1950s, as observed in the previous chapter, several studies framed within what came to be known as status attainment research highlighted schooling's continuing association with substantial socio-economic inequalities. Moreover, people's life experiences did not always accord with emergent expectations. As schooling and the ideologies surrounding its social benefits gained in prominence, it became easy to blame individuals for their failure to take advantage of opportunities for socio-economic advancement.

However, schooling itself also proved to be vulnerable to criticism. On the one side, such critics as Hilda Neatby (1953), in her controversial *So Little for the Mind*, attacked schools for straying from their intellectual roots by catering to an overly broad range of interests. The problem, viewed from this perspective, was that schooling was becoming too diverse, weakening its ability to provide a common core of essential knowledge and values. Other critics, by contrast, maintained that schools were not keeping pace with changing socio-economic realities. They saw it as essential for schools to offer socially relevant knowledge, vocational training, and courses related to new employment requirements. These demands intensified after 1957, when the Soviet Union's launch of the Sputnik satellite prompted fears that North America was losing its technological advantage to new superpowers. Educational institutions came under fire for their failure to produce technically sophisticated and innovative graduates.

Elementary and secondary schools responded by revamping their curricula, giving emphasis to programs in mathematics and the natural sciences. Enhancement of scientific and technical training, prompted by federal funding initiatives, also fuelled post-secondary educational expansion. Nationally, the number of bachelor's degrees awarded in mathematics and the physical sciences increased substantially, from 1,617 in 1960–1 to 7,730 a decade later (Dominion Bureau of Statistics, 1963; Statistics Canada, 1973). Enrolment was encouraged by the addition of programs and research facilities to existing institutions as well as by the creation of several new technical institutes and community colleges throughout the nation. Between 1960 and 1970, education spending increased from 14 per cent of all government expenditures in Canada to 21.6 per cent (Lockhart, 1979: 229), and by 1975 there were 170 public community colleges in Canada compared to just one a decade earlier (Dennison, 1981: 213).

Post-secondary educational growth in the 1960s and 1970s was further advanced with increased demands for workers in the social and human services that accompanied the expansion of the welfare state. In Canada, the number of bachelor's degrees awarded in education increased 5.8 times between 1960–1 and 1970–1, while those in law increased by a factor of 5.2 times, those in nursing 4 times, and those in the physical sciences 4.9 times; over the next decade, the number of social work degrees awarded increased by nearly 5 times. Educational and occupational growth in these areas was especially important for providing opportunities for women. The proportion of bachelor's and first professional degrees awarded to women doubled from one-quarter to one-half between 1960–1 and 1980–1. By 1980–1, women received 73.5 per cent of Bachelor of Education degrees (compared to 37.2 per cent in 1960–1), 77.3 per cent of Bachelor of Social Work degrees (44.3 per cent in 1960–1), and nearly all of the degrees awarded in nursing. While only 5 per cent of recipients of Bachelor of Law degrees in 1960–1 were women, that proportion had climbed to over 33 per cent two decades later. By contrast, however, women received only 8.4 per cent of bachelor's degrees

Box 3.3 Education problems in Canada, 1958

After World War II, educators, policy-makers, and media reports high-lighted the need to link education with technological advancement. Following the development of nuclear weapons and the launch of the Sputnik satellite by Russia, educational reformers advocated the adoption of education systems like those in the Soviet Union and other nations, and increased investment in human capital, to encourage the expansion of scientific and technical expertise. In 1958, the Canadian Teachers' Federation, the Canadian Manufacturers' Association, the Canadian Labour Congress, and other organizations sponsored a national Conference on Education, described here by the then-president of the British Columbia Teachers' Federation (Cottingham, 1958: 398–9, 407), to reassess educational practices and establish new educational priorities:

> For years people closely connected with education have been increasingly alarmed about the magnitude of the task which we have set ourselves in Canada—to provide the maximum formal education at public expense for every man's child. Perhaps those with most reason to be alarmed at the growing crisis have been the teachers and professors who face their classes every day and know to what extent the time and talents of students and instructors are being wasted or used to best advantage, despite the rising costs of education. Never in the history of our country have so many boys and girls been kept in school and university so long at such great expense as now. Never have teachers and professors been in such short supply. Never have their tasks been so heavy. Never has the supply of well prepared professional, industrial, and technological workers been so far short of the needs of our society.
>
> No matter how critical the problem, in a democratic nation the solution must await the awakening of public opinion and only through the time-consuming democratic process can action be effected. . . .
>
> This conference was planned long before USSR launched its Sputniks into outer space, but these evidences of scientific achievement on the part of our northern neighbor increased the significance of this national discussion on the problems of education in Canada, where our strange scale of values causes us to spend twice as much on liquor and tobacco as we do on formal education and almost four times as much on defense.
>
> Dr Wilder Penfield, distinguished brain specialist and Director of the Conference, gave the keynote address. 'Dissatisfaction with the support of education and the performance of educationists has led

Box 3.3 continued

to this meeting', he said, 'and the educationists have it in their power to mould our future.' Dr Penfield had visited USSR two years ago. There he found the prestige and the level of pay for teachers and professors considerably higher comparatively than they are in Canada. Russia had a better system of scholarships for its able students and its training of prospective teachers and university professors was far more rigid and exacting. However, he suspected that in Russia students specialize too early without being grounded in the humanities.

'The specialist who has a broader educational basis leads a better life.' At the same time Dr Penfield felt that more emphasis should be put on trade schools and technical colleges in Canada.

He set the whole problem squarely before the delegates when he said:

'Looking to the future we face two possibilities; the ending of this civilization such as it is, or its final flowering and fulfillment in greater progress. Education is our only hope, our challenge in the peaceful competition of the future. But, if war should come, our wits might well save us. We would be well advised to spend on the cultivation of those wits a sum comparable with what we are spending on explosive defense.' Especially in the field of higher education, Dr Penfield felt that financial support must be doubled, but that support must leave these institutions complete freedom of development. Responsibility for support of teaching at all educational levels rests with the provinces, but industry, labor and the federal government could provide scholarships. . . .

awarded in engineering and applied sciences, and 29.6 per cent of first degrees in mathematics and physical sciences in 1980–1 (calculated from Dominion Bureau of Statistics, 1963: 22, 44–9; Statistics Canada, 1973: 456–8; Statistics Canada, 1984: 69–74).

These trends illustrate the strong paradox that characterizes formal education. Expansion of post-secondary education after World War II offered legitimacy to the belief that formal education could provide individuals with meaningful social and economic opportunities. The attainment of higher education credentials not only enabled individuals to gain access to secure and well-paying jobs, but it also opened up possibilities that were not previously available to women and members of other minority groups. At the same time, the issues of who could achieve educational success and what kinds of educational programs were available to different groups remained problematic. As formal education came to be relied on more frequently as a screening mechanism for entry into jobs and other social venues, there was a danger that disadvantaged groups could be left even further behind when socio-economic inequities were reproduced. Social advancement became that much more difficult for people who, for various reasons, were denied educational success. Moreover, as revealed in the distribution of university degrees to men and women, education itself remained highly stratified, producing different opportunities and career prospects for different social groups. While increasing numbers of people were attaining higher levels of formal education, there were considerable discrepancies in the kinds of benefits that people received from their educational credentials.

Educational Crisis and Reassessment

Debate and controversy over educational priorities were not restricted to labour markets and credentials. The increasing centrality of education to social life drew attention also to the educational process and to people's experiences within educational institutions. By the end of the 1960s, popular demands for educational reform intensified in an atmosphere characterized by sensitivity to drastic social changes and critical questioning of fundamental social institutions. Technological developments were altering how people lived and worked. Media coverage of international events, particularly United States involvement in the Vietnam War, made startlingly evident the significance of global events for everyday life. University campuses and other educational sites were crucial nurturing grounds for the emergence of anti-war protests, radical student movements, and feminism. Many of the concerns were motivated by increasing awareness of the reality that graduates were not getting the kinds of jobs and social opportunities they felt they had been promised through education.

Schooling, in this context, came under attack from nearly all sides. Left-wing and radical movements, while often mobilized and empowered by educational experiences, dismissed schooling as a bastion of bureaucratic traditionalism that stifled, rather than enhanced, creativity and genuine opportunity. The ideas of such writers as Ivan Illich (1970), who advocated alternatives to schooling that required the dismantling of the present education system, gained popularity as well as notoriety both within and beyond educational circles. From the right, critics argued that social radicalism itself both produced and was a product of educational failure. Formal education had strayed from its disciplinary and instrumental purposes, according to this viewpoint, and needed to return to fundamental values, knowledge, and respect for authority in order to prevent social breakdown.

Officially, though, the most successful educational ideology was embodied in liberal and human capital positions. Both educators and policy-makers revealed renewed interest in issues of equality of opportunity and educational progressivism, modified to meet contemporary demands. Several influential reports presented in the late 1960s and early 1970s, such as those known popularly as the Hall-Dennis Report in Ontario (1968) and the Worth Report in

Alberta (1972), stressed that child-centred learning opportunities and educational flexibility were crucial elements in people's ability to adapt to a changing society.

The spirit of change embodied in recommendations contained within the various reports was translated into a flurry of initiatives to restructure schooling and educational practices across Canada. Where resources were sufficient, students were presented with many new options beyond the traditional core curricula in areas such as law, family life, sex education, band and music appreciation, psychology, creative arts, and social studies in order to broaden their development and to better prepare them for the diverse demands of a post-industrial society. Experimental and innovative practices were encouraged in educational circles to overcome what came to be regarded as overly rigid and outmoded pedagogical models based on military and industrial principles. Schools were designed or modified to incorporate open classrooms and learning resource centres to counteract the rigid, box-like structure of existing school spatial organization; boundaries between disciplinary subjects and grade levels were broken down; student evaluation and reporting came to emphasize a wide range of skills, competencies, and subjective observations rather than strictly letter or numerical grades; and teachers were encouraged to draw out the child through critical thinking and social interaction rather than focus strictly on cognitive knowledge and prescribed curricular content.

Some of the changes had immediate impacts on educational practices and outcomes. Curricular revisions and modification of programs and practices to meet local needs or to improve responsiveness to disadvantaged groups, for instance, were long overdue. However, there was considerable resistance to the process of change, and in many cases little evidence to support widespread perceptions that schooling was being transformed in fundamental ways. Many teachers felt that educational reforms had been imposed on them with little consultation and inadequate training and resources to implement them properly. Traditionalists pointed to the chaos, wasted time, and lack of tangible results as evidence that educational liberalization was a drastic failure, which provoked demands for centralized curricula with a 'back to the basics' emphasis. Still other critics pointed out that the changes, as dramatic as they appeared to be, were mostly cosmetic and did not reach the real sources of social and educational problems, thereby perpetuating socio-economic inequalities and failing to acknowledge that the school-age population and their needs were undergoing transitions (Tomkins, 1981: 147–9). 'In short,' as one commentator observed in the early 1970s, 'having failed to satisfy the exaggerated expectations created by its promoters, education is now enjoying an excess of abuse for its considerable shortcomings' (Meyers, 1973: 11).

A recurrent problem with educational reform has been that too much attention was focused inside the education system without consideration of crucial social, economic, and political factors that limited what formal schooling could do. Initiatives like the ones outlined above, which were intended to broaden the scope of education, were introduced during a period of fiscal restraint and reorganization of public services. Debate over educational goals and relevance exposed education as a vulnerable target for state measures to control public expenditures (Lockhart, 1979). From the late 1960s into the early 1970s, governments took several steps to contain education that included the introduction of legislation to cut back wages and other resources in the education sector and moves to centralize control over educational decision-making. Teachers' organizations in several provinces, notably British Columbia, Ontario, and Quebec, became increasingly militant in response to the deterioration of teaching and working conditions (LeBlanc, 1974; Repo, 1974). Symptomatic of the position of education generally, teachers felt that they were being made scapegoats for much deeper social and economic problems.

In fact, educational change in recent decades has been indicative of a broad reshaping of the Canadian social landscape, affecting both the character of the nation and the experiences of individuals. People's working and private lives are affected by significant economic and labour market transformations (Li, 1996: 136–45). Growth in the service industries, relative to manufacturing and primary industries, has been complicated by government measures to constrain employment in state services at the same time as overall demands for both low-skill and highly qualified labour have increased. Women's labour force participation has increased steadily, doubling from 20 to 40 per cent between 1941 and 1971, reaching current rates of about 60 per cent by 1991, which has contributed to shifting social relations and divisions of labour in both the workplace and households. Canada has also imported substantial numbers of workers from other nations, turning since the late 1960s especially to many non-traditional sources of immigration, including Asia, Africa, and the Caribbean, to meet demands for highly skilled and professional labour. Since the early 1970s, multiculturalism has became a new policy emphasis that, along with political demands for recognition of unique rights for francophones and Aboriginal peoples, has been associated with periodic political tensions around race and ethnic relations. The uneasy relationship between group and individual rights has also emerged in several political debates, including initiatives to negotiate a new constitution and provisions for a charter of individual rights and freedoms.

Other demographic shifts have affected schooling through changes in the size, concentration, and composition of student bodies. Once the children born in the postwar baby boom made their way through the school system by the early 1970s, elementary and secondary school enrolments declined while post-secondary attendance increased (more detailed data are presented below, in Table 3.1 and the discussion in the next section). Processes of rural-to-urban migration have made it difficult to offer educational services in regions experiencing declining populations while there are pressures to build new schools or expand educational offerings in growing suburban and inner-city areas. Linked with these trends is a growing concentration of immigrant populations in larger cities, creating demands both for increased institutional space and for programming and services that address the needs of diverse student bodies.

Contemporary Canadian Education Systems

Formal education in Canada is a collection of diverse systems rather than a single system. As the preceding historical discussion has emphasized, most formal education has come to be regulated and operated through the state, although there is increasing pressure to deregulate and privatize educational services. In addition to *formal education*, which refers to organized study through state-certified institutions, normally oriented to a degree, diploma, or certificate, Canadians engage in a broad range of educational activities. *Non-formal and adult education* refers to courses, educational activities, and training programs organized through clubs, associations, and workplaces to augment formal credentials or meet selected personal or employment-related needs and interests. *Informal education* generally encompasses all learning activities that occur outside of formally organized educational sites. Informal learning is normally focused on the acquisition of specific knowledge or skills in ways that are more structured than the everyday or incidental learning that occurs through socialization processes (Livingstone, 1999: 14). While most of the discussion in this book concentrates on formal education, it is impor-tant to acknowledge that the growing emphasis on notions such as lifelong learning and educational choice has been accompanied by increased partici-pation both in non-formal and informal education and by increasing inter-action among all three types of educational practices for nearly all members of industrially developed societies (ibid.).

Formal education is a provincial jurisdiction under the terms of the 1867 British North America Act and the subsequent Constitution Act of 1982. However, in practice, several agencies and levels of government are involved in the organization and delivery of education. Much of the responsibility for the actual delivery of educational services lies at the local level. School boards, along with recently recognized First Nations educational authorities, gener-ally are accorded the most active role in the day-to-day operations of ele-mentary and secondary schools. Both public and private interests operate post-secondary educational institutions, which are supported by a combina-tion of grants from federal and provincial governments, tuition fees, and funds from corporate and private sources. Increases at all levels in the num-ber of private schools, training institutes, and programs, and the expansion of educational programs outside formal educational institutions, have added to the diversity of educational service providers in Canada.

Figure 3.1 provides a broad overview of the structure of formal education in Canada. The diagram indicates the general transition process followed by individuals through major levels of the education system. Elementary and

Figure 3.1
The Learning Continuum

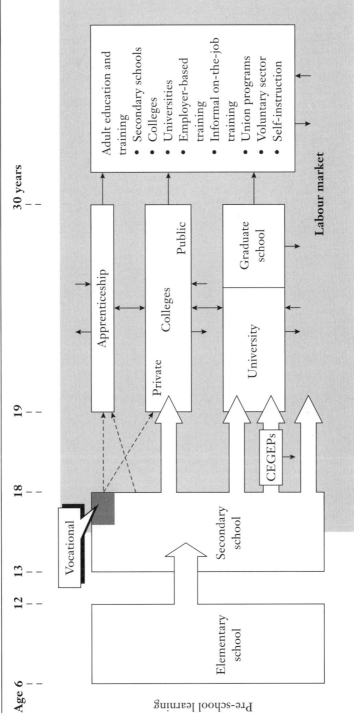

Source: Reprinted from Industry Canada (1992: 17). Reproduced with the permission of the Minister of Public Works and Government Services Canada, 1997.

secondary schooling constitutes the largest component of the education system. Most students are introduced to the formal education system at the elementary school level (although an increasing number of children are likely to have had some experience in preschool programs), which begins in kindergarten or grade 1 and continues to grades 6, 7, or 8 in most provinces. Curricula at those levels tend to be focused around a limited number of subjects, where all pupils are exposed to core areas, including language, mathematics, science, social studies, creative arts, physical education, and possibly a few other options. In the early grades, students often receive instruction from only one or two teachers. More distinct boundaries between subjects and exposure to greater numbers of teachers generally prevail by the middle grades. In some provinces, junior high schools serve students between grades 6 or 7 to grades 8 or 9 to provide a transition period into high school.

Secondary or high school, which normally continues to grade 12, is organized around more distinct subject areas, providing core courses and electives associated with specific streams tailored to requirements and interests for academic, vocational, career, and other paths. High school graduation is generally required for admission into post-secondary educational programs. In Quebec, however, students proceed from grade 11 to programs in a CEGEP (collège d'enseignement général et professionnel) that are preparatory for entry to either university education or particular vocations. Post-secondary education includes universities, which are institutions that grant degrees, and community colleges, which offer diverse programs that may lead to transfer to a university program or to diploma certification. Once they are accredited through provincial legislation, post-secondary institutions usually are granted considerable autonomy to set programs and course requirements, hire faculty or instructors, and establish and enforce academic standards. Finally, trades or vocational training incorporates specific programs, usually of short-term duration, for which high school graduation is not necessarily a prerequisite, that are oriented to qualification for specific trades or occupations (for details, see Canadian Education Association, 2001: 13–15).

The data in Tables 3.1 and 3.2 allow for a more detailed look at some important dimensions of each level of education, providing a sense of how patterns in educational enrolments and expenditures changed over the second half of the twentieth century. The figures document the significant increases in the size and cost of the education system since the early 1950s. Combined enrolments have increased by 2.4 times while total educational expenditures have increased 151.6 times (not taking inflation into account) in the past five decades.

Elementary and secondary schools constitute by far the largest sector of the education system, but the most extensive growth has occurred in post-secondary education and trades and vocational training. The share of enrolment in community colleges (non-university post-secondary) increased from about 1 per cent of total enrolment in 1950–1 to just over 6 per cent in the late 1990s, while the proportions of full-time students who were enrolled in

Table 3.1
Full-time Enrolment in Canada, by Level of Study, Selected Years, 1950–1 to 2000–1 (000s)

	Elementary/ Secondary Total (%)	Non-university Post-secondary Total (%)	University Total (%)	Total
1950–1	2,625 (96.6)	28 (1.0)	64 (2.4)	2,717
1955–6	3,291 (96.9)	33 (1.0)	73 (2.1)	3,397
1960–1	4,204 (96.2)	49 (1.1)	114 (2.6)	4,368
1965–6	5,201 (95.0)	69 (1.3)	204 (3.7)	5,475
1970–1	5,888 (92.5)	166 (2.6)	310 (4.9)	6,364
1975–6	5,595 (90.4)	222 (3.6)	371 (6.0)	6,188
1980–1	5,106 (88.8)	261 (4.5)	383 (6.7)	5,750
1985–6	4,928 (86.2)	322 (5.6)	467 (8.2)	5,717
1990–1	5,141 (85.7)	325 (5.4)	532 (8.9)	5,998
1995–6	5,431 (84.9)	391 (6.1)	573 (9.0)	6,395
2000–1	5,389 (84.4)*	407 (6.4)**	591 (9.3)**	6,387**

* Figures for 2000–1 are estimates.

**Latest figures are for 1999–2000.

Sources: 1950–1 to 1970–1 compiled from Statistics Canada, *Historical Compendium of Education Statistics* (Ottawa: Minister of Industry, Trade and Commerce, 1978), cat. no. 81–568; 1975–6 to 2000–1 compiled from Statistics Canada, *Education Quarterly Review* (Ottawa: Minister of Industry, Science and Technology, various issues), cat. no. 81–003.

universities, relative to other education levels, increased nearly four times, from 2.4 per cent to just below 10 per cent over the same period. With some fluctuations, the relative share of educational expenditures at the community college and university levels and on trades and vocational training has increased while, proportionately, spending on elementary and secondary education has declined (Table 3.2). Although complete data are not available and therefore not included in Table 3.1, full-time enrolments in trade and vocational programs increased less dramatically than did expenditures, from about 190,000 in 1960–1, peaking at 306,500 in 1993 before declining more recently to about 240,000 (Dominion Bureau of Statistics, 1962; Statistics Canada, 2003d: 53).

These trends can be explained, in part, by demographic changes. Elementary and secondary school enrolment increased substantially as children born in the post-war baby boom reached school age and progressed through school from the mid-1950s to the early 1970s. By the early 1970s— the point at which educational expenditures reached their highest levels as a proportion of the gross national product—individuals from this cohort were graduating from high school and entering universities, community colleges, and trade programs. Similarly, declining birth rates since the mid-1960s have contributed to decreases in the numbers of school-age children in most subsequent cohorts.

Table 3.2
Expenditures on Education in Canada, by Level, Selected Years, 1950–1 to 2000–1 ($ millions)

	Elementary/ Secondary Total (%)	Trade/Vocational Total (%)	Non-university Post-secondary Total (%)	University Total (%)	Total	Total Education Expenditures as % of GDP*
1950–1	359.1 (81.8)	12.8 (2.9)	11.6 (2.6)	55.2 (12.6)	438.8	2.4
1955–6	674.4 (81.3)	19.2 (2.3)	31.0 (3.7)	104.4 (12.6)	829.1	2.9
1960–1	1,328.3 (77.9)	47.2 (2.8)	57.6 (3.4)	272.9 (16.0)	1,706.0	4.4
1965–6	2,410.8 (70.9)	153.4 (4.5)	98.8 (2.9)	736.6 (21.7)	3,399.5	6.1
1970–1	4,880.4 (63.6)	574.8 (7.5)	430.0 (5.6)	1,790.8 (23.3)	7,676.0	9.0
1975–6	8,433.8 (64.8)	841.8 (6.5)	975.7 (7.5)	2,760.5 (21.2)	13,011.7	7.8
1980–1	14,730.4 (66.1)	1,309.3 (5.9)	1,822.8 (8.2)	4,437.7 (19.9)	22,300.2	7.2
1985–6	21,946.6 (63.5)	2,832.9 (8.2)	2,783.9 (8.1)	7,000.6 (20.3)	34,564.1	7.2
1990–1	30,681.2 (63.0)	4,019.6 (8.3)	3,566.6 (7.3)	10,410.4 (21.4)	48,677.9	7.3
1995–6	36,425.3 (61.8)	6,185.2 (10.5)	4,531.8 (7.7)	11,802.0 (20.0)	58,944.3	7.3
2000–1**	39,738.9 (59.8)	8,669.9 (13.0)	4,923.2 (7.4)	13,168.3 (19.8)	66,500.2	7.1***

* Figures from 1950–1 to 1975–6 are for gross national product, producing figures that tend to be slightly higher than for gross domestic product.

** Figures for 2000–1 are estimates.

*** Latest available figure is for 1998.

Sources: 1950–1 to 1970–1 compiled from Statistics Canada, *Historical Compendium of Education Statistics* (Ottawa: Minister of Industry, Trade and Commerce, 1978), cat. no. 81–568; 1975–6 to 1990–1 compiled from Statistics Canada, *Education in Canada* (Ottawa: Minister of Supply and Services Canada, various years), cat. no. 81–229; 1995–6 and 2000–1 compiled from Statistics Canada, *Education Quarterly Review* 9, 1 (Feb. 2003), cat. no. 81–003.

Demographic factors do not, in themselves, account for the growth of the education system. When the two sets of trends on enrolments and expenditures in Tables 3.1 and 3.2 are compared, it is evident that disproportionate amounts of funding have been directed to post-secondary and vocational educational programs relative to elementary and secondary education. In the 1990s and early twenty-first century, about 85 per cent of all full-time students, compared to well below two-thirds of educational expenditures, are at the elementary and secondary levels. This is partially due to the fact that education at higher levels costs more because of the higher price of qualified instructors, infrastructural support, research facilities, and other operating costs. However, it also reflects a growing commitment, especially since the 1960s and 1970s, to investment in higher education. As discussed in the previous chapter, human capital theory had currency during this period as a means to justify substantial expansion of the education system to produce a more highly qualified labour force. Substantial funding, enhanced by new expenditure programs supported by the federal government, facilitated the introduction of new institutions and programs at the community college and university levels to promote the development of knowledge and workers, particularly in scientific and technical fields. Since the early 1990s, the federal government, in common with most other highly developed nations, has elevated education and learning-related activities to a major priority as part of its innovation strategy to undertake investment for a knowledge-based economy (Wolfe, 2002).

The figures in Table 3.3 indicate the changing basis of educational finance in Canada since 1950. The most striking feature is the overwhelming extent to which education is financed by governments rather than private sources. Consistent with constitutional responsibility for jurisdiction over education, over half of all spending on education is by provincial and territorial governments. Until the 1980s, provincial governments assumed growing fiscal responsibility for education, but since that time there has tended to be increased devolution of costs to local or municipal governments. While several recent government initiatives and fiscal policies seem to indicate the likelihood of a continuing pattern of downloading of costs for education and other social spending programs to both local and private sources, there is also a countertendency towards centralization of educational planning and programming both federally and provincially. It is likely that further variations in these patterns will occur as governments move to streamline expenditures and consolidate their spheres of operations. Since the late 1990s, several provinces have adopted measures to tighten control over educational spending. Most of these reforms have been concerned to limit discretionary funding by school boards, to cut back on the number of schools boards (see Table 3.4), and to ensure that public bodies are more accountable to those who pay for government services (Council of Ministers of Education Canada, 2001: 18–19).

Table 3.3
Expenditures on Education, by Direct Source of Funds, 1950–1 to 2000–1 ($000)

	Local Governments Total (%)	Provincial and Territorial Governments Total (%)	Federal Government Total (%)	Non-governmental (Private) Sources Total (%)	Total
1950–1	199,303 (45.4)	172,864 (39.4)	20,717 (4.7)	45,867 (10.5)	438,751
1955–6	343,265 (41.4)	342,806 (41.3)	56,755 (6.9)	86,304 (10.4)	829,132
1960–1	653,207 (38.3)	729,243 (42.7)	132,218 (7.8)	191,318 (11.2)	1,705,986
1965–6	1,036,126 (30.5)	1,588,303 (46.7)	368,606 (10.8)	406,470 (12.0)	3,399,505
1970–1	1,719,354 (22.4)	4,315,985 (56.2)	930,061 (12.1)	710,649 (9.3)	7,676,049
1975–6	2,433,192 (18.7)	8,392,561 (64.5)	1,197,078 (9.2)	988,891 (7.6)	13,011,722
1980–1	3,846,131 (17.4)	14,819,995 (66.3)	1,912,817 (8.5)	1,721,237 (7.8)	22,300,180
1985–6	5,495,687 (15.9)	22,362,954 (64.7)	3,663,792 (10.6)	3,041,638 (8.8)	34,564,071
1990–1	9,809,301 (20.2)	29,269,135 (60.1)	4,896,816 (10.1)	4,702,655 (9.6)	48,677,907
1995–6	12,779,830 (21.7)	32,170,932 (54.6)	6,754,132 (11.5)	7,238,811 (12.3)	58,943,705
2000–1*	10,709,356 (16.1)	38,418,850 (57.8)	5,568,454 (8.4)	11,803,552 (17.7)	66,500,252

* Figures for 2000–1 are estimates.

Sources: 1950–1 to 1970–1: Statistics Canada, *Historical Compendium of Education Statistics: From Confederation to 1975* (Ottawa: Minister of Industry, Trade and Commerce, 1978); 1975–6 to 1990–1: Statistics Canada, *Advance Statistics of Education* (Ottawa: Minister of Industry, Science and Technology, various years); 1995–6: Statistics Canada, *Education Quarterly Review* 5, 3 (Mar. 1999); 2000–1: Statistics Canada, *Education Quarterly Review* 8, 3 (June 2002).

Shifting patterns in educational spending also point to the changing nature of federal government participation in education. Under the Canadian constitutional framework, the federal government's role in education is limited to matters that relate to minority languages, denominational schooling, and the education of designated groups under federal jurisdiction, such as registered Indians, the armed forces, and penitentiary inmates. In some of these areas, federal involvement has diminished through program reductions and jurisdictional transfers, particularly as First Nations and the Yukon, Northwest Territories, and Nunavut have gained responsibilities broadly comparable to provincial powers with respect to education and related areas.

Table 3.4
Numbers of School Boards, by Province

Province	Numbers of School Boards	
	Mid-1990s	2001–2/2002–3
British Columbia	75	60 (59 public, 1 francophone education authority)
Alberta	181	62 (41 public, 16 Catholic, 5 francophone)
Saskatchewan	121	99 (78 public, 20 separate, 1 francophone)
Manitoba	57	39 (38 public, 1 francophone)
Ontario	172	106 (31 anglophone and 4 francophone public, 29 anglophone and 8 francophone Catholic, 34 school authorities)
Quebec	158	72 (60 French, 9 English, 3 special status First Nations)
New Brunswick*	18	14 (9 anglophone and 5 francophone)
Nova Scotia	22	8 (7 regional and 1 provincial francophone)
Prince Edward Island	5	3 (2 anglophone and 1 provincial francophone)
Newfoundland and Labrador	27	11 (10 anglophone and 1 provincial francophone)

*School boards were abolished in 1996 and reinstated in 2001.

Sources: Canadian School Boards Association (1999), Cross-Canada Chart, Education Governance in Canada, and information from provincial education departments and school board associations.

More generally, however, the federal presence has expanded in education. Arising out of attempts to stimulate the development of various training initiatives and to co-ordinate labour market development strategies, the federal government has initiated several types of funding arrangements and programs, particularly in relation to post-secondary education, vocational training, and research and development initiatives. The federal government has also taken a leading role in promoting educational activities in areas such as multiculturalism. Consequently, the federal government's overall share of educational funding more than doubled, from just under 5 per cent of the total in 1950–1 to over 12 per cent two decades later. Federal funding now accounts for less than 9 per cent of all spending on education in Canada. Federal involvement in education is likely to remain highly contested and uncertain in the context of ongoing pressures to reorganize and streamline educational finance and service delivery, demands for the co-ordination of educational programming and standards on a national level, and periodic constitutional negotiations that involve, in part, differing conceptions of federal and provincial jurisdictions.

Efforts to reappraise and restructure education systems have drawn increased attention to privately funded and operated educational institutions and programs. Traditionally, in Canada, education by or within the private sector has been heavily overshadowed by public education. Governments have been reluctant to extend support and endorsement for private education beyond nominal levels on the grounds that schooling is a public enterprise that provides common learning experiences and opportunities for all segments of the population. The creation of local school boards and implementation of property-based taxation to support schools were designed to ensure that residents could gain input into and have a stake in educational matters. Without these measures, early school reformers feared that private and sectarian interests would dominate and fragment schooling, keeping it out of reach of much of the population.

One type of compromise that emerged in several provinces to accommodate demands by organized religious minorities (usually Roman Catholic and occasionally Protestant denominations) for instruction appropriate to their beliefs was the establishment of provisions to allow for publicly funded and regulated separate or denominational schooling to operate parallel with public school systems (Wilson, 1981). Normally, however, parents or groups that sought alternative forms of education were forced to finance these themselves with no assurance that programs and credentials would be officially certified or recognized. Therefore, as shown in Table 3.3, funding from nongovernment sources, such as tuition fees and private donors, has constituted a relatively small part (about 10 per cent) of educational finance, declining especially as a consequence of government expenditures to stimulate educational expansion in the 1960s and 1970s.

It is noteworthy that the relative share of private funding has gradually increased, from a low of 7.6 per cent in 1975 to an estimated 17.7 per cent in 2000–1. Between the early 1970s and the mid-1990s, student enrolment in private elementary and high schools nearly doubled while public school enrolments declined slightly (Pagliarello, 1994). Private schools have continued to grow, now accounting for about 5.6 per cent of total elementary and secondary school enrolment in Canada, about 1 per cent more than a decade earlier (Statistics Canada, 2003d: 53). Much of this growth has been facilitated by legislative changes in many jurisdictions, beginning with the western provinces and Quebec since the late 1960s, to provide public funding for private schools that meet provincial criteria in prescribed areas like curriculum and teacher certification. While the strongest impetus for private schooling has come from religious organizations, there are several types of private schools, including elite or 'preparatory' schools, alternative or 'free' schools, and schools oriented to distinct cultural traditions. Also, a growing array of private institutions provides or sponsors educational services in post-secondary programs, vocational and career training, and adult education. The expansion of private education has been hastened by government funding constraints in education and interrelated concerns about educational quality, programming options, and standards, as well as gaps in the programming options available through public educational institutions (Sweet and Gallagher, 1999).

The growth of private schooling and the increased involvement by non-government organizations in education have several important, often fiercely debated, implications for educational organizations and practices. Advocates promote private schooling on the basis that choice is necessary to provide a range of educational options that cannot be accommodated or afforded in a single, public educational system. Private schooling, viewed this way, promotes both human rights and free-market principles by enabling parents and learners to select the kind of learning environment most suited to their beliefs and interests. Critics argue, to the contrary, that the privatization of education contributes to fractionalization and reduced opportunities for much of the population. Education is not a commodity meant to be governed by price and market forces but a complex endeavour that contributes to human development and social responsibility as well as to the acquisition of knowledge and skills. Agencies that fund and operate private educational services are often more interested in their own profitability or are governed by specialized interests that run contrary to broader public concerns. As private operations, they are not subject to the same scrutiny and regulations that prevail in state-operated educational institutions to ensure that standards are met and public input is maintained.

Recent policy and institutional changes and program initiatives make it difficult to provide a comprehensive overview of contemporary educational patterns in Canada. However, several distinctive and competing tendencies are evident. On the one hand, educational restructuring driven by fiscal rationales and neo-liberal ideologies has contributed to institutional downsizing and reorganization, amalgamation and centralization of educational administration and program delivery, the transfer of educational funding and programming from the public to the private sector, the reduction of curricula to 'basic' or 'core' areas, the definition and measurement of specified learning standards that are used to determine achievement and placement in and beyond education programs, and intensified measures to scrutinize and control the activities of educators and learners (Livingstone, 1987: 57; Wotherspoon, 1991: 17; Taylor, 2001). On the other hand, a wide range of public, community-based, and private educational initiatives has emerged to serve diverse educational requirements. Programs and services tailored for socially and educationally disadvantaged groups, such as children living in poverty, learners designated 'at risk' for school failure or early school leaving, and cultural minorities, coexist with expensive training programs oriented to narrow, specialized markets. Public educational institutions continue to be governed by principles of effective community participation, relevance to heterogeneous constituencies of learners, and responsiveness to changing social and occupational demands.

More Canadians than ever before are engaged in formal and non-formal educational activities, but there is strong public concern over illiteracy, school dropouts, and lack of educational achievement. Educational reform is driven by dynamics of global competition, post-industrialism, and postmodernism, but prevailing structures and orientations that underlie contemporary education are rooted in a period of early capitalist development and industrialization. Education is directed towards the transformative potentials in human beings and their societies, but it is organized and structured in such a way that routine, standardization, and restrictions of opportunity are likely to prevail. Ultimately, the varied educational systems and practices that have arisen in the midst of recent socio-economic transformations and challenges are not a consequence of any single evolutionary historical process; rather, they represent what education fundamentally is: a somewhat paradoxical and contentious network of social relations and institutional structures.

Comparative Educational Growth

Canada's education systems have their own distinct characteristics, but they are highly influenced by education systems and advancements in other nations. In its earliest stages Canadian schooling drew heavily from European forms of school organization and curricula, particularly from France and the British Isles. The historical development of education more generally is highly diverse and uneven. Collins (2000: 214) observes that education today has not emerged through a linear evolution; rather, the history of education reveals varied fluctuations and interactions among different forms. He outlines at least four main educational models, including age cohort (such as adolescent initiation rites), private apprenticeship, professional licensing and university degrees, and bureaucratic schools derived from imperial and religious practices in China and Japan. Globally based patterns of economic development, colonial systems of rule, and expansion of market forces have created some convergence among education systems, but substantial variations and inequalities in education remain both within and across nations.

Education, both in developing and in highly industrialized nations, is guided by core concerns about how to meet basic skill and citizenship needs particular to local, regional, or national priorities and how to ensure training and skill enhancement for competitive economic growth. Historically, the

Box 3.4 Real costs of amalgamation becoming evident

The following press release from the Manitoba Association of School Trustees (2003) illustrates some of the problems posed by changes in educational organization and finance:

The strike of support workers that began this morning in Sunrise School Division is a foreseeable consequence of the forced amalgamation of school divisions enacted by the province last year, and one which may be repeated in other jurisdictions as more unions and school boards work towards contract harmonization. That was the view expressed today by Garry Draper, President of the Manitoba Association of School Trustees (MAST).

Mr Draper declined to comment on specifics of the labour dispute in the Sunrise School Division, but noted that the situation there could be 'the tip of the iceberg' for future collective bargaining and labour relations matters in the other twelve divisions that were formed or affected by amalgamation.

'School division amalgamation was legislated without a plan, and without adequate consideration of the financial consequences of the mergers,' said Mr Draper. 'The government is providing $50 per student over three years, but in most instances, that money will only partially offset costs such as systems integration and facility rationalization. It will not begin to cover labour relations costs such as an upward harmonization of wages or benefits.'

The situation is being exacerbated, he added, by provincial underfunding of the public school system which has led to a steady decline in the portion of educational costs being borne by the provincial government. 'For most school divisions, the increase in provincial funding announced for the 2003 school year was less than the amount needed to address inflationary costs and normal collective bargaining outcomes. The higher-than-average costs facing amalgamated school divisions will be borne entirely by local ratepayers.'

'The combination of chronic underfunding, forced amalgamations, and union expectations for increased wages and benefits have put many school boards and their ratepayers in an untenable situation,' Mr Draper concluded. 'Property taxpayers already shoulder an unfair proportion of education costs. Now school boards are having to decide between a course of action that will drive taxes even higher, or risk the potential of a labour dispute within the school system.'

development and growth of education systems have tended to be marked by a shift in emphasis from the first to the second of these priorities. Many governments, for instance, have adopted policies to ensure that education enhances particular kinds of skill development or channels people directly into the labour market. However, recent educational planning efforts by major international bodies and their participants have tended to pose these objectives as complementary to each other. While the expansion of higher-end skill development and advanced education remain vital priorities within most nations, parallel concern has emerged for the large segments of populations who have limited levels of education, literacy, and other basic skills.

Nations with highly advanced economies, including the OECD countries, have identified enhanced educational development beyond compulsory schooling, through post-secondary education and adult education and training, as a major priority to drive further economic growth and social development (OECD, 2001b: 151). Governments and economic agencies in Western nations have intensified their demands for educational reforms, motivated in part by the experience of nations like Singapore, referred to as Asian Tigers, which experienced significant growth in knowledge-based industries in conjunction with strategies to create strong public- and private-sector linkages among education, training, and economic growth (Ashton and Sung, 1997). National and international attention has also shifted to the need for educational improvement at the lower end, both to ensure that all persons have basic education and, especially among those who typically are marginalized from education and labour market participation, to foster continuing education (Bowers et al., 1999).

It is crucial, in a context in which lifelong learning and higher education are stressed, to recognize that significant proportions of the world's population have limited education and face continuing barriers to educational participation. The World Educational Forum, organized in conjunction with the United Nations, in 2000 identified three goals that it sought for all nations by 2015—the achievement of universal primary education; the elimination of gender disparity, first (by 2005) in primary and secondary education and later in other education levels; and the achievement of 50 per cent improvement in adult literacy levels. UNESCO (2002: 15–16) reports that while 83 nations have already achieved these goals or are on target to do so by 2015, over two-thirds of the world's population is concentrated in nations that are likely to fall short in at least one of these areas by the target date, including 28 countries (with one-quarter of the world's population) that face a serious risk of failing to meet any of the objectives.

Education, throughout the world as in Canada, has emerged over the past several decades as a vital tool for social and economic participation, and as a core priority area for public policy. This reality carries mixed significance in that the benefits that accompany education, for societies as well as for individuals, simultaneously expose education as a focus of ongoing political and economic contestation.

Box 3.5 Global inequalities in basic education

Although considerable attention is given to the importance of advanced education and skills in the global economy, over 115 million school-age children, 56 per cent of whom were girls, were not attending school in 1999, while 862 million people over the age of 15 in the year 2000 (about 20 per cent of the adult population in the world) did not possess recognized levels of literacy. These categories and their global distribution are shown in the two figures below from a UNESCO global monitoring report (2002: 7, 9) on education:

Out-of-School Children: Distribution by Region (1999/2000)

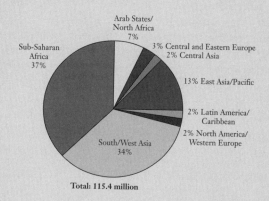

Total: 115.4 million

Adult Illiterate Population (2000)

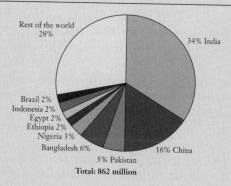

Total: 862 million

Source: UNESCO (2002: 7, 9).

Conclusion

This chapter has emphasized patterns associated with the significant growth of education systems, from a varied patchwork of programs and institutional arrangements in the nineteenth century to the massive public undertaking, supplemented by diverse alternative and private options, in what has come to be known today as the knowledge society. Associated with its scope and prominence, the education system is the site of considerable controversy and struggle over its mandate and direction.

In the course of continual economic, political, and social changes, a familiar pattern to educational reforms and debates has reappeared with startling regularity over recent decades. Demands to expand the scope of formal education by adding new programs and institutional services have run up against pressures to downsize schooling and focus on 'the basics'. Uncertainty over educational practice has been exacerbated by periodic disagreement and sometimes conflict among educators, policy-makers, and other interest groups over the goals and purposes of schooling. Education repeatedly has been blamed for a wide variety of social ills, including illiteracy, the production of individuals whose work skills did not match available job demands, rising government spending, and declining moral standards.

There has been a tendency since the middle of the twentieth century for public expressions of general concern or dissatisfaction with education to increase. In response to a Gallup Poll question asking, 'Do you think children today are being better educated or worse than you were?' 33 per cent of respondents in 1976, compared to only 12 per cent in 1948, indicated that they felt children were worse educated, while the proportion who felt children were better educated declined from 74 per cent to 49 per cent over the same period (Canadian Institute of Public Opinion, 1976: 2). Those general sentiments intensified between the early 1970s and mid-1990s. The proportion of respondents indicating that they are, on the whole, dissatisfied with the education children receive increased steadily, from 41 per cent in 1973 to 53 per cent in 1978 and 58 per cent in 1994, before declining to 48 per cent in 1999 (Edwards and Mazzuca, 1999b: 2). Similarly, Livingstone, Hart, and Davie (2001: 7) observe in their surveys of Ontario residents' attitudes towards education that, while slightly more respondents indicate they are satisfied (44 per cent) than dissatisfied (37 per cent) with the education system overall, the gap has narrowed since the late 1970s, when half of respondents indicated they were satisfied compared to 30 per cent who were dissatisfied.

We will return to these issues in the last chapter, which offers a more thorough examination of the reasons for these sentiments as they are expressed in recent demands for educational reform. For now, it is important to stress that formal education is, by nature, a political endeavour subject to competing priorities and objectives. Whether viewed as preparation for work, preparation for life in general, or an essential activity in its own right, education both reflects and influences the social world of which it is a central component. We have seen throughout this chapter that the formal education system, through its ongoing interactions with changing social, economic, and political relations, has grown to encompass a diverse array of curricular programs and social learning experiences far beyond those that appeared in the earliest schools. Expressions of public dissatisfaction about formal education reflect, to a large extent, conflicting and contradictory expectations about what education is and what it can accomplish. The next chapter explores these complex dynamics further by taking us inside educational processes.

Annotated Further Readings

Paul Axelrod, *The Promise of Schooling: Education in Canada, 1800–1914*. Toronto: University of Toronto Press, 1997. The book provides a concise overview of the early history of education in Canada, emphasizing how education has been shaped by and has affected complex class, gender, racial, ethnic, cultural, and political factors.

Neil Guppy and Scott Davies, *Education in Canada: Recent Trends and Future Challenges*. Ottawa: Minister of Industry, 1998. The authors present a detailed picture of historical educational development and recent trends in Canada, drawing from census data covering various dimensions of educational participation, outcomes, finance, and contextual factors.

John W. Friesen and Virginia Lyons Friesen, *In Defense of Public Schools in North America*. Calgary: Detselig, 2001. The authors make the case for the benefits of public schooling, presenting a concise summary of the history, purposes and outcomes of public schooling in Canada, an overview of contemporary educational issues and problems, and a critique of alternatives advocated by critics of public schooling.

Ronald A. Manzer, *Public Schools and Political Ideas: Canadian Educational Policy in Historical Perspective*. Toronto: University of Toronto Press, 1994. The author examines the development of Canadian education through the interaction of political, economic, and ideological forces.

Alan Sears, *Retooling the Mind Factory: Education in a Lean State*. Aurora, Ont.: Garamond, 2003. The nature and impact of various dimensions of educational reform are examined critically in the context of political and economic transformations driven by neo-liberal policies and the expansion of market forces.

John Young and Benjamin Levin, *Understanding Canadian Schools: An Introduction to Educational Administration*, 3rd edn. Scarborough, Ont.: Thompson Nelson, 2002. This book provides a comprehensive overview of school organization and administration in Canada, addressing issues such as school policy, educational structures, the nature and role of various educational participants, and school reform.

Key Terms

Adult education and training Educational and training activities engaged in by persons, normally aged 17 and over, who have completed their basic or initial schooling.

Curriculum Programs, courses, and materials arranged and presented formally to meet the objectives of educational institutions.

Educational attainment The highest level of education that a person has completed, usually expressed in terms of numbers of years of formal schooling or the highest credential achieved by those who are not currently enrolled in an educational program.

Indigenous knowledge Systems of knowledge and ways of knowing, premised on the interrelationships among humans with one another and the environments of which they are part, transmitted among generations through integrated cultural traditions and social systems.

Informal education Learning activities undertaken as part of a conscious or organized effort to gain new knowledge, skills, or competencies outside of programs organized by an institution or agency for specific credit or credentials.

Moral regulation Processes by which notions of right and wrong, and the sense of how to act in manners deemed to be socially appropriate, come to be internalized as part of individual personalities.

Post-secondary education Formal education leading to degrees, certificates, or diplomas beyond high school graduation levels, normally through universities, community colleges, or other accredited institutions.

Private schools Educational institutions, which may or may not receive government funding, administered or operated by individuals, associations, or agencies outside the public school system.

Public education Educational institutions and programs that are organized, administered, and funded by governments or state agencies.

State apparatus Institutions, agencies, and regulations established, organized, and administered by governments.

Study Questions

1. How and why did elementary and secondary schooling in Canada and comparable nations come to be organized through the state rather than privately?
2. Which social and economic factors have had the greatest impact on the massive expansion of education systems and educational attainment levels over the past five decades?
3. What challenges have education systems been confronted with by periodic growth in the school age population and the increasing lengths of time that people stay in school?
4. Who makes the major decisions about educational resources, curricula, and program requirements? What are the implications of these decision-making arrangements and power structures for different social groups?
5. How are educational institutions being influenced by recent emphasis on lifelong learning and global competitiveness? What educational alternatives are viable to meet these challenges?
6. Discuss the impact that social diversity among student populations has had on educational practices and outcomes.

4

The Process of Schooling

Introduction

One of the remarkable features of schooling is its consistency over time. Despite the many changes that have occurred in educational philosophies and practices over several generations, educational institutions and classrooms have retained a distinctive quality that makes it difficult for them to be mistaken for any other setting. Children who are driven to spacious, well-equipped urban composite schools replete with innovative technological devices may not immediately identify with the experiences of ancestors who walked or rode horseback to attend one-room schoolhouses with few books and blackboards made of tarpaper, but people's reminiscences of their school days tend to evoke common themes regardless of when and how they were educated. This commonality is, in part, a consequence of the integral role that schooling has come to play in developmental processes associated with childhood and adolescence and its importance in the transmission of basic knowledge and beliefs from one generation to the next. It is also a product of the massive scale of educational bureaucracies and institutional enterprises. Despite periodic modifications, fundamental patterns of classroom interaction, school organization, and curricula in Canada have remained relatively faithful to nineteenth-century roots. The school system's resistance to particular kinds of change is the focus of extensive discussion and controversy as educators, policy-makers, and various social groups struggle with the issue of what schooling should be like to ensure it remains relevant to the needs of contemporary societies.

This chapter explores the main patterns of activity that occur within educational processes, examining their significance both for individuals and for more general social relations. Although schools are likely to reveal features that are peculiar to the demographic and social characteristics of the communities they are located in, the school system as a whole is one of the most socially inclusive agencies in contemporary societies. The face of the student body has changed significantly, through patterns of immigration, lengthened periods of education from early childhood to adult education, integration of students with disabilities and others who often were excluded from regular schooling, and shifting cultural practices and expectations. The focus of this chapter is to work towards an understanding of how educational institutions variously include and exclude particular individuals and groups throughout the schooling process.

The Multi-faceted Nature of Educational Practices

A common characteristic in traditional sociological research on education, as observed in Chapter 2, has been a tendency to concentrate either on the details of life within schools or on the expectations that are placed on schooling through external social pressures and organizations. This dualism of focus is in part an expression of debates over whether human agency or social structures play the greatest role in influencing social life and human behaviour. In practice, internal and external forces, agency, and structure all are important determinants of educational realities. Some aspects of these dynamics, and in particular how they contribute to making educational practice such a varied and often contradictory endeavour, are discussed below and expanded on in subsequent sections of this chapter.

Structural analysis stresses the ways in which labelling and hierarchy, as employed both formally and informally within educational settings, contribute to the reproduction of the social order. The standard imagery, from this vantage point, portrays classrooms structured by rows of desks occupied by students facing a teacher or professor at the front of the room. Education is viewed as little else than a form of preparation for work or socialization for adult life. Whatever the variations on this theme, the image conveys certain salient features of much educational life—schooling is organized around expectations of conformity, compliance, and standardization, whereby the instructor's position and authority are privileged in comparison with those of the learners. Despite their analytical differences, both structural functionalist and Marxist theorists of education share the position that student classification and streaming are central functions of schooling driven by the requirements of advanced industrial or capitalist social structures. Educational practices are examined not for their intrinsic or unique characteristics, but for their ability to produce individuals who are ready and able to occupy the social positions that await them after they leave the education system.

Interpretative analysis, by contrast, with its emphasis on human agency, portrays labelling, categorization, and social identities within schooling as more fluid and changing processes that are often expressed in terms used by educational participants themselves. High school pupils in Newfoundland and Labrador surveyed by Martin (1982), for instance, viewed classroom culture as a series of practices constructed around two main categories of pupils—'teachers' pets' and 'class victims'. Students also categorize themselves and others through various designations, based on factors like academic performance, cultural identification (signifying recreational pursuits, musical or sports-related interests, racial or ethnic identities, drug or alcohol preferences, or gender and sexual identities), or physical characteristics. Teachers also apply labels to pupils as they differentiate between 'good kids', 'troublemakers', 'bullies', 'yahoos', 'overachievers', 'underachievers', and so on. Many of these labels, and the social interactions they are associated with, reflect or contribute to more enduring patterns of success and failure, but they are also important signifiers of the ways educational settings are constituted as rich and varied sites of social activity.

The failure in many studies of schooling to integrate analysis of activities inside the classroom—and other sites where educational interactions occur— with life beyond the classroom, and to comprehend the relationship between official and unofficial school activities, parallels more general boundaries and distinctions that characterize common perceptions about schooling. People tend to accept formal education as an inevitable part of their lives. When individuals do talk about schooling, it is usually with reference to people they hung around with, interesting or embarrassing moments, successes and failures, and overall impressions rather than about curricula and content that was learned. People are sometimes uneasy because these informal considerations seem to be at odds with the identification of school as the official world of lessons, homework, tests, rules, school-sponsored organizations, and other scheduled activities.

When asked to describe the purpose of schools, for instance, students often revert to language that could almost be quoted from official school documents, even though most students never read such statements. A typical conception of schooling, in this case from a grade 12 female student interviewed in the course of my own research, is that 'School is a place of learning, a place where we learn to interact with people and learn skill[s] that will help us deal with the problems in life with basic reason and understanding.' Whether or not they agree with particular features of schooling, people rarely question the legitimacy of formal education as a mechanism to structure learning, regulate lives, and confer credentials. This acceptance is based on distinctions we make that place boundaries between school and other aspects of our lives. As another student, this one a grade 9 male who generally had a positive orientation to school, observed, 'I dislike the hard work and homework because I like to go home and watch TV and go hang around with my friends.' In other words, for students the official part of schooling is important, but it is not the same as, and sometimes interferes with, 'real life'. Schooling overlaps substantially with people's social lives to the extent that much school time is occupied by 'joking around', finding ways to pass the time, and discussing parents, relationships, parties, and personal problems with friends, yet these events are typically discounted as irrelevant or incidental to education (McLaren, 1998; Contenta, 1993). Students often internalize responsibility for educational success or failure as a personal responsibility, regardless of personal circumstances, as observed in this account from a First Nations student in grade 12: 'I think if I experienced difficulty [in school] that would be [because of] a low expectation of myself. I have two children, I have a son and a daughter and I have a babysitter, and it takes more responsibility to get them to daycare, to get myself to school and if I can't do that then that's my fault. . . . I can't make excuses, I can't use them as an excuse because it's something I did and it's my responsibility to get my education regardless.'

It is crucial to recognize that schooling, in all of its routines as well as its more unique or exciting moments, is an important social activity in its own right even as it serves as a conduit into other spheres of social activity. Life in educational institutions carries its own rhythms and meanings, but it also reveals the pervasive influence of the world beyond the classroom door. The sometimes chaotic experiences of organized schooling leave indelible impressions about what is possible and expected in people's social lives.

Much recent sociological analysis of classroom processes has explored the linkages between social interaction in educational settings and more general historical and structural arrangements. Given the strong correlation that exists between social privilege and success in education and life beyond school, what is it about schooling that preserves this relationship in spite of the supposed role that education plays to provide equal opportunities for all? What are the features of schooling that produce relatively enduring patterns of success and failure? To what extent, and in what ways, does education impose control over people, and how much does it provide opportunities to empower them? Critical inquiry has attempted to address these issues by moving beyond individual determinants of educational attainment and school success to highlight the linkages between human agency and social structure and between formal and informal aspects of educational practices.

The Contribution of Schooling to the Development of Human Subjects

The observations made in the previous section suggest that the analysis of schooling, both in itself and through its wider social relations, must recognize formal education as having, in several significant ways, a dual character. Schooling contributes to formal learning and the attainment of knowledge and credentials that can be concretely defined and measured, but it is also characterized by more indefinite tasks associated with its human interactive and social dimensions. As was pointed out in Chapter 2, many important

Box 4.1 Aboriginal students' perceptions of a positive school climate

Several initiatives have been implemented by school systems to address persistent concerns about the lack of educational success among Aboriginal students in Canada. The experiences described by Aboriginal youth in a Saskatchewan high school that has modified its programming, organizational structure, and social relations to take into account difficulties students often encounter both in and out of school demonstrate how students can benefit from a proactive, positive school climate:

A. When teachers are teaching they always refer to something to do with Aboriginal people, all the time. If it's Psychology, if it's something, because there are always Aboriginal students that go here . . . they use examples or bring up First Nations because everybody gets a little taste of it.

B. [In this school] everybody gets by, everybody has a story, the teacher has a story, they know more about the students than a regular teacher would. . . . The classes are smaller, you get to know everyody real quick. . . . [there is] more of a holistic way of teaching, not just straight out of the textbook, more Native teachers to explain the difference between the traditional and the contemporary.

C. Lots of times [in other schools] the teachers don't understand the situations or they don't understand certain people, they are used to seeing their middle class kids attending and being good students. I guess if one of those teachers came into this school, their head would spin off their shoulders because there are so many different people with different problems and mostly everybody has some problem because most of the students are young parents. Eighty per cent of the student population here . . . is considered at risk.

D. . . . most of the teachers here will help you out if you have the time to go early . . . it's not just, 'do your work', they take the time to help you.

E. [I can] almost identify the school as a community. . . . The people are really friendly, and I know [it] kinda has a bad reputation . . . but that's always not true, there's a lot of people that have come here and they say it's so mellow and there's like no fighting, you're not really in little groups. Everybody is friends with everybody. There's no prejudice . . . it's small and caring.

school lessons are derived from a hidden curriculum with little apparent connection to formal or overt educational objectives. We learn about such things as competition, success, failure, gender roles, racial identities, cultural understandings, and our place in society through our participation in the daily rituals of schooling. In other words, in addition to its roles of transmitting knowledge and bestowing status, schooling contributes to personality formation. Expressed another way, schooling is involved in the process of *individuation*, which refers to how our identity is constructed through notions of ourselves as distinct subjects.

The idea that our personalities are not fully formed from birth but are shaped as we interact with other people in particular circumstances is a central insight of sociology. Functionalist, interpretative, and critical sociologists all emphasize, from different perspectives, the importance of formal education in the process of making us *social* beings. We are expected, through schooling, to develop patterns of co-operation with others and to gain sufficient understanding that we will comply with certain social expectations. Ironically, a fundamental part of our social identities in advanced capitalist societies is oriented towards individualism as a core value. We tend to view successful educational and social outcomes, essentially, as the product of initiative, aptitude, intelligence, and other attributes associated with qualities of the individual, while factors that contribute to failure commonly are given psychological explanations and persistent problems are regarded as ailments in need of treatment. The sociological critique of individualist positions emphasizes that individuals are shaped by society not merely because our social lives are conducted in relation to one another, but also in the sense that individualism itself is constructed through social processes.

It is important, in developing a sociological understanding of individual identities and orientations, that we do not dismiss entirely the social role played by individual actors. Fundamental to notions of human agency is the acknowledgement that each person must accept some responsibility for his/her decisions and actions as well as for the consequences that follow from them. At the same time, however, we must be attentive to how schooling and other social circumstances set parameters around which those decisions, actions, and consequences can be meaningful and effective.

Educational practices play a major role in the process by which people's lives and identities are constructed as individual subjects. Most school learning revolves around individual competencies. The individual pupil is monitored, expected to complete assignments, graded, promoted from one grade to the next, and disciplined. Educational credentials are acquired on a competitive basis, separating and distinguishing the identity and performance of each person from all others. We therefore come to identify success and failure, and learn to deal with them, as products of our own efforts. A continual focus within schooling on individual characteristics, efforts, and achievements reinforces similar orientations prevalent within the mass media, workplaces, families, and other social sites, creating an impression that the individual is the natural, inevitable basis of social existence. School knowledge involves the development of an identity based on a modified sense of place or position in society. Education sorts students through continuous assessment and evaluation of pupils within schooling and in the presentation of grades and credentials for the outside world. The operation of the hidden curriculum and the informal interactions among educational participants also serve to construct and reinforce identities both within and beyond schooling.

The processes by which formal education contributes to personality and character formation can be illustrated with reference to the historical example of boarding and residential schools for children of Aboriginal ancestry. Boarding schools, operated by religious denominations, and residential schools, operated by the churches under federal government standards and with government funds after the mid-nineteenth century, were oriented to the assimilation of First Nations children into the dominant social order. Children were separated—sometimes forcibly—from their families for at least 10 months a year. The schools were organized in accordance with the principles of what Goffman (1961) terms *total institutions*, which are isolated from external social settings and governed by strict regimes of administrative scrutiny and control. Authorities in residential and boarding schools had complete control over children's lives for the duration of schooling. In addition to class work, their social lives and labour time (justified as necessary to provide essential job skills) were highly regimented and regulated. They were treated as inmates, subject to extreme scrutiny and strict disciplinary measures for transgressions such as speaking their indigenous language. The schools were organized to alter the children's identities away from their original cultures to one that was regarded by authorities as appropriate for life in the dominant society. The intended transformation was a radical one, as described by the Royal Commission on Aboriginal Peoples (1996a: 365):

> At the heart of the vision of residential education—a vision of the school as home and sanctuary of motherly care—there was a dark contradiction, an inherent element of savagery in the mechanics of civilizing the children. The very language in which the vision was couched revealed what would have to be the essentially violent nature of the school system in its assault on child and culture. The basic premise of resocialization, of the great transformation from 'savage' to 'civilized', was violent. "To kill the Indian in the child", the department [of Indian Affairs] aimed at severing the artery of culture that ran between generations and was the profound connection between parent and child sustaining family and community.

'The result', according to Kirkness and Bowman (1992: 12), 'was a tragic interruption of culture' that produced a legacy 'of cultural conflict, alienation, poor self-concept and lack of preparation for independence, for jobs and for life in general.' The residential schooling experience not only affected students directly, but contributed to a legacy of destruction and 'cycle of abuse' whose powerful impact remains deeply embedded in many Aboriginal communities (Royal Commission on Aboriginal Peoples, 1996a: 379; Schissel and Wotherspoon, 2003: 60–3).

Boarding and residential schools are not necessarily representative of schooling in general, given the extreme circumstances in which they functioned as total institutions oriented to the modification of individual personalities, in this case from their grounding in Aboriginal knowledge systems to identities viewed by officials as being more suited for life in Euro-Canadian society. Nonetheless, there are parallels among all types of schooling. Formal education, by its nature, shares the general objective to transform individual character and consciousness. It has been pointed out in Chapter 3 that concern for classroom order and discipline is a fundamental characteristic of formal education. While the structure of many classrooms continues to resemble late nineteenth-century factory organization, school regimentation comes from roots that precede mechanized industrial production.

Nineteenth-century school reformers, in particular, were blunt in their assessment that mass public schooling should involve discipline and habit at least as much as it should be concerned with the acquisition of knowledge and work skills. Schools were consciously constructed to mould the individual and foster new loyalties and allegiances. Educational authorities devised measures, such as the timetabling of the school day, the physical organization of the classroom, and monitoring and assessment of both pupils and teachers, in such a way to ensure that schooling produced disciplined individual subjects (see, e.g., Corrigan et al., 1987; Curtis, 1988; Wotherspoon, 1993). Today's schools may be less overtly concerned with discipline and personal virtues—in fact, as will be considered later in this chapter, schools are often criticized for being too undisciplined and disorderly—but issues of character, order, and hierarchy remain fundamental to schooling processes.

As these insights demonstrate, it is important to recognize how practices that occur in educational sites both shape and are shaped by what happens outside schooling. The activities we engage in and the identities we develop tend to be mutually reinforcing. Both individually and socially, educational outcomes tend to be affected more deeply by 'things that happened' than by 'what we learned in school'. The extent to which these events may become meaningful depends, in turn, on such factors as our relations with parents and family members, out-of-school interests and obligations, racial and gender characteristics, and the social and economic resources available to us.

Regulation and Resistance in Schooling

One way in which sociologists have attempted to make sense of educational dynamics is to conceptualize schools as sites in which regulation and resistance occur. Schools regulate individuals and social activities as they fulfill tasks associated with their varied expectations, including the dissemination of knowledge, the development of student skills and aptitudes, the production of recognized credentials, and the shaping and provision of direction to individuals' lives. In its most extreme and visible forms, such as in the case of residential and boarding schools, regulation is evident through rules, disciplinary procedures, the organization of time and space, and scrutiny by school officials over pupils' activities. Regulation also occurs in subtler forms, such as the recognition of some forms of knowledge and viewpoints as valid and the denial of alternative frameworks and experiences. In schooling, as in any regulative institution, however, official objectives and practices are not always passively accepted by participants. Educators and learners alike use varied strategies and coping mechanisms as they attempt to make their lives alternatively meaningful or simply bearable. Students may mock teachers they dislike, for instance, overtly flout school rules, or vandalize school property, just as teachers may introduce materials not on the curriculum, refuse to carry out official regulations, or employ a wide repertoire of other actions in expressing their responses to either specific or general features of schooling. Notions of resistance, whether they reside in disillusionment, optimism, rebellion, or even ridicule and humour, point to the ways in which educational practices can be indeterminate and contested, regardless of the limitations imposed by dominant educational structures and the agents who act on their behalf.

The discussion thus far has portrayed life in educational institutions as a volatile combination of formal and informal, official and unofficial, and determinate and indeterminate features. These educational realities create opportunities for individual and social transformation at the same time as they contribute to the reproduction of existing social circumstances and structures. People carry with them into schooling various background characteristics and predispositions—such as race, gender, income, employment status, parental support, family responsibilities, and emotional states—that both affect and are shaped by their educational experiences in complex ways. One of the most difficult tasks in the analysis of education is to isolate the relative impact of these various influences on people's life conditions, choices, and chances. As noted in Chapter 2 (and elaborated in Chapter 7), there are strong correlations between educational experiences and outcomes and social characteristics such as class, gender, and race. Social forces interact with unique aspects of our lives to produce distinctly different opportunity structures. As a consequence, regardless of our individual predispositions, our experiences are also strongly affected by whether we are male or female, Aboriginal or non-Aboriginal, poor or wealthy, of urban or rural origin, and so on. Similar interrelationships operate within the education system. Within Canadian education, for example, most senior-level teachers and administrators are men, while women are concentrated in lower-level teaching positions. To understand this reality, it is not sufficient to consider the specific elements that influence day-to-day decision-making within the scope of the classroom or other aspects of individual teachers' lives. We must also know something about how such factors as gender discrimination and differential labour market opportunities for men and women have contributed to the historical development of teaching. While particular career paths are the result of unique experiences, those experiences are preconditioned by strikingly regular patterns defined by social boundaries and expectations.

By recognizing these boundaries and the interactions that take place within them, we can come to an understanding of how relations of regulation and resistance may produce distinct social and educational outcomes. In subsequent sections of this chapter, these dynamics are explored through discussion of four significant types of practice that structure educational experience: (1) *streaming*, whereby students are channelled into distinct learning groups and programs; (2) an emphasis on *official knowledge*, which designates the kinds of topics, information, and content considered to be legitimate or worth knowing within schooling; (3) *hegemony*, through which domination comes to be experienced in people's everyday life experiences; and (4) *silencing*, which refers to processes through which particular kinds of social experience and alternative voices are devalued, marginalized, or denied a place within educational practice.

Streaming

Streaming refers to the placement of students into different programs based on their aptitude, ability, or special interests and needs. Streaming is most visible in situations where learners are differentiated into broad program areas such as vocational or academic streams. Streaming occurs between schools both when the choice of a school is related to the programs it offers and when it is recognized (by teachers, students, and parents) that the nature and quality of education varies from one school to the next. It also takes place within schools and classrooms in the form of various measures such as ability grouping in which pupils are divided into regular, remedial, or advanced streams in basic subject areas.

Streaming tends to be more voluntaristic and less systematically co-ordinated in Canadian schools in comparison with nations such as the United Kingdom, Japan, and Germany, where highly structured educational streams are prevalent, and even the United States, where tracking (grouping within classrooms) and stratified institutional arrangements are widely practised. Pedagogical justifications for streaming are based on arguments that students of similar backgrounds, interests, and abilities can be taught more efficiently and effectively than is possible in mixed classes. According to this justification, pupils receive instruction and assignments appropriate to their levels of interest and understanding, thereby facilitating success and making the educational process more rewarding for the individual. Streaming is also promoted for its potential to make education more relevant to the learner and better oriented to student futures. It is sometimes argued that educational and individual resources are wasted when all students are expected to be taught from the same curriculum at the same pace. This position asserts that people should receive training directly related to the kinds of jobs and futures that they can expect.

Critics of streaming contend that these arguments confuse important issues while they hide the damaging realities of streaming. Much of the problem, at least on a day-to-day basis, is associated with the labels and identities that accompany student categorization. Students are highly aware of their status in relation to others and look for cues such as the classroom or work group they are placed in to identify where the system has slotted them. Responses like 'How come I'm with the dummies?' or 'I'm here because I want to go to university' signify pupils' attentiveness to groupings that may not even be officially acknowledged to the students by teachers or administrators. While the occasional placement of students in particular groups may not be highly significant, students' educational careers are given shape by recurrent labels and groupings that affect their self-concepts and educational performance. As noted in Chapter 2, the complex workings of the self-fulfilling prophecy, in which students eventually adopt behaviours consistent with the perceptions and expectations of their ability and roles held by teachers and other officials, have been demonstrated repeatedly through classroom research (Rosenthal and Jacobson, 1968; Stebbins, 1975; Contenta, 1993; Martel et al., 1999).

A regular consequence of streaming is that it does not affect students randomly but, instead, produces results that tend to correspond to existing patterns of social inequality, particularly in terms of race, class, and gender. This operates in several ways.

Gender relations illustrate both how streaming can affect students on a differential basis and how processes related to streaming can change over time. Nearly all school programs are open to males and females alike, but often there are pronounced differences in the kinds of schooling that boys and girls, and men and women, experience. Consequently, as Jane Gaskell (1992: 37) emphasizes, 'Gender itself matters' in the education system:

> At the university level, the small number of women enrolled in engineering and science has frequently been noted. Women are much more likely than men to be enrolled in nursing, education, the fine arts, and most humanities disciplines. At the college level, women are under-represented in trades training and in technologies, but are over-represented in community services and in secretarial and accounting courses. In high schools, the differences occur not so much between academic and non-academic courses, where racial and class differences are found, but within each. Young women are more often in senior French and history courses than in senior physics and computer science courses. They are more often in domestic science and business education than in industrial education.

Gender differentiation is produced by a combination of individual choices and organizational features of the school and wider society. Directions and comments from parents, teachers, guidance counsellors, peers, and others reinforce differential expectations about what kinds of behaviours and choices are appropriate for boys and girls. Many researchers have observed that teachers interact differently with boys and girls. Eyre (1991), observing students in a grade 8 home economics program, notes that boys tend to dominate discussions, are more likely to be acknowledged by teachers, and are permitted higher levels of boisterousness than girls. In contrast to this situation, in which teachers have modified the curriculum to attract the attention of boys, McLaren and Gaskell (1995: 152) observe in a senior physics class little effort by teachers or students (male and female alike) to empower girls, challenge male authority, or even confront harassment of female students by some of the male students.

Recent research findings and media attention have posed significant challenges to feminist critiques of gender-based differentiation in education. Feminist analysis initially highlighted mechanisms within education and career pathways that undermined girls' educational achievements or diverted women in directions that did not match their aspirations or capabilities. However, a powerful discourse has emerged since the mid-1990s in Canada and many other nations to suggest that boys, not girls, have become educationally disadvantaged. These claims are based on several types of evidence, including standardized test results that repeatedly show girls outperform boys overall on reading and literacy measures, higher school dropout rates for boys relative to girls, post-secondary enrolment and graduation trends in which females outnumber males in most programs, and the preponderance of female students as recipients of major academic awards. Schools have come under pressure from media voices, policy-makers, educators, and parent advocacy groups to tailor programs, teaching styles, and curricular activities to boys' interests and needs, reminiscent of efforts in previous decades to make schools more 'girl friendly'. The prominence given to standardized test results led to broader scrutiny about issues such as boys' loss of interest in school matters, lack of reading interest, and stages of developmental progress. In 2001, Durham District School Board in Ontario gained extensive national exposure after it implemented guidelines requiring schools to develop action plans to address systematically the problem of boys' educational difficulties. The board identified several factors, such as the need for 'longer, more complex written assignments from boys; increased use of libraries by boys for recreational reading; more boys in academic after-school programs; more boys being celebrated for reading achievements', which were translated in turn to specific strategies, such as the use of role models to encourage boys, scrutiny of reading materials for gender bias, public acknowledgement of boys' reading achievements, and establishment of after-school programs to attract boys (Fine, 2001: A7; Bauer, 2001).

The introduction of a discourse that has posed boys as educationally disadvantaged has been accompanied by considerable controversy. Many educators are reluctant to embrace strategies to improve boys' educational performance for fear that efforts to target any specific group will reinforce stereotypes about gender and other discriminatory groupings, and undermine efforts to promote education that is inclusive of all students. Some critics link the focus on male disadvantage to a backlash against feminism that blames previous efforts to make schooling more accessible and rewarding to girls for going too far. There are also concerns that the reframing of the positions of boys and girls in schools reinforces a traditional gender duality that identifies the masculine as the rational and the feminine as the irrational. Walkerdine (1998: 168) observes that:

> The ideal child it seems is still a boy, a boy indeed with potential, whose success is being thwarted by women and girls, indeed by the very notion of female success. It is instructive therefore to examine the discourses through which this situation is understood and the way in which what at first appears as a problem with and for boys is too easily translated into a female problem: such a translation certainly accords with educational discourses which target mothers, female teachers, and of course, latterly, feminism.

In practice, the purported reversal of the gender gap can be understood fully only after several key questions are asked about such factors as the basis of comparisons, the processes that contribute to students' selection of particular subject and academic programs, the relative status attached to specific subjects, and the employment and life prospects that follow from specific educational outcomes. Kenway and Willis (1998: 57) illustrate, in part, how these mechanisms may operate:

> Although not wanting to draw attention to themselves as high achievers, many students try to avoid being labeled as low achievers by enrolling in higher status subjects. Thus many—predominantly boys—enroll themselves in physics and chemistry with little chance of success. In contrast, a lack of confidence or ambition—or both—are perceived by many teachers to prevent girls from enrolling in physics and chemistry when they *are* able to cope with them. Gender policies and programmes which define able students' choices as acceptable when they are based on physical science and high-level mathematics, and less acceptable when they are not, serve to privilege success in male and academic terms and to devalue success in other areas. Overwhelmingly, this works against girls, who recognise that their futures are not likely to be the same as those of boys. Less obviously, it also works against 'less able' boys, who inappropriately choose subjects which are not likely to match the kinds of post-school options which will be available to them.

While boys and girls alike may be encouraged to aspire to careers in math, science, business, or health care, individual aspirations come to be modified by specific experiences of success or failure in the classroom, cues received from others about the appropriateness of particular goals, and growing sensitivity to categories produced by gender stereotyping. Despite increasing sensitivity to gender variations, it is still true, for example, that men are much more likely to be engineers and computer programmers while women are more likely to be secretaries and nurses.

Gender-based educational streaming and inequalities are strongly inter-related with other significant processes of social differentiation. While much attention has been paid to the differences between boys' and girls' test results in mathematics and literacy, for instance, more substantial variations are pro-duced by social class and inequalities in parental backgrounds (Kenway and Willis, 1998). Assessing the results of the Program for International Student Assessment (which in 2000 measured reading, mathematics, and science scores of 15-year-olds in 32 OECD nations), Bussière et al. (2001: 46–7) observe that the lower average performance by boys relative to girls on read-ing levels is a matter of some concern for policy-makers, but continue by emphasizing that contextual factors related to school, family, and commu-nity—notably socio-economic status and reading encouragement in the home—were the most powerful determinants of student test results.

Box 4.2 Barriers to the achievement of anti-racism in schools and universities

Henry et al. (2000: 55–7) identify several forms of discourse and coded language that contribute to racism and inequality despite formal com-mitment to equality of opportunity. These barriers include:

The Discourse of Denial
This discourse reflects a refusal to accept the existence of racism in its cultural and institutional forms. 'I am not a racist, and racism is not a problem in this school.' The evidence of racism in the lives and on the life chances of children of colour is indicated by the effort made by the educator and the school to suppress the processes of 'othering'—the marginalizing effects of ignoring the experiences, histories, and cultures of minority students in the classroom, texts, and classroom pedagogy.

The Discourse of Decontextualization
In this discourse, there is an acknowledgement of the existence of racism but it is interpreted as an isolated and aberrant phenomenon limited to the beliefs and behaviours of deviant individuals. It is believed that 'students enter the school with "blank slates".' The position of power and privilege that white educators enjoy in the classroom is neither acknowledged nor understood. Their own racial and cultural identities are generally invisible. Thus racism is decon-textualized in terms of what counts as knowledge and how it is taught.

Box 4.2 continued

The Discourse of Colour Blindness

Educators' attitudes toward racial minorities are expressed in assertive statements about colour blindness, neutrality, and objectivity. 'I never see a child's colour. I treat all children the same.' The refusal of educators to recognize that racism is part of the 'baggage' that racial-minority children carry with them, and the refusal to recognize racism as part of the daily policies, programs, and practices of the educational system, are part of the psychological and cultural power of racial constructions on the lives of students of colour as well as educators . . . .

The Discourse of 'Blame the Victim'

This discourse is framed around the notion that equal opportunity is assumed to exist in all areas of the educational system. Thus, the lack of success of black students, for example, is often attributed to dysfunctional families or culturally deficient or disadvantaged communities . . . . This view is reflected in statements such as: 'Education is not really valued in the black community as it is in "Canadian" culture.' At the level of the university, this discourse is articulated in relation to questions of representation and meritocracy. Proactive measures to ensure that barriers to minorities are dismantled have led to the common refrain: 'We must not lower our standards. All hiring and promotions should be based on merit.'

The Discourse of Binary Polarization

This is the discourse of fragmentation into 'we'–'they' groups. 'We' represent the white dominant culture of the school; 'they' are the students, families, and communities who are the 'other', possessing 'different' values, beliefs, and norms. 'The problem with "our" black/Asian students is that they do not really try to fit in.'

The Discourse of Balkanization

The view here is that paying too much attention to 'differences' leads to division, disharmony, and disorder in society and in the classroom. 'First they want us to do away with Christmas concerts. Soon we'll be wearing turbans. Before long, we won't know what a Canadian is' . . . .

The Discourse of Tolerance

The emphasis on tolerance suggests that while one should accept the idiosyncrasies of the 'others' (students or faculty who are

Box 4.2 continued

culturally or racially 'different'), the dominant way is superior. 'We try to accommodate their different norms, but it is not always possible or desirable.'

The Discourse of Tradition and Universalism
This form of resistance is formulated on the premise that the traditional core curriculum should remain unchanged. 'Western civilization represents the best of human knowledge and forms the basis of cultural literacy and educational competence.'

The Discourse of Political Correctness
Demands for inclusion, representation, and equity are deflected, resisted, and dismissed as authoritarian, repressive, and a threat to academic freedom. 'The standards, values, and intellectual integrity of the university are in danger.'

Class and racial and ethnic relations are reproduced in similar ways, as will be discussed in more detail in Chapter 7. Working-class children predominate in lower streams while children of professionals and those from more privileged families tend to be placed in academic streams and schools that are better equipped to produce success (Curtis et al., 1992). Educational experiences and attainments are also highly segmented through similar processes that operate along racial and ethnic lines (Li, 1988; Young, 1987). Henry et al. (2000: 239–40), in a summary of Canadian research findings, observe that streaming repeatedly works to the detriment of immigrant and visible minority students, often as a consequence of assessment and decision-making processes related to the placement of students in particular streams. They cite as prominent cases the disproportional placement of black students in low-level academic programs and vocational programs, and the concentration of Southeast Asian students in mathematics, science, and computer post-secondary programs. The impact of streaming also extends beyond the allocation of students among distinctive programs or courses. Often, when programs and services such as English/French as a second language or anti-racism programs are created in response to the needs of specific student groups that may otherwise face educational disadvantage or discrimination, they remain vulnerable to cutbacks through resource constraints and educational restructuring decisions (Canadian Race Relations Foundation, 2000: 9).

The contradictory dynamics that operate within formal education are evident within streaming. Practices that are overtly concerned with grouping learners and providing instruction appropriate to their aptitudes and competencies can also operate insidiously to reinforce or produce systematic patterns of inequality. To the educator and educational administrator, grouping and categorization are likely to signify viable practical and pedagogical responses to differences among students that do not necessarily imply any inherent advantage or disadvantage for one category relative to another. At the same time, the direct and indirect messages sent to students, in conjunction with disparate resources and opportunities associated with each stream, have important consequences that contribute to inequalities in educational experiences and outcomes. These dynamics are explored further with respect to the importance of official knowledge and hegemony in schooling and the silencing of particular voices in the educational process.

Official Knowledge

Education is centrally concerned with issues related to knowledge. We commonly view educational institutions as sites in which knowledge is transmitted or disseminated to the learner from teachers, textbooks, and course materials. In fact, knowledge relations in education are much more complex than they appear to be. Knowledge is not simply conveyed from the top down in a strict one-way flow and accumulated through what Freire (1970) calls a 'banking' approach to learning. Instead, it is dialogical and interactive in the sense that all educational participants, whether they acknowledge it or not, share in the ongoing transfer and interpretation of knowledge.

The revitalization of debates over school curricula and standards has opened up important questions about what kinds of knowledge, and whose knowledge, are part of the educational process. Periodic calls for 'back to basics', teaching to a standardized curriculum, or reliance on a selected list of core reading materials are opposed by competing claims that the curriculum is too narrowly framed and unrepresentative of student, community, and cultural diversity.

We must recognize that knowledge is not only disseminated, but also produced, in educational settings. This is most evident in universities and other post-secondary institutes that encompass within their mandates an ongoing involvement in research and scholarly work. However, all participants at every level of the education system contribute to knowledge production in a variety of ways through discussions, problem-solving, and engagement in everyday activities. Knowledge is shaped not only as it is continuously interpreted, processed, and reinterpreted in the interactions among instructors and learners in educational settings, but also through the experiences and understandings brought in from outside of schooling.

The top-down view of knowledge dissemination that dominates conceptions of formal education originates in our relatively unchallenged acceptance of official knowledge. As opposed to recognition of knowledge as something that arises from social interactions in everyday life in and out of school, emphasis on official knowledge gives legitimacy only to those ideas and beliefs that are in some way authorized by designated officials or agencies. What this means is that not all knowledge counts as 'true' or 'real' knowledge. Relations of power and authority act to differentiate between official knowledge, which is regarded as a valued commodity, and knowledge that we use in our everyday experiences, which tends to be devalued or treated as common sense (Apple, 2000: 42–4). The learned or knowledgeable individual, viewed in these terms, is someone who has book learning or formal educational credentials, whereas a person who has considerable expertise in practical matters or know-how is not recognized in the same way if these skills have not been formally acquired or certified (Jackson, 1993: 170–1).

Educational institutions are centrally implicated in the process whereby official knowledge is distinguished from and given privileged status over other forms of knowledge. This occurs in part because of the imperative for formal educational institutions to maintain their own legitimacy so that they are not undermined by other social sites that might wish to disseminate knowledge and bestow educational credentials.

The state plays a central role in granting legitimacy to educational agencies by establishing, co-ordinating, and regulating standards for the recognition of curricula, programs, and instructors. In Canada, provincial education departments are normally responsible for the formal approval of elementary and secondary school curricula and textbooks and, either directly or through bodies they authorize, for the certification of teachers and the establishment of procedures and standards for evaluation, promotion, and graduation. Provincial governments also grant accreditation to universities, colleges, public schools, and some private educational institutions, enabling them to structure their programs, hire qualified instructors, and grant certificates and degrees.

Because the state is expected to act as an arbiter among competing groups and interests, there is a legitimacy to educational practices and forms of knowledge incorporated within these formal structures of governance that is absent in less official social settings. Schools operate within an ideology of value neutrality in the sense that the curriculum is supposed to convey beliefs and knowledge representative of the society as a whole. Education's apparent objectivity is reinforced by the dismissal of ideas that are seen to represent overtly the views of 'special interest groups'. Many school boards have policies that forbid explicit product advertising or the display of corporate logos, for instance, while curriculum materials that depict gay lifestyles or readings produced by groups such as pro-life or pro-choice advocates are commonly protested if not banned from classrooms.

In practice, what comes into the schools is filtered through a selection process influenced by power relations and idea systems that prevail in the wider society. Schooling, like other social sites, conveys particular representations of reality that are not neutral in their origins and impact. This is not always readily apparent, nor is it a simple matter of one group imposing its ideas and values on all others. Several steps within educational and curricular processes allow for input and participation by diverse social agents, contributing to prospects for control by dominant groups as well as to resistance and unanticipated consequences. Apple (2000: 50–9) shows how textbooks can contain ideas that support dominant interests (by presenting one-sided, uncontested views of controversial or complex issues) at the same time as they depict the events and experiences that are meaningful to subordinate groups. Curricula that allow for discussion of issues like working-class history, gay rights, and racial and gender equity can be used in ways that are exploitative as well as progressive. What matters is how the material is used and integrated into other personal and educational experiences.

There is considerable flexibility and variation in the framing and delivery of school curricula. In Canada, most decisions about curricula and textbooks are made in the first instance by committees in various subject areas composed of administrators, teachers, specialists, government officials, and often representatives from universities, parent groups, and other community organizations. Curriculum-established limits to what is officially considered to be 'school knowledge' will vary from setting to setting, depending on such factors as the range of choices that teachers are given in lesson planning, frameworks established through specific core curriculum requirements, and the presence or absence of standardized or provincial examinations based on prescribed content or learning objectives. Teachers, working within curriculum guidelines, generally have high degrees of discretion to determine what, when, and how particular material will be taught. Curricula and teaching effectiveness are shaped further by informal and unstructured classroom interactions. Classroom practices are marked by a meandering, often indeterminate path that wanders between what is represented as official knowledge and the lessons and understandings that students exhibit after they leave their schools and classrooms.

Box 4.3 The elders' knowledge and the curriculum framework

The introduction of a new mathematics curriculum in Nunavut, as outlined by Yamamura et al. (2003: 45), demonstrates how indigenous knowledge can be integrated into contemporary curriculum requirements:

> The development process for the curriculum framework focused on discussion to help elders and teachers understand how mathematics was used in traditional Inuit society. During these conversations, it became evident that traditional Inuit used mathematics in a very holistic way. This relationship was repeated throughout the meetings with the discussions ultimately defining six principles, as described below:

Box 4.3 continued

1. Transmittance/Transference
This principle relates to the fact that much of the knowledge and stories of the elders were passed on from their own parents or siblings. In terms of the mathematics curriculum, the principle of transmittance underlies the act of transfer of knowledge to students from elders, teachers, parents, community members and classmates. There are many ways that this knowledge can be transferred, whether it be verbally, pictorially, graphically or experientially.

2. Preparedness
For traditional Inuit, being as prepared as possible for changes in weather, changes in migration patterns of caribou, and shifting ice conditions was critical for survival. In the present day, it is also important for students to be prepared for survival, whether through education or through the development of skills conducive to earning a good living.

3. Inseparability
The use of numbers or mathematical skills was inherent to traditional Inuit life through the construction of sleds, sewing of clothing and building of iglus. In a similar fashion, mathematics is inherently present in all aspects of life in our modern society. This inseparability of mathematics from all aspects of daily life serves to emphasize the importance of students achieving a working level of mathematical literacy.

4. Solution Seeking
Throughout traditional Inuit culture, survival depended on the ability to find solutions to problems. For Inuit, the focus was more on the solution than on the actual problem. One of the primary goals of the new mathematics program will be to help students become critical thinkers who are able to seek solutions in order to overcome difficulties or deal with modern survival issues.

5. Relevance
Traditionally, mathematics in Inuit culture was so integrated with everyday life that it was not considered a separate entity. In this way, mathematics was just part of all the relevant aspects of life that were so critical to survival. For any new math curriculum, it is vital that a focus on relevance for students be key to their successful mastery of mathematical and critical thinking skills.

Box 4.3 continued

6. Experimentation

Learning in traditional Inuit culture was based on experience, experiment, and practice. By focusing on these aspects of the learning process, young people are inclined to adapt techniques more consistent with their individual differences and then practise to hone their skills.

With these principles, curriculum developers now have a key element on which the mathematics curriculum will be based. These fundamental principles will be incorporated throughout the curriculum, thereby providing a direct connection between modern theory and traditional Inuit beliefs, culture, values and way of life.

At the same time, distinctions made between what is and is not considered valid educational content have important implications for different educational participants. Many students, particularly those from white middle-class families, arrive in school with a strong familiarity with the language and operations of the classroom. The greater the correspondence between what schools expect and students' background experiences, the less likely the pupils will be to have difficulties with understanding school rules and course materials. Conversely, students who lack the 'cultural capital' underlying educational practices are likely to be at a relative disadvantage.

Basil Bernstein, a British sociologist of education, offers useful insights into the ways in which cultural capital is related to power and control in educational processes. His work, in part, proceeds from a distinction between 'visible' and 'invisible' pedagogies (Bernstein, 1977). Visible pedagogies are educational processes in which there are obvious hierarchies of authority and knowledge; teachers have explicit control over pupils; the curriculum is organized, directed, and transmitted by teachers; and pupils are monitored and evaluated by teachers in accordance with relatively explicit standards. Invisible pedagogies, by contrast, are characteristic of more open teaching/learning situations in which teacher control over pupils is more implicit; children have greater apparent opportunities to select, arrange, and pace their activities and social interactions; and there is greater concern in teaching and assessment of students with process than with specific measurable outcomes.

Bernstein's analysis focuses on the development of what at the time were newer forms of open preschool classes that came to be based more on activity and play than on work, but it does have relevance for schooling at other levels as well. The open classroom seems progressive because it allows greater flexibility and concern for the learner than is possible under more authoritarian models of schooling. However, Bernstein argues that, under visible pedagogies, students (and parents) recognize explicitly what is expected of them, even if their ability to succeed depends on culturally biased materials and expectations that favour the middle classes. Under invisible pedagogies, by contrast, the standards are much less clear and, moreover, more of the child's activity becomes exposed to the scrutiny of the teacher. Successful performance now requires that students have the know-how or skills to uncover hidden rules and expectations. This educational structure gives a tremendous advantage to children (particularly those whose parents are of professional backgrounds) who have insight and experience to point them in the direction of activities and behaviours that are rewarded rather than penalized.

Hegemony

Critical sociology often makes reference to the concept of hegemony to illustrate how social structures give shape to our daily activity. Hegemony, as elaborated in the work of Antonio Gramsci, refers to a process of domination by consent, in which the general population adopts a world view that reflects the interests of the dominant classes (see, e.g., Gramsci, 1971: 12ff.). This analysis allows us to see how our common-sense way of looking at things, which we derive from our traditions and experiences, is constructed so that ruling practices are maintained without usually being evident to us.

Two examples illustrate how educational practices are hegemonic. The first is the way that knowledge is organized and presented in the classroom. The curriculum is usually understood, arranged, and transmitted to pupils, and often even to teachers, in the form of prearranged units of information. Facts, ideas, and subjects are divided and separated from one another in such a way that they sometimes seem to bear no relationship to each other, with little reference to the context within which they emerged and came to be seen as important. Assignments and tests are often based on recall and reference to discrete bits of information. The learning process comes to be narrowly defined around material that can be readily presented and retrieved (Apple, 1979). Schools are hegemonic insofar as they contribute to a taken-for-granted sense of the world by failing to encourage critical thinking and a sense of how various practices and ideas are interconnected.

A second example of how hegemony is produced in the schooling process is the ethic of individualism referred to earlier in this chapter. As we have already observed, we are taught—through schools, the media, and other venues—that our social position and worth are based on individual effort and initiative. This view, for many of us, is beyond question; we accept it because it seems natural to us. In doing so, however, we fail to consider seriously any alternative viewpoints there might be. Individualism is an ideology that draws attention away from the social origin of practices and ideas. In fact, many elements of our realities are socially constructed—they are produced through the interplay among human actors, social forces, and already existing social structures. Viewed in this way, individual ability and initiative count, but they can only be made sense of against a backdrop that places strict limitations on what is possible for any given individual. To ignore these aspects of reality leads to sets of beliefs and circumstances that favour those social interests that are dominant at any given point in time.

Schools are hegemonic institutions to the extent that they do not address or encourage the posing of fundamental questions about the nature of our social reality. They are not necessarily organized to favour explicitly the interests of the wealthy and powerful over the poor and disenfranchised, but when social inequality is not discussed as a central part of curricula and when the world is seen as a collection of individuals rather than as a system based on distinct social positions, one consequence is that prevailing patterns of domination and subordination come to be understood and experienced as natural and inevitable rather than as something to be questioned. As we have acknowledged repeatedly, formal education also affords the possibility for alternative ways of seeing the world and for resistance to official knowledge and hegemony. These will be discussed later in this chapter, following the consideration of another process—silencing—that limits the scope of learning and understanding in educational practices.

Silencing in Educational Processes

Silencing operates in two interrelated ways. First, it exists when particular issues are excluded from or discouraged in the classroom. Second, silencing also occurs when the lives, interests, and experiences of particular educational participants are made irrelevant to the schooling process. By dealing with 'the curriculum' or 'the business at hand', schools and other institutions send clear messages about what is and is not important. In the process, some topics and experiences, however central they may be to students' lives, are placed outside the boundaries of what comes to be defined or understood as legitimate areas of classroom discussion.

As we observed with respect to the official knowledge that is central to educational processes, some forms of knowledge and behaviours are rewarded while others are marginalized. Considerable attention has been given in recent years to the cultural bias inherent in standardized curricular material and instruments like aptitude and intelligence tests. Test items, like many classroom activities, often rely on knowledge or experiences that may seem to the teacher or tester to be universal but that in fact reflect a particular orientation to reality not shared by all groups. What occurs is that some world views are given voice, or legitimized, while others are silenced. Many common-sense approaches to problems are dismissed as irrelevant or inappropriate for the classroom. An Aboriginal child from a northern reserve and a black pupil in an inner-city school, for instance, may possess considerable knowledge about complex social activities that they encounter daily outside the school setting, whereas in school their worlds are rarely acknowledged. This is not necessarily a deliberate or calculated attempt to privilege one group over another, yet it has the effect, especially when reinforced over time, of compounding the disadvantage faced by subordinate groups.

Analysis conducted through various critical perspectives demonstrates that silencing operates in numerous ways to control classroom interaction and regulate individual identities. Talking in the classroom is commonly discouraged, unless it is directed by teachers and authorities who are lecturing or giving instructions, or where students are allowed to conduct discussions related to a specific pedagogical task (Shor, 1980: 72). Silencing may operate more symbolically than literally in the sense that students, when they do respond to teachers or professors, may subordinate language or dialect they employ informally in favour of patterns of discourse that are rewarded in educational settings. Remaining silent also functions as a way students may protect themselves from scrutiny by educators or from embarrassment at exposing too much of themselves and their lives (Ellsworth, 1992: 104–5). Bourdieu and Passeron (1977) examine how 'self-silencing' occurs as a result of 'symbolic violence' in the education system. Students who are unfamiliar with or unable to meet the demands that arise from educational standards and expectations are likely to undermine their own capabilities and personalities if they cannot change to achieve conformity. Rather than question how and why such standards reflect social privilege associated with dominant social groups, the individual internalizes educational failure while reinforcing existing power relations.

Proponents of inclusive education and anti-racism in schooling and other institutional settings point out the deep impact that silencing can have on people's lives. For some persons, challenges to or devaluation of their lived experiences can have damaging psychological consequences. Invisible messages transmitted in the classroom that are based on white, male, middle-class standards, for instance, can lead minority students to see their own identities as undesirable or unacceptable (Ng, 1991). Silencing produces invisibility, which through normal school practices results in negations of self and identity that 'erase the social, cultural, historical, and political realities of marginalized groups in society through the exclusive practices of Eurocentrism' (Dei et al., 2000: 172). Pupils, in response to these processes, may become marginalized and withdraw from participation in school activities, especially if there are conflicting messages between home and school about what is culturally and socially important. Such withdrawal, in turn, can lead to social isolation or to incorporation into alternative groups such as youth gangs or 'counter-school cultures' that define themselves through their defiance against authority (Willis, 1977).

The lack of connection between schooling and student background is a major contributing factor to educational problems experienced by Aboriginal and visible minority children and youth. Schools and other educational sites that fail to do so, or are not able to make a connection between what they do and the lives of the students and communities they work with, increase the likelihood that students will become disengaged from, or disaffected with, their education. Highlighting the gap that Aboriginal youth frequently identify between life in and out of school, the Royal Commission on Aboriginal Peoples (1996b: 482) observes that, 'Education as they experience it is something removed and separate from their everyday world, their hopes and dreams.' Sometimes, even content specific to students' cultural backgrounds can pose confusion or mystification when school representations conflict with what students are told at home. The comments of one grade 12 First Nations student in a Prairie inner-city school are typical of this concern: 'There is quite a contrast [between what I am told in school and what my people tell me], like the Crazyhorse, the old people know, like my grandpa used to talk about them a lot, and then when you learn about them in school . . . it's a lot different, and I was saying, ok, somebody is lying to me.' Dei et al. (2000: 20–1) contrast educational practices that exclude and marginalize minority students with inclusive schooling, in which educational personnel and practices acknowledge students' cultural backgrounds and integrate the community into the school context.

Like other hidden aspects of schooling, therefore, silencing can deeply affect both the schooling experiences and the social futures of students. Beyond the content and skills directly transmitted through the curriculum, the knowledge, attitudes, and emotions that are absent from or subordinated within educational practices convey to educational participants critical signals about how the world is organized and should be encountered. Both overt and silent understandings in the classroom contribute to a complex process of manoeuvring and differentiation in which the successful or 'good' students come to be distinguished from those characterized by alternative or deviant labels and identities.

Student Response and Resistance

Students must become accomplished actors in a number of ways in the course of their schooling experiences. Their actions contribute to the continuously changing nature of classroom activity. The school day is rarely the smooth-flowing progression of tightly integrated lessons and transitions between classes that appears in official accounts of schooling. Instead, it involves uneven pacing, constant interruptions, and shifting back and forth among planned and unplanned occurrences. Within even just a few moments, students are likely to alternate their behaviour to reflect varying degrees of attentiveness, boredom, overt and covert gestures, dialogue with teachers, and exchanges with other pupils. In contrast with common conceptions of pupils as passive consumers of curricular knowledge, students are continuously engaged in shaping and making sense of the educational process. As Michael Apple (2000: 57) observes, 'students are active constructors of the meanings of the education they encounter.'

Box 4.4 Student resistance

Resistance by students to school rules and authority takes many forms, ranging from minor acts of disruption in the classroom to more aggressive acts. Here, Peter McLaren (1998: 208–9) discusses the responses of black female students in grades 5 and 6 to their schooling in an inner-city Toronto elementary school in an area known as the Jane-Finch corridor:

Although many of the Jane-Finch girls suffered the indignities of poverty, racism, sexism, physical abuse, and, in some cases, the culture shock of recent immigration, they managed to create and maintain a distinct subcultural resistance to the consensually validated norms of the school—norms which attempted to make girls into passive, pliable, docile, tidy, neat, and diligent workers. In order to resist this conventional version of femininity, designed to nurture their 'domestic instincts', the girls developed attributes that were drawn from working-class culture in general: toughness, aggressive sexuality, distrust of authority, rebelliousness. The girls then resisted the contradictory myth that schools function as agencies of equality, that educational institutions possess the power to help disadvantaged students bridge the chasm of opportunity that separates them from their more affluent peers. Because the school system is structured tacitly to reinforce and reward middle-class values, attitudes, and behavior (and thereby penalize the 'deprived' by omission), educators and the public alike often assume that the failure of the schools to educate disadvantaged girls is really the failure of the girls themselves. The girls fail because they are perceived to be mindless, shiftless, worthless, pathological, burdened by dubious hereditary traits, or the products of deviant home backgrounds. We blame the victim rather than looking for ways in which the class and educational systems militate against the success of those who are economically powerless and who are disadvantaged by gender and race.

So pervading and intransigent is this myth of equal educational opportunity that many working-class girls come to believe that their school failure is their own fault, that they must be 'stupid or something'. In their day to day behavior, the Jane-Finch girls resisted what they unconsciously felt to be an oppressive situation; yet paradoxically, because school did not provide the rhetoric with which to articulate the experience of this oppression, they blamed themselves.

Box 4.4 continued

The liberal ideology that promises success to anyone who is prepared to work and sacrifice prevented the girls from understanding how they were being fed into a preordained future by the patriarchal, economic, and cultural forces of consumer capitalism. Paralyzed by the belief that they lacked the intelligence of the more affluent girls, many of the working-class girls gave up. (Naturally, there were some exceptions. But since bookish intelligence was equated with middle-class status, most girls soon abandoned any attempts to please teachers or achieve academic excellence. Instead their attention was soon diverted to the enhancement of their subcultural status.) For the most part, their class/cultural identity became defined for them by dirt-stained high-rises, unemployment, sexism, the strip-plaza splendor, and the general failure of educators and politicians to redress their plight. This led to strong emotional bonding, as networks of 'girlfriends' were created collectively to resist the world of the dominant class. Many of the girls had a sense that the cards were stacked against them from the very beginning. After all, did not the legacy left by our ancestors emphasize the superiority of one class of people over another? And one sex over another? And what more natural reaction to this predicament than to jettison the official ideology of the school through rituals of resistance?

When we embrace the derisory ideology that conceives of disadvantaged girls as under-socialized, as 'unfinished products' on the conveyor belt of social success, we place a veneer on the basic class structure and gender bias of society and obscure the ways in which the structure of the system determines to a great extent which class and gender will be successful and which will fail. In this way, the educational system ensures the hereditary transmission of the status quo—by appearing neutral, by concealing its social function of reproducing class relations by constructing technologies of gender, by perpetuating the myth of equality of opportunity based on scholastic merit.

Researchers who analyze educational settings frequently employ the concept of 'resistance' to understand how students engage in and respond to their schooling experiences. Most of this research is focused on adolescents at the stage where resistance tends to be most overt. The notion of resistance conveys most immediately a sense of rebellion or rejection of schooling as demonstrated through such acts as vandalism and destruction of school property, overt disregard for school rules, defiance of teachers' authority, refusal to complete assignments, absenteeism, or dropping out. However, students often exercise resistance in subtler ways. Lack of attentiveness to lessons and instructions, whispered comments and notes passed to other pupils, informal mocking of teachers, repeated errands and trips to the washroom, and pressure to discuss issues not on the formal curriculum all can signify reactions against school activities that students consider boring, meaningless, or oppressive.

The concept of resistance adds to our understanding of school processes a sensitivity to the unofficial and interpersonal elements of schooling. Educational dynamics are characterized by continual dialogue and interchange, both verbal and non-verbal. Students, far from being passive recipients of schools' efforts to shape and control the individual, are highly implicated in the directions that their schooling takes and the outcomes to which it contributes.

The presence and significance of resistance should not be exaggerated. Deviant forms of behaviour such as bullying or resentment against authority are often confused with resistance to schooling (Giroux, 1983; Lynch, 1989: 15; McLaren, 1998: 191). Resistance is more appropriately understood as student responses to the dehumanizing and restrictive aspects of schooling that diminish creativity, enlightenment, and self-worth or that devalue meaningful social experiences. Such resistance is usually individual in nature, but it may also be collective. Sometimes, collective resistance is spontaneous, such as when a group of students supports a pupil they feel is being picked on unfairly by a teacher, or when students persuade their teacher that playing ball would be more beneficial than doing a math quiz on a sunny day. Woods (1979) emphasizes how both students and teachers employ laughter and other apparent deviations from the formal curriculum as means to negotiate daily classroom interactions. School resistance can also be more organized, as when students engineer a walkout from class or circulate a petition to complain about such issues as overly harsh school regulations or the transfer of a popular teacher to another school. In these kinds of situations, it is noteworthy that student actions generally tend to be accommodative to schooling, with resistance limited to specific instances or features of educational practices.

There is considerable debate about the meaning of different forms of resistance. Kanpol (1992: 57), for instance, distinguishes between institutional political resistance, which is directed against specific features of particular schools or educational environments, and cultural political resistance, which involves movement from critique of education towards the formulation of alternative ideas and practices. Many educators, politicians, and media analysts point to school violence, vandalism, and lack of student respect for authority as alarming indicators of the extent to which educational and social standards have declined in recent years. Other commentators, particularly those who adopt a critical pedagogy orientation, portray student resistance as an outcry against oppression or a noble struggle to preserve their humanity in a dehumanizing world. Schools and school rules, in this view, signify externally imposed authority structures that are threatening to students, particularly those for whom access to meaningful participation in secure jobs and influential social positions seems unattainable.

Several researchers have commented on the frequent tensions that arise between teachers and students around issues of physical appearance. Even schools that do not have strict dress codes have unspoken or informal standards regarding appropriate kinds of clothing, hairstyles, and student demeanour. Students, however, often adopt non-traditional styles of dress and attitudes that enable them to express their sexuality and assert a rebellious stance against school authority. This is especially true for students from working-class and minority backgrounds, as such writers as McRobbie (1978) in the United Kingdom, Connell et al. (1982) in Australia, and McLaren (1998) in Canada have observed. In more general terms, though, schools are gathering places that often crystallize distinct youth cultures built around such designations as punks, metalheads, freaks, skids, skaters, ravers, gangsta' rappers, hackers, and many others commonly drawn from popular entertainment and sports. These identities may encourage a degree of peer acceptance and 'acting out' of tensions and resentment against a social environment that students otherwise perceive as meaningless or actually hostile to them.

It is important, as well, not to confuse symbolic expressions of adolescent concerns with resistance to schooling. Despite the frequent attention given to more extreme forms of resistance and deviance such as gang membership, vandalism, and violence, research that has explored in a systematic way what students think of their schooling experiences has shown that they respond to formal education—and other facets of their lives—in mixed and often contradictory ways. Schissel (1997) argues that common public images portraying contemporary youth as out of control and excessively engaged in deviant and criminal activity are the product of a socially constructed 'moral panic' directed especially at disadvantaged groups. Some of these studies, particularly the growing body of research findings that has emerged recently with respect to two sets of issues—early school-leavers and school-to-work transitions—will be discussed in more detail in Chapter 6, which explores the relationship between schooling and students' post-school lives. For now, it is crucial to recognize that student acts are not always what they appear to be.

A useful categorization of student responses is presented by Connell et al. (1982), who suggest on the basis of their interviews with Australian high school students about 14 years of age that, in addition to resistance, there are at least two other main types of student–teacher relations. The first is compliance, in which students accept school rules and express enthusiasm for their schooling as a way of gaining rewards. The second response is pragmatism, in which students engage in required activities only to the extent that they are seen to be required for achieving objectives, such as passing grades and receiving credentials.

Many other researchers have observed similar processes. McNeil (1986) and Weis (1990), studying American high schools, stress how the ritualistic nature of classroom practices emerges as part of an unspoken agreement between students and teachers. By the time they reach high school, students typically tend to be passive and docile. While the occasional outburst of energetic protest may erupt over particular issues, especially when pupils feel they are being unfairly dealt with by teachers who exercise excessively harsh discipline, double standards, or poor teaching methods (Connell et al., 1982: 84), students rarely challenge either teachers or the school authority structure. Instead, students agree to carry out at least minimal requirements to complete work assignments and keep an orderly classroom—in other words, to do what they think is expected to help the teacher do his or her job properly. In exchange, they expect to get through school with respectable treatment and acceptable grades.

This accord channels potential student dissatisfaction and resistance in such a way that the legitimacy of the education system, and the social system as a whole, is not called into question (see, e.g., Aronowitz and Giroux, 1993; Willis, 1977). Students to a large extent 'buy into' the education system, viewing educational success as desirable for social success and blaming themselves for many of the occasions that they experience failure. Even where more severe problems begin to appear, taking the shape, for instance, of frequent skipping of classes, overt resistance, conflict with teachers, or resignation, students are hesitant to express doubt about the school system except when they are probed or encouraged to speak out. Interviews with early school-leavers, such as those conducted by Crysdale and MacKay (1994) in Toronto, Samuelson (1991) and Tanner et al. (1995) in Edmonton, Randhawa (1991) in Saskatchewan, and Crysdale et al. (1999) in Alberta and Ontario, reveal that those who drop out blame the school for producing boredom, alienation, rejection, or lack of preparation for work, but they also express self-doubt and regret over personal factors that contributed to their decision to quit school. The mixture of hope and despair, self-blame and bitterness against the school system expressed by students who fail or drop out before finishing high school is not markedly different from more general student commentaries on their educational experiences.

The Concern for Safe, Inclusive Educational Environments

Students hold sophisticated and often contradictory attitudes with regard to their schooling experiences. These paradoxical stances reflect students' central but subordinate place within educational structures, their changing roles and expressions as children and adolescents, and their uncertain place in broader social and economic structures. Children and youth tend to be more optimistic than pessimistic about their futures, hold high educational aspirations, and are generally positive and accepting of their school experiences, although they are not hesitant to point out numerous issues that concern their lives in and out of schools (Bibby, 2001: 133–56; King et al., 1999: 11–25; Schissel and Wotherspoon, 2003: 82–92). They often identify grievances

Box 4.5 Students experience a variety of pressures at school

Although students generally express positive assessments of their schooling, they also encounter numerous pressures arising from their school work, relations with other persons, or bullying, as evident in the findings from a cross-national study of student health presented by King et al. (1999: 21, 23):

> Students from the English-speaking countries, England, the United States and Canada, appeared to experience greater pressure from school-work expectations. Students from the Scandinavian countries and Germany were notably lower on this indicator. There is little evidence that the amount of school-related pressure felt by students contributes to higher achievement on international tests of science and mathematics.

Fifteen-year-olds who felt a lot of pressure because of their school work, by country, 1998 (%)

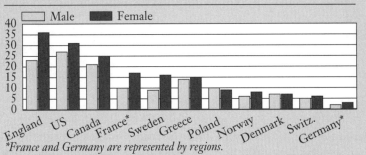

France and Germany are represented by regions.

Bullying is not a universal concept and so comparisons across countries must be cautiously undertaken. Ironically, countries where more students are viewed as kind and helpful also seem to have more problems with bullying, for example, Germany, Switzerland and Denmark. Although Canada ranks in the middle on this indicator, the proportion of students who have been bullied is still high enough to view this behaviour as a social problem.

Thirteen-year-olds who were bullied in school this school term by country, 1998 (%)

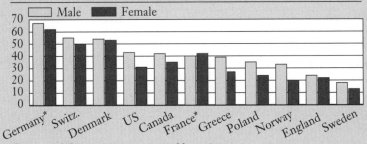

France and Germany are represented by regions.

against outdated curricula, unfair expectations from teachers, lax standards, or lack of opportunities to pursue information and activities that they prefer, but they tend not to challenge the structures of authority and rewards either within or as represented by schooling. There is a general sense that 'that's just how things are', even when students retain an uneasiness about their lives and futures that transcends anything they can do to make them better.

Students are more diverse, sophisticated, and concerned about social, economic, environmental, and political issues than they are commonly portrayed. They are highly aware of and concerned about many of the issues that are given high profile in both popular and alternative media, including bullying and youth violence, substance abuse, matters related to sex and sexuality, labour market options, consumerism, poverty, social disadvantage, and social justice. Their schooling is a crucial but not isolated part of their lives. It is valued for its contributions to knowledge, skills, social connections, and life prospects, but it is also most effective when it is connected with realities outside the classroom. The educational environment, particularly in situations in which schooling is compulsory and there are few alternatives, can be intense, competitive, alienating, and even terrifying for students who are rejected, picked on, or abused by other students and teachers. Alternatively, schools and the students within them are most likely to succeed when schooling becomes a place in which participants find security, acceptance, validation, and encouragement.

Conclusion

This chapter has considered how the profusion of incidents and the shifting pace of structured and unstructured activities that constitute the school day come to be channelled into diverse but relatively predictable social outcomes. Since its inception over a century ago, public schooling has changed substantially in several highly visible ways, including subjects taught, curricula, school facilities, classroom resources, background and qualifications of teachers, and dress and demeanour of students. However, basic classroom structures and aims and orientations of schooling have remained remarkably resistant to change. Schools continue to be regarded as factories for producing products—the schooled individual, credentials, and other end results—just as they are sites for human social development. The varied purposes and practices of schooling are not accidental by-products but direct reflections of the contradictory nature of public education.

Annotated Further Readings

Sandro Contenta, *Rituals of Failure: What Schools Really Teach*. Toronto: Between the Lines, 1993. In a highly readable and engaging book, the author discusses the ways in which schools' hidden curricula both restrict future prospects for many students and limit the extent to which true education is accomplished through schooling.

Bruce Curtis, *Building the Educational State: Canada West, 1836–1871*. London, Ont.: Althouse Press, 1988. This book provides extensive insights into how the dominant model of Canadian school organization came into practice in the nineteenth century as a mechanism to discipline and regulate individuals and create a stable social order.

Peter McLaren, *Life in Schools: An Introduction to Critical Pedagogy in the Foundations of Education*, 3rd edn. New York: Longman, 1998. The author, drawing on his experiences teaching elementary students in a Toronto inner-city school, explores the foundations of a critical pedagogy approach by framing an account of daily school practices within a broader social, economic, and political context.

Wilfred Martin, *The Negotiated Order of the School*. Toronto: Macmillan, 1976. The author offers a detailed symbolic interactionist account that understands the schooling process as the outcome of complex layers of interactions and negotiations among various school participants

Bernard Schissel and Terry Wotherspoon, *The Legacy of School for Aboriginal People: Education, Oppression, and Emancipation*. Toronto: Oxford University Press, 2003. The book combines an analysis of how residential schools and other educational developments have contributed to the subjugation of Aboriginal people in Canada with an overview of recent initiatives and commentary from Aboriginal students that highlight how educational promise may be fulfilled in the future.

Key Terms

Credentials Qualifications achieved through formal education or training programs and recognized in the form of degrees, diplomas, certificates, or other legitimate awards.

Dropouts Students who leave school without completing requirements for secondary matriculation or high school graduation. This term is often replaced with 'school-leavers' in order to take into account the many students who interrupt their schooling and return at one or more later stages to complete further education.

Hegemony Domination by consent, or ideologies that foster belief in the legitimacy of existing power relations.

Hidden curriculum The understandings that students develop as a result of the institutional requirements and day-to-day realities they encounter in their schooling. This term typically refers to norms, such as competition, individualism, and obedience, as well as a sense of one's place in school and social hierarchies.

Individuation The process by which people come to see themselves, and are seen by others, as autonomous individuals rather than with reference to the social relations of which they are part.

Moral panic The creation of widespread fears built around images of threats to public safety or order, often related to violence, deviant activity, or health concerns, generated especially by exaggerated or erroneous media and political accounts.

Silencing Mechanisms that restrict student voices or prohibit the inclusion of topics and material that are important to students' lives within the schooling process.

Socialization The ongoing process of learning and discovery through which people internalize the norms and expectations about cultures and their place within their societies.

Streaming Formal and informal educational mechanisms that sort students based on ability, social background, or other characteristics into groups, programs, or institutions that have differential status.

Total institution A self-contained institutional setting, detached from the outside world, regulated by formal routines, procedures, and scrutiny with the intent to reshape those who reside, work, or are housed or detained in them.

Study Questions

1. What are the predominant social features of elementary and secondary school classrooms? What explanations can be provided for how these features came about?

2. Critically discuss the nature and impact of residential schooling for Canada's First Nations.

3. Discuss the impact that everyday routines of classroom life have on educational outcomes for different groups of students.

4. What is the hidden curriculum? Discuss its importance, relative to the formal curriculum, for what students learn and retain from their schooling.

5. Which elements of schooling inhibit student participation and engagement? Which ones contribute to greater participation and engagement? Discuss the significance these factors have for students from different social and cultural backgrounds.

6. To what extent are schools self-contained institutions as opposed to sites that are highly influenced by their external environments? Discuss the significance of these circumstances for what students learn in schools.

5

The Politics of Teaching

Introduction

Teachers, like students, are central agents in educational processes. Their prominent role in the delivery of educational services makes them nearly synonymous with schooling in the eyes of students, parents, and community members. However, teachers also occupy a somewhat paradoxical position in and out of the classroom. They represent the school and its authority structure to pupils and parents, but they are subordinate to principals and senior administrators in educational hierarchies. They must be highly skilled and competent to gain public confidence to educate and discipline learners behind classroom doors, but they are also subject to public scrutiny with regard to what and how they teach as well as to their overall moral character. They are highly regarded as professionals, but they do not have the autonomy, authority, or status held by doctors or lawyers. They are advocates for educational causes and learning issues, but they are also waged employees of public or private educational bodies. In short, consistent with the complex nature of the education systems teachers work within, teaching is a highly contradictory occupation.

Willard Waller (1965: 49), in his classic analysis of schooling, *The Sociology of Teaching*, concisely summarizes the special nature of teaching through his conception of the teacher as 'stranger' in the community:

> The teacher stereotype is a thin but impenetrable veil that comes between the teacher and all other human beings. The teacher can never know what others are really like because they are not like that when the teacher is

watching them. The community can never know what the teacher is really like because the community does not offer the teacher opportunities for normal social intercourse.

Waller was writing mostly about teachers in small communities at a time (the book was first published in the early 1930s) when there were likely to be few other relatively highly trained professional workers active in the human services. His observations continue to hold relevance by pointing to the combination of respect and devaluation that today accompanies teachers' work and lives, constituting what Lortie (1975: 10) calls a 'special but shadowed social standing'. Mass media and popular culture, such as movies and television programs, typically portray teachers and the work they do through both positive and negative stereotypes that influence how people think of teaching (Weber and Mitchell, 1999). At the same time, teachers and the work they do are continually shaped and reshaped through their interactions within schooling and broader social and economic transformations (Tardif and Lessard, 1999).

Box 5.1 Teaching consists of a wide range of diverse activities and experiences

This excerpt from a Saskatchewan teacher's diary of daily activities (Saskatchewan Teachers' Federation, 1995: 34) illustrates the varied nature of teaching:

As I sit here ready to go home, and try to reflect on my day—only fleeting images come to mind:
- several 'broken' zippers that got fixed
- reminders to use a Kleenex
- reminders to get new rulers, erasers, etc. for school
- passing out notes to take home
- secretary telling me to pass out more notes tomorrow because she won't be here
- two children whose homes burnt down a week apart. One happened at 3 am—I could smell the smoke on her when she came to tell me about it
- learning the new library computer prog. during our library period so that I could operate it when the secretary/librarian isn't here
- cramps in my shoulders and neck from too many hours bent over books
- the feeling of a small hand sliding into mine and the upturned face and smile that went with it
- having to 'feel' several sets of cold ears to let me know how 'cold it is out there'
- the cries of 'neat' when new things were heard about penguins

Despite the multi-dimensional nature of teaching, the title of this chapter may seem somewhat misdirected for many readers because teaching is often considered to be anything other than political. This chapter highlights the diverse and often contested nature of teaching. Following a profile and history of teaching in Canada, consideration will be given to the changing nature of teaching as a particular form of work. While there are some common elements to all forms of teaching, this chapter is most concerned with teachers in public elementary and secondary schools. The vast majority of educators in Canada are public school teachers who, unlike most teachers at other levels, require specialized teacher training and certification. Moreover, public school teachers are primarily concerned with teaching and pedagogy, in contrast with university professors or vocational educators, whose work is defined more in terms of such other responsibilities as research or applied skills.

Teachers and Teaching in Canada

Nearly half a million persons work as teachers in formal educational institutions in Canada. Statistics Canada (2003d: 54) reports that there were close to 306,000 full-time elementary and secondary school teachers in 2001, with about 33,800 full-time unversity faculty and 27,800 instructors employed full-time in community college, vocational, or trade instructional institutions in 1999. In addition, growing proportions of teachers are working on a part-time basis. The number of part-time teachers in public elementary and secondary schools (over 46,000) rose by more than 10 per cent between the mid- to late-1990s, while there were over 28,000 part-time university faculty, showing an increase of nearly 10 per cent during the course of the 1990s (Statistics Canada, 2002b; Statistics Canada, 2001a: 174).

Teachers are a diverse group, with varying backgrounds, positions, and work experiences. While all teachers may share many common concerns about workloads, student demands, pedagogical techniques, and other aspects of their work, there are significant differences in qualifications and conditions associated with teaching at different levels and institutions and in different subject areas. Teachers at each level and jurisdiction are represented by specific organizations. These are usually called federations or associations, avoiding identification—with the exception of Nova Scotia teachers—as a 'union'. Elementary and secondary teachers are represented by a single organization in most provinces and territories, but there are also distinct organizations for specific groups of teachers in some provinces. Ontario and New Brunswick have separate associations for francophone teachers, while Quebec and Ontario have, in addition to their provincial associations, distinct associations for Protestant and Catholic teachers (as well as an Ontario association for English Catholic teachers). Nationally, the Canadian Teachers' Federation and the Canadian Association of University Teachers bring together affiliate members from particular organizations and institutions (Canadian Teachers'

Federation, 2003). Many subject and specialist groups also exist apart from, or in conjunction with, the major educators' organizations. In addition, teachers are often active in the initiation or operation of diverse organizations oriented to educational reform and other matters relevant to education.

Teaching is a diverse occupation because it is oriented to a variety of educational goals and objectives. Three key themes that emerge in the sociological analysis of teaching will be explored in the remainder of this chapter: (1) the development of teaching as a profession; (2) the importance of gender relations in teaching; and (3) the specific nature of teaching as a form of work. Emphasis is given to the ways in which teaching exists as a contradictory form of work organized around competing demands. In some ways these demands are similar to changing patterns of work in general, yet they are uniquely shaped by educational priorities.

Teaching as a Profession

A prevalent theme in the sociological analysis of teaching is an attempt to understand teaching as a profession. The three most common ways of depicting teaching as a profession lie in approaches characterized as *professional trait, historical, and pressure group theory* (Ozga and Lawn, 1981). As will be shown below, each of these approaches offers useful insights into the development of teaching as an occupation, but each leaves important questions unanswered.

Teacher professionalism is commonly understood through trait approaches that begin with an assessment of how professional occupations differ from other types of work. Major traits that characterize professions usually include such features as formal credentials based on a body of advanced knowledge, social recognition as high-status work, high degrees of decision-making authority in the workplace, and an altruistic commitment to careers and clients (Carr-Saunders, 1966). Authors who employ this approach tend to use recognized professions like medicine and law as a standard of comparison against which to assess the extent to which teaching is a profession. On this basis, it is commonly concluded that teaching falls short of full professional status because it lacks autonomy and prestige, or that teaching is at best a semi- or quasi-profession that remains constrained by external forces such as other professions and bureaucratic school authority structures (Anderson, 1968; Henchey, 1977).

Teaching is often understood through historical accounts, which are related to trait approaches to professionalism. Studies of this type emphasize the evolutionary strides teachers have made towards professional status. Paton (1962), for instance, outlines four historical phases within which Canadian teachers have organized and sought to achieve professional standing:

1. 1850–1914, during which teachers were brought together principally through meetings conducted by school inspectors and senior educational authorities to inform them of new developments in education and reinforce their loyalties to the school system;

2. 1914–35, a period in which teachers organized to promote teaching and improve their welfare and working conditions;
3. 1935–55, characterized by struggles on the part of teachers' organizations for official recognition and greater participation in educational policy-making processes;
4. 1955–75, during which teachers sought professional status through improved occupational powers and responsibilities.

Many other studies, such as accounts by Chafe (1969) and Chalmers (1968), respectively, of the development of the Manitoba Teachers' Society and the Alberta Teachers' Association, Skolrood's (1967) study of the British Columbia Teachers' Federation, and Phillips's (1957) overview of the role of teachers in Canadian education, concur with the overall assessment that teachers have progressively gained professional status through better training, improvements in teaching and learning conditions, and greater input into sophisticated educational matters, despite barriers to the fulfillment of some of their aspirations.

A third group of studies related to teacher professionalism concentrates on the dynamics of teachers as organized lobby or interest groups. This approach, like the historical studies, emphasizes how teachers have struggled collectively to better their professional status and occupational welfare (Downie, 1978; Martin and Macdonnell, 1982; Muir, 1968). However, the analysis of teachers' organizations as interest groups highlights two aspects of teaching that indicate there is more to the occupation than simply the desire to be recognized as professionals. First, teachers have often found they can pursue their occupational interests more successfully through collective bargaining, labour militancy, or political mobilization than through any kind of acknowledgement that they have achieved professional status (see, e.g., Ungerleider, 1994; CEQ, 1974). Second, because teaching is highly constrained by state regulation, such as provincial legislation that outlines the duties and responsibilities of teachers, the degree to which the occupation can influence educational policy and practice is limited (Lawson and Woock, 1987).

The combined impact of these factors has led to a state of affairs in which there is confusion over the nature and direction of teaching as an occupation. Canadian teachers' organizations have gained widespread notoriety as powerful lobby groups, due especially to their periodic regional or provincial support for selected political parties, their involvement in a number of important social justice initiatives, such as anti-poverty organizations, and their role in separatist movements in Quebec. Lockhart (1991: 17) observes that teaching in Canada is in crisis, signified by teachers' search for strategies that will allow them to gain professional control in the face of conflicting forces, such as fiscal cutbacks in education, public concern for accountability and quality in education, and the bureaucratic organization of schooling. Teachers are criticized periodically by governments, media representatives, and other groups for their political stances or their status as public-sector workers.

Box 5.2 The impact of education reforms on teaching and learning conditions

Education reforms, including funding cutbacks, centralized control over teachers' working conditions, and restrictions on the autonomy of teachers and school boards, have a significant impact on teaching and learning conditions, as this press release from the British Columbia Teachers' Federation (2003) suggests:

Province-wide polling reveals that more than two-thirds of British Columbians believe learning conditions for students have deteriorated since the BC Liberals stripped the teachers' collective agreement of provisions protecting class size and services to students.

'Education Minister Christy Clark claims that our education system is getting better every day, but these results show that people throughout our province are clearly seeing the negative impact of her government's policies on students' educational opportunities,' said BC Teachers' Federation President Neil Worboys. 'With larger classes, 2,000 fewer teachers, and $210 million cut, how can education possibly be getting better? We can't do more with so much less.'

In January 2002, the government pushed Bills 27 and 28 through the Legislature in a single weekend. The bills imposed a contract on teachers and eliminated provisions protecting learning conditions.

Asked about the impact of removing class-size limits and student-teacher ratios for specialists such as counsellors and special education teachers, almost 69 per cent of respondents said that learning conditions are now worse for students. Less than 4 per cent said conditions are improved.

Significantly, almost 47 per cent of respondents who identified themselves as Liberal voters also believe that learning conditions have deteriorated. Less than 9 per cent of Liberals thought they have improved.

'It just goes to show that Christy Clark can't even convince her own party supporters that her policies are taking education in the right direction', Worboys said. 'The minister should listen to parents and the public who are pleading with her to reinvest in education.'

The question was part of an omnibus poll conducted in April by McIntyre & Mustel Research Ltd. The firm polled a random sample of 501 adults throughout BC during the week of April 7, 2003. The results are considered accurate within ±4.4 per cent, 19 times out of 20.

Considerable evidence supports the claims made in the literature that Canadian teachers have made significant progress over the past century towards the achievement of professional status. Whereas most teachers received little formal training at the turn of the century, today teachers in nearly all provinces require a minimum of three to five years of university education to qualify for a teaching certificate, with recent pressures to extend and intensify pre-service training. Teachers' pay scales, which were once set at the discretion of trustees who were often unwilling or unable to secure funds to pay teachers adequately, are now bargained collectively and reflect differences in levels of professional training and experience. Teachers are represented on curriculum committees and other educational bodies that set or influence policies relating to schooling. They are recognized, through their professional training and school legislation, as professionals who make decisions regarding such matters as curricular planning, pedagogy, discipline, and evaluation of students. Teachers' associations have developed codes of ethics regarding professional conduct and have been actively involved in professional development activities for their members. Teachers have also participated in a wide range of educational decision-making activities that were once left to the discretion of legislators, school trustees, and educational administrators.

Despite marked improvements in the professional status of teachers, factors other than professionalism operate to shape teaching. As noted above, legislative and bureaucratic frameworks pose serious limitations to teachers' abilities to act as autonomous professionals. Teachers themselves commonly report frustration in their work roles, particularly as they are perceived by persons outside the occupation. Among teachers surveyed in a national study commissioned by the Canadian Teachers' Federation in the early 1990s, only about half felt that members of their profession were respected in their communities, and even lower proportions (ranging between 17 per cent in the Yukon and 44 per cent in New Brunswick) viewed community media coverage of teachers as fair (King and Peart, 1992: 141). Frequent media reports on the theme of 'what's wrong with the schools' reinforce the notion that teachers are not doing an adequate job of keeping order or teaching students proper skills for life in the technological age. Nikiforuk (1993: 112) encapsulates much public sentiment in his observation that 'Self-absorbed, poorly led, and often lacking in self-criticism (criticism now equals self-esteem bashing in some quarters) the profession or trade tends to prize its contributions too smugly.' However, especially in jurisdictions like Ontario where provincial governments have intervened heavily to tighten constraint over educational regulations and finance, teachers have maintained high public support. Livingstone et al. (2001: 8), for instance, observe in their survey of public attitudes towards education that, whereas fewer than half of all respondents expressed satisfaction with the education system in general, close to two-thirds (63 per cent) of all respondents (67 per cent of parents and 84 per cent of teachers in their sample) were satisfied with the job that teachers were doing.

Teachers' organizations are often criticized in the same regard, by many teachers as well as by those outside the education system, as being too rigidly structured, too union-oriented, and more concerned about wages and workers' rights than with professional issues such as curriculum, classroom conduct, and student services. Regardless of whether teachers are blamed for educational failure or treated sympathetically for their awkward position within the education system, there is a sense of powerlessness that has a demoralizing impact on teachers. The Council of Ministers of Education (1996), summarizing teaching conditions across Canada, points to increasing problems of teacher morale, stress, and concern about such issues as increasing demands on their time and energies in and out of the classroom, limited preparation time, fiscal and political attacks on education and educational employees, and isolation from crucial educational decision-making. In general, teachers in recent years have tended not to be as militant as other public-sector employees, but they have continued to fight against educational cutbacks and to serve as strong advocates for educational issues in many provinces (Ungerleider, 1994). In a full-page advertisement in *The Hill Times*, which reports on the activities of the federal Parliament in Ottawa, the president of the Canadian Teachers' Federation observes that schools are having difficulty in recruiting and retaining teachers because of government measures to undermine teaching and public educational quality, educational cutbacks, new societal demands, poor employment conditions, and uncompetitive salaries (Willard, 2001).

The significance of the challenges that teachers face in their work and in establishing an occupational image suggests that a focus on trying to determine whether or not teaching is a profession is misdirected. What does it mean to acknowledge that any occupation is a profession? Professionalism is not something that is static or absolute. Recent measures to restructure health care, for instance, mean that even established professions like medicine are in danger of losing much of the autonomy and respect they once held. In the continually changing world of education, teachers are subject to similar challenges, with the consequence that they are deprofessionalized in some aspects of their work at the same time as they may gain professional powers in others. Moreover, the nature and organization of teaching are governed by factors that both transcend and shape the nature of professionalism. Two of these are considered below—the importance in teaching of gender relations, and pressures in the direction of what has been conceptualized as the proletarianization of teaching.

Gender and Teaching

One of the most striking features of the teaching force is its highly segmented gender composition. Women are concentrated in elementary school

Box 5.3 Two views on teachers' right to strike

Debates over teacher professionalism and the nature of teaching are focused on such issues as whether or not teachers should have the right to strike, as argued here in two articles from the Vancouver Sun (30 Mar. 1991):

By Helen Raham
Kelowna elementary school teacher and executive director, Society for the Advancement of Excellence in Education.

Students and taxpayers are the losers under the present system of bargaining between teacher unions and school boards.

Teacher unions are clearly the winners. And school boards, having lost the power struggle to maintain control of the public education tax dollar, may be the ultimate losers when their authority is revoked.

The government of British Columbia granted teachers full collective bargaining rights in 1988, with changes in legislation that permitted local teacher associations to unionize.

This may prove to have been a grievous mistake. It has resulted in interruptions of service to students and skyrocketing public education costs for taxpayers, which do not necessarily translate into improved classroom instruction.

For years, teachers had been demanding the right to strike in bargaining their working conditions and wages. The government may have conceded prematurely. Across the province, news of job action and classroom closures assault parents and taxpayers daily. . . .

The present system of bargaining for teacher contracts is dysfunctional because the industrial model is being employed. The strike weapon as a bargaining tool is inappropriate to education. It harms the student, provides a poor model of conflict resolution, and has resulted in unmanageable costs to taxpayers. . . .

Teacher strikes mean failing grades for the public education system. Unless changes are made, the future looks bleak for taxpayers and students.

By Dan Blake
English teacher at North Surrey secondary school who is active in the Surrey Teachers' Association.

There is no doubt that teachers should have the right to strike. The Charter of Rights guarantees that all citizens shall have the same rights. If every other employee has the right to strike, then so should teachers.

Box 5.3 continued

As with any right in a democratic society, the right to strike must be exercised judiciously. It must be the last recourse of an employee group.

Going on strike means lost wages and pension benefits. It creates disruption in families as members try to adjust to sudden total income loss. For teachers, there is the added concern of a disruption in their relationship with their students.

When reason fails to convince school board negotiators, the choice for teachers is either to abandon their legitimate bargaining objectives or to strike. . . .

What could be more professional than forgoing salary and pension benefits, and trudging through the rain and snow several hours a day, for the purpose of creating a better learning environment for your students? Being professional means caring about the quality of the job you do. . . .

Teachers should not have to strike to make school boards and the government see reality, but if a strike is the only way left to achieve an acceptable learning environment, they will not be found wanting.

classrooms while men are concentrated at the post-secondary level and in senior administrative positions. More than three out of five full-time teachers in elementary and secondary schools are women; the number and proportion of male teachers is expected to drop further based on demographic trends and enrolment patterns in teacher training programs. The concentrations of women teachers in post-secondary institutions are also increasing, but remain well below those of men, with women representing two out of five full-time community college instructors and only one out of four full-time (compared to two out of five part-time) university faculty (Statistics Canada, 1999: 29). Within each educational level there are even more substantial differences. A report commissioned for the Canadian Teachers' Federation in the early 1990s indicates that women constituted 94 per cent of teachers in kindergarten to grade 3, 72 per cent of teachers in grades 4–6, but only 53 per cent of teachers in grades 7–9 and 46 per cent of those in grades 10–12, including the Ontario Academic Credit (OAC) level (King and Peart, 1992: 20). Despite the preponderance of women teaching in schools, they constitute only 22 per cent of principals and 36 per cent of vice-principals in Canadian elementary schools, and 8 per cent of principals and 17 per cent of vice-principals in high schools (King and Peart, 1992: 146). No more than 6 per cent of district superintendents or directors of education in all provinces (with the exception of New Brunswick, where the corresponding figure was

24 per cent) were women (Rees, 1990). These trends continue despite a gradual increase in representation by women within educational administration.

At the university level, three-quarters of tenured faculty, about 60 per cent of faculty in positions leading to tenure, and nearly 90 per cent of faculty at the highest academic rank of full professor are men (Canadian Association of University Teachers, 2003: 13; Statistics Canada, 1999: 31). Among full-time university faculty, women are much more likely than men to be concentrated at the lowest academic ranks, although this gap has declined in recent decades (Ornstein et al., 1998: 18). Male and female teachers are also concentrated in particular subject areas in accordance with traditional divisions of labour so that, for instance, most teachers in mathematics, sciences, and engineering are men while most teachers in general classrooms, health care (other than medicine), business education, and household sciences are women.

Differences in the kinds of teaching positions that men and women occupy are reflected in teachers' salaries. Men earn considerably more, on average, than women at all levels and ranks of teaching. Among full-time university faculty, the average salary for women in 2001–2 was nearly $12,500 (or about 14.5 per cent) below comparable levels for men, while at the full professor rank, the salary gap was just over half that, at about $6,635 (or about 6.5 per cent) (Canadian Association of University Teachers, 2003: 7). Much of the disparity can be accounted for by differences in rank, qualifications, age, and experience. Personal factors, such as family commitments, specialized interests, and background in particular subject areas, and age-grade preferences also often contribute to distinct career choices and teaching priorities among men and women. Taken together, however, these elements are indicative of how individual and structural forces combine to produce unequal opportunities for men and women in teaching, as in many other occupations and spheres of life.

An overview of the historical development of public school teaching in Canada offers some insight into how gender inequities have come to be incorporated into the occupation. Table 5.1 provides an overview of the gender composition of the national school teaching force since Confederation. In contrast with recent experience, in which women have constituted between one-half and two-thirds of the teaching force, most teachers until the late 1860s were men. During the first quarter of the twentieth century, fewer than one in five teachers was male, although the relative proportion of male teachers gradually increased from a low of 16.6 per cent in 1920 to nearly 45 per cent in the early 1980s, before dropping to current levels of just over one-third.

The national trends illustrated in the table do not show provincial and regional variations in the feminization of teaching. By the time of Confederation, the numbers of male and female teachers were roughly equal in most jurisdictions. In Quebec and many regions of Ontario, however, women teachers outnumbered men by large margins much earlier; in much

Table 5.1
Full-time Teachers in Elementary and Secondary Schools, by Gender,
Canada, Selected Years, 1867–1999*

Year**	Male (%)	Female (%)	Total
1867	3,312 (53.8)	2,840 (46.2)	6,152
1870	5,143 (38.6)	8,180 (61.4)	13,323
1875	5,338 (34.1)	10,329 (65.9)	15,667
1880	6,181 (35.1)	11,411 (64.9)	17,592
1885	5,772 (28.2)	14,719 (71.8)	20,491
1890	5,797 (25.7)	16,753 (74.3)	22,550
1895	6,069 (24.5)	18,652 (75.5)	24,721
1900	6,205 (22.7)	21,164 (77.3)	27,369
1905	6,392 (19.8)	25,818 (80.2)	32,210
1910	7,849 (19.4)	32,627 (80.6)	40,476
1915	8,789 (17.5)	41,453 (82.5)	50,242
1920	9,600 (16.6)	48,178 (83.4)	57,778
1925	12,069 (18.9)	51,771 (81.1)	63,840
1930	14,255 (20.3)	55,990 (79.7)	70,245
1935	18,492 (25.3)	54,593 (74.7)	73,085
1940	19,417 (25.8)	55,970 (74.2)	75,387
1945	17,415 (22.5)	60,064 (77.5)	77,479
1950	24,064 (26.8)	65,618 (73.2)	89,682
1955	31,058 (26.8)	84,777 (73.2)	115,835
1960	44,593 (29.1)	108,447 (70.9)	153,040
1965	67,832 (34.4)	129,261 (65.6)	197,093
1970	100,820 (38.4)	161,637 (61.5)	262,457
1975	110,429 (41.8)	153,833 (58.2)	262,262
1980	121,537 (44.4)	152,170 (55.6)	273,707
1985	119,400 (43.9)	152,659 (56.1)	272,059
1990	119,143 (40.1)	177,963 (59.9)	297,106
1995	113,198 (37.9)	185,478 (62.1)	298,676
1999***	110,834 (35.8)	198,759 (64.2)	309,593

* Data not available for Nova Scotia and Quebec in 1867; Prince Edward Island in 1875 and 1895; Manitoba and British Columbia until 1885; data for Alberta and Saskatchewan not included until 1905, Newfoundland until 1950, and Yukon and Northwest Territories until 1960.

** School year beginning in the year shown.

*** Figures are estimates.

Sources: For 1867–1975, F.H. Leacy, ed., *Historical Statistics of Canada*, 2nd edn (Ottawa: Statistics Canada, 1983), W150-2; for 1980–90: Statistics Canada, *Education in Canada* (Ottawa: Minister of Supply and Services Canada, various years); for 1995–9: Statistics Canada, 'School Enrolments and teaching staff', *The Daily*, 18 Sept. 2003, 1.

of western Canada, men predominated until at least the 1880s; and there were more men than women teaching in Prince Edward Island schools until after the turn of the century (see, e.g., Danylewycz et al., 1991; Leacy, 1983: W150–91). Among rural school districts in many provinces, particularly those that employed teachers working in one-room schools, men tended to out-number women until late in the nineteenth century. In such districts, gender parity often continued for several years after that, although there were vari-ations in the trends from one region or school district to another (Danylewycz et al., 1991).

Danylewycz and Prentice (1986: 60–1) emphasize that many commenta-tors hold mistaken views associated with historical processes through which teaching became feminized. One such myth is that the preponderance of young female teachers at the turn of the century devalued teaching and made it susceptible to extensive regulation by educational authorities, thereby delaying or preventing the occupation from becoming a full profession. While it is true that teachers were frequently subjected to paternalistic con-trol by educational administrators, it is also important to emphasize the strong professional commitment demonstrated by many early women teach-ers in their efforts to provide effective education despite personal and occu-pational difficulties (Poelzer, 1990; Prentice and Theobald, 1991; Wilson, 1991). Sometimes, young women entered teaching on a temporary basis until they were married, but many teachers saw the occupation as a lifelong voca-tion. A spirit of adventure and the ability to innovate were often essential ingredients for the success of those who assumed teaching positions in remote rural areas. Although such teachers initially may have lacked formal training and experience, they played a crucial role in promoting public education and maintaining the school as a vital part of social development in many com-munities across Canada.

A second misconception related to the feminization of teaching concerns the devaluation or invisibility of teaching as a form of work (Danylewycz and Prentice, 1986: 61). Teaching traditionally has been discounted as some-thing less than a 'real job' or else has been analyzed separately from other work by virtue of its nature as non-manual labour performed primarily by women. Instead, it is often considered as an extension of unpaid social roles associated with mothering and domestic work (Gaskell and McLaren, 1991). In addition to undermining teaching as work, these views have been used to justify discriminatory practices in teaching, including the maintenance of pay schedules in which female teachers were paid less than men until the mid-twentieth century, as well as the periodic requirement of provincial gov-ernments and school boards for women to resign from teaching positions upon marriage. Despite persistent realities to the contrary, female teachers have been depicted by many administrators and policy-making bodies as less dedicated and well-trained than males, and less in need of income and careers to support themselves or their families (Arbus, 1990; Reynolds, 1990).

An analysis of the historical development of teaching in Canada yields important insights about changing gender relations within the occupation. Both men and women have played central, although often distinctive, roles in all phases of Canadian schooling. Gendered divisions of labour were established early. In New France, distinct schools for boys and girls tended to be run, respectively, by parish priests and female teaching orders in the seventeenth century (Johnson, 1968: 8–9). Beyond elementary schooling, at least until the nineteenth century, teaching tended to be conducted by men for men, usually by clergy in colleges or seminaries that offered professional training or by highly educated men who provided elite training to other men of privileged classes.

In general, two kinds of schooling, associated with distinct classes of teachers, prevailed prior to the late nineteenth century. Grammar schools or those established by particular organizations sought teachers who were somewhat qualified and loyal to the goals of the sponsoring authorities. Common schools open to all children in the community were initially established by anyone who claimed to be a teacher or who could hire others to teach. The former tended to be somewhat better paid and more highly regarded than the latter, although there were frequent reports of public disdain for, if not hostility against, teachers in general (Phillips, 1957: 546–7).

One of the main objectives sought by advocates for a system of free public schools in the nineteenth century was the establishment of a stable, highly respected teaching force. This desired form of school organization had contradictory implications for teachers, whose role came to be that of 'subordinate partners' in the education system (Wotherspoon, 1993). Teachers gained some degree of job security and occupational legitimacy through the introduction of measures to ensure that communities had schools operated with public funds and other forms of state support. Teachers also experienced increasing status through the expectation that they would promote public education and be entrusted to supervise and teach children. At the same time, though, teachers were more fully monitored by school inspectors and regulated by state educational administrators. Thus, although they had considerable autonomy and authority in the classroom, teachers became public servants in the sense that their primary obligations and loyalties were to the 'public good' rather than to any specific social interest.

School promoters and educational administrators were interested in developing a teaching force that met their ideals of public education. Repeatedly, in the speeches, reports, and writings of such educational leaders, the ideal teacher was presented as a relatively well-educated and self-disciplined man of high moral quality (Corrigan et al., 1987; Love, 1978). While educational authorities were not opposed to female teachers, they sought males, who they felt would be more committed to public education as a project of state formation. From its beginnings, then, a paternalistic model of authority was incorporated into the public education system so that senior administrators and state officials were almost exclusively men, as were secondary school teachers and senior teachers in larger schools, while women taught in the elementary grades or in ungraded rural schools.

The development of the Canadian teaching force, like many other aspects of education, involved a constant tension between educational ideals and practical considerations. One of the persistent limitations to the fulfillment of educators' visions of the education system was the lack of an adequate supply of suitable, fully qualified teachers. This problem was itself often the consequence of other difficulties within the education system, including negative public images of teachers and low teacher salaries. These factors often reinforced one another. Public schools, by the late nineteenth century, were supported by provincial government grants intended to be supplemented by locally raised funds. The latter, however, were frequently scarce, contributing to inequalities between rural and urban schools and among school districts. Collection of school funds could not always be enforced, especially in poorer regions or districts where the public had little interest in or support for the school system. Therefore, teachers were often paid less than amounts they had been promised, however inadequate those salaries were to begin with (see Wotherspoon, 1993). Teachers' salaries, on average, were lower than the wages of unskilled labourers at the turn of the century (Phillips, 1957: 551–2) and they remained well below average occupational salaries until after World War II, when factors such as the consolidation of school districts, increased allocation of central government funding for education, and aggressive collective bargaining by teachers began to stabilize teacher incomes.

Table 5.2

Average Elementary and Secondary School Teachers' Incomes in Comparison with Average Income in Canada, by Gender, Selected Census Years, 1921–2001

	Teachers			All Occupations		
	Male	**Female**	**Total**	**Male**	**Female**	**Total**
1921	$ 1,395	$ 818	$ 914	$ 1,057	$ 573	$ 954
1931	1,575	917	1,066	927	559	848
1941	1,416	793	962	993	490	755
1951*	2,673	1,915	2,050	3,468	1,788	2,898
1961	4,712	3,176	3,734	3,679	1,995	3,191
1971	8,420	5,532	6,424	6,574	3,199	5,391
1981	24,039	15,142	18,111	16,988	8,863	13,635
1991	41,266	27,938	31,864	29,847	17,751	24,329
2001	46,356	38,449	40,751	38,347	24,390	31,757

* For 1951, figures are for median income; for teachers, data for Quebec are not available.

Sources: Compiled and calculated from census data; for 1951, data on teachers are from Dominion Bureau of Statistics, *Survey of Elementary and Secondary Education, 1950–54* (Ottawa: Queen's Printer, 1959).

This situation exacerbated gender-based differential pay rates for teachers. Table 5.2 reveals that women have been paid about two-thirds to three-quarters of what men received until relatively recently. However, while teachers experience greater gender parity than other Canadian workers, as a whole, the average income for female teachers remains just over four-fifths of that for male teachers. Altenbaugh (1995: 83–4) indicates that differences in pay among men and women throughout North America stemmed in part from the likelihood that male teachers had more formal training and teaching experience and were concentrated in high schools, where salaries tended to reflect higher qualification levels and where teachers were better able to organize to protect their occupational interests. However, as Altenbaugh also emphasizes, gender discrimination played a more fundamental role in teaching, as evident in the fact that women were paid less even when they were teaching high school or had more education and experience than men. It has been noted previously, for instance, that gender differences were institutionalized through separate and unequal pay scales for men and women that were systematically maintained by provinces and school districts until the 1960s.

Gender factors also entered into the regulation of teaching by educational administrators and government officials. Public or common schooling, of which teachers were the most visible representatives in local communities, signified the presence of state rule in everyday life. This placed teachers in a position in which their lives and characters were under surveillance away from school as well as at work. The lack of teachers with adequate training and of presumed character to meet the ideal desired by educational authorities posed a dilemma that resulted in new ways of monitoring and managing the teaching force.

In the late nineteenth and early twentieth centuries, legislators and educational administrators introduced several measures to regulate teaching. Many of these initiatives were directed in particular towards the preponderance of young women who entered the teaching force to meet the demands of a growing school system. A system of school inspection was implemented so that state authority would be represented in schools on a periodic basis to compensate for the difficulties involved in monitoring classroom activity on an everyday basis. The school inspector was instructed to assess the character as well as the competency of teachers. The traumatic nature of school inspectors' visits—and the mysterious authority they represented—has become a recurrent theme in Canadian fiction as well as in biographical accounts of students and teachers (see, e.g., Braithwaite, 1979). The system of classroom inspection had the additional effect of reinforcing paternalism and gender-based divisions of labour within educational hierarchies by creating a career path in which it was possible for loyal male teachers to be promoted to the rank of inspector (Fleming, 1986). In the larger urban schools, supervision of teachers was often more directly accomplished through the presence of principals, head teachers, and subject specialists (Danylewycz and Prentice, 1986: 70).

The inspection function was complemented by a second form of control under the guise of legislation and regulations to govern the character and work of teachers. Teachers' duties came to be specified in law and other directives passed down from both the provinces and school boards. Thus, as exemplified in the regulations of British Columbia in 1875 (see Box 3.2), the teacher not only had to teach 'diligently and faithfully' the curriculum set by boards of education, but was also required to promote 'both by precept and example, CLEANLINESS, NEATNESS, AND DECENCY . . . TRUST AND HONESTY' (British Columbia, 1875: 47). Teachers' duties and the demands on their time expanded in conjunction with increases in school size and enrolment, the duration of school attendance, and the scope of the curriculum. In addition to growing class sizes and the requirements to teach new subjects, teachers were faced with paperwork, documenting everything from student attendance and progress to homework and classroom activities (Danylewycz and Prentice, 1986: 66–8).

However, as the quotation above reveals, teachers' personal attributes and lives, more than just their school-related work, were subject to external scrutiny by educational authorities. This applied to both men and women. School officials frequently criticized male teachers for their apparent lack of commitment to teaching or carelessness in their work and personal habits. The lives and habits of female teachers were subjected to even closer scrutiny. Akin to forms of patriarchal regulation of women's sexuality and social activities that prevailed in the family, school board regulations and teachers' contracts stipulated how female teachers should dress, prohibited them from keeping company with men, proscribed the hours they were to be at home, and made them subject to dismissal if they drank, smoked, or married (see, e.g., Apple, 1986: 72–4; British Columbia School Trustees' Association, 1980). The teacher—especially the female teacher—became a public figure who was governed by specified notions of morality as determined by state authorities.

A third form of regulation oriented to the governance of women teachers was the regularization and expansion of teacher training programs. Until the early part of the twentieth century, the qualifications and training required to become a teacher were highly irregular. While many private and secondary schools were able to attract and pay adequate salaries to persons who had undertaken university studies, common schools often hired whomever they could to ensure an adequate supply of teachers. Initially, a person might be considered eligible to teach simply by virtue of having more schooling than the students being taught (or even claiming to have more). State officials, concerned about the quality as well as public perceptions of the school system, promoted the establishment of formal teacher training programs. Teacher training institutions called normal schools, which provided prospective teachers with knowledge about curricular subjects and the 'art' and practice of teaching, were introduced as early as 1836 in Montreal and 1847 in Upper Canada and New Brunswick (Johnson, 1968: 156). Over the next

Box 5.4 Serious issues affect teachers in many nations

In many countries, teachers' efforts to gain full professional recognition for their work and qualifications are undermined by educational reforms, funding crises, and other serious issues. Funding cuts and legislative changes affecting teachers and education have produced teacher layoffs and school closures, increased class sizes, limited or rolled back salary increases for educational workers, restricted teachers' collective bargaining rights, and threatened teachers' right to strike. Items that have appeared in recent news and government reports demonstrate that teaching faces severe challenges, such as the following:

- teachers across Russia in 1999 engaged in strikes, rallies, information meetings, and work suspensions to protest delays in the payment of wages or substitution of food for monetary salary;
- teachers in Guatemala engaged in strike action in 2003 to demand increased spending for textbooks, desks and chairs, school meal programs, bilingual education programs, and other improvements to the education system promised by the government;
- school and university teachers in Zimbabwe were dismissed in 2002 after engaging in strikes to protest lack of action to address a serious gap between wages and price increases;
- teachers in Honduras engaged in strike action in 2003 to protest lack of pay for periods of up to four months;
- teachers in France, Austria, and other European nations engaged in protests and strike action in 2003 to fight government proposals to scale back or eliminate pension and retirement plans;
- teachers in Zambia and other African nations are experiencing high rates of infection and death from AIDS.

several decades, provincial governments and school boards made periods of training in normal schools, usually in conjunction with some high school attainment, a requirement for teacher certification. Nonetheless, as Phillips (1957: 579) observes, 'actually, in all provinces before 1900 a large proportion of elementary school teachers had no more than two years' secondary school education, and either no professional training at all or no such training at the normal school level.'

Normal schools had as their objective the production of a corps of teachers that could at least approximate the ideal advanced by educational authorities. However, they also reoriented their focus to the reality that most persons who were entering the teaching force were 'raw, untrained' young women, as they were characterized by at least one school official (British

Columbia, 1904: A65). Consequently, normal school training came to emphasize the cultivation of feminine dedication and loyalty to the public educational enterprise as much as practical classroom knowledge. These paternalistic aims were directed by male administrators in both the school system and the normal schools (Wotherspoon, 1989: 151).

It is necessary to recognize several fallacies contained in the portrayal by education officials of teachers, and women teachers in particular, as compliant and incompetent novices. First, while there were many 'green' teachers who did enter the classroom with little formal training, most school districts had several examples of teachers who, over the course of extended careers, made significant contributions both to the education of several generations of youth and to the increasing public respect that came to be accorded the school system overall. High teacher attrition rates were at least as likely to be the result of inadequate pay or working conditions, or regulations such as the one to force women to resign their positions upon marriage, as the consequence of individual failings.

Second, teachers were, as they generally continue to be, much more resourceful than they have been given credit for. Teaching, in common with other occupations considered to be 'women's work', such as clerical work, involves highly complex attributes that tend to be discounted as skills (see, e.g., Jackson, 1994). There is considerable skill involved, for instance, in the day-to-day ability to organize and manage classrooms. Especially in poorly equipped schools or those located at a distance from major towns and cities that have libraries and other forms of resource support, teachers have had to develop their own materials and techniques to convey the curriculum and maintain student interest.

Teachers also possess expertise in their ability to facilitate interpersonal relations in and out of the classroom. As this book has emphasized, the often indeterminate nature of life and social dynamics within schooling is a vital part of educational processes. The teaching relationship includes such things as sensitivity to students' emotional states, informal counselling and advising, mediation between competitive or antagonistic students, and other nurturing activities. These aspects of teaching are often devalued and discredited as real skills because of their parallels with mothering and domestic labour, forms of unpaid labour that are considered natural. Nonetheless, the 'caring' dimensions of teachers' work remain central to capacities regarded as essential for good teaching. Acker's (1999: 195) observations with respect to one school are applicable to many teaching situations:

> The fact that most of the teachers were women was also one of its strengths. Many of the women had in the past, or were having concurrently, experience in managing homes and families and balancing competing commitments. They seemed well adapted to the flexibility and tolerance for change required for a successful teacher at the school.

A third problem is the image of docility associated with a highly feminized teaching force. The very fact that educational administrators and teacher-training officials introduced a broad and frequently changing range of regulations to govern teaching signifies that the teaching force was not readily subordinated. Many teachers demonstrated courage and determination simply to maintain their positions in the face of parents, trustees, and other officials hostile to them or the school. Teachers adopted both formal and informal means to resist measures they felt were extreme or unfair. Women teachers not only advanced struggles for pay equity, improvement of teaching conditions, and curricular change within the school system, but they were also engaged, often in leadership roles, in the suffragist and later feminist movements as well as in other organized groups in pursuit of social justice. Moreover, women did have some formal opportunities to influence the profession more directly. Although women with university degrees and other superior qualifications were more likely to be bypassed for promotion in favour of men, they were not always completely excluded from administrative and senior teaching positions.

These observations are important in helping us to reconceptualize the notion of professionalism. In contrast to approaches concerned with the question of whether or not teaching is a profession, historical evidence suggests that professionalism can more appropriately be understood as a strategy or ideology employed by various forces and agencies, both within and external to teaching, in order to shape the occupation in particular ways (Warburton, 1986). In the same way that school officials continually had to revise how they regulated teaching because it was not possible to construct a teaching force of idealized teachers, diverse images and consequences of professionalism have contributed to the development of teaching in Canada.

Some school officials, for instance, were opposed to female teachers because they saw the influx of young women as a deterrent to the achievement of professional status by teachers. Viewed in this context, the introduction of normal schools was a way to upgrade teacher professionalism by providing specialized training and improving teacher qualifications, but it was intended to scrutinize teachers and inculcate in them an appropriate orientation to the school system before they entered the classroom. Similarly, teachers working in different educational settings had unique professional needs. For relatively well-paid, highly qualified secondary school teachers, professionalism was a way to increase their status and power in the education system, while teachers in poorly equipped remote rural schools were more likely to see professionalism as a tool for attaining fundamental improvements in teaching and working conditions. Professionalism, as an ideology, has had a moderating impact by restricting the extent to which teachers have adopted overtly political and militant actions, but it has also been influential in raising teachers' occupational profile, sometimes by their aggressive pursuit of policies and practices that go beyond school-specific issues.

The tendency for many teachers, as well as legislators, administrators, trustees, parents, and the media, to establish boundaries that define legitimate spheres of activity for teachers and distinguish these from areas that teachers should not be engaged in continues to have important consequences for gender relations in teaching. Teachers who have advanced equitable treatment for women in teaching, for instance, have sometimes also been leaders in wider feminist movements. Some have encountered criticism from within and outside teaching for dealing with issues characterized by critics as political rather than educational in nature. Frequently, both educational administrators and leaders of teachers' organizations have dismissed demands by teachers to address issues such as pay inequity, racism and sexism in the classroom, and concern about poverty in the community as 'unprofessional'. These tendencies have made it difficult for teachers' organizations to take decisive action on such problems as sexual harassment, maternity leave, inequitable assignment of duties, competing demands between home and school, and other concerns that emerge through women's experiences in teaching.

The continuing division of labour along gender lines in teaching is clearly illustrated by the data on the positions occupied by men and women in the education system presented at the beginning of this section. In general, it remains the case that most teachers in the lower grades and subordinate positions are women, while most teachers in high school and administrative positions are men. Although women have come to have a much greater impact on educational decision-making than in the past, partly reflected in increased participation rates in senior positions, substantial gender inequality within teaching and educational administration continues (Canadian Teachers' Federation, 1993; Young and Levin, 2002: 182–3). Employment equity programs, increased recognition of the need for women to take more central roles in educational planning and management as well as delivery, and the leadership that some women have provided to change educational realities and serve as successful role models have had an impact on creating more favourable conditions for gender equity. Various factors, including personal choice, positive and negative attitudes of teachers and administrators, and the ways in which teaching-related activities are differentially recognized in career and promotion decisions within teaching, have contributed to the mixed success in achieving equity objectives (Rees, 1990; Canadian Teachers' Federation, 1993).

Teaching is posed with additional scrutiny and challenges in relation to the increasing racial diversity within Canadian schools. Teachers are expected to reflect many of the major characteristics of the communities they work in and to play a leadership role by fostering learning environments that are sensitive to the students and communities they work with. With few exceptions (notably visible minorities teaching at the university level), the proportion of teachers and educators at all levels who are visible minorities or Aboriginal has not kept pace with comparable growth in the student body and the general population (Guppy and Davies, 1998: 41–3). This is clearly shown, with regard to Aboriginal teachers, in Figure 5.1. Racial minority groups, especially within black and Aboriginal communities, frequently cite the lack of representation within the teaching and educational administrative work-force as a serious deficiency in the creation of a racially tolerant and cultur-ally supportive atmosphere (Canadian Race Relations Foundation, 2000: 8–9). Many visible minority and Aboriginal teachers express concern about their work placements, job expectations, and lack of acceptance by other school and community personnel. Broader concerns are also evident as teach-ers are mandated to implement anti-racist or culturally inclusive program guidelines despite having limited background knowledge, administrative sup-port, resources, and time for preparation. These problems coexist with sev-eral promising initiatives in which teachers are strongly supported and com-mitted to develop strong connections and relationships with the communities in which they work (Dei et al., 2000: 141ff.; Schissel and Wotherspoon, 2003: 116–19).

The Proletarianization of Teaching

In contrast to the view that teaching can be characterized by its strong progress towards professionalism and gender equity, some commentators argue that the dominant tendency is one of proletarianization. Proletarianization refers to the processes whereby teachers, like workers in many industries, are subject to increasing, externally driven forms of control and pressures to intensify their work.

One of the primary claims for recognition of teaching as a profession has been the continual increase in educational qualifications required for teacher certification. Whereas at the turn of the century it was not uncommon for teachers to have less than high school completion, secondary education and a period of specialized teacher training were required by the early part of this century; by the mid-1970s, teacher training in most provinces was established in university degree programs, and now most Canadian jurisdictions require a minimum of four to five years of university education, including one or more years of professional studies, prior to certification. Most administrative positions and some secondary teaching positions are restricted to persons with a master's degree or higher in combination with other forms of profes-sional development (Canadian Teachers' Federation, 2003). By the early 1990s, two-thirds of all teachers who taught at the kindergarten to grade 3 levels and over 70 per cent of teachers in the higher grades (increasing by level) held university degrees (King and Peart, 1992: 22). Despite these improvements in formal educational qualifications, a common complaint of teachers is that there is a disjuncture between their training and the expecta-tions placed on them in the classroom and in other aspects of the job. Those who argue that teaching is becoming proletarianized rather than profession-alized emphasize the necessity for examining how teaching is organized and

Figure 5.1 Aboriginal Population and Teacher Representation by Province and Territory, 1996

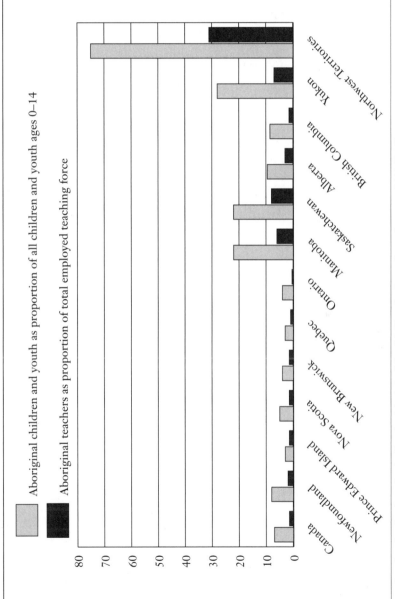

Aboriginal children and youth as proportion of all children and youth ages 0–14

Aboriginal teachers as proportion of total employed teaching force

Source: Data from Steering Group for the Situational Analysis of Canada's Education Sector Human Resources (2002:15–16).

regulated as work, rather than what the formal entry requirements are, in order to assess how 'professional' teaching has become. Moreover, when teaching is analyzed as work, the reasons for teachers' involvement with organized labour and their adoption of trade unionist strategies become more readily apparent.

With respect to teaching, proletarianization can be analyzed in several different ways. In the most general sense, the concept refers to the attributes that teaching shares with other forms of work that are regulated and controlled by employers or managers outside the occupation. Braverman (1974), in one of the most influential analyses of contemporary labour processes, argues that no occupation is immune from proletarianization and the related process of deskilling, in which workers lose their ability to plan, make decisions, and use a wide range of skills to carry out their work tasks. As was observed in Chapter 2 and will be expanded upon in the next chapter, increases in formal educational credentials and training requirements in many occupations do not necessarily mean that workers use the acquired skills and training on the job. This phenomenon is significant for teachers in two ways: (1) in terms of how teaching is organized as work, and (2) in terms of their responsibilities to educate students whose own work futures are uncertain.

All jobs are organized around the completion of particular tasks. In the case of teaching, the main activities tend to be considered as mental rather than manual labour. Teachers are able to make claims to professionalism in part because many aspects of their work are difficult to codify. This stands in contrast to many other jobs, such as those involved in the making or selling of commercial products, in which employees are expected to follow explicit instructions in accordance with their job descriptions. Teaching, though, is also organized around several technical functions, such as designing lesson plans, grading students, keeping records of student attendance and progress, and following rules and procedures regarding student discipline. For each of these activities, there is likely to be considerable variation from one teaching situation to another with respect to how closely teachers are monitored and expected to perform specified duties or how much leeway teachers have to alter their practices.

Proletarianization occurs as teachers are subject to increasing levels of external control by supervisors or administrators, or when their work is reorganized to minimize the discretion they have over their activities. When standardized curricula or exams are introduced into schooling, for instance, there is potential to assess teachers' performance as much as that of students. Educators' reliance on curricula and lesson plans based on rigidly defined behavioural objectives, or on student workbooks that follow a specified progression of lessons and exercises, requires little input from the teacher in the curricular planning and delivery process. While most teachers are likely to use these materials in conjunction with other resources and to innovate in their lesson planning, the likelihood that they will come to depend on prescribed materials (if, indeed, they are not overtly directed to adopt these materials) increases as class sizes and demands on their time grow. Runté (1998) observes in one Canadian jurisdiction that even when teachers have some discretion over what is taught and how it is taught, the imposition of centralized examinations and standardized tests removes effective education-planning and goal-setting from the school level to more centralized authorities.

Apple (1986: 41ff.) refers to the process of intensification to demonstrate how important aspects of the work of teachers and other professionals can be proletarianized or deskilled. Intensification occurs when the demands associated with a job are increased. Apple (1986: 41) observes that intensification:

> has many symptoms, from the trivial to the more complex—ranging from being allowed no time at all even to go to the bathroom, have a cup of coffee or relax, to having a total absence of time to keep up with one's field. We can see intensification most visibly in mental labour in the chronic sense of work overload that has escalated over time.

As school districts reduce teaching and support staff and increase class sizes, for instance, teachers are required not only to teach more pupils but also to perform more duties that were once done by other workers. Changes to school budgets and programs mean that many have to teach in areas for which they have little or no training, especially if subjects outside of the core areas, or a full range of extracurricular activities, are to be retained. New curricula and modified learning objectives require the introduction of new subjects and materials with which teachers have to keep up to date. However, these changes place increased demands on teachers' time in and out of the classroom, especially when there is limited funding and time for in-service training.

These trends are not just hypothetical. Educational researchers and teachers' organizations in many nations have pointed to growing concerns about teacher workload, stress, and other problems associated with new demands imposed on teachers through educational reform and changing school contexts (Smyth, 2001; Whitty, 1997).

Research into teaching tends to contradict common perceptions of teaching as a job conducted in the classroom within the confines of the school day and school year. For Canadian teachers, like people in many other occupations, one of the biggest issues is time—time in the classroom to meet the demands of the curriculum and attend to the diverse needs of students, administration, and other school-related responsibilities; and time outside the classroom to plan lessons, meet with parents, engage in organizational activities, manage extracurricular activities, and upgrade their professional skills and knowledge related to their jobs. Major studies of teaching in Canada reveal that, nationally, teachers' average workload increased by 1.5 hours per week between 1982 and 1992 (Schembari, 1994: 11). Smaller et al. (2000) observe that, in addition to an average work week of 47 hours reported by teachers, full-time teachers spend several hours on a weekly basis in both

Box 5.5 Trends associated with the restructuring of teachers' work

Teachers in Canada and other nations are experiencing significant changes in their work amid global economic restructuring. Smyth (2001: 38–9), writing from an Australian perspective, summarizes many of the prevalent forces and trends:

- [Education] is being constrained by the intrusion of external agencies who require that schools operate in the 'national interest', a claim that is invariably couched in the economic imperative of increased international competitiveness.
- The fiscal crisis of the state is reducing funding to schools, in contexts in which schools are exhorted to 'do more with less'.
- The breakdown of other social institutions is occurring at the same time schools are expected to take on a wider and more complex range of functions.
- Control is being re-centralized, having the effect of conveying the message to teachers that they cannot be trusted and that their work is devalued—this happens in contexts in which it is made to look as if teachers are being given more autonomy, self-control, and decision-making power at school level.
- Schools are expected to operated more like private enterprises, to market themselves, to compete against one another for students and resources—functions that take them increasingly away from the reasons for which they exist, namely, teaching and learning.

All of the matters just alluded to are ripe with implications for teachers' work and have resulted in a number of policy initiatives that:

- require teachers to work within more rigidly defined policy frameworks and guidelines, of one kind or another;
- place greater emphasis on determining the worth of teaching in terms of measurable outcomes;
- supposedly make teachers more accountable by linking outcomes to the actions and activities of individual teachers, classrooms, and schools;
- move teachers and schools in the direction of processes that are more appropriate to those of the corporate and industrial sector—performance appraisal, curriculum audits, quality assurance, and the like;
- preach the virtues of education and schooling as being no different than any other commodity—to be measured and calibrated

Box 5.5 continued

according to quality standards; packaged and delivered to targeted audiences; and haggled over in the artificially constructed 'user-pays' marketplace of education.

On the other hand, there is another set of tendencies and trends appearing to point in the opposite direction. These all have the sounds of pseudo-participation and quasi-democracy about them: devolution; competition; choice; autonomy; collegiality; collaboration; self-management; liberation management; teamwork and partnerships; networking and collegiality; flexibility; responsiveness.

While the tendencies just listed might look and sound as if they are about giving teachers more control over their work, and in some cases it is true that they do, it is more a matter of appearances in most instances. There is a substantial contradiction. The work of teaching is increasingly brought under the influence of politicians, policy-makers, and the captains of industry at the same time as claims are made that teachers and schools should take greater control of their own destiny: deciding on local priorities; exercising greater self-management; breaking away from expensive and inefficient bureaucratic forms of organization; and making schools into leaner organizations able to be more responsive.

formal and informal learning related to their work and other interests. A study of Saskatchewan teachers, conducted in 1994–5, indicates that teachers are working even more hours than previously reported and are experiencing considerable stress associated with multiple and often competing demands for their time (Gallen et al., 1995). The authors observe that 'Teachers describe a relentless pressure to take care of school work even when they are in poor health or experiencing personal difficulties' (ibid., 56). Naylor and Schaefer (2002: 35), reporting on a study of British Columbia teachers that echoes issues raised in many other jurisdictions, highlight the growing stress that teachers experience as a consequence of several factors, including:

- a large volume of work;
- a wide range of workload duties that have changed over time;
- changing class composition;
- seasonal pressures, with intense periods of work in addition to regular loads;
- extensive curriculum changes; and
- a wide range of expectations from government, employers, school administrators, and parents.

Teachers' experiences of stress and other pressures, as well as their working patterns within teaching and competing commitments outside of their work, are highly influenced by such factors as gender, marital status, teaching level, and career stage (see also King and Peart, 1992; Canadian Teachers' Federation, 1993). Because of this diversity within the teaching force, many research findings on teachers' work are contradictory. Female teachers, particularly those who teach kindergarten and early elementary grades, for instance, are less likely to report that they have adequate preparation time during the day, but these teachers are also the least likely to report themselves as being in the high-stress group (Canadian Teachers' Federation, 1993: 62, 68–9). However, female teachers tend to be disproportionately affected by the combined impact of shifting forms of workplace control, emerging educational demands, responsibilities associated with caring for children and other dependants, domestic work, and community activity (Naylor, 2002: 140–1). Overall, though, teachers remain highly committed to their work and the students they work with. Despite increased concern about intensification, growing fears about physical safety in schools, legal action for child abuse, and attacks on the teaching profession by politicians and media reports, about three-quarters of Canadian school teachers surveyed by King and Peart (1992) indicate that they 'look forward to coming to work each day', and a majority of teachers report that they would choose teaching even if they could begin their career again.

To understand the apparently paradoxical ways in which teachers describe their work, it is instructive to consider the observations made at the beginning of this chapter. The characterization of teaching as a contradictory endeavour has been a recurrent theme in the analysis of education whether the focus has been the classroom, the school authority structure, the community, or the teaching occupation itself. In this context, we can understand teaching as an occupation subject to diverse and often competing forces. Consequently, proletarianization and professionalization are not necessarily mutually exclusive. This is why it becomes possible for teachers to view additional demands on their time, involving such tasks as learning techniques to manage larger classes or developing lesson plans around new curricula, as an extension of their professional competencies at the same time as their work is being intensified and deskilled. If teachers feel that their expertise and professional judgement are being used in the process of educational change, they may be more willing to endure increased workloads even when it means they are working harder or putting in longer hours. Apple (1986: 45), describing the situation in a school in which much of teachers' work was reorganized around standardized packages of skill-based worksheets, observes:

> Professionalism and increased responsibility tend to go hand in hand here. The situation is more than a little paradoxical. There is so much responsibility placed on teachers for technical decisions that they actually work harder. They feel that since they constantly make decisions based on the

outcomes of these multiple pre- and post-tests, the longer hours are evidence of their enlarged professional status.

These factors become even more significant when we come back to the point that teaching tends to be characterized more by social relationships than by strictly technical operations. The human or interpersonal dimensions of relationships between teachers and students (who most often are children or young adults) are defining features of interaction in classrooms and other educational settings. These social aspects of teachers' work are so obvious that they are easy to take for granted in the analysis of teaching. However, by drawing attention to their importance, we can begin to understand how proletarianization and professionalization interact in teaching.

One of the characteristics that makes it possible for teachers to claim professional status, and thereby to seek improvements in their terms and conditions of work, is the fact that they are working with human beings. From an early point in the establishment of a system of mass public education, teachers had to gain public confidence that they were sufficiently competent, trustworthy, and reliable to manage a classroom of children. Gradually, standards of certification and training, backed by legislation and regulations, ensured that teachers were authorized to conduct classes, evaluate pupils, and perform a wide range of other educational functions.

This legitimacy to work with and assess individuals has had a dual significance for teachers. On the one hand, it has given teachers a privileged status that distinguishes them from laypersons and other workers in the community because it allows them to claim expertise over professional matters such as child development, discipline, pedagogy, and curricular content. As certified representatives of the school system, they have a public responsibility, in contrast to parents and other community members whose interests appear to be more fragmented and private. On the other hand, this responsibility, combined with the fact that they are employees, has meant that teachers are also subject to moral regulation and intense administrative and public scrutiny even when they are not directly observed performing classroom duties. Teachers are as likely to be monitored informally, through rumours and conversational accounts of their activities in and out of school, as through more formal kinds of assessment. Thus, while school board regulations concerning teachers' dress and public conduct may not be as stringent as they once were, their moral character, as much as their teaching ability, remains the focus of considerable public interest. Inside the classroom, fears of the school inspectors' visits have been replaced by worries over allegations of sexual abuse, while teachers' social lives continue to be constrained by the dangers of being seen doing the wrong things in the wrong places by students, former students, parents, school officials, and the media.

Recognition of the dual nature of teaching also allows us to understand how technical regulation and intensification occur. Because it is difficult for educational managers and administrators to monitor and assess many of the interpersonal aspects of a teacher's work, demands for increased educational quality and output tend to be met by looking at measurable factors, such as standardized test scores and class sizes. Increases in workloads, however, make it less possible for teachers to attend to the varied needs of all students as well as to other responsibilities. As class sizes go up, for instance, it is tempting, for the sake of both classroom control and pedagogical efficiency, for teachers to rely more heavily on lectures, pre-packaged textbooks and assignments, and standardized group activities than on interaction with small groups or individual pupils.

The examples cited above reflect a tendency in which educational productivity is measured in quantitative terms, to favour technical over subjective or interpersonal dimensions of teaching. Chapter 8 will consider in more detail how contemporary demands for measurement and accountability in education favour limited conceptions of what goes on in schools over approaches that view schooling as a process that contributes to meaningful social participation and opportunities.

Conclusion

This chapter has examined teaching as a highly complex occupation characterized by several paradoxes. Teachers are professionals, but they are also workers whose professionalism is highly constrained. Their special status and responsibilities leave them subject to extensive public scrutiny and criticism. They are expected to perform their work with specialized skills and knowledge, but they work under conditions in which they may not be able to put their capabilities and training to use. They are potentially curriculum planners and innovators who at the same time face or succumb to pressures to routinize their activities to the point of monotony and dehumanization. They are in positions in which they are expected to be community leaders and role models for children and other learners, but they also experience restraints and receive criticisms from people who do not fully understand what schooling and teaching are all about.

These contradictions can be understood as inherent characteristics of the teaching occupation rather than as unfortunate or accidental by-products of the school system. Like other workers, teachers are paid employees who are subject to extensive administrative or managerial control governed by demands for efficiency, accountability, and order. Unlike many other workers, though, teachers are entrusted to work intensively in a formative way with other human beings. It is the uncertain nature of these social characteristics that makes teaching both a potentially rewarding and satisfying occupation and one that can often be frustrating and over-regulated.

Annotated Further Readings

Sandra Acker, *The Realities of Teachers' Work: Never a Dull Moment*. London: Cassell, 1999. The author provides an in-depth study of the working relationships and lives of teachers at an elementary school, highlighting the complex interactions in and out of the classroom that are vital parts of teaching.

Michael W. Apple, *Teachers and Texts: A Political Economy of Class and Gender Relations in Education*. New York: Routledge & Kegan Paul, 1986. This analysis of economic and cultural pressures to transform education includes a detailed discussion of the changing nature of teaching as a particular, highly feminized, form of work.

Ivor Goodson and Andy Hargreaves, eds, *Teachers' Professional Lives*. London: Falmer, 1996. Contributors from several nations identify core issues that are central to the work and lives of teachers, with a focus especially on diverse models of professionalism.

Alexander Lockhart, *School Teaching in Canada*. Toronto: University of Toronto Press, 1991. This is one of the few studies to examine teaching across Canada, addressing the historical development of teachers' associations, the nature of teachers' work and working conditions, characteristics of the teaching force, and challenges faced by teachers.

Susan Robertson and Harry Smaller, eds, *Teacher Activisim in the 1990s*. Toronto: James Lorimer, 1996. Several contributors demonstrate the impact of educational reform, driven by global economic restructuring, on teachers, teachers' organizations, and schools in Canadian provinces and other nations.

John Smyth and Geoffrey Shacklock, *Re-Making Teaching: Ideology, Policy and Practice*. London: Routledge, 1998. The book addresses the powerful impact of global economic change on educational reform, emphasizing the pressures to reshape and undermine teaching and vital elements of the teaching process in various national contexts.

Key Terms

Collective bargaining A process by which members of an occupational group, normally represented by a union, enter into agreements with employers on such matters as wages, benefits, and terms and conditions of employment.

Division of labour The differentiation and distribution of jobs and tasks at different levels, which can occur globally or across a society, within a particular form of work or activity, or among social groups.

Feminization The concentration of women within particular occupations or groups, often discussed in conjunction with gender-based forms of discrimination.

Intensification A process through which workers lose privileges and autonomy through rules and procedures intended to increase productivity and tighten control over work outcomes.

Moral regulation Scrutiny of teachers and other workers based on expectations related to their personal characteristics, habits, beliefs, and behaviour.

Normal schools Teacher training institutions that operated from the mid-nineteenth to mid-twentieth centuries to provide beginning teachers who had limited educational qualifications with information, guidance, and practical experience related to the varied dimensions of teaching.

Professionalization A trend in which a particular occupation gains status and recognition through specific credentials, specialized knowledge, or access to specified rights and privileges.

Proletarianization A process in which workers lose control over core aspects of their work, or one in which self-sufficient workers are replaced by employees in subordinate positions.

Teachers' associations Organizations that represent teachers in collective bargaining over salaries and conditions of work and provide teachers with opportunities and resources for professional development, advocacy for public education, and services to support teaching and teachers' well-being.

Working conditions The varied dimensions of schooling and educational organization that affect teachers' work, such as overall workload, class size, preparation time, teaching assignments, supervision of students during the school day, participation in extracurricular activities, and resources to support teaching in particular school contexts.

Study Questions

1. Discuss the extent to which school teaching is or is not a unique occupation in comparison with other forms of work.

2. Critically discuss the question of whether teachers should have the same right as other workers to engage in strikes and other job actions in relation to contract disputes over wages and working conditions.

3. How representative is the teaching force in relation to the social composition of Canada's population? What is the significance of this relationship for the education of diverse groups of learners?

4. What factors account for the fact that most Canadian school teachers are women? What implications does the gender composition of the teaching force have for teaching as an occupation?

5. Many governments and media analysts have blamed teachers for the poor quality of education and other social problems. Critically discuss these arguments, and provide an explanation for negative public perceptions about teaching.

6

Schooling and Work

Introduction

It is widely accepted that a major purpose of schooling is to prepare people for work. This task is carried out both directly, in the provision of skills and knowledge necessary for work, and indirectly, through the development of aptitudes and credentials whose importance is recognized for employment. Current debates over education have called into question the relevance of schooling in a world in which educational reform has not necessarily kept pace with fundamental transformations in the nature of work and labour markets. Frequent criticism has been levelled by employers, government agencies, and labour organizations, as well as parents and students, over the presumed failure of schools and other educational institutions to offer the kinds of preparation that workers require in order to find jobs and succeed in today's globally competitive society. Education critics contend that schooling is not only contributing to a mismatch between workers and jobs, but that it is also remiss in its efforts to prepare people to adjust to the social realities of a new economy transformed by rapid technological innovation and global economic change.

This chapter provides a critical analysis of the relationship between schooling and work. It begins with an overview of contemporary demands for educational reform targeted to prepare students for work in a globally competitive environment. Major economic changes are making it imperative that students have access to educational services that provide them with both skills and orientations to learning that will enable them to make successful life decisions under highly uncertain circumstances. At the same time, some of the claims made about the apparent inability of formal educational institutions to adjust to economically driven forces are called into question through an understanding of the complex historical factors that have shaped the relationship between schooling and work. Contemporary critiques of the education system's ability to deliver the kinds of work training sought by many segments of society echo those that have been raised on several occasions for more than a century. Educational planning and practices encompass conflicting priorities that cannot be reduced to a simple economic rationale. It is important, ultimately, to understand the various contributions that schooling makes to labour markets and jobs as phenomena characterized by the competing visions and contradictions inherent within all educational endeavours.

Contemporary Demands for Educational Reform: The 'Mismatch' between Schooling and Jobs

The promotion of educational reform has become an increasingly central component of labour market development strategies in Canada and other advanced industrial nations. The emergence of new forms of work and investment strategy marked by rapid developments in information technology, technological innovation leading to increased productivity, and intense global competition has fostered renewed interest in human capital. Education figures prominently into the equation for its significance in ensuring basic knowledge and social skills for potential workers and consumers, its contributions to advanced levels of training, its integration into a broad array of lifelong learning choices, its value as a commodity within business and other enterprises, and its contributions to innovation. The Organization for Economic Co-operation and Development (OECD, 2001: 56) summarizes the importance that solid educational foundations hold for emerging economic priorities:

> In the knowledge-based economy, providing everyone with at least a basic educational background has become more important. To be employable and productive, young people must be equipped with at least upper secondary education (or an apprenticeship certificate). In recent years, completion rates of upper secondary education have increased in all OECD countries. Still, more has to be done since completion rates vary considerably across the OECD area.

The central place that education holds in discourses and strategies associated with the knowledge economy carries mixed significance for education, educators, and learners. There is the promise that the promotion of educational priorities will be accompanied by enhanced awareness, resources, and revitalization for educational institutions, mitigating some of the most severe attacks and cutbacks they have endured in previous years. Teachers and other educators may gain some influence and status in the process, while educational programs may benefit from new partnerships with business, governments, and communities. Many proposed educational reforms and calls for enhanced early childhood education and improved support services, including those for disadvantaged groups, echo concerns long held by educators. However, the knowledge or learning agenda also signifies major shifts in existing educational priorities and directions. It increases public expectations about education, posing intense pressure on educators and the institutions they work in to fulfill promises that are not always clearly understood or adequately supported with essential resources. The 'new economy' discourse contains both explicit and implicit indictments of educators and the systems in which they work: its implementation involves measures to contain costs, ensure accountability, outline explicit performance indicators, and align education more closely with market-based economic activities. Schools are attributed full or partial blame for alienating youth before graduation or producing graduates with low literacy levels, inability to integrate into labour markets, and limited capacity or aptitude for innovation and entrepreneurship.

A steady flow of reports and position papers distributed by governments, corporate bodies, think-tanks, and lobby groups since the mid-1980s outlines the expectations that the new economy holds for education and training in a context driven by globally competitive economic development. Typically, such reports begin with an overview of the nature and size of the 'education industry', acknowledging that levels of educational expenditure, involvement, attainment, and outcomes in Canada rank at or near the top, relative to other OECD nations. Education is then posed in terms of productivity, quality, and returns on investment, with emphasis on the need to raise the bar in order to retain a competitive advantage.

During the early 1990s, as public concern mounted over government deficits and spending, the education system was challenged to account for questionable results. 'Why', asked a report by the Economic Council of Canada (1991: 168), did 'Canada, as a nation, not appear to be getting a greater economic return on its substantial investment' in formal education? Similarly, a federal government consultation paper entitled *Living Well . . . Learning Well* highlighted the issue of 'underdeveloped and underutilized' human resources, signifying that the 'fundamental problems with learning in Canada are that, compared with other countries, there is not enough of it and we do not take seriously enough what we have. Our prosperity depends on major improvements in the general level of skills held by all Canadians, as well as on having many more people with advanced and specialized skills' (Canada, 1991: v). These assessments of the situation point to two apparent problems associated with the education system: (1) excessive spending on education and other public services has been a detriment to Canada's ability to invest in more productive sectors; and (2) education must be reshaped to overcome substantial limitations in its ability to meet contemporary labour force requirements.

Box 6.1 The skills challenge

The rapid advancement of a knowledge-based economy is accompanied by calls such as this one—outlined in the Canadian government's innovation strategy (Government of Canada, 2001: 19–20)—for significant increases in the levels of education and skills training across the population:

Canada's educated population and highly skilled work force are key strengths in the global economy. However, our supply of highly qualified people is far from assured in the medium term. Canada will have great difficulty becoming more competitive without a greater number of highly qualified people to drive the innovation process and apply innovations, including new technologies.

Skill requirements in the labour market will continue to increase at a rapid pace. Firms will be looking for more research personnel—technicians, specialists, managers—to strengthen their innovative capacity and maintain their competitive advantage. Universities, colleges and government laboratories have already begun launching a hiring drive to replace the large number of professors, teachers, researchers and administrators reaching retirement age. This will result in a huge demand in Canada for highly qualified people.

On the supply side, Canada has experienced sluggish growth in higher education participation rates in recent years. In addition, we do not compare well to other countries in terms of upgrading the skills of the existing work force through employee training. While our track record in attracting skilled immigrants is good, we will need to more aggressively seek out highly qualified immigrants in the next decade. If we do not address these issues, Canada will face persistent shortages of the skills required for success in the knowledge-based economy.

Shortages will be exacerbated by international competition for talent as the most advanced economies experience many of the same economic and demographic pressures. If Canada does not take measures *now*, we will certainly face critical shortages in the talent we need to drive our economy.

The Skills Challenge: Canada must ensure that in years to come it has a sufficient supply of highly qualified people with appropriate skills for the knowledge-based economy.

More recent policy statements have shifted emphasis from a portrait of education's failure to meet its fundamental objectives to its role as a partner in the pursuit of higher levels of training and excellence. Formal education has come to be placed into a continuum of lifelong learning, running from early childhood through schooling and into workplace training, adult education, and numerous alternative learning sites. A federal government statement on Canada's innovation strategy begins, in part, as follows:

> Canada is consistently near the top, and often at the top, of international rankings of the best countries in which to live. We have built a strong and vibrant society with culturally diverse, dynamic communities and enviable education, health, social, and economic systems. . . . Canada is well positioned to enjoy continued social and economic prosperity in the new century. . . . Countries that succeed in the 21st century will be those with citizens who are creative, adaptable and skilled. The so-called 'new' economy is demanding new things from us. The need for ingenuity, creativity and hard work has not changed. How we do our work has. Today's workplace requires higher levels of education and skills. . . . To seize the opportunities before us, learning must be available to all Canadians throughout their lifetime, so that everyone has the opportunity to reach his or her potential. . . . We can and must do more, together. (Government of Canada, 2002: 5–6)

There is a simple appeal in these claims. Widespread acceptance of the view that education is positively associated with socio-economic success is borne out by statistical evidence that, in general, the more education one has the greater the likelihood of labour force participation, the lower the rates of unemployment, and the higher the average incomes. Figures for early 2001, for instance, reveal that, in comparison with a national unemployment rate of 6.1 per cent, only 5.1 per cent of graduates from post-secondary programs, as opposed to 10.1 per cent of persons who did not have a high school diploma, were unemployed (Statistics Canada, 2003g: 55).

Moreover, there is a general sense that the importance of education for jobs and work is growing. Livingstone et al. (1999: 19) report in their survey of public attitudes towards education that the proportion of Ontario residents who indicated that having a post-secondary education was very important increased from about one-third in 1979 to nearly three-quarters in the late 1990s, while almost four out of five respondents in the mid-1990s, compared to just below two-thirds in 1986, felt that the percentage of jobs that would require a university degree or college certificate would increase in future years. There is also growing public support for the view that college diplomas in a technical area are at least as important as university degrees in the sciences for labour market success (Livingstone et al., 2001: 38). In short, considerable evidence demonstrates that most Canadians agree with the assessment that job-relevant education and training are critical components of both personal and national success in a global economy.

The other factor that is central to the ideology of educational reform—that schools are failing to provide the kinds of training necessary for today's job market—is much less certain in the public's view than it may appear in the documents produced by government and corporate groups. While only

Box 6.2 Growth in highly skilled occupations

As Statistics Canada (2003c: 7) indicates in this profile of change and continuity in the Canadian labour force, highly skilled occupations that require a university education are leading the way in the growth of the workforce:

As of May 15, 2001, Canada's labour force consisted of almost 15.6 million people, up 9.5 per cent from 14.2 million a decade earlier. The number of women in the labour force grew at twice the pace of men, increasing 13.8 per cent to 7.3 million. The number of men increased by 6.0 per cent to 8.3 million.

More than 90 per cent of the 1.3 million overall gain in the labour force occurred in the last half of the decade, as the economy rebounded from the recession of the early 1990s.

Of the 15.6 million people in the labour force, more than 2.5 million were in highly skilled occupations that normally required a university education. This was a 33 per cent increase from 1991, triple the rate of growth for the labour force as a whole.

Highly skilled occupations accounted for almost one-half of the total labour force growth over the decade. As a result, there has been a shift in the skill makeup of the labour force. In 2001, people in highly skilled occupations normally requiring a university education accounted for 16 per cent of the total labour force, up from 13 per cent a decade earlier.

Skilled occupations—those usually requiring a community college diploma or apprenticeship training—grew at less than a third of the pace of the labour force as a whole. The census enumerated nearly 4.7 million people in such occupations, a 3.3 per cent increase from 1991. As a result of this slow growth rate, occupations usually requiring a college education or apprenticeship training accounted for 30 per cent of the total labour force in 2001, down from 32 per cent a decade earlier.

Within the skilled occupations, there was a 3.8 per cent decline in the number of people in occupations normally requiring apprenticeship training, such as skilled trades. In particular, the number with skills in certain construction trades plunged by between 40 per cent and 60 per cent.

In contrast, the number of skilled occupations usually requiring a college education increased 6 per cent during the decade, two-thirds the pace of the total labour force. Within this skill group, there was a strong increase in childcare workers and administrative officers.

Box 6.2 continued

The census enumerated 6.8 million people in occupations normally requiring at most a high school diploma. The rate of growth for these occupations was 5.4 per cent, much slower than total labour force growth. As a result, their share of the labour force in 2001 was 43 per cent, down from 45 per cent in 1991.

The number of managers increased 17.2 per cent over the decade to just over 1.6 million in 2001. These occupations accounted for 18 per cent of the growth of the labour force.

Highly Skilled Occupations Usually Requiring University Educations Have Led the Growth Over the Decade

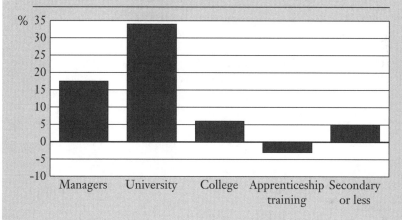

about 38 per cent of respondents to a national poll in 1999 agreed that high schools were doing a good job of preparing students to enter the contemporary labour force, this was about 12 percentage points higher than the proportion who agreed in 1993 (Angus Reid Group, 1999: 14–15). However, a slight majority of respondents also expressed satisfaction with the public school system overall, while many of those indicating dissatisfaction—particularly in Ontario—were more concerned with the harmful impact government policies were having on education than with the education system itself (ibid., 9–10). A survey undertaken in 2003 revealed that just over half of parents of school-age children in Canada were satisfied with schools' ability to meet their top-ranked objective of achieving a good understanding of the basics, but only about one-third were satisfied that their children were developing satisfactory skills for a job or university (Ipsos-Reid, 2003: 1). These findings are broadly comparable to the views expressed by respondents to a survey of the general public in southwestern Saskatchewan, where fewer than one-quarter of respondents indicated they felt that the quality of education in elementary and secondary schools had declined in recent years, compared to nearly three out of five who indicated that the quality of education had remained the same or improved (Wotherspoon, 1998: 140). These results suggest that, while there may be some general public uneasiness about the quality and job-specific relevance of education, there is nowhere near the consensus surrounding the view that schools are failing in their central missions that is assumed in the rhetoric to promote economically driven educational reform.

Box 6.3 Comparative school-to-work transitions

Education systems and their role in the transition to work differ across nations. Kerckhoff (2000: 472) examined the educational systems of Germany, France, the United States, and Great Britain and concluded that 'the transition process varies greatly among those four societies'. Here he summarizes the two different models he found:

> From the review presented, it is possible to construct two ideal types of educational systems. Type One systems are highly standardized and stratified, and their educational credentials recognize vocational specialization. Type Two systems are relatively unstandardized and unstratified and their credentials have little vocational relevance. It appears that Type One societies have a stronger education-occupation association, lower rates of return to full-time school, fewer increases in educational credentials, fewer job changes, and lower rates of early occupational mobility. In effect, the transition from school to work is more orderly and stable in Type One societies.
>
> Germany comes closest to having a Type One educational system, and the United States comes closest to having a Type Two educational system. France and Great Britain have mixtures of the characteristics used in this typology.
>
> Difficult problems in studying the transition from school to work still remain. One is finding a definition of the first job that is wholly adequate for comparisons across societies. A related problem is the societal variation in the opportunities for increasing one's level of educational credentials while in the labour force rather than only while outside the labour force.

The vigorous emphasis on education's significance for economic development strategies highlights an exchange among educators, business leaders, and government officials that has often been uneasy and uncertain. There are numerous visions of the appropriate linkages between schooling and work just as there are different models in which those relationships are applied. In

North America, unlike nations such as Germany or Japan, there is little direct relationship between schooling and employment. Employers and educators often regard one another with skepticism or distrust, with the former assailing schools for their inability to produce the kinds of workers and skills they demand while the latter condemn business for its skewed sense of education and its failure to see that schooling is concerned with much more than simply training for employment and profit. The absence of dialogue and engagement among employers and educators is often posed as an obstacle to effective educational reform. However, this has begun to change through several new partnerships and growing integration of schooling and work through co-operative learning, internship, and other innovations. The consequences for education and students are mixed, as will be observed later in this and subsequent chapters.

The Relationship between Schooling and Work

The expectation that schools should be evaluated in terms of how well they are doing to prepare youth for work appeals to the logic that schools exist primarily to channel people into the world of work. However, formal education is about much more than job training. It is a contradictory endeavour that is oriented to education in a broad sense, including personal development and other social capacities not strictly governed by labour markets and workplaces. Viewed in this way, it is worth posing a different set of questions that enables us to consider as problematic the extent to which, and in what ways, schools contribute to work preparation, and how these forms of preparation are related to competing educational objectives.

The following discussion addresses these issues by examining, initially, the kinds of contributions schools do make to work preparation, including (1) the granting of credentials; (2) curricular knowledge relevant to participation in the labour force; (3) the relationship between work and organizational features of schooling that are part of the hidden curriculum; (4) social features of the hidden curriculum related to individual characteristics and interpersonal relationships; and (5) general contributions that schools make to the economy as mass markets and workplaces. It will be seen that a substantial degree of 'correspondence' exists between educational structures and processes, on the one hand, and economic productivity and work training, on the other.

However, there are at least three important limitations to the view that schools should be more responsive to requirements for work preparation. (1) Historical evidence demonstrates that mass public schooling, from its inception, was not intended to be governed narrowly by jobs or economic considerations. (2) Continuing debate and alternative views identify schooling as an endeavour that must be responsive to diverse educational objectives beyond training for work. (3) There are barriers to the extent to which schooling can and should be the most effective institution for labour market preparation.

The Contributions of Schooling to Work and the Economy

Formal educational institutions make several direct and indirect contributions to labour markets and wider economic processes.

(1) One of the central functions of schooling is to bestow diplomas, certificates, degrees, and other credentials upon successful completion of particular educational programs and levels of study. Many hiring and promotion decisions, as well as eligibility requirements for certain jobs, are based on specified types of educational achievement or credentials earned through education and training programs. Educational credentials become relevant to employment decisions in different ways. In some instances, possession of a credential implies that the individual has acquired particular kinds of knowledge or met standards of rigour deemed to be essential for a job. In many other cases, educational achievement is used as a screening mechanism to limit the number of qualified applicants seeking particular jobs, regardless of whether the education or training is directly relevant to the work positions. These issues are discussed below, briefly, and developed more fully later in this chapter in the context of debates about work skills.

(2) Another important function of education and training programs is to transmit knowledge and skills related to employment situations and the workplace. This knowledge includes information that may be necessary for specific occupations as well as general know-how considered valuable by employers and that therefore makes a person employable. The most direct and apparent relationship between formal schooling and jobs tends to be in vocational training, certification, and professional degree programs required for entry into specific occupations such as welding, hairdressing, law, and medicine. These kinds of programs are organized in accordance with technical specifications and requirements for licensing or certification that are deemed critical for practice in the specified field. Outside of these areas, other courses, subjects, and programs are usually seen to have a looser connection with jobs, providing either a general background in an area or offering fundamental knowledge desired by employers, beginning with basic competencies like the ability to read, write, and compute through to more advanced, abstract, or specialized types of knowledge and skills.

Sensitivity to employers' needs has been a long-standing current in educational thinking. It is instructive to note the similarities between the following passage, a call for the introduction of technical and industrial training in the schools issued over a century ago in the report of the Royal Commission on the Relations of Capital and Labour in Canada (1889: 119), and contemporary demands for educational reform:

> To be successful competitors with foreign manufacturers we must have workmen as highly skilled in their respective callings as those with whom they have to compete. To do so, the same facilities must be provided to give the cultivation and training necessary to acquire skill and knowledge as the workmen of other countries have.

The fact that similar statements have been made repeatedly over the years seems to indicate that schools have not responded well to demands that they become more relevant to employers' needs. Despite this impression, though, several curricular reforms have been justified by their contributions to changing job markets. Sutherland (1976: 155ff.) documents how schools introduced subjects such as agriculture, industrial arts, domestic science, bookkeeping, and other forms of vocational and technical education following vigorous pressure for change from various lobby groups in the nineteenth and early twentieth centuries. More recently, courses in computers and natural sciences have been introduced or modified to keep pace with technological developments and demands for highly skilled scientific workers. Table 6.1, which outlines some of the most important subjects introduced into school curricula over the past century, demonstrates the periodic introduction of vocational subjects into programs initially dominated by academic subjects.

Table 6.1
Summary of Major Changes and Additions to Curricula in Canadian Elementary Schools

1825–50:	reading, writing, arithmetic, religion (Bible reading), needlework, cooking
1850–75:	grammar, geography
1875–1900:	kindergarten classes, literature, history, music, drawing
1900–25:	nature study, art, manual training, physical training, hygiene, household science
1925–50:	social studies, science, industrial arts, home economics, health, physical education, enterprise, languages, phonics
1950–75:	French and French immersion, business and commercial education
1975–current:	whole language instruction, language arts, computer studies, technological education, Native studies, technical vocational education, hospitality and tourism, life transitions, wellness.

Sources: Phillips (1957: 433); Katz (1969: 67); various provincial curriculum guides.

Despite periodic curricular modifications and innovations designed to reflect vocational and employment concerns, educators have tended to oppose the idea of turning schools into training factories. In some cases, vocational and career-oriented courses were introduced more for the pragmatic consideration of gaining employers' support for the school system than for enthusiasm over the academic or curricular merits of the subjects. Vocational and technical subjects continue to remain distinct from core areas of the curriculum in schools with academic programs. Moreover, there are often considerable discrepancies between the formal listing or presentation of a subject in a curriculum description and the actual teaching of that subject in the classroom. These issues, as will be discussed later in the chapter, make the relationship between schooling and work preparation more problematic than it might otherwise appear to be.

(3) Beyond the teaching of vocational and career-oriented knowledge or subjects, formal education contributes to labour force participation in many indirect ways. As observed in Chapter 4, student school experience is shaped at least as much by everyday practices, unwritten rules, and informal expectations as by the overt transmission of knowledge and skills. This hidden curriculum is defined by Apple (1979: 14) as 'the tacit teaching to students of norms, values, and dispositions that goes on simply by their living and coping with the institutional expectations and routines of schools day in and day out for a number of years.'

The 'expectations and routines' that constitute the hidden curriculum—in terms of both the organizational and social characteristics of schooling—are heavily influenced by work. The spatial and temporal structure within most educational institutions has a great deal in common with nineteenth-century factory organization. Physically, schools tend to be arranged as a series of box-like classrooms or special-function areas (gyms, libraries, art rooms, resource centres) that are oriented to regimentation and control. There are also strong parallels between schooling and industrial work organization in terms of models of supervision and assessment, the division of classes by grade and subject, streaming within grades or subject areas, and the hierarchy of authority that prevails both administratively and in the conduct of classes.

Workplace discipline is also reflected in the regulation of school time. The day is broken into distinct periods, usually signified by the ringing of bells. Students' bodily functions, including eating, are directed by timetables and school rules, and pupils frequently are required to seek permission to use the washroom or get a drink of water. These arrangements are structured in such a way that students come to internalize routines associated with the day-to-day patterns of life in many workplaces.

(4) The hidden curriculum is oriented to individual as well as organizational characteristics. Writers working within both traditional (e.g., Jackson, 1968; Dreeben, 1968) and critical (e.g., Bowles and Gintis, 1976; Willis, 1977) perspectives agree that much of the social reproduction accomplished within schooling occurs through the cultivation of dispositions and attributes necessary to function in contemporary society (Lynch, 1989). This analysis stresses that what is important is not so much the specific knowledge required for any particular job or social position as the general preparedness and ability to meet expectations that are attached to out-of-school roles. Through their schooling, students encounter circumstances such as competition, success and failure, deference to authority, deferral of gratification, and other situations that prepare them for later social experiences. They must also develop an awareness of how the world is structured and how it operates in order to ease their transition into work and other social settings.

Lesley Andres Bellamy (1993, 1994) adopts the concepts of 'habitus' and 'cultural capital' developed by Pierre Bourdieu (1977, 1984) to analyze how Canadian students make choices about their post-high school futures. *Cultural capital*, understood in conjunction with economic capital and other social resources, refers to the attitudes, behaviours, preferences, and general sense of how things operate that individuals must possess to be socially successful. Constituted in this way, cultural capital is neither neutral nor equally accessible to all social groups. Andres Bellamy (1994: 122) observes that, for Bourdieu, 'the culture that is transmitted and rewarded by the educational system reflects the culture of the dominant class.' This places students who possess the prior knowledge or sensitivity to the qualities that enable them to meet educational expectations in an advantaged position in comparison with students who lack cultural capital. The related concept of *habitus* refers to a 'system of dispositions' produced by our past experiences, which are embedded into our perceptions and interact with new social circumstances. It operates as a kind of internal code that affects how we approach and understand everyday practices.

Using data from interviews with British Columbia high school students, Andres Bellamy (1993) argues that schools reinforce cultural capital in such a way that students view their choices about work and post-secondary studies as an unproblematic part of their normal progression from family life. Schools, in this way, contribute to labour force reproduction by fostering dispositions regarding success, failure, and future plans even if they are not directly involved in job training and employment selection. This insight complements the findings of other influential studies, such as those of Willis (1977), Anisef et al. (2000), and Lareau and Horvat (1999), which demonstrate that school organization, social background, and students' lived circumstances affect one another in such a way that students often 'choose' predictable futures without being directly pushed into those positions.

(5) Schools and other educational settings serve a purpose that is more than merely preparatory for work in the sense that substantial economic activity takes place within them. Schooling contributes to economic relationships in two important ways beyond its role in preparing individuals for entry into the labour force—educational institutions themselves are workplaces as well as markets in which billions of dollars are spent annually on goods and services.

Educational institutions are workplaces that employ both directly and indirectly large numbers of teachers, administrators, maintenance and support staff, purchasing agents, and other personnel. As the previous chapter on teachers has emphasized, educational workers are subject to many of the same dynamics that operate within wage employment in general, even though educational work also contains unique characteristics related to educational processes. Besides their work with students or educational clients, educational workers engage in economic production insofar as they develop products, knowledge, and skills that may be of benefit to particular employers, corporations, or social interests. While this activity is most evident at the post-secondary level, where faculty members and other researchers are expected to cultivate and disseminate knowledge, classrooms and education systems at all levels are open to experimentation and innovation, the benefits of which may extend beyond the education system.

Education also has economic significance as a site responsible for the purchase of massive quantities of goods and services. Given its size and, in some instances, centralized decision-making, which leads to the adoption and purchase of textbooks, course materials, technologies, and supplies for entire school districts, post-secondary institutions, or even provinces, the educational market is a highly lucrative one. Educational institutions also stimulate economic activities in other ways, beyond their importance for the consumption of instructional resources. The construction of educational facilities, especially during peak growth periods such as the 1960s and 1970s, has had a significant economic impact on communities. Even when few new schools or universities are being built, employment is created through the maintenance and repair of educational facilities, as well as in their day-to-day operation. The food and beverage industry is supported directly by school cafeterias, while there tends to be a concentration of restaurants, bars, bookstores, and entertainment and service operations around universities and community colleges. Large corporations have found schools and universities such lucrative markets that they have entered into sometimes controversial agreements to provide funding for scholarships, sports, and other programs in exchange for exclusive agreements to sell their products. The economic spinoff from education is also important in other respects. The computer industry, for instance, has pursued the educational market aggressively in part because it is recognized that many students and parents will purchase hardware or software packages compatible with new technologies employed in the classroom.

The role of business and industry in the classroom has long been debated by educators. As education systems are confronted with declining levels of government funding, prospects for reliance on materials and services that are donated, purchased in bulk, or provided at low cost from corporations and other external agencies are likely to increase. Many corporations introduce curricular materials or sponsor school teams and events, such as essay-writing competitions, that may produce a favourable climate or corporate image at the same time as potential recruits or ideas are being harnessed for corporate objectives (Apple, 1993: 119–20; Regnier and MacLean, 1987). While corporate partnerships have promoted some areas of innovation and access to resources that would not otherwise be available to support students, programs, and research in public educational institutions, many educators and observers point to the growing danger that reliance on corporate bodies and fiscally driven planning are skewing educational priorities so that basic educational services directed towards a wide range of learning needs and community interests will be sacrificed to more glamorous initiatives based on narrow and unrepresentative agendas (Axelrod, 2002; Currie and Newson, 1998; Robertson, 1998).

Clearly, in a growing number of dimensions, education is highly integrated with economic activity. Through direct labour force preparation and participation, as well as through more general involvement in the production and consumption of particular commodities, education can be considered an industry essential for economic advancement of both individuals and societies. Nonetheless, there is considerable tension between the view that schooling should become guided more fully by economic considerations and the position that education must remain oriented to other principles than commercial ones.

Limiting Factors in the Relationship of Schooling, Work, and Economic Activity

While the evidence presented so far suggests that there is considerable merit to the idea that schooling has a central role to play in the reproduction of the labour force and in the stimulation of economic activity in general, it is necessary to address some of the limitations to this relationship. In particular, schooling has been responsive to competing priorities that place emphasis on personal and social development as well as economic factors.

1. *Education and morality*. Mass public schooling, from its inception, was not strictly concerned with labour force preparation. Early educational officials cautioned against the dangers of reducing schooling to its economic functions. Writing in the early 1880s, for instance, New Brunswick's chief superintendent of education contended that 'The primary function of the public school should not be subverted to provide technical instruction'; rather, 'the public school is primarily an agency for the general education of all classes of youth', where such basic training consists of the elements of physical health, intelligence, and character (cited in Lawr and Gidney, 1973: 93–4). As Table 6.1 indicates, the core areas of the curriculum have been concentrated in academic areas (such as reading, writing, mathematics, languages, sciences, history, and geography) or subjects oriented to personal development (health, physical education, drawing, and music) rather than workforce training. Certainly, each of these areas contributes in a general way to labour force development, particularly through the provision of basic skills, discipline, and orientations to work required for the performance of wage labour. However, social and political objectives, at least as much as economic ones, figured prominently in the origins and rise of mass public schooling.

In many ways, the Church rather than the factory provided the inspiration for a formal system of public education, although not in a direct way. Order, discipline, and habit may have been amenable to industrial work, but they were more explicitly promoted as essential attributes for individuals who were attuned to life in a new social and political order. Corrigan, Curtis, and

Lanning (1987: 21, 24) argue, for instance, that early school reformers were concerned with 'the creation of particular kinds of political selves' in the form of individuals who would engage in social relations through 'willing' or 'cheerful obedience'. The school's mission, like that of the Church in this regard, was to produce morally regulated individuals. Such morality, however, was to be produced in the public realm, with adherence to the bourgeois state rather than to any particular religious denomination. Across Canada, legislation concerning the establishment and maintenance of public schools addressed this objective by the creation of highly centralized provincial educational administrations, although room was allowed for diverse community input through delegation of many responsibilities to local and district school boards (Tomkins, 1977: 11–14).

The location of educational authority within the state was intended to counter the overt influence of groups considered to have narrowly defined interests, including religious denominations as well as business and industry. Industrial leaders were often indifferent to or had little regard for public schooling. During the rise of the factory system, especially into the late 1860s in the more industrialized areas of central and Atlantic Canada, schools were perceived as intrusive to employers who relied on children as a low-cost labour force. The main value of schooling, from this point of view, was as a vehicle for social control to keep idle children from engaging in crime or other mischief on the streets when they were not working. Ironically, much of this 'idleness' was a consequence of children's decision to leave schools that did not provide them with sufficient job-specific skills (Houston, 1982: 139–40). Educational authorities were sensitive to these trends, sometimes seeking reforms intended to win the support of employers for educational causes, but they continued to ensure that schooling could not be reduced to any kind of crude vocational training.

2. *The right to learn*. Public education, since its origins, has continued to be driven by competing forces that are not restricted to training for work or other economic purposes. Carnoy and Levin (1985: 14) point out that schools are driven by the contradictory dynamics of what they call a capitalist imperative and a democratic imperative. They contend that, 'On the one hand, schools have traditionally reproduced the unequal, hierarchical relations of the nuclear family and capitalist workplace; on the other, they have represented the expansion of economic opportunity for subordinate groups and the extension of basic human rights.'

These dynamics themselves are subject to debate and contestation. Included within the capitalist imperative, for instance, are employers' demands for appropriately disciplined and skilled workers and working-class demands for education and training that will result in meaningful, well-paid employment (Livingstone, 1987: 62–3). The issue of who benefits from education extends beyond class lines, encompassing demands for opportunity and representation coming from various groups, including women, racial and ethnic minorities, residents of rural areas and remote communities, and many others. Competing interests are reflected in debates over major issues, including what is taught in schools and how extensive the provision of public education should be, as well as more specific concerns such as the length and timing of the school year or what kinds of reading materials are included in school libraries.

A brief look at the major objectives of schools and education systems reveals how diverse educational aims are. The Report of the Royal Commission on Education for British Columbia (1988: 68) observes that, for more than a century, extending their central mandates as 'agencies of learning':

> schools have been viewed as multi-purpose institutions whose endeavours go far beyond educational functions—various public elements at various times have seen schools as agencies for civic development, as laboratories for democratic practice, as institutions to sustain a common culture and common values, as places to remediate the behaviour of wayward youngsters, and as centres for community life. Within the public imagination, the potential of schools has sometimes seemed boundless; we have turned to schools to reduce crime, improve public health, inspire patriotism, minimize civil strife, eradicate prejudice, promote social justice, set children on the 'right road,' and, in the long run, even contribute to international understanding.

The degree to which these varied objectives are given priority varies over time and place as well as among social groups. Coulter (1993: 71, 81) reports that Canadian youth in the 1930s expressed serious concern about unemployment and skill development, but by the mid-1940s a national survey of youth revealed that job preparation was ranked below both 'helping to think clearly on the problems of life' and 'helping to understand modern society and the responsibilities of a citizen' as key purposes of schooling. Nearly three decades later, a national survey conducted by the Canadian Education Association indicated that the top two reasons for schooling were the attainment of self-satisfaction and the goal 'to get along better with people at all levels of society', while only 18 per cent of respondents suggested that the primary reason for schooling was 'to get better jobs' (Lauwerys, 1973: 14). In 1999, over half of respondents to a national survey indicated that schools needed to devote greater attention to 'the basics' such as reading and writing skills rather than computer skills, whereas a slight majority felt that youth should be encouraged to learn specific trades or skills in community colleges instead of pursuing a general university education (Angus Reid Group, 1999: 5, 17).

One pattern that emerges in surveys of this nature is that job preparation and training gain force as priorities in times of high unemployment and uncertainty or transitions in labour markets. This helps to explain why these issues have once again moved to the forefront in recent debates over educational reform. Employers' concerns to have access to a supply of adequately qualified labour converge with individuals' expectations that education will lead them to a stable employment future at a time when most people have been exposed to harsh realities associated with occupational restructuring and the threat or experience of joblessness.

3. *Job training in the schools.* Despite the force of recent arguments that schooling should be doing more to help prepare individuals for the labour market, the question remains as to how effective schools could be even if this endeavour were to become their primary orientation. There are several impediments to the ability of formal education, as it is currently structured, to direct and place students into jobs. Considerable changes occur in personal aptitudes, labour markets, and employment needs over the normal period of 12–13 years that it takes an individual to proceed from kindergarten to high school graduation. Even if it could be assumed that schools were vocational in nature (thereby ignoring the varied purposes of public education), it is doubtful whether they would have the resources and ability to meet labour market requirements, particularly in a context in which jobs, technologies, and skills are continually being redefined and reorganized. Several critical questions would need to be addressed:

- Should people be educated for self-employment or wage labour and, if the latter, would major corporations or small businesses prevail?
- Which skills would be common to all pupils and which would be developed within particular educational streams and at what levels?
- Would individual or community interests be outweighed by employers' interests?
- What kinds of credentials and expectations would there be regarding prospects for employment after the completion of formal education?

Many of these issues are currently at the centre of both public policy discussions and academic analysis of work-school linkages. The notion of 'transitions' has replaced a long-standing sense that there is a linear transition process as people move through their life courses from family to school to work to retirement (Ashton and Lowe, 1991: 1–2). The rethinking of school-work linkages is given focus by emphasis on lifelong learning, innovations in areas such as adult and continuing education, and the rapid expansion of alternative forms and sites of educational delivery. Given these concerns, discussion turns in the next section to contemporary changes in work as they pertain to education.

Education and Work in Canada

The Canadian labour force and the kinds of jobs that workers have been engaged in have changed significantly over the past few decades. As shown in Table 6.2, shortly after the end of World War II, one-quarter of all workers were involved in agricultural work and nearly one-third were blue-collar workers, while fewer than two out of five were classified as white-collar workers.

Box 6.4 Employment in the service sector

The dramatic rise in service-sector employment has been accompanied by uncertainty and variable working conditions for many Canadians, as Crompton and Vickers (2000: 7–8) observe:

By the beginning of the 1970s, the services-producing workforce totalled over 4.8 million, or 62 per cent of Canadian employment. In 1999, employment in services accounted for more than 10.7 million jobs and 73 per cent of total employment. The biggest employers in the sector were retail and wholesale trade (2.2 million workers), health and social services (1.4 million) and education (983,000).

Although the services-producing sector includes the highly unionized public-sector industries, many service jobs are not as secure, offer fewer full-time positions and generally are lower-paying than jobs in the manufacturing sector. But recent research shows that, while job stability varies within and between different service industries, it is not much different than the goods-producing sector. For example, jobs in business services and distributive services are just as stable as those in manufacturing; on the other hand, those in consumer services have high turnovers like those in fishing, forestry and construction, although their stability seems to be improving.

There is no doubt, though, that services-producing jobs are less likely to be full-time jobs. Only 77 per cent of service jobs were full-time in 1997, compared with 92 per cent in the goods-producing sector. Not surprisingly, nine in 10 part-time workers are employed in the services industries.

The impact of fewer hours of work can easily be seen in the average weekly earnings reported for the two sectors: $554 for services-producing versus $777 for goods-producing in 1998. The same pattern plays out between the service industry groups, in which industries with the highest rates of full-time employment have the highest average pay. For example, in 1999, weekly earnings in finance, insurance and real estate averaged $760 and business services somewhat less at $700. In contrast, earnings reported in food and beverage services, an industry where almost half the employees are part-time workers, amounted to just over $210 weekly.

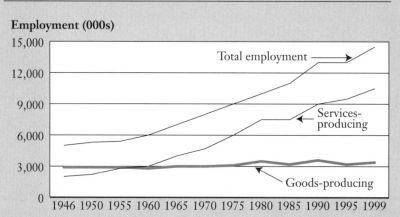

Box 6.4 continued

Services-Producing Industries Have Been Canada's Main Employer
Since the Late 1950s

Note: Total employment data from 1976 on have been rebased to the 1996
Census of Population. A change in the industrial classification system in
1987 resulted in a slight shift in employment from the goods- to the services-producing sector.

By 2002, however, only about 2.1 per cent of workers were part of the agricultural labour force and the proportion of blue-collar workers was about one
in five, but nearly three out of every four workers were involved in white-collar work. This has meant, at least in a general way, that types of work that
typically require formal educational credentials have become increasingly
central to the labour force as a whole.

In the same way that the occupational classifications of workers have
changed, the nature of work and the composition of the labour force have
become much more diverse. New technologies, services, product lines, and
forms of work organization have altered the jobs we do and the way we work.
The transformation of working arrangements, in turn, affects and is shaped
by shifting patterns of employment and demands for distinct kinds of workers. Canada's paid labour force, which at the time of Confederation consisted
predominantly of men of British and French origin, has become increasingly
feminized as well as more racially and ethnically heterogeneous. Today, most
men and women, regardless of age, marital status, and social origin, are labour
force participants. At the same time, the changing occupational structure has
meant that the prospects for and future of work are highly uncertain for substantial proportions of the population. This is particularly true for youth who
are about to enter into the workforce and for minority group members who
have historically experienced marginal labour force participation.

Table 6.2
Employment by Industry, Selected Years, Canada, 1946–2002 (% of total)

Industry, by Sector	1946	1951	1956	1961	1966	1971	1976	1981	1986	1991	1996	2001	2002
PRIMARY													
Agriculture	25.4	18.4	13.9	11.2	7.4	6.2	4.9	4.4	3.9	3.5	3.0	2.1	2.1
Forestry	1.8	2.3	2.1	1.4	1.1	0.9	0.7	0.7	0.6	0.5	0.8	0.6	0.5
Fishing, trapping	0.6	0.6	0.4	0.3	0.4	0.3	0.2	0.3	0.3	0.4	0.2	0.2	0.2
Mining, quarrying, oil wells	1.6	1.5	2.1	1.3	1.7	1.6	1.5	1.9	1.6	1.4	1.3	1.2	1.1
Primary total	29.4	22.8	18.5	14.2	10.5	9.0	7.4	7.3	6.4	5.8	5.3	4.1	3.9
SECONDARY													
Manufacturing	26.0	26.5	25.7	24.0	24.4	22.2	20.3	19.3	17.3	15.1	13.9	14.9	14.9
Construction	4.8	6.8	7.4	6.2	7.0	6.1	6.7	5.9	5.4	5.7	5.6	5.7	5.9
Secondary total	30.8	33.3	33.1	30.2	31.4	28.3	27.0	25.3	22.7	20.8	19.5	20.6	20.7
TERTIARY													
Transportation, communications	7.4	7.8	7.8	8.1	7.6	7.7	7.5	7.1	6.7	6.3	4.8	5.0	4.8
Public utilities	0.7	1.0	1.2	1.2	1.1	1.1	1.2	1.2	1.0	1.1	0.9	0.8	0.8
Trade	12.3	14.1	15.8	16.9	16.5	16.5	17.3	17.1	18.0	17.6	15.0	15.4	15.3
Finance, real estate	2.7	3.0	3.5	3.9	4.3	4.8	5.3	5.5	5.7	6.1	6.0	5.5	5.5
Service*	16.8	18.0	20.3	19.5	22.7	26.2	27.1	29.6	32.6	35.4	39.4	41.4	41.8
Public administration	—	—	—	5.9	5.9	6.5	7.2	7.0	6.9	6.8	5.7	4.9	4.8
Tertiary total	39.8	43.9	48.5	55.5	58.0	62.7	65.6	67.5	70.9	73.3	71.8	73.0	73.0
Total (per cent)	100	100	100.1	99.9	99.9	100	100	100.1	100	99.9	96.6	97.7	97.6
Total number (000s)	4,666	5,097	5,585	6,055	7,121	7,958	9,776	11,398	12,095	12,916	14,899	16,246	16,689

* Includes public administration until 1961.

Sources: For 1946–91: Bernier (1996); for 1996–2002: *Labour Force Historical Review* (2002) CS71-0004/2002-MRC.

Important social and economic transformations have been mirrored in the changing relationship between schooling and work. In the nineteenth century, schooling had little importance for the majority of the population except as a brief point of contact to gain basic reading, writing, and social skills. Other than for the select few persons who entered professions, such as medicine, law, teaching, and the clergy, education bore little formal relation to the kinds of jobs most people worked at, such as farming, fishing, mining, manufacturing, and commercial work. The primary importance of schooling was in its service as a socially stabilizing force, keeping young people occupied and off the streets. As we have seen, however, the importance of formal education increased through the twentieth century to become a major conduit for entry into the labour market.

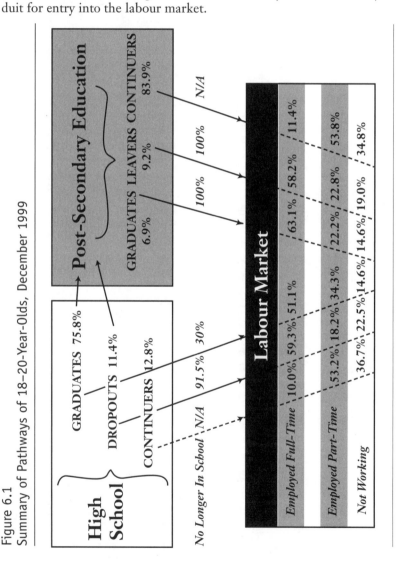

Figure 6.1
Summary of Pathways of 18–20-Year-Olds, December 1999

Source: Brink and Dhawan-Biswal (2002:19).

In recent years, there has been a further reassessment of the social and economic purposes of schooling. What had come to be regarded as a relatively fixed pattern of progression through the major individual life roles has been redefined as a process of multiple transitions in the context of global economic changes (see, e.g., Anisef and Axelrod, 1993). As Figure 6.1 demonstrates in part, there is not so much a single point of entry into labour markets as a persistent shifting from one educational or work setting to another. Just as increasing numbers of students seek part-time employment to gain experience and support themselves during the time that they are engaged in formal studies, they are also more likely to return to educational programs after they have started work in order to upgrade their credentials or retrain for new lines of work. Movement between part-time work and studies, periodic unemployment, changes in the nature of work, and changing educational requirements have altered traditional relations between schooling and work. We are being told more frequently that 'lifelong learning' has become the norm that will govern our educational futures and that adaptability is the key to success (Livingstone, 1999: 14–15).

Table 6.3
Educational Attainment and Labour Force Participation, Canada, 2002

Highest Level of Educational Attainment	Labour Force Participation Rate (%)			Unemployment Rate (%)		
	Total	Males	Females	Total	Males	Females
0-8 years	25.1	34.8	16.6	13.4	13.1	14.0
Some secondary	52.3	61.3	43.0	13.9	14.3	13.3
High school graduate	71.7	80.1	64.2	7.4	7.7	7.0
Some post-secondary	69.3	73.6	65.3	8.7	9.0	8.5
Post-secondary certificate or diploma	77.2	82.2	72.4	6.0	6.4	5.5
University degree	81.2	83.4	78.8	5.0	5.1	4.9
Total	66.9	73.3	60.7	7.7	8.1	7.1

Source: *Labour Force Historical Review* (2002) CS71–0004/2002–MRC.

In general, evidence points to the likelihood that people with higher levels of education and diverse educational backgrounds will be more successful in job markets than those who have more limited educational credentials. Education is positively associated, for instance, with the chances of finding a job, having more meaningful work, and securing better incomes. Tables 6.3 and 6.4 provide indications of the relative return from education in relation to labour force participation and income. It must be recognized, however, that labour markets continue to be characterized by substantial gender inequities. Similar trends hold true for other minority groups, including

Table 6.4
Average Earnings by Gender, Highest Level of Schooling
and Work Activity, 2001

Work Activity and Highest Level of Schooling	Average Earnings ($)			Earnings Ratio*
	Men	Women	Total	
Worked full year, full-time in 2000				
Less than high school graduation certificate	36,193	24,914	32,242	68.8
High school graduation certificate and/or some post-secondary	41,217	29,818	36,278	72.3
Trades certificate or diploma	44,494	28,602	40,017	64.3
College certificate or diploma	49,231	34,456	41,825	70.0
University certificate, diploma, or degree	71,957	48,257	61,823	67.1
Total	49,198	34,642	43,231	70.4
All Earners				
Less than high school graduation certificate	25,485	15,190	21,230	59.6
High school graduation certificate and/or some post-secondary	30,870	19,952	25,477	64.6
Trades certificate or diploma	38,478	21,669	32,743	56.3
College certificate or diploma	41,250	26,270	32,736	63.7
University certificate, diploma, or degree	60,480	36,721	48,648	60.7
Total	38,347	24,390	31,757	63.6

* Women's earnings as a percentage of men's earnings.
Source: Statistics Canada, 2001 Census, Catalogue no. 97F0019XCB01002.

immigrants and Aboriginal peoples (Li, 2003: 110–12; Schissel and Wotherspoon, 2003: 111–14).

The importance of education for job prospects takes on greater significance in light of recent evidence that it has become increasingly difficult for young adults to achieve a secure position in the labour market. Crompton (1996: 17) observes, on the basis of data collected between 1979 and 1993 on the labour market experiences of young adults, that 'For 25- to 29-year-olds, who have reached an age when the transition from school to work should be over, finding work has become more difficult; for those with jobs, the income earned . . . is substantially less than it used to be.' As the twentieth century drew to a close, the situation appeared even more dismal for many young labour market entrants. Bowers, Sonnet, and Bardone (1999: 39) emphasized that 'The economic state of the average young person in OECD countries falls short of what is desirable. Despite a decline in the relative numbers of youths and the proliferation of programs aimed at young people in the past two decades, their employment and earnings position has worsened, in some countries substantially.'

As labour markets become more volatile and competitive, there is additional pressure to achieve greater levels of education and training. Just as workers who enter job markets with strong educational credentials have greater employment and career opportunities than those with less education, a growing body of evidence points towards the importance of both formal and informal job-related education and training in maintaining employment success. While individuals with a broad range of educational backgrounds are engaging in such training, the benefits are not equally shared among all labour market participants. Lowe and Krahn (1994: 7), for instance, found from a sample of Edmonton youth that young workers with relatively high levels of education are the main beneficiaries of further education and training. Livingstone (1999: 26, 27, 30) reports significant increases in adult and continuing education among virtually all social groups, particularly among young adults or those who had previously dropped out of school, but cautions that 'Those who have higher levels of formal schooling are more likely to participate in most forms of further education.'

This evidence seems to reinforce the general argument that individuals, even if they are already highly educated, require extensive educational credentials and continual upgrading to remain competitive in today's job market. By implication, those who fail to achieve high levels of education and up-to-date training are relegated to the growing pool of marginal or long-term unemployed workers. These factors point to two common claims regarding educational restructuring: (1) that efforts to improve credentials are an individual responsibility, and (2) that governments and employers must work more actively to overcome the mismatch between workers and jobs.

Box 6.5 Participation in adult education in Canada

Canadians from all backgrounds participate in adult education and training beyond their initial formal education. However, as documented in a report from Statistics Canada and Human Resources Development Canada (2001: 18–19), significant variations in participation rates are influenced by such factors as social background, education, and region:

The influence of family background is . . . visible in the strong relationship between initial educational attainment and participation in adult education. [The figure below] shows total participation by initial educational attainment. The rates vary from a low of 11 per cent among those who did not complete high school to a high of 48 per cent among Canadians with a university degree. Four distinct categories of participation seem to be closely related to levels of initial

Box 6.5 continued

education. At the bottom are those who have not completed high school. High school graduates and people with trade certificates fall into the second level, with a rate of 12 to 15 percentage points higher. About the same increase in the rate of participation can be observed between the former category and those with a community college background. At the top with a markedly higher rate come the university graduates.

Percentage of Adult Population Participating in Adult Education and Training, by Level of Educational Attainment, Canada, 1997

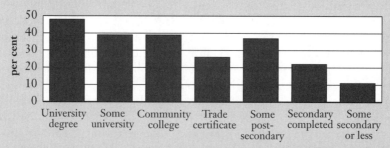

The general 'law of inequality'—which suggests that the higher the educational attainment the more likely a person is to participate in adult education—holds up to scrutiny in all regions of Canada. However, the data in [the following figure] suggest that some provinces appear more successful than others in attracting participants with low levels of school attainment. Because of small sample sizes, the Atlantic provinces are grouped together.

Adjusted Odds Showing the Likelihood of Adults Receiving Adult Education and Training, by Province and Level of Educational Attainment, 1997

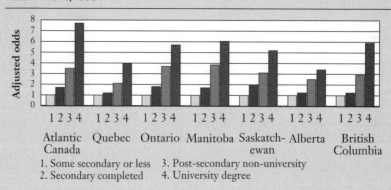

Box 6.5 continued

In the Atlantic provinces, the odds of participating in adult education and training for those with a university education are 13 times higher (unadjusted odds ratio) than for those who had not completed high school. In Alberta, the odds ratio is equal to 5—by far the lowest difference in likelihood of participation by education level in the country. Manitoba and Saskatchewan show relatively large differences in participation by education level, while Quebec, Ontario and British Columbia experience smaller differences—but substantially more than in Alberta. When factors like demographic and labour market structures are taken into account, the differences in inequality across Canadian provinces are reduced. This is particularly true for Quebec whose adjusted odds ratio for university graduates (4.0) is close to that of Alberta (3.4). The high level of participation and somewhat lower level of inequality in Alberta might be a result of the province's long history of community-oriented programs of adult education. The reason for the Quebec figure might be that Quebec has a strong tradition of social movement involvement in adult education. A closer examination of the training effort by province shows that the most educated people participated more but also spent more time on learning activities.

Unfortunately, the description of the trends outlined above does not offer any indication of the extent to which education and training are actually required on the job. We need to consider, in other words, whether the increase in educational credentials is a function of the growth of more sophisticated jobs or whether it is, instead, a consequence of credential inflation and other factors beyond work-related skills and training.

Proponents of the first thesis point to the impact of information technology on the creation of jobs that require a more highly educated and trained labour force. The expansion of jobs that require high qualifications occurs in two ways—through the creation of new jobs in high-level professional and service work, and through upgrading and new skill demands in already existing jobs. Advanced education is required as work-related tasks become more specialized and sophisticated. Since the mid-1980s, job growth in Canada, the United States, and other highly developed nations has been clustered in industries that possess high concentrations of 'knowledge workers', i.e., professionals, engineers, scientific and technical workers, computer specialists, senior managers, and the self-employed who possess high levels of training, specialized skill, and/or decision-making authority. Statistics Canada (2003c: 7), reporting on the 2003 census, observes that:

Of the 15.6 million people in the labour force, more than 2.5 million were in highly skilled occupations that normally required university education. This was a 33 per cent increase from 1991, triple the rate of growth for the labour force as a whole . . . . Highly skilled occupations accounted for almost one-half of the total labour force growth over the decade. As a result, there has been a shift in the skill makeup of the labour force. In 2001, people in highly skilled occupations normally requiring a university education accounted for 16 per cent of the total labour force, up from 13 per cent a decade earlier.

The growth of highly skilled jobs and knowledge work is necessary, advocates claim, to drive productivity for both large and small firms in a highly competitive economy. Education and training can increase the degree of complementarity between the interests of workers and employers because they not only assist individuals in their ability to secure employment but also to influence the wages, personal benefits, and working conditions of employees. Bowlby (1996: 35) indicates that, in addition to receiving higher wages, 'Graduates with a direct education-job relationship are the most likely to be satisfied or very satisfied at work, much more than graduates in unrelated jobs.'

A less optimistic view, however, is taken by those who emphasize that the categorization of jobs or industries by job titles and education levels is highly misleading if we do not examine how work is actually changing. Recent economic restructuring has been characterized by the disappearance of stable, better-paying work and the proliferation of low-end jobs as businesses pursue strategies that will reduce labour costs. In traditional industries and businesses, existing jobs often are phased out or deskilled while newer jobs, particularly in the service sector, are concentrated in low-skill, low-paying occupations. Education serves as a screening device independent from competencies required on the job. As general education levels rise and job descriptions change, employers are able to keep wages low through competition generated by labour surpluses, claims that available workers do not have suitable skills to match the available work, new labour-saving technologies, and the transfer of production from regions or nations with high-cost labour to those with lower labour costs and living standards. Much recent employment growth has been in service industries characterized by part-time, temporary, or insecure work, low wages, few benefits, and often poor working conditions. Increasingly, the absence of secure, high-status jobs drives workers into jobs and fields where they are unable to use their capacities and skills. In 2000, for instance, one-third of Canadian workers aged 20–9 with post-secondary educational credentials indicated that they were overqualified for their jobs (Crompton, 2002: 23).

Recent evidence on the changing nature of employment has pointed to a much more complex picture than that revealed in the two arguments outlined above. Much attention has been focused on the tendency towards polarization of job growth distributed among high-end and low-end jobs, with a corresponding decline in the share of employment held by mid-level jobs (Economic Council of Canada, 1991; Beach and Slotsve, 1996). This analysis highlights the decline of employment in goods-producing industries relative to substantial increases in service-sector employment. Both sectors, in turn, are characterized by diverse clusters of internal characteristics. Demand for highly educated, skilled, well-paid employees in many industries has increased as a consequence of new production and information technologies. However, increased productivity, workplace restructuring, and corporate and public-sector downsizing have also contributed to large-scale layoffs, intensification of work, and deskilling. In the process, several prevalent trends emerge, most notably including the expansion of white-collar work (in managerial, administrative, professional, clerical, sales, and service occupations), the growth of part-time and self-employment relative to full-time paid employment, and deepening problems for the most vulnerable segments of the labour force (Heisz et al., 2002; Kerr, 1997).

It is often tempting, in the analysis of labour force trends, to look at these patterns in an abstract way as if they affected all workers equally. In fact, however, labour market changes have very different implications for distinct categories of workers. Since the mid-1980s, the degree of labour market polarization, or the gap between the highest- and lowest-paying jobs, generally has dropped for women, grown for men, increased substantially for workers less than 35 years of age, and remained high for visible minority groups and Aboriginal people (Human Resources Development Canada, 1996: 6; Canadian Council on Social Development, 2000: 21–3). Hughes and Lowe (2000) conclude that such factors as the gender and age of workers and occupational conditions are more likely than computer technology to contribute to polarization within the labour market. Occupations associated with high job vacancies also tend to be polarized among those with relatively high skill requirements and those that are not unionized and have low wages. Galarneau et al. (2001: 33) observe that, 'Even in periods of strong economic growth, a substantial share of job vacancies are outside the high technology sectors. In 1999, more than 40 per cent of job vacancies and 50 per cent of long-term job vacancies of profit-oriented establishments were in the retail trade and consumer services industries.'

Some commentators, therefore, have argued that the structure of work is best characterized in the form of a segmented or dual, rather than a unified, labour market (Piore, 1979; Clairmont and Apostle, 1997). This kind of analysis seeks to explain how members of subordinate social groups, notably visible minorities as well as female workers, are concentrated in lower-paying, more insecure jobs in contrast to white men, who tend to be concentrated in the better jobs. A primary labour market, in which relatively highly qualified and unionized workers are able to demand better wages and working conditions from larger employers, is distinguished from a secondary market in which smaller, more competitive businesses seeking cheaper labour costs require a more unstable labour force. Segmented or dual labour market models are useful in demonstrating that not all workers are competing for the same jobs, and also offer some insight into how educational qualifications can be used to differentiate distinct pools of workers. The practice of streaming in Canadian schools, for instance, operates to select students for particular positions within segmented labour markets (Curtis et al., 1992).

Despite the insights they offer, segmented labour market theories do not provide a complete explanation of inequalities within labour markets. Labour markets are both more diverse and less static than depicted by this approach. The face of work has been altered in many ways by changes in the organization of work, new technologies, demographic shifts, and labour market dynamics. The demise of jobs in traditional labour markets such as manufacturing, combined with the growth of small business and increasing employment in non-traditional occupations, has also blurred the boundaries between primary and secondary segments of the labour force. Immigrant selection criteria increasingly have emphasized skills, qualifications, and other human capital attributes even though many immigrants continue to face specific social or race-based barriers (Li, 2003: 122–3).

Significant continuity and changes in gender segmentation also are evident. Whereas fewer than 20 per cent of women aged 25 and over participated in the paid labour force in 1946 and only about one-third did in the late 1960s, nearly 60 per cent of women were labour force participants in 2000. Men's participation rates have declined somewhat over the same time period but still remain relatively high, at about 90 per cent in 1946, 85 per cent in the late 1960s, and just under 75 per cent in 2000 (Bernier, 1996: A48–9; Statistics Canada, 2001b: 12, 17). As data in Table 6.5 indicate, women are represented in substantial numbers and proportions in a wide range of occupational groups. Women's participation in many higher-paying fields, such as managerial, administrative, and professional occupations, has increased in conjunction with more open access to advanced levels of education. However, the data also show that women are most highly concentrated in only a few areas, notably clerical, sales, and service occupations characterized by low wages and relatively little autonomy. Moreover, comparisons among persons who work full-time on a full-year basis show that women earn on average only two-thirds of the wages earned by men, with the lowest ratios of women's to men's earnings tending to be in sales, services, and other occupations in which there are high concentrations of female workers. The segmentation of the labour force along gender lines is even more pronounced when part-time and temporary workers are taken into consideration, given that much of this labour is performed by women working for relatively low wages and benefits. Vosko (2003: 27) observes that, despite significant shifts in the nature of work that have created some advances for female workers, women remain highly vulnerable because 'the erosion of minimum standards legislation, the deterioration of collective bargaining, unemployment insurance reforms, and cutbacks in the federal public service are fuelling new

Table 6.5
Full-time and Part-time Employment, by Gender, Industry, and Occupation, Canada, 2002

	Women 000s	(%)	Men 000s	(%)	Total 000s
INDUSTRY					
Agriculture	65	24.3	203	75.7	269
Other primary industries	36	13.8	224	86.2	260
Utilities	30	23.4	98	76.6	128
Construction	61	7.5	750	92.5	812
Manufacturing	624	27.8	1,620	72.2	2,244
Trade (wholesale & retail)	730	41.6	1,023	58.4	1,754
Transportation and warehousing	126	18.8	544	81.1	670
Finance, insurance, real estate, and leasing	423	55.4	340	44.6	763
Professional, scientific, and technical services	340	39.5	522	60.6	861
Management of companies and administrative and other support services	191	42.8	255	57.2	446
Educational services	464	61.4	292	38.6	756
Health care and social assistance	951	79.6	242	20.3	1,194
Information, culture, and recreation	233	44.5	291	55.5	524
Accommodation and food services	336	56.2	262	43.8	598
Other services	228	43.4	297	56.6	525
Public administration	327	45.0	399	55.0	726
TOTAL, ALL INDUSTRIES	5,165	41.2	7,362	58.8	12,527
OCCUPATIONS					
Management	415	32.1	876	67.9	1,291
Business, finance, and administrative	1,571	68.4	727	31.6	2,298
Health	486	77.4	142	22.6	628
Social science, education, government service, and religion	524	60.6	340	39.4	864
Sales and service	1,306	52.2	1,194	47.8	2,500
Trades, transport and equipment operators, and related occupations	103	5.1	1,924	94.9	2,027
Processing, manufacturing, and utilities	348	28.9	857	71.1	1,205
TOTAL, CLASSIFIED OCCUPATIONS	4,753	44.0	6,060	56.0	10,813

(continued)

Table 6.5
(continued)

	Women 000s	(%)	Men 000s	(%)	Total 000s
PART-TIME EMPLOYMENT					
INDUSTRY					
Agriculture	33	53.2	29	46.8	62
Other primary industries	6	50.0	6	50.0	12
Utilities	3	75.0	1	25.0	4
Construction	27	38.0	44	62.0	71
Manufacturing	44	53.7	38	46.3	82
Trade (wholesale & retail)	453	67.0	223	33.0	676
Transportation and warehousing	42	48.8	44	51.2	86
Finance, insurance, real estate, and leasing	92	69.2	41	30.8	133
Professional, scientific, and technical services	85	64.4	47	35.6	132
Management of companies and administrative and other support services	86	58.9	59	40.4	146
Educational services	204	78.5	56	21.5	260
Health care and social assistance	370	89.6	44	10.7	413
Information, culture, and recreation	103	56.9	78	43.1	181
Accommodation and food services	269	66.3	137	33.7	406
Other services	131	80.0	37	22.0	168
Public administration	36	69.2	16	30.8	52
TOTAL, ALL INDUSTRIES	1,984	68.8	900	31.2	2,884
OCCUPATIONS					
Management	46	56.8	35	43.2	81
Business, finance, and administrative	371	81.9	82	18.1	453
Health	206	90.7	21	9.3	227
Social science, education, government service, and religion	156	74.6	53	25.4	209
Sales and service	999	69.8	432	30.2	1,431
Trades, transport and equipment operators, and related occupations	39	25.5	114	74.5	153
Processing, manufacturing, and utilities	24	46.2	28	53.8	52
TOTAL, CLASSIFIED OCCUPATIONS	1,841	70.6	765	29.4	2,606

Note: Numbers are rounded.

Source: *Labour Force Historical Review* (2002) CS71–0004/2002–MRC.

patterns of gendered labour market inequality.' Armstrong and Armstrong (2001: 66) emphasize that, despite improved educational and employment opportunities, women continue to be segregated in jobs that parallel the kinds of personal service and domestic labour they carry out in the household. Educational participation has created new social and employment opportunities for women, but traditional gender roles are also reproduced through demands and responsibilities that occur through the intersection of household, schooling, and workplace (Gaskell, 1992).

Box 6.6 Youth in the labour market in OECD countries

This excerpt from the proceedings of an OECD conference on *Preparing Youth for the 21st Century* (Bowers et al., 1999: 14, 17–18) notes that while young people today are staying in school longer and consequently are better educated than those of a generation ago, their employment prospects have not improved. Indeed, in some instances, the likelihood of youth finding meaningful employment is less than it was a generation earlier:

> Despite declines in the relative size of the youth cohort . . . and increases in the level of educational attainment in the past two decades in most OECD countries, the employment and earnings of young people have not improved. Youth labour force participation and employment rates fell across a large number of OECD countries over the period, and the earnings of young workers declined relative to those of older workers in most countries. In several countries, the deterioration of the position of youths on the labour market shows up mainly in relatively high unemployment rates and low employment/population rates. In others, it shows up mainly in falling relative wages for young workers. But in most countries, there is a group of disadvantaged youths facing both kinds of deterioration. Only part of this is due to rising education enrolments as the largest negative trend in employment is among young men not in education . . . . [K]ey . . . facts about school-leaving and labour market outcomes for young people today compared with the late 1970s/early 1980s [are summarized as follows] . . . :

> *They are more educated . . .*
> * More youths remain in education beyond compulsory schooling: on average across OECD countries 34 per cent of youths aged 22 were attending school in 1997, compared to 19 per cent in 1984.
> * Consequently, there are fewer early school-leavers. For instance, the proportion of 18-year-olds not attending school was 33 per cent in 1997, compared with 50 per cent in 1984.

Box 6.6 continued

- There are slightly fewer youths neither in initial education nor in a job: 14 per cent of 16–24-year-olds were not at school and not employed in 1997, compared with 22 per cent in 1984.
- Young people facing the largest barriers to a stable entry into the labour market are more and more those who complete school with qualifications ill-suited to employment or dropouts with no qualifications.

. . . but their labour market prospects have not tended to improve.
- Youth employment rates are lower: in 1997, 44 per cent of the 15–24-year-olds were in employment, compared with 52 per cent in 1979.
- Out-of-school young men have fared particularly badly, as evidenced by a strong trend decline in their employment prospects.
- The employment gap between the youth cohort and the adult cohort has widened.
- Youths in the labour force are more likely to be unemployed: the OECD average unemployment rate for 15–24-year-olds was 16 per cent in 1997, 4 percentage points higher than in 1979.
- While the experience of unemployment is widespread, it is highly concentrated among a disadvantaged group of young people.
- Youths are confronted with stagnant or declining earnings relative to adults, a rather unexpected twist that could have major longer-term consequence in terms of lifelong earnings.

Persistencies across the past two decades:
- Transition processes and outcomes differ greatly by country, gender and, often, educational level.
- In many countries, being in full-time education is more common than combining education and work.
- Combining work with schooling is a feature either of apprenticeship countries or of countries with a relatively high incidence of part-time employment.
- Teenage and young adult women perform better at school and have seen a long-term trend increase in their employment prospects compared with their young male counterparts.
- Apprenticeship/dual-system countries clearly do better at getting young people a firm foothold in the labour market.
- Those who fail to get a firm foothold in the labour market form a 'hard core' of disaffected young people, a stigmatized minority with cumulative disadvantages, often related to intergenerational factors such as poverty, unstable family backgrounds and life in communities with high overall unemployment.

As the evidence and trends outlined in the preceding paragraphs suggest, labour markets are highly complex and changing entities. The possibility that a person will find relatively secure employment with limited education or can follow an educational track that leads to clearly definable, rewarding career opportunities is becoming increasingly remote for labour force entrants. This situation creates heightened uncertainty and stress for individuals who are considering or reassessing their employment prospects. As Osberg et al. (1995: 182–3) conclude in their analysis of case studies of changing Canadian workplaces in the 1990s, problems of 'increasing unemployment, the polarization of incomes, rising poverty, and greater dependence on transfer payments—all have their special complexities, but there is a root problem, a lack of jobs.' Bibby (1995: 99), for instance, reports that 42 per cent of Canadian respondents employed full-time—45 per cent of women and 40 per cent of men—expressed concern about keeping their jobs. Young workers, who are especially vulnerable to economic shifts, must rely on part-time work, periodic retraining, or jobs that do not match their qualifications in order to break into the labour market (Lowe and Krahn, 1994: 5; Human Resources Development Canada, 2000).

One of the major contradictions evident in these trends is the coexistence of large numbers of workers who are undereducated and underqualified for available jobs along with a substantial pool of labour market participants who are overqualified and underemployed. Statistics Canada data concerning employment experiences of graduates of post-secondary programs reveal, in general, that those with the highest levels of formal education tend to show the strongest match between job skills and education, with a slightly higher degree of fit for women relative to men (Finnie, 2001: 14).

Since the late 1980s, periods of economic restructuring and recession made it increasingly difficult for graduates of trades and vocational programs, who might be expected to have work directly linked to their training, to find and keep such jobs (Bowlby, 1996: 38). Myles and Fawcett (1990: 16), presenting data from a national survey conducted in the early 1980s, indicate that nearly one-third of workers reported they were overqualified for their jobs. These proportions were even higher for high-growth sectors like personal services work, and were highest among women and young workers. Lowe and Krahn (1994: 5) indicate that, a decade later, while most workers felt that their work was appropriate to their education, just under one-quarter of all workers, one-fifth of university graduates, and nearly one-third of high school graduates expressed the feeling that they were overqualified for their jobs.

Livingstone (1999), through his own research and in summaries of other findings, demonstrates the simultaneous existence of two large groups of workers—those whose formal educational credentials exceed their job requirements and those who feel they do not have sufficient skills or training to carry out all their job tasks. More specifically, he shows that underemployment and subemployment are themselves subdivided among distinct categories of labour force participants, depending on such factors as the levels of qualifications workers have, the credentials required for entry into certain occupations, the knowledge and skills employed on the job and those that workers have but cannot use in their work, and workers' perceptions about the relationships among these factors. Between one and three out of five workers in North America are likely to be underemployed according to various dimensions based on the reality or perception that they have recognized skills and credentials they are not able to employ in their jobs, at the same time as these workers are engaging in more formal and informal training on and off the job (Livingstone, 1999: 94–5).

In summary, it is difficult to make comprehensive judgements about the degree of match or fit between education and jobs because of the highly complex and changing nature of work and labour markets. Even those individuals who are in a position to make long-term plans for their career futures are subject to the possibility that credential requirements may change or that certain jobs may be substantially reorganized or disappear altogether before their formal education is complete. The discourse of lifelong learning, acknowledging ongoing transformations in the nature of work and periodic transitions among diverse employment circumstances and learning sites, has replaced conventional notions of a pathway that leads from schooling into a clearly defined career path. In general terms, it is clear that individuals with the highest levels of formal education are in the best position to benefit in terms of finding stable, well-paying, meaningful work. However, even among highly educated workers there is a strong possibility of no available work relevant to their training, while pressures mount for continuous retraining and upgrading. By contrast, those with limited amounts of formal education are more likely to have difficulty finding and keeping work, but when they do, in many cases even they may be overqualified for their jobs. For youth faced with the prospect of seeking work, regardless of their levels of educational attainment, the pressing question of what kinds of jobs are available is becoming increasingly uncertain.

Conclusion

This chapter has addressed issues related to the relationship between schooling and work. While the goal of preparing youth for entry into the labour force has long been a central concern of educators, just as it has been a recurrent matter for public debate, the chapter has emphasized that there has never been a strict correspondence between formal education and work training. Labour market preparation has been only one of several objectives of education systems. This, combined with the varied demands of employers, the changing nature of most occupations, and the complexity of transition processes between schooling and work, means that there are limits to the responsiveness that formal education can maintain to labour market demands.

While recently there has been considerable attention in policy discussions and the media on the apparent failure of formal education to produce the kind of workforce required in a competitive global economy, much of that emphasis has offered a relatively uncritical analysis of the kinds of job choices and school-work connections that labour market entrants are confronted with. Clearly, many improvements are needed in the ways that schools approach labour market preparation. It is not sufficient, however, to lay blame with schools or individuals for the mismatch between workers and jobs. A combination of factors that links individual life circumstances and choices with structural characteristics of education and work opportunities contributes to the kinds of life courses that people follow. These features are the subject of Chapter 7.

Annotated Further Readings

Paul Anisef, Paul Axelrod, Etta Baichman-Anisef, Carl James, and Anton Turrittin, *Opportunity and Uncertainty: Life Course Experiences of the Class of '73*. Toronto: University of Toronto Press, 2000. This book offers one of the few systematic long-term studies of the educational, occupational, and life pathways followed by students as they complete their schooling and move through adolescence into adulthood.

Stewart Crysdale, Alan J. King, and Nancy Mandell, *On Their Own: Making the Transition from School to Work in the Information Age*. Montreal and Kingston: McGill-Queen's University Press, 1999. The authors report on a study based on youth accounts of their varied schooling and labour market experiences, highlighting social background and educational factors that make for successful integration as well as issues that mark uneven transitions.

D.W. Livingstone, *The Education-Jobs Gap: Underemployment or Economic Democracy*. Toronto: Garamond Press, 1999. Offering a comprehensive analysis of the relationship between education and work in contemporary economic contexts, this book demonstrates how the broad range of educational experiences and capacities is not given sufficient recognition and scope in many jobs and labour market situations.

Graham Lowe, *The Quality of Work: A People-Centred Agenda*. Toronto: Oxford University Press, 2000. The author examines contemporary trends and attitudes regarding the changing nature of work, building from critique towards a framework for the creation of meaningful work opportunities that address people's concerns for greater personal development and fulfillment.

Richard Marquardt, *Enter at Your Own Risk: Canadian Youth and the Labour Market*. Toronto: Between the Lines, 1998. The book examines the uncertainty and risk that characterize current labour market conditions for Canada's youth, placing education and employment in a broader historical context.

Key Terms

Capitalist imperative   Pressures to reproduce hierarchy and inequality through schooling and other institutions in order to ensure profitable production and other needs associated with capitalist economies.

Democratic imperative Pressures to ensure that schools and other agencies are governed by priorities for widespread participation, expanded socio-economic opportunities, and social justice for all groups.

Deskilling A process in which workers lose control and autonomy over their work, either through the centralization of decision-making in management and new technologies, or the fragmentation of jobs into more simplified and directed tasks.

Habitus Relatively stable systems of dispositions, habits, or tastes that constitute the basis for how we understand the world.

Knowledge workers Workers, generally with high levels of skills and qualifications, who are engaged in the production, manipulation, and dissemination of knowledge, often involving extensive use of information and communication technologies.

Lifelong learning The notion that learning extends on a continuum from early childhood through adulthood, occurring in a variety of institutional and informal settings rather than being confined to formal learning within selected programs, institutions, and age cohorts.

New economy A term used to highlight the shift in emphasis from industrial production within specific industries, firms, and nations to economic activities driven by information and high-level technologies, global competition and international networks, and knowledge-based advancement.

Transitions The pathways that people follow from family life, into and out of education, and into various jobs or other social situations throughout their life course.

Underemployment A situation in which a person has educational credentials, skills, or other capacities that are not required for or used in her/his jobs.

Vocational education Education and training programs that lead to certificates or other credentials oriented to specific occupational requirements.

Study Questions

1. Critically discuss the argument that 'Education is failing in its primary purpose to provide the skills and training that individuals require for competitive performance in the new economy.'

2. Outline and explain the impact that changing job structures and labour market requirements have had on educational practices over the past century.

3. Discuss the extent to which education systems across Canada and other nations should or should not be harmonized with one another in order to provide job skills that are transferable from one setting to another.

4. Critics from various perspectives have suggested there is a strong mismatch between education and jobs. Critically compare and contrast the main competing orientations to this mismatch, indicating the extent to which each is supported by available evidence.

5. Outline and explain the degree of correlation between levels of education and levels of employment, income, and labour market success.

6. Debate exists over the question of whether work is becoming more highly skilled or workers are increasingly deskilled. Compare and contrast these positions with reference to research findings and recent trends related to work in Canada.

7

Educational Opportunity and Social Reproduction

Introduction

One of the primary themes in the sociological analysis of education is the assessment of contributions made by formal education both to social inequality and to socio-economic opportunity. This interest runs parallel to high social expectations about the value of schooling as a vehicle for social mobility. There is widespread faith in the ability of education to elevate living conditions and advance individual opportunities for all participants. International comparisons of social and economic development among nations, for instance, regard the general levels of education attained by a population as one of the most common indicators of the advancement of a society (UNESCO, 2002) in the same way that learners and their parents tend to regard schooling as a key determinant of an individual's future success.

While there is little question, in general terms, about the importance of the connection between education and socio-economic opportunity, the degree to which education has been able to contribute effectively to greater social equality has been subject to repeated challenge from different ends of the political spectrum. Compulsory education, along with social welfare, income and tax transfer programs, and other state policies devoted to minimize the impact of poverty and reduce social inequality in Canada, the United States, and other industrial democracies, has not eliminated pronounced gaps that separate the advantaged from disadvantaged segments of the population. Empirical evidence demonstrates that education on a global scale in many cases has had an uneven or ambiguous impact on development, although there continues to be high public confidence in education's ability to drive economic, political, and cultural development (Chabbott and Ramirez, 2000). This apparent failure has been accompanied by recurrent debates over the causes of social inequality and related demands for reforms in education and other social programs.

This chapter focuses on central debates and issues related to the relationship between formal education and social inequality. It addresses questions such as the following:

- Who benefits from education and what kinds of return do individuals and groups receive from their formal schooling?
- How much does formal education contribute to the reproduction or the eradication of social inequality?
- What are the limitations of education's ability to fulfill its promise of better social futures for individuals and social groups?
- What are the prospects that social and educational reform can overcome these limitations?

The Nature and Causes of Social Inequality in Canada

Canadians often pride themselves on the observation that their nation ranks ahead of most other nations on indicators that concern standards of living, quality of life, and relative equity among groups. Extreme gaps between the haves and have-nots are not nearly as visible as they are in most parts of the world, whether in developing or developed regions. Nonetheless, social inequality in Canada is prevalent along several dimensions. These include disparities in the possession of or access to income and wealth, political power, and ideological power (see, e.g., Curtis et al., 1999).

Regardless of which measure is considered, Canadian society is highly stratified according to inequalities of gender, race and ethnicity, class, region, age, and many other social factors (Bolaria, 2000). Women, who earn on average less than three-quarters of the average incomes of men, continue to be concentrated in subordinate roles in both the household and workplace (Armstrong and Armstrong, 2001: 66). People of Aboriginal ancestry and members of groups considered visible minorities frequently are marginalized and limited in their ability to gain access to important economic and political positions. While wealth is concentrated among a small core of individuals and firms, large disparities between the privileged and underprivileged are growing. Rice (2002: 117) observes that the new economy, in addition to perpetuating earlier divisions between 'good jobs and bad jobs', is also blocking social mobility, with the consequence 'that Canada will continue to develop two economies, one for the haves and one for the have-nots. Opportunities will flow to those who have the advantage of educated or well-off parents, while those with poor parents will have limited opportunities.' Households headed by young adults, lone parents, seniors, and Aboriginal peoples (especially among women in each of these groups) are much more likely than other households to be living in poverty, often for extended durations (National Council of Welfare, 2002).

The chances of finding secure employment, decent wages, and access to adequate living conditions and social support also vary according to where people live. Regional inequalities are acknowledged in government policies that distinguish between the 'have-not' provinces—notably in Atlantic Canada—that receive equalization payments from the federal government and the 'have' provinces (historically Ontario, and often Alberta and British Columbia). There are also significant inequalities within regions, frequently though not exclusively on a rural/urban and north/south basis. Historically, for instance, the sovereignist movement in Quebec originated out of contradictions, most evident in terms of disparities among anglophones and francophones, both within the province and between Quebec and the rest of Canada (Denis, 1995).

Several competing explanations for the persistence of inequalities like the ones outlined above are evident in both public policy debates and social analysis. Different theories of social inequality are not only linked with particular assumptions about how the world is organized, but they also carry distinct implications regarding prospects for social change. If we assume, for instance, that inequality is a necessary feature of human societies or that it is the product of individual characteristics, we may be inclined to believe that little can be done to alter existing social arrangements. By contrast, if we view inequality as the product of social factors, we are more likely to support social policies or government actions such as proposals for affirmative action or tax benefits for the poor. In fact, while various and wide-ranging theories attempt to explain inequality, the most common variants in these debates are positions that, on the one hand, emphasize individual or cultural factors and, on the other hand, stress social structural factors (Bolaria, 2000).

Individual explanations of inequality regard each person as responsible for his or her own success or failure. Disadvantage and poverty are viewed as consequences of low ambition, inadequate skills or abilities, or some other faulty personal characteristics, while those who succeed are considered more capable or talented, exercise personal drive and good judgement, and demonstrate good work habits. These capacities are seen to reside in either the biological or personality structures of individuals.

Social Darwinism, which was popular in the late nineteenth century, for example, promoted the view that individuals were sorted according to their abilities or 'fitness' to succeed. The notion of 'survival of the fittest' was introduced by sociologist Herbert Spencer (not Charles Darwin, as is often supposed) to indicate how social progress required a naturally competitive selection process to enable the strongest (i.e., those who could contribute the most to socially desirable outcomes) to succeed while the poor and weak should be left to fend for themselves (Ritzer, 2000: 32).

Although this view is highly controversial and has lost favour among most analysts, it continues to appear in various guises, particularly among the political right. In recent decades, widespread attention has been given to the view that intelligence is distributed and inherited unequally among the population, thereby accounting for higher rates of educational and socio-economic failure among visible minority populations such as blacks in the United States (Jensen, 1973; Herrnstein, 1973; Rushton and Bogaert, 1987). Herrnstein and Murray (1994) reignited controversy in the 1990s by arguing in *The Bell Curve* that because of a 'cognitive partitioning', through which the population comes to be subdivided into distinct intellectual categories, often on racial lines, it is not possible for everyone to benefit from education. They contend that only select groups should have access to higher education, while those with low IQs should not be expected to graduate from high school.

The views outlined above are among the most extreme examples of the individualist orientations to social inequality. They have been widely criticized on several accounts, including their failure to question faulty assumptions about how social characteristics like race, gender, and intelligence are defined and measured, problems with their methodologies and use of data, and their lack of attention to structural factors like social policy or legislation that restrict opportunities for particular groups (see, e.g., Fraser, 1995). Fischer et al. (1996: 18), observing the impact of social policies and other factors that perpetuate social inequality, state emphatically that 'It is not that low intelligence leads to inferior status; it is that inferior status leads to low intelligence test scores.' Nonetheless, this approach shares much in common with the widely held liberal assessment that social rewards are allocated on the basis of merit through competition among individuals. The relative success people have in attaining particular social or economic positions is therefore seen to be determined by ability, effort, and personal achievement. This analysis presupposes that social structures and institutions such as education are relatively open, accessible, and fair to all persons.

A variant of the individualist position is found in cultural theories of inequality, which argue that some cultures are more oriented than others to traits that are rewarded in advanced societies. According to this view, persons from modern cultures are better situated than those with a traditional value orientation to identify with goals and adopt characteristics that lead to social and economic success. Traditionalism, 'cultures of poverty', and lack of an achievement orientation are presented from this viewpoint as impediments to progress, thereby contributing to the subordination of the culture as a whole as well as the limitation of opportunities for individuals within those cultures (Hurst, 1992: 229–30).

Structural orientations to social inequality do not share the assumptions made by individual and cultural theories. A structural approach does not 'blame' individuals or their cultures for possessing deficits or failing to live up to the standards and expectations by which success is determined. Instead, inequality is regarded as a phenomenon that is socially produced and reproduced on at least two levels. First, structured inequalities permeate social systems and institutional processes. Second, social groups do not share equal

Box 7.1 Girls and basic education in Ghana

Schooling in many nations is constrained by significant barriers to participation, programming, and advancement. Stephens (2000: 46) summarizes issues and policy implications that arise in the education of girls in Ghana, demonstrating the combined impact of schooling and the environments in which schools operate:

Home

That home life for many schoolgirls is shaped by matters of kinship, descent and the extended family. The practice of fostering and the work expected of many girls has implications for the development of compulsory schooling.

That recognition be given to the cultural values inculcated in the child at home. Obedience and deference to elders, for example, will have implications for those keen to develop more child-centred teaching methods.

That the situation of rural girls be accorded particular attention, e.g., in the development of non-formal provision for girls working as domestic servants in urban homes.

Economy

That the concept of the 'girl child' be extended to include the 'girl child at risk'. It is clear that 'dropping out' is not an event but a process, and often involves very small amounts of money. The question of 'safety-net' provision at national and local level needs to accompany policies to increase participation in schooling.

That macroeconomic policies such as structural adjustment create an array of 'winners' and 'losers', particularly at the micro level of extended family. The encouragement of the free market has also led to a realization for many that being out of school is more profitable for their child than being in.

That in many poor homes the sole breadwinner is the girl child at school. Recognition of this needs to be accompanied by more flexible school timetabling and a reappraisal of vocational training.

School

That schools are still places where many children spend significant periods of time doing nothing and learning very little. Many of the cultural core values . . . translate into how the teacher behaves and how he or she expects the child to learn.

That little attention is paid to the 'culture of the classroom' where issues of attitude to knowledge, teaching methodology and language policy constrain efforts to implement reform.

That the life of the teacher is still very hard, with many perceiving their profession as low status. Improving the position of teacher requires not only better conditions of service but the development of professional practices within schools. Such a task falls to the head teacher well supported by district education offices.

Box 7.1 continued

Home	Economy	School
That attitudes towards the education of girls still raise questions of parental awareness of the benefits of schooling, the necessity of examining the support available for poor families to send girls to school, and the broader question of the amount and flexibility of schooling provided.	That the introduction of school fees has meant that 'success' is now a question of return on an investment. The 'culture of failure' in many schools with excessive and poorly administered assessment procedures can have major consequences for the underachieving child. That solutions to these problems lie in both the hands of policy-makers and in the creative way many girls and young teachers juggle the relationship between the world of school and the world of work.	That the experiences of the child in school be accorded more importance. The frequency of punishment, support in the learning of literacy and numeracy, and the existence of successful women teachers as role models for girls and boys are areas mentioned by many children. We need to listen to what the young people are telling us about their educational experiences and the solutions provided by them.

access to opportunities, positions, and rewards that accompany those systems and processes. Success and failure, in these regards, are determined by factors other than individual characteristics and efforts. The social system is organized in such a way as to define and produce failure in particular ways, which in turn creates advantages or disadvantages for some groups relative to others.

In Canada, numerous discriminatory policies at the federal, provincial, and municipal levels have restricted opportunities or prohibited access to services on the basis of race, gender, and other social characteristics. Historically, for instance, there have been policies to prohibit women and people of Asian ancestry from attending universities or registering in specific programs and to limit the length of time that registered Indians could attend public schooling. Similarly, lack of access to material resources has restricted the ability of members of socially disadvantaged groups to achieve success in important political, economic, and social spheres of activity.

Competing individual and structural explanations of inequality extend beyond academic analysis into social policy considerations. Various policy alternatives are organized around issues such as what role the state should play in regulating people's lives, providing human services, promoting personal incentive, and recognizing individual or collective rights. Over the past century, intense contestation over these questions frequently has accompanied the rise of—and subsequent efforts to reshape or dismantle—the welfare state.

Formal education is implicated in these debates because of its importance as a state-managed mechanism to transmit values and regulate credentials and access to highly valued social and economic positions. In these regards, concern has been mostly focused around the meaning and nature of educational opportunity. Lessard (1995: 178–9), citing Lévesque (1979), outlines three distinct meanings of the concept of educational opportunity—equality of access, equality of treatment, and equality of results, each of which corresponds with different political philosophies.

The first meaning, equality of access, refers to the notion that all individuals should be guaranteed little more than the opportunity to attend schools or other formal educational institutions. This view is associated with a conservative or a laissez-faire approach that emphasizes individual responsibility. The state's role is limited to assurances that schools and other vital public services are available to all citizens and that the rules governing these services are fairly applied. Beyond that, people should be expected to look out for their own welfare and be held accountable for their own success or failure. This ideological position, especially when it is combined with concern about government debt, has driven recent reforms to downsize the welfare state through funding and program cuts in education as well as in related areas such as social welfare, health care, and unemployment insurance.

The second concept, equality of treatment, corresponds with a liberal philosophical orientation that stresses that the state must take a more proactive role with respect to education and other social services. Consistent with cultural explanations of inequality, this view argues that persons from varying social backgrounds have distinct needs, interests, and characteristics that have to be taken into account in the planning, delivery, and evaluation of educational programs and services. It is not sufficient simply to 'bring people to the classroom door'; instead, the opportunities presented can only be taken advantage of when there are assurances that they are meaningful and relevant to the needs of learners and other clients.

The third approach to educational opportunity, which emphasizes equality of results, emerges from a critical or social democratic philosophy grounded in a structural explanation of inequality. In contrast with the first two orientations, this position demands an even greater sense of social responsibility on the part of both the state and the more privileged groups within society. People tend to be poor, unemployed, or socially disadvantaged not through any fault of their own but rather because the social system produces poverty, unemployment, and structural inequality as conditions of its ongoing existence. Individuals should not be blamed, for instance, for being born into poor families or for living in communities in which factories close down or fisheries are jeopardized. Therefore, a proactive approach is required to ensure that all members of a population have access to a wide range of educational and social services and programs to guarantee them at least minimum standards of living and opportunities for success.

The politics of education in Canada, often parallel to the development of the welfare state, have been characterized by struggles over the extent to which educational opportunity should be guaranteed and extended by the state. The introduction of mass public schooling in the nineteenth century was itself supported by arguments that all children, regardless of class or social background, should have access to common educational experiences. State-supported schooling ensured that children would be able to attend school even if their parents could not afford to pay tuition costs. Compulsory attendance legislation from the late nineteenth and early twentieth centuries, and later enforcement of truancy regulations to ensure that children were actually in the classroom, expanded the state's role beyond simple assurances that all children had access to schooling. Opposition to these initiatives was countered by arguments that schooling was necessary for the public good and that its domain superseded the interests of any particular individuals or groups. Until recently, the status of education—as one of a limited number of universal social programs available on an open, affordable, and accessible basis to all eligible Canadian residents—has been relatively unchallenged (Rice and Prince, 2000: 169).

The justification of schooling as a resource for the common good has been the basis of repeated attempts (not all of which have been successful) to introduce, modify, or delete particular curricula, programs, and services because they were targeted at other than the general clientele of the public school system. Over the years, courses in areas such as physical education, family life, citizenship education, multicultural studies, Aboriginal studies, computer and technological education, and anti-racism education have been added to curricula. Schools have come to take on diverse new roles, including counselling, public health, and other social services. At the same time, education systems remain vulnerable to lobbying to remove curricula, programs, personnel, or materials deemed too costly, unnecessary, or offensive to certain groups.

Debates over the ability of formal schooling to provide conditions for equality of opportunity must take into consideration the ideological nature of claims about the 'common good'. Such claims typically are made on the basis of interests expressed in accordance with the requirements or demands of particular social constituencies, posed in such a way as to represent the general interest. In the most general terms, for instance, there is likely to be widespread agreement with the idea that schools should teach literacy and mathematical and social skills, among other things. However, the kinds of curricula, teaching approaches, learning materials, and modes of evaluation that are used in the teaching of these areas, and how these are combined with other aspects of the schooling process, involve choices to be made from a range of alternatives. In this way, what is taught, how it is transmitted, and what is conveyed to the learner are rarely universally representative but, instead, are reflections of inequalities and power arrangements that operate both within the education system and through the wider society.

The issue of educational equality also raises questions about the extent to which all students should be subjected to identical educational experiences. The argument that it is sufficient for schools to present a common curriculum to all students places the onus on students, regardless of their social backgrounds, to compete with one another on the basis of universal standards. School programs that provide for integration or mainstreaming of children who come from families that do not speak the language of instruction or of physically or mentally disabled students, for instance, are founded on notions that equate equality with 'sameness' of treatment. An alternative position recognizes that different groups have distinct needs to which education must respond. Curricula and teaching methods that fail to take social differences into account are disadvantageous to minority students. 'Anti-racism education' is based on the view that educators must incorporate into educational processes both acceptance and understanding of racial diversity and pedagogical strategies to combat systemic oppression (Dei, 1996). Similarly, feminist pedagogy emphasizes that gender disparities are reinforced when educators fail to recognize how male and female students have different social experiences that translate into different learning styles.

Current debates over social and educational inequality are shaped by conflicting demands from various interests and perspectives. Governments in several nations, including Canada and its provinces and territories, have been increasingly responsive to neo-liberal and individualist arguments that the state should not, and cannot afford to, offer too broad a range of programs and services in public enterprises like education when these are targeted to the needs of what have come to be defined as 'special interests'. Affirmative action, education equity, inclusive curricula, multicultural education, English as a second language (ESL), and arts and music programs are some of the areas singled out by such critics as 'frills' that are costly, socially divisive, and counterproductive to educational needs in a highly competitive economic environment. Members of minority groups and other people most affected by lack of access to meaningful social and economic opportunity, by contrast, have become increasingly more vocal about their rights and entitlements. These concerns are frequently raised as a consequence of experiences of continuing discrimination and obstacles to the fulfillment of equity objectives. Cutbacks in programs and state services designed to enhance educational and economic opportunities have placed the least privileged segments of the population in an even more vulnerable position when they cannot gain access to the programs and resources required for competitive success.

Differing interpretations of the meaning of educational opportunity and inequality are also associated with differences in how educational opportunity is assessed or measured. The remainder of this chapter will focus on the most common determinants of inequality, addressing such factors as educational attainment, participation rates of different social groups, and relationships among education and income, labour force participation, and other relevant measures.

Before these indicators are examined, however, it is important to emphasize that educational success or failure cannot be understood only in quantitative terms. Acknowledgement must be given to the human and social dimensions that contribute to differing educational experiences and outcomes. Education is not an abstract process but a composite of lived practices that have real consequences for people's lives and futures. As emphasized earlier in this book (Chapter 4), schooling is characterized by a complex array of day-to-day occurrences in educational settings that intersect with external demands and structures. Success and failure come to take on differing interpretations just as they are produced through the interaction between personal experiences and social structural forces. For instance, we tend to place the greatest social and economic value on the attainment of a university degree, yet the completion of a high school diploma may be a major accomplishment for a person who has returned to school much later in life after being forced in youth to work to support a family following an interruption such as the death of a parent or an unplanned teen pregnancy. Similarly, a mid-range grade may be viewed as a failure by a student whose parents expect nothing less than performance that will lead to admission to an elite university, but the same grade may be a triumph for a student designated by school officials as 'at risk' or another for whom English is a second language.

The Assembly of First Nations (1988: 72) points out that notions of educational quality from which measures of success and failure are derived are culturally laden, and emphasizes that educational success from a First Nations perspective should be based on the following goals: '(1) education should prepare children to gain the necessary skills for successful living and to contribute to community and (2) education should reinforce the student's cultural identity.' Educational opportunity and performance, viewed this way, situate educational practices and student experience in an overall social context; they are not merely objects to be measured in quantitative terms. Regardless of how they are defined or interpreted, they have a material and psychological impact on people's lives.

Dimensions of Educational Inequality

This section examines the most prevalent indicators associated with educational inequality, taking into account that schooling and its outcomes cannot fully be understood in isolation from the social practices that constitute or contribute to school life. The discussion highlights questions about who is enrolled in educational programs, what the characteristics are of students who enrol in and graduate from particular programs, and what the benefits of formal education are for people from particular social backgrounds.

The question of who goes to school can be answered simply, at least in general terms. Almost every Canadian, with the exception of the very youngest and most elderly, is engaged in some educational activity on a regular basis. Nearly one-fifth of the total population is enrolled in full-time formal educational programs. About 19 out of 20 children aged 6 to 16 attend school on a full-time basis. Among young adults in the 20–4 age group about 40 per cent enrolled in full-time educational programs and an additional 8 per cent engaged in some formal schooling in 2000–1. In addition, close to 350,000 adults attend post-secondary educational programs on a part-time basis, about one-quarter of employed adults participate in job-related adult education and training programs, substantial proportions of the adult population are involved in other non-formal educational programs out of general interest or for personal reasons, and at least three-quarters of Canadians regularly engage in informal learning activities (Statistics Canada, 2001a: 30–3; 94–108; Statistics Canada and Human Resources Development Canada, 2001: 18; Statistics Canada, 2003e: 14; Livingstone, 1999: 36–7).

The compositions of school-age populations and student bodies have undergone significant transformations. Immigration has contributed significantly to the linguistic, racial, and cultural mix in Canadian schools, especially in the largest metropolitan centres. In Toronto and Vancouver, for example, 17 per cent of school-age children in 2001 had immigrated to Canada over the previous 10-year period. Immigrants arrive from diverse places and backgrounds; over half of recent arrivals were born in Asia, and between two-fifths to two-thirds of school-age immigrants speak languages other than English or French at home (Statistics Canada, 2003b: 8–9). Aboriginal people are also becoming more concentrated among school-age populations, especially in the Prairie provinces and northern regions. Aboriginal people represent about 3.3 per cent of the Canadian population, but the proportion rises to 5.6 per cent among children aged 14 and under, including about one-quarter of children in Manitoba and Saskatchewan (Statistics Canada, 2003a: 7–8). In addition to racial, cultural, and linguistic diversity, schooling incorporates large proportions of students who encounter various social, economic, and physical challenges. About one in five Canadian children lives in a low-income household, and about one in four children who was under the age of eleven in 1997 exhibits one or more learning or behavioural problems (National Council of Welfare, 2002: 7; Willms, 2002: 54; Zeesman, 2001: 5). Whereas children with special needs were previously segregated into specialized classrooms or excluded from schools, by the mid-1990s nearly 60 per cent of students who received special education for learning disabilities, emotional and behavioural problems, speech impairment, intellectual or physical disabilities, or other problems were integrated into regular classrooms for most of their instruction and school-related activities (Bohatyretz and Lipps, 1999: 9). Parallel trends in the growth of student diversity are exhibited, in many cases, within post-secondary and adult training institutions.

Educators and educational institutions face a significant challenge to balance student diversity, through strategies that promote integration and inclusion, with external demands for differentiated social and economic outcomes. The sections below highlight the persistence of major discrepancies in educational participation, performance, and outcomes, concentrating on dimensions of educational inequality associated with gender, racial and ethnic minorities, Aboriginal peoples, social class, and region.

Gender

Gender-based inequalities are less evident within enrolment patterns than in terms of what happens within educational processes. Because almost all children attend school, there are no significant gender differentiations in enrolments at the elementary and secondary levels. Long-standing gender inequities in post-secondary enrolments have shifted. Overall, proportionately more men than women were enrolled in post-secondary programs until the mid-1980s, after which time the number of women has exceeded the number of men. For example, the ratio of female to male full-time undergraduate university students was 0.8 to 1 in 1977, but by the end of the 1990s this ratio had climbed to nearly 1.3 to 1. Women's participation rates are even higher when part-time students are taken into account. The only level at which men have continued to outnumber women has been in full-time graduate studies, where the proportion of women was 32 per cent in 1977, but even at this level the proportion of women (48.3 per cent) was close to equity by the end of the twentieth century (Canadian Education Statistics Council, 1996: 123; Statistics Canada, 2001a: 54). Some critics, such as Hoff Summers (2000), view these kinds of trends as evidence that schools, influenced by feminism, have contributed to ideologies and practices that produce disadvantage for males. The evidence, however, points to a much more complex picture.

Gender emerges as a significant factor when areas or programs of study are examined. Women's increased overall educational participation has been characterized by growing proportions of women in nearly every field of study, as the data in Table 7.1 indicate. Since the early 1980s, women have predominated numerically in several areas, while approximate gender parity has been reached in such traditionally male-dominated fields as agriculture and medical studies. Despite women's increased educational participation and attainment, however, the data indicate the continuing existence of considerable gender segmentation. Women constitute at least three-quarters of the students enrolled in fields such as nursing, education, secretarial science, household science (home economics), and social work programs, all of which lead to jobs traditionally regarded as 'women's work', while two-thirds or more of students in areas such as physical sciences, engineering and applied sciences, computer science, and mathematics are men (Statistics Canada, 2001a: 60–5).

Table 7.1

Full-time Enrolment in University Undergraduate Programs and Career Programs of Community Colleges by Fields of Study and Gender, Selected Years

Field of study	1982–3				1992–3				1998–1999			
	Male	Female	Total	Female as % of total	Male	Female	Total	Female as % of total	Male	Female	Total	Female as % of total
UNIVERSITY UNDERGRADUATE												
Agriculture and biological science (total)	9,488	10,895	20,383	53.5	13,306	19,139	32,445	59.0	13,976	24,514	38,490	63.7
Agriculture	2,895	1,715	4,610	37.2	1,871	1,690	3,561	47.5	1,981	2,512	4,493	55.9
Biology	4,423	4,227	8,650	48.9	8,109	10,433	18,542	56.3	8,580	14,289	22,869	62.5
Household science	120	3,157	3,277	96.3	371	3,632	4,003	90.1	246	3,145	3,391	92.7
Other	2,050	1,796	3,846	46.7	2,955	3,384	6,339	53.4	370	927	1,297	71.5
Education (total)	12,104	26,174	38,278	68.4	18,285	36,700	54,985	66.7	15,736	38,487	54,223	71.0
Education	6,704	20,021	26,726	74.9	9,908	28,776	38,684	74.3	8,159	27,678	35,837	77.2
Physical Education	5,400	6,153	11,553	53.3	8,377	7,924	16,301	48.6	7,577	10,809	18,386	58.8
Engineering and applied science	37,285	4,686	41,971	11.2	37,003	8,397	45,400	18.5	37,745	10,720	48,465	22.1
Fine and applied arts	4,982	8,052	13,034	61.8	6,293	10,439	16,732	62.4	6,489	11,902	18,391	64.7
Health professions (total)	8,188	14,834	23,022	64.4	8,754	18,373	27,127	67.7	7,693	19,637	27,330	71.9
Dental studies and research	1,523	476	1,999	23.8	985	700	1,685	41.5	953	857	1,810	47.3
Medical studies and research	4,997	3,333	8,330	40.0	4,527	3,958	8,485	46.6	3,454	3,779	7,233	52.2
Nursing	177	6,409	6,586	97.3	566	7,241	7,807	92.8	815	8,068	8,883	90.8
Pharmacy	919	1,739	2,658	65.4	1,280	1,980	3,260	60.7	1,052	2,182	3,234	67.5
Rehabilitative medicine	261	2,189	2,450	89.3	688	3,340	4,028	82.9	753	3,171	3,924	80.8
Other	311	688	999	68.9	708	1,154	1,862	62.0	666	1,580	2,246	70.3
Humanities	10,336	14,519	24,855	58.4	20,410	32,118	52,528	61.1	16,875	27,987	44,862	62.4
Mathematics and physical sciences	19,460	7,516	26,976	27.9	19,232	8,205	27,437	29.9	22,049	9,547	31,596	30.2
Social sciences	55,917	48,289	104,206	46.3	71,767	85,807	157,574	54.5	63,167	87,598	150,765	58.1
Arts/science (general)	35,076	34,833	69,909	49.8	27,617	36,193	63,810	56.7	27,265	39,792	67,057	59.3
Not reported	7,294	6,286	13,580	46.3	8,603	10,601	19,204	55.2	8,824	10,948	19,772	55.4
Total	200,130	176,084	376,214	46.8	231,270	265,972	497,242	53.5	219,819	281,132	500,951	56.1

(continued)

Table 7.1
(continued)

Field of study	1982–3				1992–3				1998–9			
	Male	Female	Total	Female as % of total	Male	Female	Total	Female as % of total	Male	Female	Total	Female as % of total
CAREER PROGRAMS OF COMMUNITY COLLEGES												
Arts	7,624	9,505	17,129	55.5	10,175	12,929	23,104	56.0	13,012	16,901	29,913	56.5
Arts and science	831	1,102	1,933	57.0	3,215	3,739	6,954	53.8	3,290	4,030	7,320	55.1
Business and commerce (total)	21,684	37,466	59,150	63.3	27,093	41,616	68,709	60.6	32,298	49,331	81,629	60.4
Management and administration	18,455	20,527	38,982	52.7	22,379	24,214	46,593	52.0	25,331	32,037	57,368	55.8
Merchandising and sales	2,427	2,927	5,354	54.7	3,294	3,147	6,441	48.9	3,691	4,326	8,017	54.0
Secretarial science	73	13,119	13,192	99.4	640	13,411	14,051	95.4	764	9,977	10,741	92.9
Service industry technologies	729	893	1,622	55.1	780	844	1,624	52.0	1,920	2,225	4,145	53.7
Engineering and applied sciences	48,659	11,464	60,123	19.1	51,706	9,988	61,694	16.2	66,558	15,271	81,829	18.7
Health sciences (total)	3,843	27,036	30,879	87.6	6,177	29,290	35,467	82.5	4,643	22,707	27,350	83.0
Health-related technologies	2,324	6,625	8,949	74.0	3,264	8,101	11,365	71.3	2,737	10,254	12,991	78.9
Nursing	1,519	20,411	21,930	93.1	2,913	21,189	24,102	87.9	1,651	11,364	13,015	87.3
Humanities	700	1,936	2,636	73.4	1,072	2,281	3,353	68.0	1,118	2,306	3,424	67.3
Natural sciences and primary industries	7,811	3,043	10,854	28.0	7,718	3,685	11,403	32.3	9,064	7,160	16,224	44.1
Social sciences and services	6,873	17,687	24,560	72.0	12,913	28,824	41,737	69.1	12,718	37,658	50,376	74.8
Educational and counselling services	841	6,159	7,000	88.0	1,187	10,236	11,423	89.6	784	8,948	9,732	91.9
Protection and corrections services	3,513	2,139	5,652	37.8	7,426	4,764	12,190	39.1	6,962	7,278	14,240	51.1
Social services	968	5,061	6,029	83.9	1,654	8,963	10,617	84.4	1,855	13,534	15,389	87.9
Other	1,551	4,328	5,879	73.6	2,646	4,861	7,507	64.8	2,774	6,219	8,993	69.1
Not reported	237	150	387	38.8	231	169	400	42.3	344	489	833	58.7
Total	98,262	109,389	207,651	52.7	120,300	132,521	252,821	52.4	143,190	155,708	298,898	52.1

Source: Statistics Canada, *Education in Canada* (Ottawa: Minister of Supply and Services Canada, various years).

There is also a high degree of gender segmentation within general programming areas. In community college programs in social sciences and services, for instance, in which three of every four students are women, women are distributed across a number of different programs while over half (about 55 per cent) of the men are concentrated in protection and correction services. In university programs in education-related studies, nearly half of the men, compared to just over one-quarter of the women, are enrolled in physical education studies, while among students enrolled in the health profession areas, over half (57.3 per cent) of the men compared to less than one-quarter (23.6 per cent) of the women are engaged in medical or dental studies and research (Statistics Canada, 2001a: 61–3). These trends carry through to graduation, which provides a more precise indicator of specified fields of study. Consistent with enrolment trends, substantially more women than men received undergraduate university degrees in 1998–9 in all disciplinary areas except for mathematics and physical sciences and engineering and applied sciences (Statistics Canada, 2001a: 140–6). There is only limited evidence that the emergence of what is often called the new economy, with its emphasis on innovation, changing business opportunities, and information technology, is contributing to some convergence in fields of study. Degrees and diplomas in fields associated with business and commerce were among the highest growth areas of post-secondary studies for both men and women during the 1990s. However, growth rates were much higher for men than for women in computer and engineering-related fields, creating possibilities that the gender divides in these areas may widen rather than narrow (Statistics Canada, 2003e: 12–13).

The literature on educational processes reveals considerable further evidence of gender segmentation within educational programs. Gaskell (1992) argues that differentiation according to gender—along with class and race—occurs both through streaming and in the different signals and messages transmitted within the educational experience. Often these signals contribute to the production of distinct educational paths or careers for male and female students. Bernhard and Nyhof-Young (1994) discuss how preconceptions held by parents and peers, an absence of female role models, distorted media representations, inadequate curricular materials, teacher biases, and insufficient school support are responsible for the low rates of participation by women in post-secondary education and subsequent careers in mathematics, science, and technology. Female students also perceive signals from teachers, in the form of comments or attitudes, to channel them into gender-segregated occupational tracks (Crysdale et al., 1999: 33). The absence of female teachers, or the clustering of female teachers in selected areas, in senior grades and post-secondary studies contributes to a lack of role models in the classroom and a potentially limited capacity for consideration of issues of critical importance to female learners. Eyre (1991), drawing on her observations of students in a grade 8 home economics class in British Columbia, demonstrates how gender segregation and stereotyping are reproduced through the experiences and interactions among boys and girls even within a single coeducational classroom. Sometimes, even efforts meant to alleviate gender inequity can have the opposite impact. Kenway and Willis (1998: 208–9) point to a 'gender/generation gap' through which some teachers maintain outdated notions of gender that do not take into account significant changes in students' lives and identities. Relatively systematic messages can be conveyed as a student's social experiences come to be shaped through interactions with parents, peers, teachers, and other people in such a way as to produce distinctive trends and patterns based on gender (Mandell and Crysdale, 1993). Moss and Attar (1999: 143) observe that efforts by schools to ensure gender neutrality in the adoption and presentation of books and reading materials may be offset by the strongly gender-specific messages students receive through popular media and books read outside of school.

Thus, while school-age youth perceive a general movement towards gender equality in contemporary society, there is an uneasy sense about unfair treatment and discrimination. The results of a survey and discussion groups involving students in grades 6–12, sponsored by the Canadian Teachers' Federation (1991: 17–18), illustrate these trends. While 91 per cent of the girls surveyed agreed or strongly agreed with the statement that 'I think women today have just as good a chance of making it in the world as men', nearly all of them revealed that they had experienced some unfairness relative to boys in such areas as sports, sexuality, and personal freedom, and many indicated that they had experienced a strong 'anti-female bias in general'. Similarly, adolescent girls are considerably more likely than their male counterparts to hold negative views about themselves and to express lack of confidence about their appearance and capabilities (Bibby, 2001: 40; King et al., 1999: 44–50).

The differential educational experiences of males and females contribute to the reproduction of important inequalities beyond the classroom. Figure 7.1 illustrates one aspect of this in the form of relations between education and income. For both men and women, average earnings increase for each subsequent level of educational attainment, but women's earnings are lower than those of men at every level. The data show that the gender gap in earnings generally decreases as education increases, with women periodically having the advantage at the doctoral level. However, relatively few women possess doctoral degrees, in part as a consequence of gender-biased channelling in earlier years of education. These trends point to the importance of understanding the intersection of family, labour market, and educational factors.

Processes that contribute to gender segregation in education also operate in a similar manner, and reinforce one another, in the spheres of work and family life. Domestic responsibilities, orientations to marriage and family, and personal experiences, among other factors, affect educational attainment and employment and career prospects (see, e.g., Wilson, 1996). The actual or projected interruption of an education program or career due to pregnancy or family considerations, for instance, normally affects women's lives and

Figure 7.1
Mean Earnings of Post-Secondary Graduates (in 1995 constant dollars)

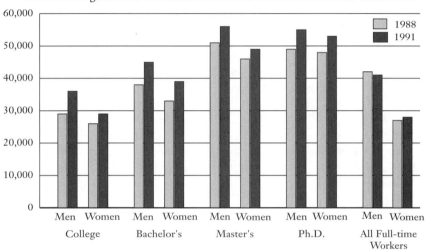

Mean Earnings of 1986 Graduates Two Years and Five Years after Graduation

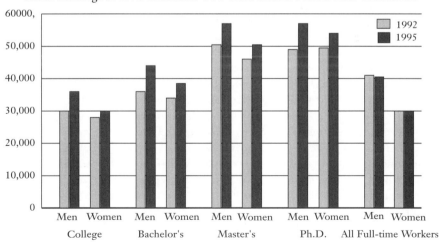

Mean Earnings of 1990 Graduates Two Years and Five Years after Graduation

Source: Data from Finnie (2000: 29, 34).

opportunities more than it does those of men. At the same time, many women have experienced benefits through access to education, both personally and in terms of their ability to acquire better-paying, more secure jobs. The enrolment and graduation trends outlined earlier suggest that education will continue to be an important basis through which women can gain entry into non-traditional positions and occupations that will contribute to greater gender parity in terms of labour force participation, wages, and other benefits.

Nonetheless, there are limitations to potential advances in these areas produced by internal labour market dynamics and persistent gender discrimination, as well as more general economic restructuring of the kind discussed in Chapter 6 that creates pressure to downsize the labour force, deskill workers, and minimize labour costs. Even when formal education has worked to the initial advantage of women who obtain relatively high-status jobs, women continue to be disadvantaged compared to men over the course of their entire careers (Boyd, 1985). Overall, despite improvements in women's educational attainment and benefits, the evidence demonstrates that gender inequalities still exist with respect to the kinds of educational credentials people receive and in the connections between education and subsequent life circumstances.

Racial and Ethnic Minorities

There are strong parallels between issues of gender and of racial and ethnic inequality in education. Evidence suggests that the expansion of educational opportunities, especially since World War II, has been beneficial for racial and ethnic minorities. However, there are important differences in the educational experiences and achievements among various racial and ethnic groups. In his landmark study of social stratification in Canada, Porter (1965) stressed that barriers to equitable educational participation have contributed to the inability of minority ethnic groups to attain proportional representation in positions of power and privilege, thereby undermining the claim that our social system is fully meritocratic and democratic. Today, although Porter's argument has been challenged and reassessed by many researchers, many of those inequalities remain. In terms of overall or average educational achievement, persons of Aboriginal ancestry (discussed more fully in the next section) have significantly lower overall rates of educational attainment and are much less likely to attend and complete post-secondary studies than other Canadians. Among other people within the adult population and in the labour force, those of Jewish and Chinese origin have the highest average years of schooling and are most likely to have a university degree. Particularly among the foreign-born, those from southern European origins tend to have the lowest levels of formal education (Li, 1988: 79–81). These patterns remained relatively enduring throughout much of the twentieth century, but there is evidence that visible minorities—especially persons from Asia—as well as southern and eastern European groups, have experienced considerable gains in their average educational attainment over the last four decades (Forcese, 1997: 116; Guppy and Davies, 1998: 23).

To a certain extent, the modified reproduction of racial and ethnic inequality can be explained by immigration policies and practices that since the late 1960s have placed increasing emphasis on the selective recruit- ment of highly qualified labour. Slightly more than half (52 per cent) of

Box 7.2 Guidelines to ensure a safe and caring environment for students

These guidelines from the Canadian Race Relations Foundation (2000: 5) are intended to help school administrators know whether their school is 'proactive' or 'reactive':

Have you ensured that . . .
• Your school has a safe and caring environment where all students are treated with care and treat each other with respect;
• Your students are aware of the school's code of conduct and that in case of misbehaviour, all students involved receive a fair hear- ing and are treated fairly and equitably;
• All your students can identify with the curriculum, are expected to succeed and are given the support to develop their individual academic competencies;
• You make all your students feel respected and dignified by deal- ing with incidents such as name-calling, racial slurs and jokes and graffiti seriously;
• Your personnel have been trained to identify and a proportion of funds has been allocated towards purchasing non-discriminatory supplementary materials;
• You have encouraged extracurricular activities where students can explore their cultural heritage and backgrounds and individ- ual differences;
• Your supervisors and curriculum developers have been directed to develop resources and materials for assisting classroom teach- ers in reducing the impact of biased materials;
• Your students have been taught positive social skills such as responsibility, problem-solving skills and respect;
• In your school, students, community members, parents and staff are involved in the writing, implementation and reviewing of your policies and guidelines;
• Your teachers have received appropriate support and in-service training to implement these policies and guidelines;
• Your school feels welcoming, inviting, and secure for all.

immigrants aged 25–64 who arrived in Canada during the 1970s and 1980s had high school or less (between 55 and 75 per cent of the general population in these age cohorts had high school or less over the same period). Among persons who immigrated to Canada during the 1990s, all but 39 per cent (compared to 46.6 per cent of the general working-age population in 2001) had attained university degrees or other certification beyond high school (Statistics Canada, 2003e: 29, 42). Recent trends demonstrate even further growth in the numbers of highly qualified immigrants, as well as higher than average participation rates in continuing education. The 1991 census revealed that 14 per cent of immigrants, compared to only 11 per cent of Canadian-born persons aged 15 and older, had a university degree. Subsequently, over two out of five (40.7 per cent) persons aged 25–64 who immigrated to Canada between the census periods of 1991 and 2001 had a university degree—nearly double the proportion of the general population in that age range (22.6 per cent) who held a degree in 2001 (Statistics Canada, 2003e: 29, 42).

The relationship among race and ethnicity, immigration, and education and the economic benefits associated with education are considerably more complex than these general trends reveal, indicating substantial variations according to class, gender, race, and other significant characteristics. Immigrants, in part due to the credentials and capacities that they bring with them, perform relatively well overall on many economic criteria. Among persons entering the labour force, immigrants tend to have higher-level jobs than those born in Canada, reflecting higher educational attainment. However, some immigrant groups—such as those of Chinese, South Asian, Filipino, West Asian, and Arab origins—are more likely than other Canadians to hold a university degree, while others, including black and Latin American men, are less likely to have a degree, and higher than average proportions of women from Southeast Asia and South Asia have less than high school. Similarly, various immigrant and visible minority groups are clustered at both professional, high-skill and (especially among visible minority women) lower-status occupational positions (Pendakur, 2000: 151–6; Guppy and Davies, 1998: 122–3). Immigrants, especially women and visible minorities, encounter selective barriers that restrict the recognition they are granted for foreign credentials, which in turn affects their prospects for occupational mobility. However, these immigrants have much greater occupational mobility than those immigrants (including women) who begin in a relatively strong employment position yet have almost no career mobility (Creese et al., 1991: 72–3; Li, 2003: 122–3). Reitz (2001), observing considerable variations both between immigrants and non-immigrants and among different immigrant groups, demonstrates that immigrants receive lower returns on both education and work experience than do persons born in Canada. Similarly, Kazemipur and Halli (2001: 234) find that while education had an impact on alleviating poverty within the general population between 1991 and 1996, that relationship did not hold for immigrants, especially those who were in visible minority groups.

Two prevalent themes emerge in the literature on race, ethnicity, and Canadian schooling. (1) Race—and, to a certain extent, ethnicity—does have an impact on people's educational experiences and social opportunities. (2) Ethnicity and race cannot be understood in isolation from social class, gender, and other important social characteristics. Several researchers have emphasized the changing nature of race and ethnic relations in Canada, documenting the ways in which family, work, schooling, and other institutional environments interact to produce continual modifications and tensions among ethnic identity, ethnic group cohesion, and diverse cultural adaptations (Fleras and Elliott, 2003). McLaren (1998: 202), observing children of West Indian origin in a North York school, notes that underprivileged black students engage in forms of resistance in opposition to dominant school and social expectations if they see that they must attempt to deny their 'blackness' to succeed. James (1993), examining the school-to-work transition process for black youth in Toronto, stresses that, while respondents he interviewed tended to assume individual responsibility for their own success or failure, their lives and self-concepts were continually affected by racist stereotypes and structures prevalent both within and beyond schooling. Visible minority and Aboriginal students, though receptive to the substantial opportunities for equity and participation afforded by schooling, remain keenly aware of the many manifestations that they and other students encounter of racism and discrimination (Bibby, 2001: 42–3; James, 2003: 131–64; Schissel and Wotherspoon, 2003: 82–3).

Much as with gender and class, with which they interact, racial and ethnic factors enter into the complex web of social arrangements in such a way as to produce differential experiences and career and educational futures for students of distinct social origins. Jackson (1987: 181) refers to these school practices, as they come into existence through the choices and actions of students and teachers, as 'differentiating practices' that emerge:

> as practical organizational solutions to the conflicts and contradictions which both school life and the labour market pose for ethnic minority students. Both the student and the educator may feel justified with their choice of practical solutions, particularly if the student experiences success in his/her courses in the short run. However, this is to disregard the 'hidden injury' of long-term educational disadvantage.

The federal government's policy of multiculturalism, in effect since the early 1970s, stands as an important institutional response to the reality of and problems associated with racial and ethnic diversity in Canada. Multiculturalism provides a good example of how state policy has shifted over time in conjunction with differing social realities and conceptions of equality. McAndrew (1995: 165) points out that multiculturalism signifies the state's response to the 'pluralist dilemma in education' whereby divergent social interests express 'conflicting visions of the role that school plays in either reproducing or transforming ethnic/religious/racial inequalities'.

Multiculturalism is intended to foster tolerance and understanding for the broad mosaic of cultural groups within Canadian society. At the same time, it represents the state's interest in perpetuating a common national purpose. In the area of education, in particular, as Fleras and Elliott (1992: 183–5) emphasize, multiculturalism signifies a pronounced change, in jurisdictions outside Quebec, from a preoccupation with integration and assimilation in compliance with English-speaking, white standards of conformity to official recognition of pluralism and diversity, encompassing among its objectives the desire:

> (a) to diminish the ethnic 'problem'; (b) to eliminate discrimination and promote intergroup harmony; (c) to foster genuine equality and justice for ethnic minorities; and (d) to improve intercultural sharing, understanding, and communication.

In education, multiculturalism has been implemented in various ways across Canada, including such measures as heritage language instruction, the development of curricula to represent diverse cultural traditions, cross-cultural training for educational workers and administrators, and the provision of specific services or opportunities for minority students. The uniqueness of multicultural educational policy and initiatives in each province or region reflects both the fact that education is a provincial responsibility and the reality whereby each jurisdiction has its own distinctive cultural composition and political climate (McAndrew, 1995: 170–4). In general terms, multicultural policy has changed in emphasis since the mid-1980s from an initial concern with cultural understanding and tolerance of racial or ethnic differences towards a more active orientation on race relations, equity issues, and institutional change (Fleras and Elliott, 1992: 68–9). Canadian schools in general have clearly become more sensitive to issues involving cultural diversity and minority learners, although it is difficult to determine how much of this, rather than being the result of the impact of multicultural policies and practices, is due to the reality that many communities are much more racially heterogeneous than they were two or three decades ago.

With respect to anti-racism education, Henry et al. (2000: 233–4) note that, despite several prominent policy statements and initiatives concerned with the eradication of racial bias and discrimination through education, racism continues to be a problem both within schools and in the communities in which they operate. Even programs like ESL, for instance, which are intended to provide training directed to the special needs of students who lack language or social skills essential for success in mainstream classrooms, can marginalize and stigmatize minority children. Rockhill and Tomic (1995: 222) observe that 'The segregation of children into special classes for ESL instruction further marks their difference from the other students. When this is coupled with being seen as having a problem, a deficiency or lack, feelings of deviance and shame are reinforced.' Multicultural and related programs, in these regards, act in a contradictory way, fostering tolerance of diversity and generating opportunities for minority groups, yet at the same time representing state efforts to manage race and ethnic relations as ongoing problems without providing assurances of full equality for all groups (Wotherspoon, 1995b).

Aboriginal Peoples

Aboriginal peoples, in general, are the most disadvantaged in Canadian society in terms of educational attainment, employment circumstances, poverty and social conditions, health status, and many other indicators, despite substantial improvements that have been achieved through many promising recent initiatives. Fewer than 17 out of 20 registered Indians aged 6–16 living on-reserve are enrolled in full-time schooling (83.4 per cent in 2000–1) compared with more than 19 out of 20 persons of comparable ages in the general population. Disparities in educational participation rates are even more pronounced at the post-secondary level. In the late 1990s, for instance, only 6.6 per cent of the registered Indian population aged 17–34, compared with 11.4 per cent of the general population in the same age cohort, were enrolled in full-time university studies (Indian and Northern Affairs Canada, 2002: 31, 36). Similar inequalities are evident in patterns of educational attainment.

Data from the 2001 census reveal that, among those aged 25–64 who were not attending school full-time, about two out of five persons of Aboriginal ancestry (38.7 per cent), compared with fewer than one-third of the general population (29.0 per cent), had high school or less, while only 7.8 per cent of the Aboriginal population as opposed to 20.2 per cent of the general population had a university degree. Table 7.2, with more detailed 2001 data, indicates, as well, important differences in educational patterns within Aboriginal populations, suggesting that we must be cautious not to overgeneralize the circumstances that pertain for any social group. Educational attainment is lowest among the Inuit and among registered Indians living on-reserve (close to two-thirds of whom have no more than high school and about 3–4 per cent have a university degree), while slightly more than half of registered Indians living off-reserve have grade 12 or less and about 7 per cent of Métis and off-reserve Indians have university degrees.

Several factors have contributed to the under-representation and under-achievement of Aboriginal peoples in Canadian schooling. As noted earlier, schooling was an important instrument both in the early colonization of indigenous peoples by Europeans and in subsequent efforts by the Canadian state to assimilate or acculturate Indians within a dominant framework often marked by racism and hostility towards Aboriginals and their cultures. As was the case for other visible minorities until well after World War II, First

Table 7.2
Education by Highest Level of Schooling Completed, Ages 15 and Over,
Aboriginal Peoples, Visible Minorities, and Total Canadian Population, 2001*

Highest Level of Education	Total Population	Visible Minorities	Total Aboriginal Ancestry	Métis single response	Inuit single response	North American Indian single response	On-reserve**	Off-reserve**	Multiple or Other Aboriginal Responses
Less than high school	31.3%	28.0	48.0	42.1	57.7	50.6	59.0	44.1	45.0
High school graduation	14.1	12.5	9.9	11.9	6.2	9.0	6.8	10.7	11.7
Some post-secondary	10.8	13.1	12.6	12.4	12.9	12.7	10.7	14.3	10.9
Trades certificate or diploma	10.9	6.6	12.1	13.6	11.1	11.5	11.8	11.3	11.8
College certificate or diploma	15.0	12.3	11.6	13.4	9.5	10.7	8.2	12.6	13.3
University degree or certificate	17.9	27.4	5.8	6.7	2.7	5.5	3.5	7.0	7.2
Total number	23,901,360	3,041,650	652,345	207,610	27,610	395,325	172,080	223,245	21,800

*Figures are rounded so totals may not add to 100.

**On-reserve and off-reserve figures are for those identifying North American Indian single response identities only.

Source: Compiled from data in Statistics Canada publications 97F0010XCB01045 and 97F0011XCB01042.

Nations have rarely been given opportunities to represent themselves and their interests in educational decision-making and curricular materials because of the dominant educational orientation towards Anglo-conformity.

In addition, for most Canadians education is a provincial responsibility, whereas education for persons defined by the Indian Act as registered Indians is under federal jurisdiction. One consequence has been separate and distinct institutional structures for Aboriginal children, including boarding and residential schools whose legacy of destruction and pain continues to resonate throughout Aboriginal communities (Schissel and Wotherspoon, 2003; Miller, 1996). This constitutional framework has also contributed to jurisdictional disputes that have restricted educational funding and services for First Nations people and produced considerable variations in the nature and quality of educational services provided to different segments of the Aboriginal population.

These factors have contributed to the variations in educational attainment among on- and off-reserve registered Indians, non-status Indians, Métis, and Inuit, as shown in Table 7.2. Compounding these legal and historical circumstances, Aboriginal students have experienced discrimination, lack of culturally sensitive curricula and learning materials, an absence of teachers trained to work with Aboriginal learners and communities, and other problems that have restricted their educational opportunities and success (Satzewich and Wotherspoon, 2000: 126–38).

Recent struggles on the part of Aboriginal peoples to gain input into and control over crucial aspects of their education illustrate the contradictory nature of the relationship between education and socio-economic opportunity. Persistent barriers to educational access and experiences of educational failure have contributed to higher than average rates of unemployment, poverty, and other types of social and economic marginalization among Native peoples. At the same time, education has been regarded by First Nations as a sphere of strategic importance in their quest for self-determination and improved socio-economic conditions. The position paper, 'Indian Control of Indian Education', presented by the National Indian Brotherhood (now the Assembly of First Nations) in 1972 and adopted a year later as policy by the federal government, outlined the principles of local control and parental responsibility that would serve as the foundation for subsequent self-government initiatives in the area of education. Since First Nations began to take control of educational services in the early 1970s, the number of band-operated schools has increased steadily, reaching 492 and enrolling three-fifths (61.3 per cent) of all on-reserve registered Indians attending kindergarten, elementary, and secondary school in 2000–1 (Indian and Northern Affairs Canada, 2002: 29, 33). The shift to band control has been accompanied by the development of new curricula and teaching/learning aids with First Nations content, cross-cultural training programs, teacher-training programs designed to increase the number of teachers of Aboriginal ancestry, school-community liaisons, and diverse initiatives designed to improve the chances of success for Aboriginal students in both band-controlled and provincial schools.

The impact of these developments has been mixed (Assembly of First Nations, 1988; Castellano et al., 2000; Kirkness and Bowman, 1992; Schissel and Wotherspoon, 2003). Growing sensitivity to the need for educational improvement among Aboriginal communities, combined with appropriate programming, services, and personnel, has contributed to increasing educational participation and attainment rates among Aboriginal populations at almost all levels. About 27,000 registered Indian students annually are now enrolled in post-secondary education programs with funding support from the Department of Indian Affairs and Northern Development (compared to about 8,600 in the mid-1980s and just over 800 in 1969–70), and in 1999–2000 over 3,500 such students graduated from post-secondary programs (Indian and Northern Affairs Canada, 2000: 35, 39). The actual number of Aboriginal students and graduates is higher than these figures indicate, since many Aboriginal students do not qualify for or receive federal funding. Significant numbers of Aboriginal people are returning to school later in life to upgrade basic education or achieve higher credentials. The 2001 census reveals that, among those aged 20–64, persons who report Aboriginal ancestry are more likely than the general population to attend school full-time, with participation rates of 8.9 per cent and 6.9 per cent, respectively. For those aged 20–4, the non-Aboriginal population has close to double the participation rates of the Aboriginal population (40.5 per cent to 24.1 per cent, respectively), but Aboriginal people have higher participation rates, by factors of two to four times for each age cohort between 30 and 64 (Statistics Canada, 2003e: 47). Despite the persistence of numerous obstacles and resistance to change, some elementary and secondary schools have made significant progress to accommodate Aboriginal learners and communities, with demonstrated improvements in student attendance, academic achievement, student motivation and work habits, staff awareness, and the incorporation of positive role models.

Several jurisdictions have begun to incorporate a comprehensive, integrated approach into their educational planning and delivery, recognizing that the most severe problems faced by learners cannot be resolved through schooling alone. Saskatchewan, for instance, has adopted a community schools policy built on a vision to provide:

> a comprehensive range of best educational practices for meeting the diverse learning needs of at-risk and Indian and Métis students. They provide a responsive, inclusive, culturally affirming and academically challenging learning program and environment and are effective in addressing the challenges of the communities they serve. As hubs for a network of community organizations and activities, they use collaborative approaches to foster the development and well-being of the entire community. (Saskatchewan Education, 1996: 6)

This vision more recently was augmented and broadened to the entire provincial school system through the adoption of a model called 'School Plus' intended to 'describe a new conceptualization of schools as centres of learning, support and community for the children and families they serve', building on partnerships with diverse communities and human service agencies (Government of Saskatchewan, 2003: 1). The Royal Commission on Aboriginal Peoples, in placing education at the core of its far-reaching aim to achieve full participation in the economy and self-sufficiency of Aboriginal people, has stimulated several innovative educational developments (Castellano et al., 2000). Insofar as there is an impetus within all levels of governance, including First Nations as well as federal and provincial authorities, to foster such an integrated approach to social and educational development, it is possible that more meaningful opportunities can be provided to large segments of the Aboriginal population.

Nonetheless, several problems remain. Kirkness and Bowman (1992: 52–3) emphasize that, along with the observed progress in meeting many of the needs of First Nations students, administrators in band, federal, and provincial schools are at least as likely to report that critical problems—poor attendance and motivation, high dropout rates, poverty and racism, tensions between schools and families, high mobility, and language difficulties— remain unresolved. Many of these concerns, along with frustration over the slow pace of efforts by Aboriginal Elders, parents, and other community members to gain effective input into and control over their education, have been repeatedly expressed to various educational and policy-making bodies, but they have met with little productive response (Royal Commission on Aboriginal Peoples, 1996a, 1996b). Aboriginal students generally express highly positive assessments of schools, teachers, and education's importance for life success, but they also encounter racism, institutional barriers, and cultural divisions that can significantly impede their educational progress (Silver and Mallett, 2002: 29–30; Schissel and Wotherspoon, 2003: 82–92). In many cases, Aboriginal people have been able to translate educational credentials, particularly in professional fields, administration, and business and commerce, into labour market and economic advances. However, the Aboriginal population, both overall and with respect to those with higher credentials, remains highly segmented, often concentrated within specific areas. Aboriginal people pursuing post-secondary studies remain relatively under-represented in the most prestigious or highly skilled fields, focusing instead in such areas as human services, trades and construction, and technologies for men and commercial and human services and clerical programs for women (Statistics Canada, 2003e: 46). Hull (2000: 108) observes that educational pathways and returns are highly mediated by class, gender, Aboriginal status, and region for Aboriginal people, concluding:

> It is clear that, by and large, registered Indian women continue to have weaker labour market participation and success than registered Indian men

Box 7.3 The educational attainment of Aboriginal peoples

The Royal Commission on Aboriginal Peoples (1996b: 433–4, 440, 476–7) describes several factors that have contributed to the restriction of opportunities for educational success and limited integration into the labour force among Aboriginal youth:

> In Aboriginal societies, as in many societies, children are regarded as a precious gift. Control over the education of their children has been a pressing priority of Aboriginal peoples for decades. This is not surprising. The destiny of a people is intricately bound to the way its children are educated. Education is the transmission of cultural DNA from one generation to the next. It shapes the language and pathways of thinking, the contours of character and values, the social skills and creative potential of the individual. It determines the productive skills of a people.
>
> Aboriginal peoples are diverse in their histories, environments and cultures, but their deep commitment to education cuts across all boundaries. In our public hearings, Aboriginal parents, elders, youth and leaders came forward to tell us of the vital importance of education in achieving their vision of a prosperous future. Education is seen as the vehicle for both enhancing the life of the individual and reaching collective goals.
>
> For more than 25 years, Aboriginal peoples have been articulating their goals for Aboriginal education. They want education to prepare them to participate fully in the economic life of their communities and in Canadian society. But this is only part of their vision. Presenters told us that education must develop children and youth as Aboriginal citizens, linguistically and culturally competent to assume the responsibilities of their nations. Youth that emerge from school must be grounded in a strong, positive Aboriginal identity. Consistent with Aboriginal traditions, education must develop the whole child, intellectually, spiritually, emotionally and physically.
>
> Current education policies fail to realize these goals. The majority of Aboriginal youth do not complete high school. They leave the school system without the requisite skills for employment, and without the language and cultural knowledge of their people. Rather than nurturing the individual, the schooling experience typically erodes identity and self-worth. Those who continue in Canada's formal education systems told us of regular encounters with racism, racism expressed not only in interpersonal exchanges but also through the denial of Aboriginal values, perspectives and cultures in the curriculum and the life of the institution.

Box 7.3 continued

The human costs of this failure are immense. It saps the creative potential of individuals, communities and nations. Yet, despite the painful experiences Aboriginal people carry with them from formal education systems, they still see education as the hope for the future, and they are determined to see education fulfil its promise. . . .

By the time they enter high school, many Aboriginal youth have spent eight years or more in an education system from which they and their parents feel alienated. In public schools, the absence of support for Aboriginal identities is overwhelming: no Aboriginal high school teachers; only a limited curriculum dealing with contemporary Aboriginal languages, cultures, history and political issues; an emphasis on intellectual cognitive achievement at the expense of spiritual, social and physical development; and the marginalization of youth in decision-making about their education.

At the high school level, most parents are even less involved in their children's education than at elementary school levels. Their exclusion from decision-making is intensified where there are no local high schools, where teachers and administrators are non-Aboriginal, and where Aboriginal parents are in a minority. Issues of culturally appropriate curriculum, language education, parental involvement, and funding for curriculum development and culture programs are all present in the education of youth, as in the education of the child. Additional challenges encountered in the education of youth are the need for youth empowerment; the need for local high schools; the opportunity to return to high school; and the transition from high school to economic activity and careers.

and that there continue to be high concentrations of men and women in particular occupations. It also appears that within urban areas registered Indians experience greater extremes of occupational success on the one hand, and government dependency on the other. These extremes are closely related to educational attainment.

In many cases, however, educational improvements have not been sufficient to overcome deeper problems like absence of sufficient jobs and discrimination. The 1991 census revealed that two-thirds of Aboriginal respondents who were looking for work indicated that they experienced difficulties due to an absence of jobs, about two out of five noted their education or work experience did not match the jobs available, and 16 per cent said that 'being

Aboriginal' produced difficulties in their search for jobs (Statistics Canada, 1993). Aboriginal people with the highest educational credentials tend to receive significant returns for their education, but considerable evidence points to the reality that Aboriginal people in general are more likely than other Canadians to experience a diminished relationship between education and social and economic opportunities (Canadian Race Relations Foundation, 2000: 24–6).

Social Class

Despite a long tradition of analysis of the relationship between social class and other dimensions of social inequality, until recently a surprisingly small body of systematic data has been available to document those relations with respect to Canadian education. This problem, in large part, is a consequence of differences in the definition and measurement of class inequality. The most common conceptions of class, derived from structural functionalist analysis, emphasize social stratification, relying on such indicators as income, occupation, parental education, and other variables that can be empirically measured and compared (Forcese, 1997: 22–8). These kinds of indicators can be readily identified, but require considerable resources and massive databases, such as census sources, if they are to be analyzed in a comprehensive way.

Alternative conceptions, including those derived from Marxist analysis or others following the critical analysis of contemporary European researchers such as Pierre Bourdieu, emphasize class as a relational concept that requires much more intensive scrutiny of what people do and how they do it in relation to other people, productive property, and labour processes (Nakhaie, 1996; Veltmeyer, 1986). This kind of analysis has rarely been applied to a consideration of educational inequality because of the detailed information required to place people in class relations and to assess their educational backgrounds, not to mention the inclination among many researchers and agencies that compile large quantities of data to disregard this conception of class. Regardless of how class is defined and operationalized, however, several important indicators demonstrate the interaction between social class and educational inequality.

In general terms, there is a strong two-way association between social background and education because social privilege increases the chances of gaining higher educational credentials, which in turn increase the likelihood of subsequent socio-economic success. As we have already observed with respect to gender, race, and ethnic inequality, nearly all groups have experienced some benefits from the expansion of Canada's education system in the latter part of the twentieth century. Porter et al. (1982: 313), in an analysis of students' educational plans and paths in Ontario, concluded that the education system is somewhat meritocratic in that, regardless of social background, students tend to have high aspirations and access to educational opportunities, and that factors like mental ability and self-concept do count. About two-thirds of all Canadians have more education than their parents, while only 7 per cent have less formal education than their parents; in 1993, 'just over half the population had attended a post-secondary institution, compared with a little over 10 per cent of their parents . . . while 70 per cent of the parents had not graduated from high school, only 30 per cent of their children had failed to do so' (Fournier et al., 1995: 24, 26).

However, these opportunities are not distributed equally. Anisef and Okihiro (1982: 131) observed that, while the rapid expansion of post-secondary education produced some relative gains in educational opportunities for women and some ethnic minorities in the 1970s, patterns of class inequality remained relatively stable. The research by Porter et al. (1982: 313) revealed that class plays a strong role in influencing students' aspirations, usually indirectly through its impact on the programs students entered into, their parents' expectations, and the self-concepts of the learners. Forcese (1997: 133) has argued that educational institutions tend to serve as 'gatekeepers to "success"' rather than as facilitators for upward social mobility because they restrict the numbers of students from lower-class backgrounds who benefit from formal education:

> Education was to have been the means of overcoming the inheritance of social class. However, as presently constituted, the educational system favours the already privileged, and screens out the already disadvantaged. Rather than defeating stratification, formal education is a cause of persisting and increasingly rigid stratification.

More recent research confirms the tendency for educational inequality to be reproduced across generations. Guppy and Davies (1998: 123) conclude from a comprehensive overview of education trends in Canada that, in comparison with gender and ethnicity, 'class background seems to be the far more enduring source of educational inequality' once general educational improvements are taken into account.

The likelihood that a young Canadian will engage in post-secondary studies, especially at a university level, increases with each successive level of parental education and household income (Knighton and Mirza, 2002). Surveys of graduates from post-secondary programs in Canada reveal that about one-third of the mothers and the fathers of university graduates, compared with about one in eight parents of trade/vocational graduates, have at least some post-secondary education, while over half of the mothers and fathers of trade/vocational graduates and about one-third of parents of university graduates had less than high school (Clark, 1991: 11). These findings indicate that there is some educational mobility—people from diverse backgrounds are represented at all levels—but they also reveal that the chances for educational opportunity are greater for those who are already relatively well situated. (see Figure 7.2)

Siedule (1992: 19), comparing the impact of various socio-economic factors including family income, family structure, province of residence, and ethnic background, demonstrates that the difference between favourable and unfavourable conditions can make a difference of up to five years in the amount of education a person attains. Research conducted in Ontario by David Livingstone and his colleagues also reveals the strong association between class background and educational success. Among the 25–34-year-old population, for instance:

> More than a third of the people whose fathers were industrial workers, or were self-employed, dropped out of high school. Nearly half of those whose fathers were unskilled workers dropped out. Those people from single-mother and poor visible-minority households probably fared even worse. On the other hand, less than 10 per cent of the people whose fathers were company managers or professionals dropped out of high school. . . . Employers' and professional-class kids are much more likely to go to university than are working-class kids—somewhere between two-and-a-half to four times as likely. (Curtis et al., 1992: 10)

Research conducted through the York University Institute for Social Research shows that, three months after university graduation, only 31 per cent of graduates who came from families with incomes under $26,000 had jobs, compared to 70 per cent of those from families earning over $100,000 and 58 per cent of graduates whose family income lay between those extremes (Grayson, 1997).

The mechanisms by which class inequalities are reproduced are highly complex, consistent with the analysis offered by such writers as Bernstein, Bourdieu, Gramsci, Apple, and others discussed in Chapter 4. Individual predispositions and experiences combine with signals from peers, family members, and educators in such a way as to lead into certain pathways or trajectories, as opposed to others, regarding such matters as how long to stay in school, what subjects to study, what careers to seek, and how much effort to apply to particular courses (Andres Bellamy, 1993). Class-related elements enter into the degree of influence that parents can have on their children's education, for instance, through the extent to which family members can provide time and money to support educational studies, and involvement in networks where interaction with other parents, teachers, and employers provides advantageous feedback and direction (Lareau, 1989: 116–19). Many other considerations, including individual self-confidence, ability to read and perform well in test situations, selective use of information from teachers and career counsellors, and job interview skills, are also likely to be associated with class (Grayson, 1997; Tanner et al., 1995: 52–4). The Program of International Student Assessment, based on reading, science, and mathematics skills tests administered to youth in 2000, found that socio-economic differences tended to be less pronounced in Canada than in most other OECD nations, and that a variety of factors, including parental interest in their children's education, reading at home, and numerous aspects of school climate, influenced student outcomes. Nonetheless, the survey also demonstrated that socio-economic status, whether determined by parental background or

Box 7.4 Educational inequalities and disadvantage in rich nations

Results from comparative tests of educational achievement indicate the varied roles that schools play, in conjunction with social, demographic, economic, and policy factors, in the reproduction of educational inequality, as illustrated in this summary of findings by the UNICEF Innocenti Research Centre (2002: 2):

- Educational performance in some OECD countries is consistently better than in others—whether measured by the percentage of students reaching fixed benchmarks of achievement or by the size of the gap between low-achieving and average students.
- A child at school in Finland, Canada or Korea has a higher chance of being educated to a reasonable standard, and a lower chance of falling a long way behind the average, than a child born in Hungary, Denmark, Greece, the United States or Germany.
- The percentage of 15-year-olds judged 'unable to solve basic reading tasks' varies from under 7 per cent in Korea and Finland to more than 20 per cent in Switzerland, Germany, Hungary, Greece, and Portugal.
- High *absolute* standards of educational achievement (measured by the percentage of students achieving a given benchmark) are not incompatible with low levels of *relative* disadvantage (measured by how far low-achieving pupils are allowed to fall behind the average).
- For the OECD as a whole, the average gap between high and low math scores in the same year is approximately nine times the average progression between one year and the next (grade 7 to grade 8).
- Between-school variance in educational performance is very much higher in some countries than in others.
- There is no simple relationship between the level of educational disadvantage in a country and educational spending per pupil, pupil-teacher ratios, or the degree of income inequality.
- In all OECD countries, educational achievement remains strongly related to the occupations, education and economic status of the student's parents, though the strength of that relationship varies from country to country.
- Inequality in learning achievement begins at an early age and attempts to mitigate educational disadvantage need to begin even before a child starts school through good quality early childhood care and education.

school composition, was one of the strongest determinants of student per-formance in all Canadian provinces and 31 other participating nations (Bussière et al., 2001: 47).

There is growing awareness of the barriers that confront people from low-income backgrounds who wish to pursue further education. Livingstone et al. (2001: 18) observe that, in a reversal of more optimistic perceptions dur-ing the 1980s, over two-thirds of Ontario residents now indicate that youth from lower-income families have a worse chance than those from upper-income families to achieve a post-secondary education. However, there is both widespread faith and a sense of urgency across social groups in which educational attainment is perceived to be a fundamental tool for social and economic participation and an avenue for advancement. Educational success remains tied to notions of individualism and competitiveness, which may serve an ideological purpose that acts in the interests of those who benefit most from existing social arrangements. Youth whose occupational opportu-nities are limited after they have dropped out of school, for instance, often blame themselves for much of their failure while they maintain faith that their own individual initiative and educational upgrading will enable them to have better chances for success in the future (Tanner et al., 1995). A follow-up study conducted four years after an initial 1991 survey of Canadian school-leavers revealed that one-quarter of the earlier dropouts had received their high school diplomas by 1995, while others were attending school or plan-ning to gain further education (Gilbert and Frank, 1998: 16, 19).

Continued belief in the legitimacy of schooling to facilitate individual access to jobs and other social rewards is based, in part, on the kinds of evi-dence outlined above, which show that many people do benefit from con-verting their educational achievements into social mobility and success. Hunter and Leiper (1993), for instance, suggest that factors like human cap-ital theory and 'market signalling', in which employers rely on educational credentials as an indication of future employee productivity, interact to pro-duce a strong relationship between formal education and earnings. Even when the evidence is contradictory and individuals are aware that significant barriers to social mobility exist, the stakes are sufficiently high to ensure that most of us play by the rules—i.e., while not all of us can achieve educational success, and educational success does not in itself guarantee a good job, the consequences of not having an education are severe enough to motivate peo-ple to get as much education as they can. Between 1984 and 1999, for instance, average family wealth increased by 53 per cent among families whose major income recipient was a university graduate compared to 22 per cent for those who were not university graduates (Morissette et al., 2002: 18).

Poverty is one of the more widely recognized costs of low educational achievement. There is a strong two-way relationship in that poverty rates are highest among those with the lowest levels of education and educational problems are often most severe among those living in poverty. In 1999, pre-tax poverty rates were 60.2 per cent for unattached persons with grade 8 or

Box 7.5 The impact of poverty on education

Poverty influences educational experiences and outcomes, and it is associated with educational attainment. In the spring of 2003, Statistics Canada and Human Resources Development Canada—at the urging of some provincial governments and influenced by research out of the neo-conservative Fraser Institute—eliminated the low-income cut-offs (LICOS) that had been used for several decades as a measure of poverty in Canada, replacing these with a 'market basket measure' of poverty that, with a single bureaucratic stroke, effectively has meant that many Canadians previously considered 'poor' no longer are, although no changes have occurred in their circumstances. Nonetheless, however politicians and public officials define the boundary between those who live in poverty and those who do not, the fact remains that education, for many Canadian children, is significantly affected by family income and material well-being. A report by the Canadian School Boards Association (1999: 7–8) outlines some of the main dimensions of the impact of poverty on education:

Poverty has a profound effect on education. Poverty is a national issue, for no community is without a poverty issue. The strength of the nation depends on the skills of its citizens.

Over 1.5 million Canadian children, more than 20 per cent, live in poverty, according to Statistics Canada. The poverty rates have grown since 1989 when the House of Commons of Canada unanimously voted to eliminate child poverty by the year 2000. Poverty means that a family's income falls below the low-income cut-offs established by Statistics Canada.

The effects of poverty include

- poor school performance
- chronic stress and adjustment problems
- greater vulnerability to stressful events in later life
- conflicts among family members
- feelings of deprivation that may lead to rage and despair
- social impairment
- psychological disorders
- health problems
- teenage pregnancy
- injury and early death

The effect of poverty begins long before children enter school, and for that reason those concerned with education have taken an increasing interest in seeing that preschool education and services

Box 7.5 continued

are in place for students living in poverty. Preschool education covers the period from birth to school entry and is known to be a time of rapid learning and development for children. If a child does not acquire sufficient skills in the preschool years, it may be difficult for the child to benefit fully from schooling.

The underlying causes of poverty are diverse and complicated. The face of poverty differs from one community to another and from one area of the country to another. The situations vary greatly, but poverty is always present, either as a cause or an effect. Poverty is not monolithic. However, there are some common effects on schools and students and common responses that schools can use to address the needs of students living in poverty.

The effects of poverty on education include

- food deprivation that influences daily concentration and learning
- inadequate nutrition that can affect the long-term development of the child
- inadequate adult supervision and child-care arrangements that limit learning experiences
- difficult behaviour in students
- low self-esteem and self-confidence due to feelings of lack of control, failure, discrimination, autocratic parenting styles, and lack of hygiene and material goods
- less stimulation, resulting in less motivation to learn and delayed cognitive development
- illiteracy and lower achievement in school
- less participation in extracurricular activities
- streaming into basic and vocational programs
- interrupted school attendance, dropping out of high school, and lower university attendance

When schools intervene for students living in poverty, the effects on the students include

- more students progressing from grade to grade at the same rate as their peers
- intellectual gains
- academic gains

less, 48.5 per cent for those with some high school, 28.6 per cent for those with a post-secondary diploma, and only 19.0 per cent for those with a university degree (National Council of Welfare, 2002: 64).

Being poor also increases the risk of further educational difficulties. The likelihood that a student will drop out before completing high school (a trend that also holds for those who do not return for additional education) is highest among those in lower socio-economic groups and those whose parents had little formal education (Gilbert et al., 1993: 23; Gilbert and Frank, 1998: 15–17). These trends reflect, in part, class-based differences both in dispositions towards education transmitted from parents to children and in the cultural and economic resources that students are able to draw upon in the classroom (Andres Bellamy, 1993).

There is growing awareness of the impact that poverty and associated 'risk factors' have both during early childhood and throughout the life course. Low income and poverty are associated with nutritional deficiencies, ill health, emotional and behavioural disorders, and social disruptions that produce frequent absences from school, attention deficits, and other factors that have an adverse effect on school performance (Council of Ministers of Education Canada, 1999: 17; Health Canada, 1999: 46–7). These problems accumulate over time, so that health risks are greatest among adults who have the lowest levels of educational attainment (Roberge et al., 1995: 17). Particularly for older students, economic pressures sometimes force youth to combine schooling and work. Although some students who combine schooling with moderate hours of work may have increased chances for high school success, those who are forced to work longer hours, thereby reducing the time available to attend class, complete assignments, or meet other school-related demands are more likely to encounter educational difficulties (Bernier, 1995: 19–20; Bushnik, 2003).

Schools themselves, as well as the circumstances of those living in poverty, can also contribute to lower educational achievement among the poor. Olson (1995: 205) argues that children from working-class and poorer families are penalized in part because schooling, teaching, and the curriculum are organized and oriented in such a way as to be irrelevant to the needs and interests of those children. Curtis et al. (1992: 66) argue that, in addition to strong class differences (along with racial, ethnic, and gender ones) in the distribution of students into higher and lower educational streams, resources are diverted from programs in vocational and general education, where the less privileged are likely to be found, into special programs like French immersion, classes for 'gifted' students, and private schools that typically serve students from more privileged backgrounds. Educational outcomes are highly affected by the complex mix of educational practices, the culture of school organizations, the extent and use of school resources, students' socio-economic backgrounds, and the mix of students within specific schools and classrooms (Frempong and Willms, 2002).

Recent trends suggest that class and educational inequalities are likely to compound one another further. With about 20 per cent of Canadian children living in poverty (Canadian Council on Social Development, 2003: 2), youth from disadvantaged backgrounds, as well as those with disabilities, are less likely than other youth to complete high school and more likely to experience difficulties in labour market participation (Human Resources Development Canada, 2000: 44). Despite consistent evidence, there has been an absence of comprehensive policy to address problems for low-income households. Individuals and their family members endure heavier responsibilities for financing their own education and securing social support as educational costs rise and government services and financial support erode.

This problem has implications for students at all levels of schooling, given the importance of fiscal and cultural capital for educational success, but it may be most visible among those who proceed to post-secondary studies. Bouchard and Zhao (2000: 28) observe that a widening gap in university participation rates, leaving students from families with the lowest socio-economic status with an increasing disadvantage relative to those from higher SES family backgrounds, corresponds with the period after 1989–90 in which tuition fees began to rise significantly. Figure 7.2 indicates the relationship between post-secondary participation and both household income and parents' education.

Tuition fees are increasing at the same time as employment opportunities are declining for young people, making it increasingly necessary for students to rely on family sources or borrowed funds to cover their educational costs. The proportion of graduates of career and technical programs who borrowed money to finance their education increased from 41 per cent of those who graduated in 1982 to 51 per cent of those who graduated in 1986. Among cohorts of university graduates, the increase was from 50 per cent to 53 per cent over the same time frame (Clark, 1991: 53). Moreover, changes to sources of financial assistance such as the Canada Student Loan Program are altering the nature and amounts of funding available to students. These trends make it more difficult for students from less privileged backgrounds to attend the post-secondary programs of their choice, or worse, they may restrict access altogether (Finnie and Garneau, 1996: 28). Levin (1990: 52–6) argues that while tuition increases alone may not reduce accessibility to university because students have generally tended to be drawn from relatively privileged backgrounds, other barriers, such as lack of services for non-traditional groups and those most in need of assistance, do restrict access.

Finally, increasing concern with trends associated with post-secondary attendance has not been matched, in Canada, with systematic attention to issues related to non-completion of university, community college, and adult education programs. Nonetheless, many post-secondary students interrupt their studies periodically, sometimes for substantial lengths of time and in other cases without returning to complete their programs, for a variety of reasons, including inadequate financial resources, isolation and lack of support networks, personal and family commitments, work opportunities, and limited commitment to or interest in their studies. Butlin (2000: 15, 20) estimates that between one-fifth and one-quarter of students who enter post-secondary programs in Canada leave prior to completion, with socio-demographic

Figure 7.2
Post-Secondary Participation Rates for Canadians Aged 18–21
and No Longer in High School, by Household Income and
Parents' Education, 1998

Participation rate (%), by household income

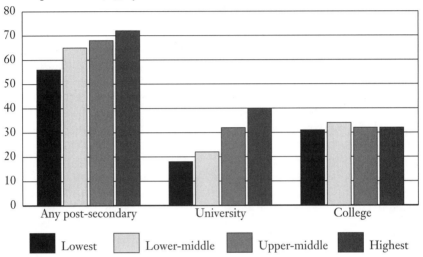

| Lowest | Lower-middle | Upper-middle | Highest |

Participation rate (%), by parents' education

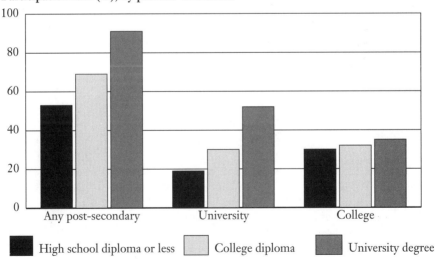

| High school diploma or less | College diploma | University degree |

Source: Knighton and Mirza (2002: 28).

factors most affecting the likelihood of leaving community college and school-related and personal factors having a greater impact on those who left university programs. However, these factors often interact strongly with one another, as illustrated by the case of First Nations students who are alienated by educational institutions that do not take into account personal, cultural, and economic factors (Monture-Angus, 1995: 81–4).

Regional Inequality

Canadians receive unequal amounts of and returns from education on the basis of where they live. These differences reflect disparities between urban and rural settings, provincial and regional diversity, and inequalities within a single geographical site such as a city or metropolitan area.

Educational indicators are generally more favourable for persons living in cities in comparison with those who reside in rural areas. Rural residents have less formal education, on average, than urban residents do. Census trends demonstrate a declining, but persistent, gap in educational attainment between rural and urban populations. By the mid-1990s, just over one-third (34.6 per cent) of persons aged 25–54 living in regions defined as 'predominantly rural' had not received a high school graduation certificate, compared to 22.7 per cent of their urban counterparts, whereas 62.8 per cent of those in urban areas and just under half (49.3 per cent) of those in rural areas had completed at least some post-secondary education (Alasia, 2003: 17). Some of these differences can be accounted for by virtue of the fact that educational institutions, especially at the post-secondary level, are concentrated in urban areas, as are jobs and services associated with higher levels of education.

Rural/urban disparities, however, also appear among the school-age population. Dropout rates, overall, are higher among rural than urban residents, and rural students who drop out of school tend to leave earlier—42 per cent of rural dropouts, compared to 29 per cent of urban dropouts, leave school prior to completion of grade 10 (Gilbert et al., 1993: 22). Among young adults, those living in urban areas are marginally more likely to participate in schooling than are those living in rural areas—37.7 per cent of the urban population aged 15–24, in comparison with 40.3 per cent of those in rural areas, were not attending school, according to the 1991 census. However, the difference lay in part-time attendance (6.8 per cent of those in urban areas versus 4.3 per cent in rural areas) rather than full-time attendance, where the rates were just over 55 per cent among both rural and urban populations. Moreover, the highest rate of full-time attendance in the 15–24 age cohort (60.8 per cent) was among those living on farms (Statistics Canada, 1994b: 10). Graduates of high schools in rural areas were slightly more likely than those from urban areas to attend community colleges, while the reverse was true for university participation, where 45 per cent of high school graduates from urban areas attended university compared to 34 per cent of those from rural areas (Butlin, 1999: 22).

Patterns of educational inequality are evident in comparisons across provinces and territories, as the data in Tables 7.3 and 7.4 illustrate. Regions that tend to be poorer, including most Atlantic provinces, Quebec, Manitoba, Saskatchewan, and Nunavut, all have average and median levels of educational attainment lower than the corresponding national figures of 12.3 years and 12.7 years, respectively, of schooling. Close to one-third of the populations in each of these provinces or regions have not completed high school, and in nearly all of them the proportion of the population that has a post-secondary diploma, certificate, or degree is below the national average of 48.9 per cent. The converse is true for the 'have' provinces of Ontario, Alberta, and British Columbia (as well as the one exception, the Yukon Territory), which meet or exceed the national average levels of educational attainment. Comparative studies of reading skills and adult literacy reveal similar trends, with persons living in rural areas and in provinces with the highest rural concentrations demonstrating lower scores than those in urban centres (Statistics Canada, 1996: 20–3; Statistics Canada, 2003h: 10–11).

Some levelling out occurs, however, when only the younger adult population is considered (the third and fourth columns in Table 7.4). In all provinces and territories except the Northwest Territories, the 15–24-year-old population has an average of close to 12 years of schooling, with a median of between 12.2 and 12.7 years. Secondary school graduation rates are higher than the national average in the Atlantic provinces, which tend to have lower overall educational attainment levels, and the proportions of persons 15 years and over who are attending school on a full-time basis are also higher than the national average in Newfoundland, Nunavut, and the Northwest Territories, as well as in Ontario, Saskatchewan, and Quebec.

There are also regional differences in people's attitudes towards schooling and educational performance. Ironically, persons living in regions with the lowest levels of education tend to have more positive views of schooling than those with higher levels. Various surveys of public opinion typically reveal that people in the Prairie provinces and Atlantic Canada tend to have more favourable attitudes about schools and improved quality of education than those from provinces with the highest urban concentrations of population (Williams and Millinoff, 1990: 37–8; Angus Reid Group, 1999: 9, 12). Such poll results reflect, at times, public reaction to unpopular educational reforms in specific provinces, such as Ontario in the late 1990s. They also reveal, though, strong convictions that education is important to the future of rural communities and to options for individuals from those communities. Rural communities face a perpetual challenge to address the reality that many of their youth look to education as a channel for educational, economic, and social opportunities that exist in cities or other regions (Knight, 1993: 306–7; Wotherspoon, 1998: 138).

Observed differences in educational attainment and attitudes towards schooling reflect several important dimensions of Canadian social reality. To a large extent, education systems in Canada have emerged and developed

Table 7.3
Educational Attainment, by Province, 2001, and Graduation Rates, 1999 (% of population aged 25 and over)

	Canada	Newfound-land	Prince Edward Island	Nova Scotia	New Brunswick	Quebec	Ontario	Manitoba	Saskat-chewan	Alberta	British Columbia
Educational attainment, 2000*											
Less than secondary	24.4	35.7	30.9	27.4	30.6	31.4	21.5	27.8	28.6	19.3	18.5
Graduated from high school	19.6	15.0	15.3	13.6	19.4	15.7	21.7	21.0	20.6	19.2	22.5
Some post-secondary	7.0	4.8	6.4	7.1	5.2	5.6	6.8	6.6	7.0	9.1	9.8
Post-secondary certificate, diploma, or university degree	48.9	44.6	47.4	51.9	44.8	47.2	50.0	44.6	43.9	52.3	49.2
Secondary school graduation rates, 1998–9 (%)**	76.7	79.5	81.3	80.4	84.8	84.2	77.3	74.3	75.0	63.3	73.4

*Population aged 25 and over.

**The sum of the age-specific ratios of the number of graduates to population for an academic year, calculated using the population as of 1 June of the school year and the number of graduates by age as of the same year.

Source: Compiled from Statistics Canada, 'Education at a glance', *Education Quarterly Review* 9, 1 (2003): 55–6.

Table 7.4
Educational Attainment in Participation, by Provinces and Territories

| | Highest Level of Schooling Attained, 1996 (Years of Schooling) | | | | % of Population 15 Years and Over Attending School, 2001 | |
| | Population 15 Years and Over | | Population Aged 15–24 Years | | | |
	Average	Median	Average	Median	Full-time	Part-time
Canada	12.3	12.7	12.3	12.5	11.6	4.7
Newfoundland	11.2	11.7	12.1	12.5	12.6	2.5
Prince Edward Island	11.9	12.3	12.1	12.4	10.9	2.9
Nova Scotia	12.1	12.5	12.1	12.4	11.3	2.9
New Brunswick	11.6	12.4	12.1	12.5	10.5	2.5
Quebec	11.9	12.5	12.2	12.6	12.0	4.4
Ontario	12.7	12.9	12.5	12.7	11.7	4.8
Manitoba	11.9	12.4	11.8	12.3	10.5	4.7
Saskatchewan	11.8	12.4	11.8	12.3	11.9	3.2
Alberta	12.6	12.8	12.0	12.4	11.4	4.9
British Columbia	12.7	12.8	12.2	12.5	11.1	6.1
Yukon	12.8	12.9	11.8	12.2	11.6	7.3
Northwest Territories	10.9	11.8	10.4	10.8	12.9	4.9
Nunavut	—	—	—	—	16.2	3.6

Source: Compiled from Statistics Canada 1996 Census (20 per cent sample data), Catalogue no. 93F0028XDB96007 and Catalogue no. 93F0028XDB96003, and 2001 Census: <www.statcan.ca/English/Pgdb/educ40a.htm>.

amid debates over the degree to which competing economic and social considerations should drive educational planning and programs. On the one hand, imperatives such as economies of scale, efficiency, and cost considerations have led to consolidation of schools and school districts and centralization of programs and resources. Regions with stronger economic bases are in a better position than poorer regions to provide both the resources to finance a strong educational system and employment opportunities for people with educational credentials. Similarly, smaller provinces and rural or isolated areas with limited populations are less likely to be able to offer a complete range of educational programs and services than are city schools or larger school districts. On the other hand, educational institutions are under pressure to be responsive to local concerns and to provide meaningful services. Schools with low enrolments may not be cost-efficient, but they may be able to offer several advantages to students and community members—greater opportunities for teacher-student interaction, sensitivity to parental concerns, and higher morale—that tend not to be found in larger school settings (Haughey and Murphy, 1983). In rural areas and smaller communities, especially, schools are essential for more than their educational offerings, serving as focal points for sports and recreation, social organizations, and cultural events that contribute to an enhanced quality of life within the community. Nonetheless, such schools often remain at risk through an absence of adequate resources and stability (Bolaria et al., 1995: 433–5).

The structure of educational finance in Canada has been shaped by efforts to compensate for some of the most severe consequences of regional inequalities. Throughout most of the twentieth century, funding for elementary and secondary education in nearly all provinces (except New Brunswick and Prince Edward Island) came predominantly from tax revenue generated at the school board or district level, augmented by grants from provincial governments to equalize school spending between poorer and wealthier districts. Federal-provincial arrangements generally have operated on a similar principle, with equalization payments and special funding programs for post-secondary education based on the transfer of funds from the federal government to ensure that the 'have-not' provinces are able to provide services equitable to those available in the 'have' provinces (Dibski, 1995: 69–70). Such programs have sought to ensure that a basic range and level of educational services, along with health care and other social services, are available to residents in all provinces and regions.

Recent changes to cost-sharing formulas and funding arrangements, however, have tended to shift the burden of funding downward, while centralizing fiscal constraints, thereby heightening fears that inequalities among districts will increase (Barlow and Robertson, 1994: 12). Several programs previously funded directly by the federal government have been merged into a single new entity called the Canada Health and Social Transfer (CHST) program, introduced as a way to attack the federal deficit by cutting social spending and co-ordinating programs. During the 1990s, nearly all provincial governments implemented parallel initiatives to restrain education spending, centralizing control over many educational decision-making matters, eliminating or placing limits on local school district discretionary spending and taxation powers, and reducing the numbers of school boards (Council of Ministers of Education Canada, 2001: 18–19; Young and Levin, 2002: 152–6). Manitoba and Saskatchewan are the only remaining provinces to maintain significant local educational taxation supported by equalization arrangements. While it is likely that these developments may produce some long overdue innovations in educational organization and programming—especially as attention has come to be refocused in the twenty-first century on the importance of strategic educational investment—they also increase the likelihood that programs and services for selected groups, such as people with special educational needs or residents in smaller communities, will be reduced or cut out altogether.

Conclusion

This chapter has examined several dimensions and consequences of educational inequality in Canada. The expansion of the education system and broadening of conceptions of educational opportunity throughout much of the twentieth century have resulted in substantial gains in educational attainment among nearly all segments of the population. This expansion has been especially important for many women, as well as for some members of visible minority and Aboriginal populations, providing access to educational programs and subsequent social and economic positions reliant on advanced educational credentials, such as law and medicine, which traditionally have not been open to them. Considerable evidence indicates that not only does education contribute to social mobility but it also limits the extent to which social inequalities are simply reproduced from one generation to the next. There is a real basis to claims that educational gains can lead to increased social and economic opportunities and that individuals can benefit from education regardless of their social background.

However, substantial obstacles continue to stand in the way of full equality of access to and benefit from education for many segments of the population. Gender equity has been achieved in participation rates at most levels of formal education, but gender segregation remains in areas of study concentration and in the ability to translate educational credentials into subsequent educational and career advancement. Similarly, visible minorities have demonstrated considerable gains in levels of educational participation and attainment, but their ability to translate those advances into socio-economic success also depends on such factors as personal experiences of discrimination and their structural location in Canadian society. With a few notable exceptions, persons of Aboriginal ancestry, in particular, remain a considerable distance away from education and employment equity with the population as a whole. Such problems as sexism, racism, poverty, and regional disparities often compound one another, contributing to distinctly different probabilities that people from diverse social backgrounds will achieve educational and social success.

In summary, then, there is a contradictory relationship between formal education and social and economic opportunity. Education is a vital ingredient in most recipes for success, sometimes as a contributing factor but more often as part of an overall package associated with relative privilege or disadvantage. Several policy and organizational changes, such as improved educational access for minorities, education equity initiatives, multiculturalism, teacher training for greater sensitivity to the educational needs of distinct categories of learners, and inclusive curricula, have enhanced opportunities for people who have been typically disadvantaged. However, schooling, both actively, in terms of how it responds to and rewards people on a differential basis, and tacitly, in terms of the gaps, silences, and failures to confront socio-economic disparities on a systematic basis, also contributes to the ongoing reproduction of social inequality.

To be sure, there will be new opportunities for some individuals as jobs are created that reward intelligence, initiative, and technical proficiency as opposed to socio-economic background. Nonetheless, recent policy and

program changes in the direction of funding cutbacks, restrictions on or dele-
tion of support services for students, greater individual responsibility for educational costs and options, and realignment of educational priorities in conjunction with wider fiscal planning are likely to minimize the chances that
those from less privileged social backgrounds will receive equitable access
to and benefits from formal education. Significant challenges, debates,
and reforms surrounding contemporary education are the focus of the next
chapter.

Annotated Further Readings

Ibrahim Alladin, *Racism in Canadian Schools*. Toronto: Harcourt Brace, 1996. The
   author demonstrates that, contrary to ideologies that emphasize equity and opportunity, Canadian schooling is infused with various racist practices.
Marlene Brant Castellano, Lynne Davis, and Louise Lahache, eds, *Aboriginal
   Education: Fulfilling the Promise*. Vancouver: University of British Columbia Press,
   2000. The authors highlight several promising developments, as well as crucial
   challenges, that characterize education for Canada's Aboriginal people in the wake
   of the 1996 report of the Royal Commission on Aboriginal Peoples.
Bruce Curtis, D.W. Livingstone, and Harry Smaller, *Stacking the Deck: The Streaming
   of Working-Class Kids in Ontario Schools*. Toronto: Our Schools/Our Selves
   Education Foundation, 1992. This is one of the few detailed Canadian accounts
   of streaming and its impact on children from different social backgrounds.
Dennis Forcese, *The Canadian Class Structure*, 4th edn. Toronto: McGraw-Hill
   Ryerson, 1997. The writer outlines the various dimensions of class-based social
   inequality in Canada, emphasizing causes and consequences associated with persistent social barriers for some groups relative to others.
J. Douglas Willms, ed., *Vulnerable Children: Findings from Canada's National
   Longitudinal Survey of Children and Youth*. Edmonton: University of Alberta Press
   and Human Resources Development Canada, 2002. This book summarizes findings from the comprehensive National Longitudinal Survey of Children and
   Youth. It covers crucial causes, consequences, and dimensions of negative life
   experiences associated with vulnerability, including racial and ethnic discrimination, parenting concerns, family violence, poverty, and learning and behavioural
   disorders.

Key Terms

Class A social grouping based on social and economic relations, defined in terms of
   people's position with respect to ownership and control of assets that contribute
   to the production of new goods and services.
Equality of opportunity The view that all persons should have the same chance to
   succeed or fail on their own merits, regardless of their social background.
Equality of results The notion that intervention by the state or other agencies is
   necessary to guarantee that all persons will achieve at least minimum agreed-upon
   standards of living and access to other essential resources and opportunities.
Gender segmentation The concentration of males and females within distinct and
   separate jobs, education programs, and other social sites, often associated with differential status and benefits.

Meritocratic The principle that persons are selected for social positions based on merit, or achievement in accordance with universal standards and criteria.

Social Darwinism A view that societies change through their internal evolutionary processes, commonly employed to justify existing social inequalities to reflect 'survival of the fittest'.

Social disadvantage Inability to attain important social and economic resources as a result of barriers or inadequate opportunities relative to standards that prevail among a nation or social group as a whole.

Social reproduction The process by which social structures and systems of inequality are maintained over time.

Socio-economic status (SES) A measure of the relative social and economic position of a person or group, determined by such factors as income, wealth, occupation, education level, family background, and prestige accorded an occupation.

Visible minority A term used in Canada to refer to non-Caucasian persons of specified racial or ethnic origins other than Aboriginal.

Welfare state A policy framework in which governments, rather than individuals, families, or other agencies, are responsible for ensuring the economic security and physical and social well-being of all citizens.

Study Questions

1. To what extent is educational achievement the outcome of individual effort as opposed to social factors? Explain your answer.
2. Discuss the extent to which education contributes to or restricts opportunities for social and economic success among diverse racial and ethnic groups in Canada.
3. Explain why, despite efforts to ensure that schooling is inclusive and responsive to all students, strong educational inequalities persist among social groups.
4. Which groups have benefited the most from educational expansion over the past five decades? Explain your response.
5. To what extent is there a gender bias in contemporary schooling that favours either girls or boys? Discuss and explain.
6. Discuss the importance of university education. To what extent is university open to and able to provide equitable opportunities for students from diverse social backgrounds?

8

Contemporary Educational Challenges and Reforms

Introduction

Educational institutions and practices are the focus of considerable controversy amid public concern over how best to achieve and advance a knowledge society. Current educational debates are much less likely to reflect the heavily critical—and at times combative—tone that prevailed a decade earlier as reflected in media accounts under headlines like 'What's wrong with our schools?' and in popular literature that carried such titles as *Class Warfare: The Assault on Canada's Schools* (Barlow and Robertson, 1994), *School's Out: The Catastrophe in Public Education and What We Can Do About It* (Nikiforuk, 1993), and *Busting Bureaucracy to Reclaim Our Schools* (Lawton, 1995). Nonetheless, education systems are challenged to rethink and reshape themselves to keep pace with volatile social, economic, and political transformations.

This chapter analyzes some of the main issues and challenges that continue to drive educational reform in Canada. The major themes examined here include the governance and financing of formal education, calls for increased accountability and choice in education, the impact of new technologies on education, and changing educational requirements for diverse groups or communities of learners. While contending visions for educational reform are sufficiently complex that they cannot be reduced to a simple polarization between different kinds of rights or imperatives, there is a strong relationship between educational tensions and the contradictory dynamics that underscore the social and economic contexts within which education operates.

Conflicting Visions of Educational Reform

Education systems have benefited in some ways from the re-emergence of discourses that place human capital development at the centre of strategies to build a highly skilled labour force. Educational expansion is a key component in the quest to adapt to a knowledge-based economy governed by advanced technologies, accelerated information processing capacities, innovation, and flexibility. This approach coincided with de-emphasis on fiscal restraint and renewed government spending in important areas of both social and economic programming, or at least it did until the diversion of state policy and resources throughout most of North America and Europe to issues related to security and the military following the 11 September 2001 terrorist attacks in the United States. Education systems have also attempted to reshape themselves to capture new resources and ameliorate criticism from public, government, and corporate interests.

Despite the apparent truce, the assault on education has not disappeared—in many ways, it has merely changed in form and emphasis. Education has not been immune to a general crisis of confidence in government and public institutions, while it has also attracted unique critiques along the way. Critics continue to level serious charges against existing education systems—our education system has not maintained competitiveness with systems in the most advanced nations; students are not learning essential skills and performing as well as they must to succeed in the global economy; schools are too costly to maintain in their present form; too much attention is placed on frivolous programs to the neglect of the basics; there is not enough discipline and respect for traditional values in the schools; education systems and personnel need to be more open and accountable to the public; schools need to be more responsive to market forces; taxpayers (or 'consumers') who are paying for education require a wider array of educational choices. The catalogue of criticisms is long.

Defenders of public education assert that the critics are creating a distorted portrayal and offering misguided proposals for educational reform that may be even more damaging than the alleged problems. By way of rebuttal, critics respond that many of the people who speak out on behalf of education systems are teachers, bureaucrats, and others whose self-interest lies in preserving the educational status quo. Governments have followed suit by implementing a variety of reforms to constrain and reallocate educational costs, expand public and parental choice, and address issues of accountability, openness, and public participation.

Overriding specific concerns, a new hegemony suggests that existing education systems must undergo more fundamental changes to align themselves with new social and economic realities. This vision advances beyond an earlier notion of basic education, combined with selection mechanisms to ensure that the most capable persons gain the capacities they require for higher-level jobs and social positions, by placing a reformed general education system into a broader continuum of ongoing training, innovation, and skill development (United Nations Development Program, 2001: 84–5). The OECD (2002: 21) poses this dilemma as a significant area of concern for contemporary societies:

> A democratic society, genuinely committed to the encouragement of life-long learning for all its people, is faced with a great challenge in the system of education it inherits from the antecedent meritocratic society. Can a system designed to sort and reward the most able be reformed in such a way as to help everyone fulfil their (very diverse) potential? Or, if reform is impossible, is a kind of educational revolution on the agenda for learning?

The vehemence with which contending views about educational reform are expressed signifies the importance of education to both public and personal life. As Chapter 3 has emphasized, many of these debates are not new—the history of public education is riddled with an ongoing litany of critiques, defences, and counter-critiques about education systems and their efficacy. Whatever positions are advocated, widespread concern clearly exists over the necessity to maintain an accessible, equitable system of quality education in the face of significant social and economic changes.

Educational debates tend to be characterized by diverse strands that emerge around fundamental contradictions between what Carnoy and Levin (1985) term capitalist and democratic imperatives in education, as discussed in Chapter 6. Apple (2000: 17–18), following Gintis (1980), argues that these educational tensions are indicative of underlying contention over *property rights*, where individual rights and liberties are governed by market relations, contracts, and the possession of private property, and *person rights*, in which people's rights and freedoms are granted on the basis of citizenship and moral claims. Support for initiatives such as market-based educational reforms, reduction of state funding for education, and an emphasis on standardized curricula exemplify some of the ways in which capitalist imperatives and property rights have begun to influence educational decision-making. On the other hand, movements to broaden public access to education, foster schools as inclusive sites that represent and serve the full range of diversity within communities, and develop curricula and programs oriented to social justice issues are indicative of approaches to educational reform guided by democratic considerations and human rights.

The Governance and Financing of Canadian Education

Education is subject to ongoing efforts by governments to restructure public service delivery and restrain or tighten control over public spending. Total education spending in Canada increased steadily, from $8.4 billion in 1971 to $25.4 billion a decade later, more than doubling to $53.1 billion in 1991, and reaching and holding steady at nearly $59 billion in the mid-1990s before climbing gradually (with some annual fluctuations) to about $67 billion by the turn of the century (Statistics Canada, 2003: 54). The recent recovery and modest growth in overall education expenditures masks diminished spending power due to inflation and rising educational costs, increased enrolments, and shifting priorities within education systems. As was observed earlier (Table 3.3), education continues to be funded predominantly by provincial and territorial governments (supplemented with transfers from the federal government), but there has been a gradual shift over the past two decades towards heavier reliance on private and local sources of funding, which, when combined, increased their share from about one-quarter of all educational spending in Canada in 1980–1 to current levels (since the mid-1990s) of one-third. Its massive size and cost (between 7 and 8 per cent of Canada's gross domestic product, second only to health as a priority for total government spending) have exposed the education system as a visible target within strategies to reduce government spending or compensate for tax cuts and spending priorities in other areas, but public education has also been defended under the guise of human capital approaches as a vital investment in the nation's future.

This double significance is reflected in distinctly different orientations to education spending held by particular social groups. Livingstone et al. (2001: 10), for instance, report that increasing proportions—nearly three-quarters of the Ontario residents they surveyed in 2000 compared to one-half a decade earlier—felt that education spending should increase beyond the rate of inflation, as opposed to only 8 per cent who indicated that education spending should decrease. Over half (53 per cent) of corporate executives in their sample agreed that there should be increased funding, a reversal of the stronger sentiment for reduced educational funding expressed by executives in the mid-1990s (ibid., 51). However, even if public opinion is softening in some respects, a general pattern is evident in which calls from business and right-wing lobby groups for major educational reform, reduced social and educational spending, and tighter educational controls are counterposed against demands from organized labour, teachers' and parents' organizations, and other community groups that education funding be maintained or increased (Lewington and Orpwood, 1993: 16–17).

Disparate views of education have been accompanied by various measures in virtually every major jurisdiction in Canada and other Western nations to modify arrangements for educational finance and governance, regulate teaching and teachers' organizations, reorganize curricula and service delivery, and implement mechanisms to assess performance outcomes and contribute to public accountability in education. There is considerable variation in the kinds of educational reforms instituted within each national, provincial, and territorial setting, and in the extent to which these reforms have altered or undermined public education—advanced most vehemently in Alberta, Ontario, and British Columbia within Canadian jurisdictions within the past decade—but the overall direction of change to create a stronger match between education and economic imperatives is remarkably uniform (Portelli and Solomon, 2001; Taylor, 2001; Brown et al., 1997).

Box 8.1 Funding cuts affect educational inequality

Educational reforms and funding cuts often increase educational inequalities, as this report from the *Toronto Star* (Brown, 2002: A1, A26) reveals:

Inadequate funding is creating a two-tier system in Ontario's grade schools, warns a report by the advocacy group People for Education.

The shortfall hits children hardest in 'have-not' neighbourhoods where parents cannot afford to make up the gap, says the non-profit organization.

'So much depends on fundraising now, for every classroom need from Kleenex and library books to paper and pencils, that parents end up becoming the food bank of the education system,' said group spokesperson Annie Kidder.

'But some schools can charge more for the same muffins than others', noted Kidder, adding some schools report being unable to raise a dime from their community, while one topped $65,000 in a single year.

The funding formula was supposed to make the system fair for Ontario's 1.4 million elementary students, she said, by making all boards wholly dependent on government grants, rather than their wildly divergent local tax bases.

'But the funding levels are so low, parents are having to make up for programs that aren't paid for—so then it depends on where you live and who you are,' said Kidder.

'There is a growing concern about equity. There is a growing gap between the "have" and "have-not" schools.'

Of the 841 schools that responded—representing 21 per cent of all grade schools in the province, including Catholic, public, English- and French-language—most said they scramble more each year to pay bills not covered by government grants, such as roof repairs, band teachers, computers and caretakers.

'But the top 10 per cent of schools raise more than the bottom 60 per cent of schools put together,' said Kidder.

Moreover, they're fundraising more and more for the basic tools of learning, because schools cannot cover the costs. For example:

- Fifty-two per cent of schools said they fundraise for classroom supplies, up from 31 per cent in 1997.
- Twenty-four per cent of schools fundraise for textbooks, up from 21 per cent in 1997.
- Sixty-two per cent of schools say they fundraise for library books, compared to 56 per cent in 1997.

Box 8.1 continued

As well, despite an increase in immigration to Ontario, the number of schools teaching English as a second language (ESL) has dropped 31 per cent in five years.

'ESL programs give every child an equal chance, but some of the harshest program cuts have been in this area,' said Diane Dyson, the group's research director. 'And there is a disturbing trend to use any warm body to teach ESL, rather than paying for someone with ESL training.'

The fifth annual survey of grade schools across the province provides the one regular, detailed snapshot from the front lines of how schools are coping under the funding formula introduced five years ago.

It chronicles schools where toilets are broken, where some families face a one-year wait for their child to see a psychologist and where pupils spend three hours a day on the bus.

But the children the system fails the most are those whose families cannot afford to augment dwindling school programs with private music lessons and sports leagues, summer nature camps, private psychological assessments and tutors, said Kidder.

Of the schools surveyed, 3 per cent said they were able to raise no money at all. Sixty-nine per cent said they raised less than $10,000 a year, and another 17 per cent were able to raise between $10,000 and $20,000, while 11 per cent raised more than $20,000.

Debates over educational funding and organization are often more about priorities than absolute spending levels. This helps to explain how funding or program cutbacks may be experienced by some educational participants or sectors even as educational expenditures rise or remain relatively constant. While there is general consensus that education is crucial for personal, social, and economic development, there is considerable disagreement about the kinds of education and educational organizations there should be.

It is often difficult to pinpoint the social bases of educational debates because views about education appear in complex and sometimes contradictory ways, incorporating persons who represent diverse social perspectives. People with a broad range of educational experiences and social backgrounds may come together, for instance, to either support or oppose a 'back to the basics' orientation to curricula, culturally sensitive educational practices, or demands for greater discipline and safety in schools.

Apple (2000: 20ff.) analyzes the impact on education of the rise of the New Right in the United States and Britain, and some of his insights apply, to a certain extent, to the politics of education in Canada. The New Right is characterized as a broad movement supporting principles of market-driven free enterprise, opposing state regulation, cynical about state officials, and fearful about loss of authority, tradition, and standards in personal and public life. Rather than operating as a unified group or force, however, the New Right is better understood as an amalgam of disparate forces such as the pro-family movement, business lobbyists, opponents of the welfare state, neo-liberal groups, right wing organizations, and other populist forces that seek a return to 'traditional' values. Education, because it touches family life, economic futures, and other concerns vital to people's lives, hopes, and aspirations, has been a prime target for reform by the New Right. Apple (2000: 22) argues that:

> The sphere of education has been one of the most successful areas in which the Right has been ascendant. The social democratic goal of expanding equality of opportunity (itself a rather limited reform) has lost much of its political potency and its ability to mobilize people. The 'panic' over falling standards and illiteracy, the fears of violence in schools, the concern with the destruction of family values and religiosity, all have had an effect. These fears are exacerbated, and used, by dominant groups within politics and the economy who have been able to move the debate on education (and all things social) onto their own terrain, the terrain of 'tradition', standardization, productivity, and industrial needs.

One of the major features that such critics of the education system point to is the size and power of the educational bureaucracy, which is often posed as a monopoly resistant to change. Fears about unchecked growth of the education system are enhanced with depictions of educational administrators, teachers, and other entrenched interest groups who are distant from the real concerns of students, parents, and community members. Journalist Andrew Nikiforuk (1993: 57), for instance, argues in his book *School's Out*:

> Just as the Canadian oil industry did during the boom of the 1970s, educators have spent, built, and added on programs and services without any coherent plan or realistic sense of limits. Unlike the oil patch today, however, educational institutions cannot be effectively regulated or reformed by market forces. As essentially social monopolies, they appear to have become unmanageable because of their autonomous nature.

Similarly, Lawton (1995: 14–15) criticizes the 'bureaucratic bondage' that has removed control over education from parents and other segments of the public into the hands of bureaucrats, professional educators, and administrators. Hepburn (1999: 1), in a report published by the right-wing Fraser Institute to make the case for school choice in Canada, states the apparent problem more bluntly: 'Canadian education is not just inefficient but seriously inadequate. Statistical evidence of poor student performance coupled with the deterioration of public confidence suggests that, if it is not to become obsolete, public education must be redesigned.'

These criticisms have a common-sense appeal because they pose a unifying framework for a series of problems that most people can identify with or have experienced in one form or another. Taken as a whole, the kinds of issues we see or hear about in our educational institutions, such as rising costs, declining standards, uncaring teachers, lack of accountability to taxpayers and communities, student violence and vandalism, irrelevant curricula, meaningless reporting practices, and wasted instructional time, may convey an image of an education system in serious crisis.

There is a danger, however, in adopting an uncritical approach to such a critique. Despite numerous concerns, no consensus necessarily exists over the idea that the education system is failing or in crisis. In fact, as has been noted on several occasions throughout this book, public opinion on most educational issues is divided and highly complex. In a social context within which public and private institutions are regarded by skepticism and declining confidence overall, public schools are rated relatively well, maintaining higher levels of confidence than nearly all other major institutions (Edwards and Mazzuca, 1999a; Guppy and Davies, 1999).

Wickstrom (1994: 6–7) identifies seven distinct models to characterize the diverse demands that exist for educational reform:

1. the factory, emphasizing productivity, uniformity, and quality control;
2. the department store or large convention, stressing variety and consumer choice;
3. the family, with a focus on love, compassion, and co-operation;
4. the garden or 'untended meadow', in which growth, interest, and beauty and diversity are crucial;
5. the Olympics, highlighting excellence and competition;
6. the freedom march, oriented according to passion and indoctrination to a specific cause;
7. the clinic, regulated by diagnosis, prescription, precision, and successive stages of sophistication.

While each of these models can be applied to specific groups or philosophies of educational change, most educational practices and opinions encompass a mixture of elements from various models. Surveys of public attitudes towards education have revealed a relatively equal and enduring split in opinion between those who feel that governments or taxpayers receive satisfactory value for education spending and those who express dissatisfaction with the value received for education spending (Williams and Minhoff, 1990: 16; Livingstone et al., 2001: 7).

The notion that the public is clamouring with one voice for particular kinds of educational reforms is ideologically and socially constructed. Educational reports, policy documents, and anecdotal evidence that highlight educational problems come to be merged into an apparent consensus dominated by business and corporate interests rather than values and practices that emerge from people's real experiences (Delhi, 1993: 116–17). Barlow and

Robertson (1994) argue that, akin to the New Right in the United States and Britain, a conservative alliance driven principally by business and religious fundamentalist interests has mobilized public opinion to promote school reforms across Canada that exacerbate class divisions and weaken the schools' ability to respond to the needs of less privileged social groups. Dominant class interests have pressured education further, both directly and indirectly, for neo-liberal reforms and market-based orientations through international and multinational trade agreements (Grieshaber-Otto, 2002: 129–30; Robertson, 1998). Within these ideologies and associated reforms, property rights gain ascendancy over personal rights by regarding individuals, variously, as consumers, clients, and products of education. Despite the emphasis on personal choice and freedom, real people and their diverse needs and struggles are regarded as abstractions, like inputs and outputs in an industrial system governed by considerations of cost-effectiveness and competitive advantage.

Educational Accountability

One set of issues in which competing educational interests and ideologies have become highly apparent is debate over accountability and choice, and related emphasis on market-driven alternatives such as charter schools, educational voucher systems, and parental choice models. Wilkinson (1994: 17) summarizes the three main factors normally involved in such debates—concern over the declining quality of education in Canada in the face of increasing international competitiveness; concern over the kinds of values transmitted through schooling; and frustration over the lack of responsiveness to change within the educational bureaucracy.

Some of these arguments have been outlined in Chapter 6 and elsewhere in this book. The issues of concern illustrate how various groups—such as business and neo-liberal interests calling for competitiveness in education and religious organizations seeking the promotion of Christian values in schooling—come to be aligned within the New Right. By contrast, many other segments of the population, including educational and teachers' organizations, organized labour, coalitions to promote social justice, and people who subscribe to more inclusive notions of social equality, have expressed considerable opposition to proposals for market-driven educational reforms.

Fundamental to these debates are competing conceptions about what the goals and purposes of education are and whose interests schooling should serve. Advocates of varying positions agree that public education requires some reform to meet the needs of diverse groups of learners in a rapidly changing social and economic context. Many critics, however, argue that extensive changes reaching beyond the current system are necessary to compensate for a lack of quality, imagination, choice, and effective outcomes in public education.

Proponents of property rights and market-based educational choice make their case by highlighting, in part, relationships between educational and economic indicators to demonstrate the deficiencies of the present system. Demands for drastic educational reform were bolstered in the early 1990s by data suggesting that Canada was receiving poor returns on its educational investments, as signified by its relatively poor or 'mediocre' ranking on labour market activity, economic performance, and student rankings in comparative scores on standardized mathematics, science, and literacy tests (Economic Council of Canada, 1992: 107; Schweitzer, 1995: 47). This critique has been tempered somewhat by more recent findings that Canadian students, both in general and within many provinces, are faring relatively better than those in most other comparable nations—and much better than in the United States.

In part, the emphasis on test scores and other indicators of educational performance reveals a desire by educators, policy-makers, and parents for systematic feedback on educational activities. In terms of assessment of and reporting on individual student performance, for instance, school jurisdictions across the country have sought compromises between those parents and teachers who want test scores that produce a numerical or letter grade purporting to show exactly where one student stands in relation to others and those who feel that anecdotal reporting and commentary about educational processes provide a truer reflection of a student's ability and progress (Lewington, 1995: A1). Just as parents wish to know how well their children are doing in comparison with others, educators and other interested groups want information about how well different education systems and their outputs measure up against one another.

Educators and education bodies have shed much of their initial reluctance to engage in comparative testing, driven both by political pressures and genuine desire for a knowledge base that may contribute to improved educational performance. Nonetheless, the results from various comparative databases remain highly volatile, particularly when they are used to promote the agendas of particular bodies, such as the Fraser Institute, which has published school-by-school 'report cards' on educational performance in Alberta, British Columbia, Ontario, and Quebec in its pursuit of market-driven educational reform. De Broucker and Sweetman (2002: 8), noting the potential that comparative educational indicators have to be employed in narrow ways by specific groups, stress that 'It is all too common to focus on problems, and they certainly exist, but problems are in fact "news" (and often covered by the news media), whereas the "un-newsworthy" is mostly good compared to that experienced by other countries.'

Since the 1990s, Canada (through various federal government departments, provincial governments, and the Council of Ministers of Education Canada) has participated in recurrent cycles of initiatives like the International Mathematics and Science Study, the Program for International Student Assessment, and the cross-Canada School Achievement Indicators Program. These programs, which variously employ standardized tests to compare mathematics, reading, writing, literacy, and science skills at particular age or grade levels across educational jurisdictions, signify a growing desire for data to provide a comparative baseline for guiding educational assessment and decision-making. Parallel to these developments are movements towards a national curriculum and core curricula in several provinces that provide specified areas of study and learning materials for all learners at particular stages of their studies. Government inquiries into education, such as Ontario's Royal Commission on Learning (1994b: 130–58) and the Royal Commission of Inquiry into the Delivery of Programs and Services in Primary, Elementary, Secondary Education (1992: 379–99) in Newfoundland and Labrador, have acknowledged that issues surrounding problems of assessment, evaluation, and reporting are highly complex in nature. At the same time, consistent with the prevailing trends, their recommendations pointed to the implementation of more systematic procedures for testing and assessing both students and education system performance that reduce these issues to quantifiable outcomes.

Many critics have pointed out that standardized tests, curricula, and performance indicators do not reflect the true nature and quality of education. For standardized tests that compare student performance in different provinces and countries to be valid and fair, there must be some assurance that students in each jurisdiction have had an opportunity to cover the material or acquire the skills being tested. Consequently, testing tends to be restricted to a narrow range of all material that is likely to be covered in a subject area. It remains highly debatable as to how accurately test scores reflect student ability either within a given subject area or in more general terms. This is further limited by virtue of the fact that testing and evaluation, particularly when they are oriented to empirical or 'objective' measures, generally focus on relatively discrete bits of information rather than on critical thinking and wider, more complex activities usually regarded as essential within educational practices. Given that the school day consists of both formal curricular expectations and social and other dimensions of the 'hidden' curriculum, there is no necessary correlation between the number of school days and the amount or quality of education in a given school jurisdiction. Moreover, test data must be carefully presented and interpreted in order to be meaningful. Media and political commentary often ignores the fact that most international and interprovincial comparisons of test results draw on different populations or subgroups of students. Some jurisdictions with lower 'average' test scores often include a wider range of students than other jurisdictions that draw from more selective student bodies that would be expected to produce higher score results (Gilliss, 1995: 121–3). Some rethinking of comparative test results has accompanied findings that demonstrate the impact of specific factors—notably socio-economic inequality—on overall performance. In particular, especially within Canada, jurisdictions that have the most favourable outcomes tend to be those in which the performance of participants from the lowest socio-economic categories do well, and which reveal the least difference among learners from the top and bottom socio-economic categories (Willms, 1997: 20; Bussière et al., 2001: 32–3).

Box 8.2 Economic advantages add up to better scores

The use of standardized test scores to measure school performance ignores the complex nature of both the tests themselves and the schooling process, as this *Ottawa Citizen* article (Hughes, 2003) argues:

Socio-economic status and language are the key factors in whether schools finished at the top or bottom of the Fraser Institute's rankings of provincial elementary schools, Ottawa educators say.

Simply put: privileged students with English as a first language do well on the province's standardized tests, while students from less wealthy, immigrant families often do not.

The Fraser rankings are based entirely on results of Ontario's standardized-testing system.

Differences in wealth and social status also appear to be reflected in the geographic breakdown of the rankings.

Schools in Toronto, especially in wealthy urban enclaves and affluent suburbs in surrounding York Region, dominated the top of the table, as did those in adjacent communities such as Ancaster, Oakville, Stoney Creek, and Burlington.

Schools in economically mixed areas such as Mississauga, St Catharines, Whitby, Pickering, Waterloo, and Windsor scored at or slightly above the provincial average. Cities with substantial working-class populations—Hamilton, Welland, Niagara Falls, Ajax, Brampton, London, Renfrew, and Sudbury—scored slightly below the provincial average.

Overall, Ottawa's public and Catholic schools scored at the provincial average. Northern schools fared the worst, scoring an average of 5.1 out of 10. One northern school board—Rainy River District, west of Thunder Bay—however, was ranked among the top 10 English boards, placing ninth with a score of 6.8.

At Katimavik, in Kanata, principal Maria Sarot said teachers at her school have very high expectations for students, as do their affluent parents.

'This school has a very homogeneous group of students as far as socio-economic standards are concerned. So, of course, high academic achievement is expected,' she said.

The French-immersion school does not face the challenges of schools that may have groups of learning-disabled students or English-as-a-second-language students. The progress of those students is evaluated with the same tool as is used for the Katimavik students, and their results suffer, she said.

Box 8.2 continued

Accommodations are made to help certain students write the tests, Mrs Sarot noted, 'but we have to ask ourselves whether, with ESL students, are we truly measuring knowledge acquisition or language proficiency?'

Mrs Sarot said she is not opposed to the testing done by Ontario's Education Quality and Accountability Office, but it is only one measuring stick.

'One snapshot is not enough. It's absolutely essential to collect several snapshots, anecdotes and personal success stories of each student, then we can have an album that we can look at and see a true picture of a child's progress.'

Danielle Cloutier, principal at Présault for four years before she retired last June, is acting principal while her successor prepares for amalgamation with another school.

She attributes the school's top rank to a dedicated team of teachers and good chemistry with students and parents. 'The community is behind us, and we have great parents here, parents who are concerned and help with enrichment programs.'

As well, 'we have eight or nine gifted students identified every year, and their results help bring up the average.'

Jim Tayler, principal at Pinecrest, and Sandra Richardson, principal at Viscount Alexander, also stressed that EQAO tests are only one indicator of progress.

'We have a lot of children that come to school without a wide range of experiences that in a lot of ways are valued and help them be successful,' Mr Tayler said. 'They don't have extra-curricular activities that many children have, and in some cases they don't have access to the local cultural resources, and the families lack the means to be involved in those kinds of things.

'That does filter into how they achieve at school.'

He said 60 per cent of his students have English as a second language—around 300 students in the 480 student school on Pinecrest Road.

'We do have children who were born here, but we also have students who are new to the system, with parents who are new to the system, so language is a huge barrier when you're dealing with something like an EQAO style of testing,' Mr Tayler said.

'However, there are other ways of measuring progress. We can look at kids who come to school knowing no English and six months later they're conversing with you in the yard. Does EQAO measure that? No it doesn't.

Box 8.2 continued

'Are we making progress? We sure are, because that young child is able to communicate.'

Ms Richardson, of Viscount Alexander, has been at the Mann Avenue school for only one year, although she's been a principal for six.

'We have a very multicultural population, which is a wonderful environment for our students, but it does bring academic issues with it,' she said.

'We're dealing with children coming new to Canada, or coming with another language as their first language of instruction or speaking at home, and we need to focus on taking them from where they are when they arrive and moving them along—and we look at the progress closely.'

Progress is not always reflected in standardized scores such as EQAO; it's more reflected in how teachers see pupils grow over the years, she said.

'That's not to say we don't focus on academics. But we focus on moving them along as opposed to necessarily expecting them to meet a standard by Grade 3 or even by Grade 6, depending on when we receive those students. Meeting the standard might come later in their academic career.'

Mr Tayler, who has been at Pinecrest for four years, said 'when you rank us against schools with students from more of a middle-class or upper-middle-class background, it stands to reason those are kids who are very well versed in the kinds of things EQAO measures and tests.'

'You look at the EQAO results each year and are certainly aware that concerns about numeracy and literacy are key issues in all schools,' he said. 'We're addressing that through excellent teachers who are committed to working with our kids.'

He said teachers help children learn to handle the EQAO tests, which are set for those whose first language is English. In spite of accommodations, many students still find it very difficult to succeed, he said.

Ms Richardson conceded her school's scores are low, 'but I look at them in the context of what I see in the building and I see successful students.'

In small schools, statistics can be misleading, she added.

Last year in Grade 3 there were only 27 students eligible for the test and only 15 actually wrote it. When you look at 15 students, two or three either way can really sway the results, so I look more at the students than the percentages,' she said.

> ## Box 8.2 continued
>
> 'One of the things we're looking at for next year is helping our students to learn how to express their knowledge, so they get credit for what they know.'
>
> This is not teaching to the test, she stressed, but working on the style of answering.
>
> Often, 'when it's your second language, you wait for the teacher to say "Can you elaborate on that or can you give me more?" In the testing situation, when they stop, that's it, we can't ask them for more.'
>
> Ms Richardson said year-to-year comparisons are difficult.
>
> 'In a community such as ours the children come and go regularly, so that by Grade 6, they're a completely different group from Grade 3. We could easily have turned over 50 per cent of those students in the three-year period.'

As has been noted throughout this book, schooling and learning are about much more than simply acquiring and repeating information. Many critics ignore the more indeterminate human and social dimensions of education as they seek to generate standardized achievement test scores and quantitative measures of educational accountability for specific ends. Evidence from New Zealand, Australia, the United Kingdom, and several American states in which educational measurement and accountability have been key elements of market-based school reforms indicates that these measures have been employed more fully to control education, discipline teachers, and appease parents than to contribute to more effective teaching and learning (Smyth and Shacklock, 1998: 96ff.). Discourses of accountability and measurement are often silent on the cultural and political dimensions to learning. Persons from distinct social backgrounds have varying degrees of access to information deemed as valuable or valid from the dominant cultural perspective. In many educational settings, not high test scores but the extent to which all students can gain access to meaningful social opportunities and experiences is the mark of student and school success. Bacon (1995: 87), expressing the concerns of many Canadian teachers, emphasizes that:

> Outcomes are not just things that are measurable. For example, appreciation of cultural diversity, adaptability to change, values clarification, a sense of personal worth and responsibility, and character development are all important outcomes but are difficult to measure. Nor are these things the sole responsibility of the school. These responsibilities are shared with parents and others in society.

One former business executive, commenting on his reversal of an earlier assessment that schools should be governed more like businesses, stresses that he has since 'learned that a school is not a business. Schools are unable to control the quality of their raw material, they are dependent upon the vagaries of politics for a reliable revenue stream, and they are constantly mauled by a howling horde of disparate, competing customer groups that would send the best CEO screaming into the night' (Vollmer, 2003: 42). Posed another way, the determination of educational quality is a highly contested process that involves several levels of human judgement:

> the common denominator among all attempts to judge educational quality is the imposition of human judgement with all of its complex and conflicted assumptions, values, biases, cultural predispositions, and so forth. In this respect, the narrowest of quality evaluation schemes founded purely on standardized tests is no more objectively valid than the most uncomplicated of holistic quality judgements. All parties to the educational process do the same thing in this matter, they impose—or attempt to impose—their ideas about the knowledge, beliefs, values, and attitudes the schools ought to foster. (Paquette, 1989: 23)

School Choice and the Educational Marketplace

Just as there is debate over how to measure and interpret educational quality and outcomes, there are also strongly divergent views about how to reform the education system to improve its performance. Some proponents of reform have argued that educational competition and accountability can be increased by implementing merit pay for teachers, basing their salaries or providing incentive bonuses in accordance with student performance or test results. Others argue that governments should issue educational vouchers that enable parents or students to select their schools (public or private), in lieu of current funding arrangements whereby grants are provided directly to school boards.

Advocates of a market or consumer choice model of education claim that educational choice is required to ensure that schools will be more flexible and responsive to community concerns (Easton, 1988: 71–6; Wilkinson, 1994). Chubb and Moe (1990), in their influential case for school choice, argue that school improvement follows as a logical outcome from the removal of constraints on parents, teachers, and schools, whereby schools (posed as distinct enterprises) would have the autonomy to make changes necessary to attract and retain students and their parents (posed as consumers).

Market-based educational reforms, both as a focus for public debate and in their implementation, appear to be less pervasive in Canada than in many other jurisdictions, including several American states. This general impression, however, obscures several significant developments and trends in the expansion of options and enrolments in both alternative school settings within public education systems and options outside of public schooling. Private schooling, along with legislation to allow or provide public funding for alternatives to the public school system, has been expanding across Canada in diverse forms and levels. The proportion of students enrolled in private schools, nationally, increased from 4.6 per cent of all children in elementary schools in the late 1980s to 5.6 per cent a decade later, reaching 9 per cent in British Columbia and Quebec (Statistics Canada, 2001). Various forms of home-based education have expanded significantly as many parents choose to keep children out of public schools for religious reasons, concerns about academic quality or learning style, flexibility, school-based victimization, and a variety of other factors. An estimated 60,000 to 95,000 elementary and secondary school-age children (about 1.5 per cent of the school-age population), or as many as 100,000 families across Canada—concentrated most heavily in Alberta, British Columbia, and Ontario—are engaged in home schooling (Priesnitz, 2003; Ray, 2001: 28). Numerous private educational alternatives are expanding, ranging from preschool programs and adult training and post-secondary options to private tutoring businesses (Davies et al., 2002).

Public school systems and post-secondary institutions have also modified and expanded how they deliver their educational programs, both to attract and maintain enrolment in competition with other agencies and in response to broader educational challenges and needs. School districts have relaxed or removed policies that previously required most students to attend their neighbourhood schools. Many school districts have introduced specialized schools targeted to particular groups, such as immigrant populations, Aboriginal inner-city youth, academically talented students or those with special learning needs, students with specific cultural and arts-oriented interests, adult learners, and students with disabilities. Publicly funded post-secondary institutions have expanded programming and developed alternative modes of course or program delivery, sometimes through contractual arrangements with private agencies.

One of the most actively promoted models of educational choice is the establishment of charter schools. Charter schools operate on the basis of a 'charter' or agreement between particular schools and governments that identify specific mandates and features of governance by which each school will operate in conformity with general principles of public education. They are premised on the notion that parents are educational consumers who should be provided with effective input and choices in order to make rational decisions about their children's schooling.

Advocates of charter schools argue that viable alternatives are needed because public schools have become too firmly entrenched in the hands of educational elites and have experienced declining educational standards by attempting to be all things to all people. Some options, such as home schooling and private or independent schooling, are beyond the reach of parents who do not have sufficient time or resources to invest in these alternatives or who do not share the values embodied in these special forms of education. Charter schools, by contrast, are promoted on the basis that they offer the best elements of both public and private schooling. Charter schools, like public schools, are funded by government grants, are ideally open to all pupils, and are subject to provincial curriculum and teacher certification guidelines. Like private schools, however, they have greater autonomy to define their own particular mandates, to make decisions about staffing, resource allocation, and instructional matters, and to ensure that parents' voices are incorporated into educational planning (Lawton, 1995: 68–9; Nikiforuk, 1993: 100–2; Raham, 1996).

Joe Freedman (1995: 40), one of strongest early promoters of charter schooling in Canada, argues that they offer a 'middle ground between choosing schools by voucher and allowing the system to fix itself'. Their success, Freedman claims, is driven by 'the challenge of removing the exclusive franchise from school boards, creating choice for parent clients, providing a focus on outcomes, establishing real autonomy through school status as a legal entity, and creating genuine accountability through the threat of school closure or loss of teaching position.'

One of the most broadly-based initiatives to introduce charter-like schooling is in New Zealand, which in 1989 required all school jurisdictions to develop charters as part of a series of initiatives to deregulate and privatize government services. Considerable pressure from interest groups in the United States has led to various forms of charter arrangements in several states, beginning with Minnesota in 1991, which was joined within the next two years by four other states (Lawton, 1995: 70–81). Within the next decade, the number of charter schools had increased to over 1,600, serving close to half a million students in 34 states (Fuller, 2000: 7). There have been several vocal advocates of charter schooling in Canada, notably in Alberta, which has remained the only province to authorize charter schools since the passage of facilitating legislation in 1994 (Bruce and Schwartz, 1997: 408). By 2001, 10 charter schools were in operation out of 12 charters granted, each oriented to particular groups or focuses including traditional 'back-to-basic' instruction, foreign language instruction, English as a second language, street youth, academically talented learners, fine arts, and science and technology (Bosetti, 2001: 103–8).

Despite the inroads and popular support it has gained in some jurisdictions, charter schooling also faces considerable opposition from educators and educational organizations, as well as from broader community and policy groups. Some opposition arises from concerns that charter schooling is an affront to public education that may undermine established educational structures and bodies. However, serious concerns also arise from prospects that charter schools can be divisive, inequitable, undemocratic, and ineffective in addressing major educational problems (Canadian Teachers' Federation, 1997). Critics argue that educational choice is already provided, or possible, within existing structures of public and private schooling and that charter schooling diverts control and resources from schools that serve the wider community (Crawley, 1995: 168–9; Friesen and Friesen, 2001).

Although charter schools may have some general appeal, advocacy for charter schools and other market models of education is being pursued most actively by individuals supported by or representing groups that have the most economic, political, and cultural capital (Robertson, 1998: 263–6). Critics contend that these advocates stand to gain the most from a bifurcated education system in terms of both individual competitive advantage and the benefits that accrue from the redirection of public funds into private hands. They add, moreover, that while public schools are intended to serve and be responsive to diverse social groups, charter schooling is likely to contribute to the diversion of resources and opportunities from disadvantaged groups that have the greatest educational needs. Finally, charter schooling and related shifts in the direction of educational accountability and measurement may contribute to the deskilling of teachers' work by setting and controlling performance standards and conduct in such a way as to restrict professional autonomy and increase workloads.

The early evidence from charter schooling and other private alternatives supports many of these contentions, though some evidence is mixed (Bosetti, 2001). Charter schools have drawn students who have been disengaged or dissatisfied with the mainstream education system as well as those from more privileged groups. Similarly, whereas public schools are most likely to enrol students from a diverse mix of backgrounds, children who attend private schools are drawn predominantly from households situated at the top and bottom ends of family income groups (Statistics Canada, 2001). Private school advocates point to data from comparative student assessment programs that indicate students in private schools achieve higher scores than those in public schools (though this trend is less pronounced in Canada than in many other nations). However, this trend tends to disappear when social class, school diversity, and other background factors are taken into account (Bussière et al., 2001: 38).

Regardless of the impact of particular types of school reform, debates over school choice will continue to be ineffectual as long as they ignore more fundamental issues, including the structural causes of poverty and social and income polarization (Fuller, 2000: 10). Without this priority, such debates may be more about competitive positioning for corporate resources and family advantage than about meaningful educational reform and improvement.

In summary, the various options promoted for educational reform and alternatives to public schooling represent divergent and ideological interests. It is important not to discount the genuine concerns that all people have to seek changes that will make education more meaningful and rewarding in its varied economic, cultural, social, and moral purposes. The kinds of reform strategies being pursued, however, follow distinctly different courses leading, in one direction, to a market-driven orientation to the education 'industry' and, in another, to a more person-centred focus on human development, opportunity, and social justice.

Education and New Technologies

The revolutionizing possibilities and imperatives associated with the 'information age' are integral to contemporary educational reform processes. Computers, advanced data-processing systems, technology transfer programs, and electronic information networks like the Internet and World Wide Web have affected our expectations about education in the same way that they have altered many general patterns of living and working. Educational institutions encounter rising expectations about their ability both to incorporate information technologies into their own activities and to train persons who have the capacity to master and develop new technologies in innovative ways. Like most educational issues, there are contradictory dimensions to how people view these developments and what their implications are for education systems.

Technological innovations have been eagerly embraced by some segments of educational communities and resisted or regarded with disdain by others. It is important to distinguish, in these varied responses, between the use and impact of technologies as they relate to individual learners and educators, and those associated with education systems or processes as a whole. Individuals may use computers or network systems, for instance, to conduct research and write term papers, to organize attendance records or grade reports, to introduce graphic presentations or simulations to classes, or to exchange information with people in other educational settings. These applications may be used as resources to facilitate administrative, teaching, or learning practices for individuals without substantially altering teaching or learning processes. Technological innovations may also be applied in a slightly more engaged manner involving changes that apply to both individuals and education systems, such as the teaching of courses in computers or data-processing or the introduction of distance education courses by television, teleconferencing, or computers, but which are still combined with more traditional educational practices.

Technological change can alter education in more fundamental ways. In the extreme, information and communications technologies suggest an imperative for new paradigms based on drastic alterations to our whole way of thinking, learning, interacting, and living. Information technologies are commonly posed as inescapable realities that set the pace and standard for work and socio-economic survival in the emergent global scheme of things. Schooling, if it is to be relevant, must ensure that students become familiar with the operation of computers and other new technologies, which means that the infrastructure must be sufficiently equipped with these technologies—and be able to adapt and innovate within ongoing processes of change. Spurred by varying forms of government support and corporate funding,

Box 8.3 Learning for work in the information society

Rapid economic and technological changes are forcing employers, governments, and educational organizations to seek alternative mechanisms to provide timely education and training such as e-learning, described here by Murray (2001: 3):

> Despite a high standard of living, Canada is falling behind other countries because of its relatively poor innovation and productivity performance. E-learning is one answer to sweeping global changes and our own labour market and productivity issues. E-learning affords small and medium-sized enterprises, as well as large organizations, an opportunity to provide workplace learning, and it gives Canada a chance to close its 'digital divide' through the development of e-literacy.
>
> E-learning is being spurred on in Canada by three broad drivers:
>
> - the global economic context;
>
> - the human capital context; and
>
> - the information and communications technology context.
>
> E-learning can be viewed as a means of delivering three key outcomes: improved and consistent rates of lifelong learning, improved productivity and improved innovation and competitiveness. Another desired outcome is increased equity. The issue of equity raises questions that need to be addressed now. Do Canadians currently have access to these learning technologies, is access to e-learning equally distributed by income, age and educational levels, and are barriers to e-learning such as cost and lack of information, time and content being addressed? E-learning, like all learning, should yield outcomes that benefit society and the economy.
>
> ### What Is E-Learning?
>
> E-learning uses information and communications technologies to deliver content (learning, knowledge, and skills) on a one-way or two-way basis. One-way (asynchronous) technologies . . . deliver content . . . one way at one point in time. They include:
>
> - Broadcast television that delivers learning content
> - Audiovisual aids
> - Film
> - Video
> - Digital video disk (DVD)
> - Computers

Box 8.3 continued

- CD-ROMS

- E-mail

- Internet/intranet/extranet networks

- Wireless technologies

    Two-way (synchronous) technologies . . . deliver content . . . two ways or more at the same time. They include:

- ICQ/IRC—interactive conferencing and chat rooms

- Teleconferencing

- Internet/intranet networks

- Web conferencing

- Wireless technologies

several initiatives have emerged in recent years to promote the introduction and use of new technologies and information-based learning systems at virtually all levels of education and training.

Educational innovations now in place or underway include the delivery of entire educational programs by computer-based curricular modules, the transformation of classrooms into fully 'wired' learning centres, and electronic networks that provide for 'virtual' campuses or schools. There is growing official support to integrate new technologies more comprehensively into education. In the mid-1990s, Ontario's Royal Commission on Learning (1994c: 26–7) stressed that 'it is crucial that every classroom in every school be part of the information highway', driven by the conviction 'that information technology is one of the engines needed to drive the necessary transformation of the education system.' By the end of the decade, initiatives like SchoolNet, organized through Industry Canada in conjunction with provincial and territorial governments, had created the mechanisms to link all public schools and libraries through the Internet with the aim to prepare learners for the knowledge-based society. These broader objectives are supported by a wide range of initiatives, including:

- purchase and action plans to incorporate computers, programs, software, and communication networks into the ongoing activities of educational institutions;
- the establishment of computer-assisted learning and computer-based training programs;

- the introduction of hands-on learning technologies in classrooms; and
- the development of electronic linkages among new institutional networks of participants in education and other fields.

The introduction of new technologies and information networks has widespread appeal because of the advantages they offer to both educators and learners. Routine tasks can sometimes be integrated into computer programs in an efficient, cost-effective manner that may both benefit and enhance the interest of the learner, teacher, or administrator. Information and materials previously beyond the reach of many educational institutions, particularly in remote areas or those with limited supporting resources, are now often readily available to all participants who have access to computer facilities or advanced communications technology. Information and service networks, learning packages in CD- or DVD-ROM form, multimedia kits, distance education programs, and on-line, wireless, or satellite transmission of information enable educators, students, and even parents to access an unprecedented range of resources. Students who acquire computer and programming skills and gain facility with information transmission and retrieval processes will be well prepared for entry into competitive job markets driven by technological change. Moreover, computer-literate students and school personnel contribute to the pool of highly qualified human capital required to advance further technological progress. Information technology and the networks it fosters also promote co-operation and innovation among educational institutions and between education and other sectors of the economy.

There are, however, several limiting factors to how far education can and should be modified by technological change. Tran (1995: 50–1) poses a number of questions that educators need to contend with as they consider the introduction of computers into the classroom. These include:

- What is the goal of education and how do computer systems contribute to this goal?
- What are the best approaches to teaching students, training teachers, and evaluating programs?
- How is computer technology related to various subject areas?
- How far can new technology be incorporated without damaging major learning objectives?

Some proponents of the expansion of computer technology in the classroom tend to portray teachers and other school personnel as uninformed or rigid detractors who resist changes that have already been embraced by students and employers (Lewington and Orpwood, 1993: 100). However, in many cases, computers and new information systems are introduced into schools without a thorough assessment of how they will be incorporated into daily school routines, how they affect teachers' work, and what kinds of training and support resources are available. Even when school systems and personnel are firmly committed to the expansion of new technologies, for instance, deficiencies in areas such as in-service training, technical support, and access to hardware and software will undermine the potential contributions these technologies can make to educational practices. Cuban (2001: 177–8) observes that, even as computer use has become ubiquitous in North American schools, there have been no clear advances in educational outcomes related to academic achievement and efficiency, no clearly defined agreement on what constitutes computer literacy, and no technological revolution in teaching and learning in most classrooms.

From the perspective of learners, new technologies constitute additional forms of cultural and fiscal capital that will differentially affect opportunities for success or failure. Growing awareness of the 'digital divide' points to the inequitable nature of information technology access, use, and returns. Increasing proportions of the population have access to computers and Internet connections at home, school, workplaces, and public sites such as libraries and Internet cafés. New technologies tend to be adopted more widely over time once their utility is established and basic start-up costs drop. At the same time, differential means and opportunities possessed by families, communities, and institutions to keep abreast of up-to-date, compatible forms of information technology and support contribute to the persistence of gaps in technological access and use. While less evident in Canada than in many other nations, significant inequalities in computer and Internet access and use are based on class, region, gender, age, race and ethnicity, language, and other important social factors, as demonstrated in Table 8.1 (see also Cuneo, 2002). Internet use has expanded significantly across all income groups in Canada, for instance, but the divide between the top and bottom income groups has persisted or even widened since the mid-1990s (Sciadas, 2002: 5). About 85 per cent of 15-year-olds in Canada, compared to an average of 70 per cent of those the same age in OECD nations, indicated in 2000 that they had access to a computer at home on a daily basis or several times per week (Statistics Canada, 2002). The same survey found that for three-quarters of Canadian 15-year-old students, computers were available in school on a regular basis, though just under two out of five of them used computers at school frequently, with girls reporting both less frequent use of computers and less certainty about the importance of computers than boys (Statistics Canada, 2002). Despite the promise that computers may hold to expand education and training possibilities, students' use of computers for personal enjoyment, gaming, and communications tends to match or prevail over word processing and other activities related to schoolwork (Corbett and Willms, 2002: 14).

Gender-related differences extend to how computers are used and the kinds of computer-related training undertaken in schooling. Males remain much more actively involved than females in computer studies and computer use at all levels of education, particularly in fields that involve computer programming and advanced applications, as opposed to data entry, word processing, or clerical uses (Collis, 1991; Dryburgh, 2002). Among Canadian

Table 8.1

Percentage of Canadians with Internet Access in the Home, by Income, 2000

Quintiles	Bottom	2nd	3rd	4th	Top	All
Education						
Less than high school	10.9	15.4	32.5	39.7	50.1	22.5
High school/college	32.2	40.9	56.7	63.9	80.1	55.4
University degree +	56.7	62.3	71.1	81.1	91.0	79.3
TOTAL	23.9	34.5	54.4	63.6	80.9	51.5
Family type						
Single family, children <18	48.0	59.3	67.0	76.6	87.4	71.4
Single family, no children <18	22.0	24.8	43.8	57.3	75.8	46.9
One-person families	13.2	25.4	49.3	58.3	60.2	28.0
TOTAL	23.9	34.5	54.4	63.7	80.9	51.5
Geographical location						
Urban (CMA)	25.9	36.4	56.2	64.4	82.7	54.0
Rural (non-CMA)	17.6	28.4	47.7	60.8	70.5	41.8
TOTAL	23.9	34.5	54.4	63.7	80.9	51.5

Note: The top 18 Census Metropolitan Areas are used as a proxy for urban areas.
Source: Sciadas (2002: 2).

teens, half or more of all males, compared to just over one-third of females, identify their computer and the Internet as a source of enjoyment, with males substantially more likely to identify video and computer gaming as a major source of enjoyment. Females, on the other hand, are slightly more likely than males to designate e-mail communications as a source of enjoyment (Bibby, 2001: 24). Differences in computer use and applications tend to be associated, in turn, with gender-differentiated labour market and employment patterns.

Much of the discussion over the implementation of new technologies in education concerns the specific advantages or disadvantages of technology while ignoring wider political and pedagogical considerations. Among the most ardent promoters of computer and advanced technological innovations in education are business interests, corporations, specialists, or government personnel whose profits or career advancement are linked with prospects for widespread adoption of their products or services in educational settings, or parents who seek competitive advantage for their children (Mangan, 1994). Education poses a highly lucrative market for business and commercial interests both directly and indirectly, through sales of information and communications technology and related products to educational institutions, broader influence over educational decision-making, and cultivation of product identification and marketing to students and their families.

The rhetoric associated with new technologies sometimes helps to foster a misleading sense of urgency in which it appears imperative for us to master technology or else become doomed to failure. As funding and program priorities shift towards an emphasis on computer technology, other programs and services may be cut or undermined. Some critics point out that it is easy to become mesmerized by graphics, simulations, and other technical capabilities, as well as imagery related to technological revolutions and information highways, to such an extent that fundamental moral and human dimensions of education are forgotten (Beattie, 1996: 104–5). In its most extreme forms, technology can decontextualize education, reduce knowledge to isolated bits or fragments of information, and undermine the kinds of face-to-face contact and social interaction that are vital to many learning processes (Nelsen, 1997).

Computers and other new technologies, as with many other factors associated with teaching and learning, play a contradictory role in educational relationships. Information technology can stimulate interest, increase access to resources and programs, enhance innovation and flexibility, facilitate connections among educational participants, and ensure that education is attuned to emergent global trends. It can also work to the disadvantage of educators and learners who do not have access to or are unable to master technological developments. It may democratize access to information, but it can also contribute to centralized control, increased monitoring of individual activity, and limits to freedom. It can open up new employment and creative possibilities, but it can also contribute to the reproduction of existing social inequalities and the emergence of new dimensions by which more privileged groups come to distance themselves from the underprivileged. Underlying all of these concerns is the recognition that schooling, by nature, tends to be highly nuanced and complex because it involves social as well as technical relationships.

Education and Social Diversity

As educational institutions struggle to remain relevant and viable, they must contend with the ongoing challenge of how best to define their mandates and serve the students and communities they intend to reach. The educational landscape is being challenged and reshaped through both internal and external transformations. In addition to the array of choices created by new institutional arrangements and programs, increased attention is being paid to various kinds of lifelong learning and informal learning that occur in community and work settings and other sites beyond formal educational institutions. These initiatives, at the same time, have exerted new pressures on public schooling and traditional modes of educational delivery to remain open, accessible, and meaningful to a diverse range of learners and their communities.

The educational world has also gained complexity as educational con-stituencies have broadened. Education is beginning earlier in life, with expanded preschool and early childhood initiatives, and continuing well beyond high school and post-secondary levels for most people. Demographic changes, immigration, increasing Aboriginal populations, changes in families and workplaces, modifications to the life course, and broader concerns about personal, community, and social security are altering the nature of student bodies and the attitudes and expectations they carry with them. Educational institutions and participants are positioning themselves to respond to admo-nitions that the stakes of getting an education—and getting the proper kinds of education—are growing.

Various educational programs and services have also emerged in response to the needs of diverse educational constituencies. These include:

- adult education, university degree programs for mature students, and integration programs for persons who return to school later in life;
- ESL, heritage language, cultural education, and anti-racism education programs;
- programs for Aboriginal students and educational institutions and ini-tiatives under First Nations control;
- educational programs and services for the visually or hearing-impaired, or for persons with other physical or mental disabilities;
- alternative schools or classes for intellectually gifted, emotionally impaired, or learning-disabled students;
- expansion of distance education, Web-based courses, and other options for students who cannot attend classes in person as a result of geography, time, mobility, or other restrictions;
- increased acknowledgement and recognition of alternative forms of knowledge, including indigenous knowledge, knowledge acquired on the job or in other social settings, and assessment and recognition mecha-nisms for prior learning;
- co-operative education and other learning programs that combine for-mal schooling with vocational training or community or work experi-ence;
- scholarship or mentoring programs to encourage female students to complete studies in fields like natural sciences and computers and to pro-mote male literacy and reading skills.

Many of these changes are positive insofar as they expand educational oppor-tunities and provide options for education and training appropriate to peo-ple's circumstances and needs. Expanded educational services may provide particular benefits for segments of the population that typically have been excluded from all but the most basic levels of education. It is crucial, at the same time, to analyze and not take for granted issues like sponsorship, con-trol, funding, accessibility, and delivery of programs and services in order to

Box 8.4 Universities facing higher expectations

People, both individually and as groups, today look to post-secondary education to fulfill rising social and economic aspirations, and consequently universities and other post-secondary institutions face pressure to accommodate the needs and interests of diverse groups, as these accounts from Manitoba reported by the Canadian Association of University Teachers (2002) clearly illustrate:

Universities and colleges in Canada must do more to encourage participation from disadvantaged groups, according to participants in a set of public hearings organized by CAUT last month in Winnipeg.

Rob Marriott, a Métis student and coordinator of the Lesbian, Gay, Bisexual, and Transgendered Collective of the University of Winnipeg, described the difficulties faced by Aboriginal students.

'Aboriginal people face many different things in a university setting', he explained. 'This includes racism, culture shock, and being considered "experts" on Aboriginal issues because you are the only Aboriginal in class.'

He also added that inadequate funding remains the most serious problems for Aboriginal students.

'Education is a treaty right of First Nations people, but the federal government is not holding up its responsibility. There are long waiting lists for funding.'

Barry Hammond of the Grove Street Teachers' Centre in Winnipeg suggested a number of ways universities could better ensure the success of Aboriginal students.

'Tuition should be balanced with the average social income of the communities from which a student comes', Hammond recommended. 'As well, smaller campuses must be designed since few Aboriginal students can succeed in a setting with over 20,000 other learners. Of course, staff must also be diversified with better representation from Aboriginal and other minority groups.'

Amanda Aziz and Lisa Stepnuk of the University of Manitoba's Womyn's Centre said that while women are attending universities and colleges in ever greater numbers, a number of inequities still exist.

'Manitoba has the highest high school dropout rate among women of any province', Aziz noted. 'Many of these young women are mothers and a significant portion is Aboriginal. If these women are dropping out of high school, most of them will never make it to university or college.'

'For those women who do get onto campus, they must also face an atmosphere that is systematically sexist and exclusionary',

Box 8.4 continued

Stepnuk said. 'Male professors and deans make up the majority of most departments so that the education we receive is almost entirely from a male perspective. Add to this the fact that the overwhelming majority of all faculty members are white and the problems become even more acute.'

Larissa Ashdown, president of the University of Winnipeg Students' Association, warned higher tuition fees are closing the doors to post-secondary education for many qualified students.

'Recent data suggests [sic] there is a direct link between funding and accessibility. We also suspect that dropout rates from Canadian post-secondary institutions are disturbingly high, largely due to the excessive financial burden placed on students and their families.'

Representatives of the faculty associations of Saint-Boniface, Winnipeg, and Manitoba also participated in the hearings.

Ranjan Roy, president of the University of Manitoba Faculty Association, said universities in Canada, encouraged by governments, are shifting priorities away from traditional liberal arts programs to 'more market-oriented programs' like computer science and business administration.

'While over the past couple of years hiring at my university has kept pace with and even exceeded the number of colleagues who've left or retired, the faculty of arts has had a net loss. Departments of English, French, Spanish, Italian, history, psychology and sociology have experienced significant cuts. Recently, $800,000 was transferred from the faculty of arts budget to a Strategic Initiatives Fund, controlled by the administration and used for more lucrative and high-profile programs.'

Representatives of a number of community organizations attended the hearings and suggested the city's universities and colleges need to develop a better relationship with the local community.

'The universities as institutions have been basically irrelevant to the community I work with', stated Marty Dolin, executive director of the Manitoba Interfaith Immigration Council. 'The perception of the folks out there is that the universities are isolated and not relevant to the Aboriginal community, the ethno-Canadian community, and the working-class community because universities themselves are not open to them.'

gain a full understanding of the nature and implications of educational change and innovation.

This is especially true of reforms that are fiscally or politically motivated, or those that treat education in an abstract way as an industry or business. Economically, it often makes sense to close community or neighbourhood schools with low enrolments, to increase class sizes or tuition fees, or to prioritize educational programs that contribute to high student achievement and employment. Canada and other jurisdictions have begun to explore mechanisms that would provide a foundation for evidence-based decision-making in education. Educators, administrators, and policy-makers, in the process, need to keep a strong perspective on the questions and limitations that surround the appropriateness and applicability of such indicators. Viewed in pedagogical and social terms, educational reform and decision-making are much more complex matters that are often compounded by uncertain or conflicting evidence. There are few absolute or readily agreed-upon answers to questions about such issues as the optimal class size for teaching and learning at different levels, the impact of mainstreaming of special-needs students within regular classrooms on different groups of students, the extent to which decisions over school closures should consider community interests as well as cost factors, the amount of formal recognition that should be given to different educational credentials, and the relative merit of training workers as opposed to educating citizens. It is likely that debates over these kinds of issues will intensify as the role of education in a globally changing society comes under further public scrutiny.

Conclusion: Conflict, Diversity, and Choice in Education

The insight that education and schooling are complex, multi-dimensional, and contradictory endeavours—one of the prevalent themes throughout this book—is an essential starting point from which to base an understanding of educational issues. Education is a social activity concerned with the development and transformation of human beings. As education is converted into various informal and institutional forms, it both reflects and modifies the social world of which it is a part. Consequently, education has personal and social importance, as well as wider economic and political significance.

These issues, in turn, point to important questions linked to social policy formulation and research in education. Some of these, as we have seen, have been addressed by research and analysis, but because all of them involve conflicting choices and interpretations, they require much more intensive scrutiny. A sampling of these questions is outlined below:

- What is really meant by quality education?
- Who should pay for education? To what extent, and at what levels, should the state cover educational costs as opposed to leaving responsibility with individuals, families, employers, or other agencies?

- To what extent should learners be segregated from, or integrated with, other learners according to ability and special needs?
- To what extent should specific groups or communities, defined by such factors as religion, cultural values, political beliefs, or economic interests, be able to establish and control their own educational institutions? If such schools are established, who should pay for them and what kinds of guidelines, if any, should be in place to ensure their consistency with federal or provincial standards?
- How should we define and measure educational success?
- To what extent should educational priorities and programs be determined by labour markets?
- How much should public education be focused on local concerns as opposed to global issues?
- How much autonomy should educators and educational specialists, as opposed to parents and community members, have to plan and deliver educational services?

While sociological analysis, in conjunction with other forms of inquiry, can help provide a foundation and tools from which to assess these issues, it cannot provide absolute answers. This book began with an overview of key debates central to sociological inquiry that must be taken into consideration when addressing questions such as the ones posed here. Our analysis should be guided by a recognition that social structures and institutions, which give shape to our experiences and provide definition for social issues, are also constructed and can be changed through human activity.

Sociology enables us to gain insights about our lives by examining the relationships between individuals and social forces. In sociological research and analysis, as with all other dimensions of human social life, we must make decisions about what to study, how to examine it, and what to do about our findings. The answers we come up with emerge only from the choices made by people as they interact with one another and their social circumstances. Education, in this sense, is a critical process in our ability to broaden our basis of social understanding, increase our ability to make meaningful life decisions, and transform our world in ways that can be beneficial to all of us.

This chapter has highlighted emergent debates and issues associated with contemporary demands for educational reform. There is a broad range of positions about what education should be about and how it should be organized. These tend to be focused on divergent views that stress, on the one hand, an understanding of education as a commodity that can be marketed like other goods and services and, on the other hand, an emphasis on the personal, transformative characteristics of education for social justice. The centrality of the diverse forms of education to human life suggests that education will continue to be contested, leaving open questions about how to ensure that all people are able to develop and use their capacities in meaningful ways.

Annotated Further Readings

Patrice de Broucker and Arthur Sweetman, eds, *Towards Evidence-Based Policy for Canadian Education*. Montreal and Kingston: McGill-Queen's University Press, 2002. Contributors from diverse academic and policy perspectives highlight relevant issues, advances, and concerns related to educational measurement and research oriented to the improvement of educational practices and outcomes.

Larry Cuban, *Oversold and Underused: Computers in the Classroom*. Cambridge, Mass.: Harvard University Press, 2000. The author investigates the claims made by proponents and critics of computers in education systems, providing strong evidence about the limits and prospects associated with the integration of new technologies within existing classroom settings.

John P. Portelli and R. Patrick Solomon, eds, *The Erosion of Democracy in Education: From Critique to Possibilities*. Calgary: Detselig, 2001. This collection draws on examples from different Canadian contexts to highlight serious concerns arising from recent educational reforms and to work towards an alternative, progressive educational vision.

Satu Repo, ed., *Making Schools Matter: Good Teachers at Work*. Toronto: James Lorimer, 1998. Contributors present examples from a variety of teaching contexts and jurisdictions in Canada to demonstrate the broad range of effective and innovative educational possibilities.

Heather-Jane Robertson, *No More Teachers, No More Books: The Commercialization of Canada's Schools*. Toronto: McClelland & Stewart, 1998. The author offers a pointed critique of the ways in which powerful lobby groups and business interests are attacking and reshaping schools in order to expand opportunities for commercialization and ensure stronger alignment with market forces.

Charles Ungerleider, *Failing Our Kids: How We Are Ruining Our Public Schools*. Toronto: McClelland & Stewart, 2003. The author, drawing on extensive experience as an educational researcher, administrator, and policy-maker, examines conflicting challenges that are posing dangers for public schools. He makes a highly informed case for the development of strong schools that can contribute effectively to economic development and informed citizenship.

Key Terms

Accountability The expectation that public education, like other state-provided services, has clearly defined objectives that members of the public can identify and assess as to how well and how cost-effectively they are being met.

Charter schools Schools based on a contract or charter that outlines specific arrangements and performance commitments, made between school representatives and school boards or government bodies.

Digital divide The gap between individuals, groups, and regions based on differential access to and use of computers and information communications technologies.

Educational governance The laws, procedures, regulations, and institutional arrangements that outline how education systems are organized and operated within a specific jurisdiction.

Inclusive schooling A concept that emphasizes schools as agencies that actively incorporate and respond to diverse student needs, regardless of social, physical, or cultural characteristics.

Marketization   A process in which social relationships are transformed by defining people as consumers and social services such as education are considered as profit-making endeavours or commodities that are produced, bought, and sold in a market environment.

Person rights   The basis for a vision of democracy in which all people are assured specific social entitlements and opportunities for meaningful participation in social, political, and economic life by virtue of their residence or citizenship within a jurisdiction.

Property rights   The notion that social, economic, and political participation are based on market relations, private property, and contractual arrangements.

Study Questions

1. Considerable recent controversy has been generated over the issue of whether there should be an overarching public system of education or a variety of educational alternatives that allow parents optimal choice for their children's schooling. Discuss whether the provision of education should be a public or a private matter, critically assessing the strengths and limitations of the main positions within this debate.

2. Critically discuss the extent to which educational practices have been affected by, and should be modified to adapt to, computerization and new developments in information and communications technologies.

3. Discuss the role of formal educational institutions in a context that places increasing emphasis on lifelong learning. To what extent should the role and mandate of school be broadened, relative to alternatives that place greater emphasis on learning at home, on the job, and in other sites?

4. Discuss the extent to which parents and other community members should be involved in decision-making within local schools. Should schools respond primarily to local interests or address broader concerns?

5. Discuss the extent to which, and the ways in which, educational reform is necessary in order to fulfill contemporary social and economic expectations.

6. Describe and explain major directions in recent educational reform, indicating which groups have had the strongest influence on those reforms.

Web Sites

www.afn.ca/Programs/Education/educationsec.htm
The Assembly of First Nations Web site includes policies, position papers, research, and resources related to education and other matters of importance to First Nations across Canada.

www.asanet.org/soe/
This site, maintained by the Sociology of Education section of the American Sociology Association, is directed primarily to professionals and researchers engaged in the field. It contains a summary description of the sociology of education and emerging issues, as well as many useful links to other databases and relevant sites.

www.caut.ca/
The Canadian Association of University Teachers, which represents academic staff at Canadian universities, reports on its Web site major developments, issues, analyses relevant to post-secondary education.

www.cepan.ca/cepan.htm
The Web site of the Canadian Educational Policy and Administration Network contains resources, discussion topics, and links related to elementary and secondary educational policy and administration in Canada.

www.cfs.ontario.ca
The Canadian Federation of Students provides a student voice and perspective on post-secondary issues, policies, and relevant matters of concern to its membership (drawn from university and college students in institutions across Canada) and others interested in educational matters. The cfs site includes position papers, research and analysis, and links to other major education information sites.

www.cmec.ca/indexe/htm
The home page for the Council of Ministers of Education Canada provides access to major reports and studies conducted through that organization, as well as links to each of the provincial and territorial ministries of education and other important Canadian and international education bodies.

www.educationcanada.cmec.ca/EN/home.php
Education@Canada, maintained by the Council of Ministers of Education Canada, provides a resource base with information on education in Canada and its provinces and territories. It offers basic information and more detailed links related to different education systems and levels across Canada.

www.eric.ed.gov/searchdb/searchdb.html
ERIC, the Educational Resources Information Center, contains a comprehensive database of information (mostly abstracts of journal articles and reports) on various aspects and fields related to education, including sociology of education. It is a valuable reference tool and starting point for research into both contemporary and historical educational issues.

www.hrdc-drhc.gc.ca/common/home.shtml
Human Resources Development Canada provides information on jobs, education and training initiatives, children and youth, Aboriginal people, persons with disabilities, and other factors relevant to workplace and community participation. The Web site contains extensive research and reports in addition to basic information about government programs and employment in Canada.

www.oecd.org/home/
The Web site of the Organization for Economic Co-operation and Development provides useful and up-to-date information for international comparisons and developments. It includes report summaries, statistics, and links to major documents on education and related thematic areas that highlight significant trends and issues for 30 member countries and several dozen other nations.

www.oise.utoronto.ca/depts/sese/csew/nall
The Web site for the New Approaches to Lifelong Learning national research network provides definitions, discussion papers, and research findings that document the nature and extent of informal learning and other forms of learning that occur outside of formal educational institutions.

www.oise.utoronto.ca/other/ien/ienpage.html
The Indigenous Education Network was started in 1989 by Aboriginal students at the Ontario Institute for Studies in Education/University of Toronto, and now includes both Aboriginal and non-Aboriginal students, faculty, alumni, community members, and others who organize events, foster collaborative work, and provide support for and public information related to Aboriginal education. Its Web site is oriented primarily to postsecondary education but includes links to numerous sites for those interested in historical and contemporary dimensions of indigenous people and their education.

www.schoolnet.ca/home/e/
SchoolNet, established by the Canadian government in the late 1990s, was the world's first initiative to link public schools and libraries in all parts of the country. The Web site is intended to provide ready access for educators, students, and numerous educational partners to common sites and to an extensive resource base to support teaching/learning and educational activities.

www.sosig.ac.uk/roads/subject-listing/World-cat/soceduc.html
The Social Science Information Gateway, based in the United Kingdom, offers a substantial and useful set of links to significant reports, databases, journals, publishers, government bodies, and other organizations pertinent to the sociology of education in numerous national settings.

www.statcan.ca/
Statistics Canada provides the most comprehensive body of data and information on education and numerous related areas on its Web site and through its links with other sites. The site includes census data, diverse databases and reports on both current and historical dimensions of Canadian social and economic life, and learning resources for students and educators.

www.tcrecord.org/
The Web site for *Teachers' College Record* offers an on-line journal, discussion groups, and other items of interest for educators, educational researchers, and students. Free registration is required for access to numerous items that are relevant to many significant dimensions of teaching and learning.

References

Acker, Sandra. 1999. *The Realities of Teachers' Work: Never a Dull Moment*. London: Cassell.

Alatia, Alessandro. 2003. 'Rural and Urban Educational Attainment: An Investigation of Patterns and Trends, 1981–1996', *Rural and Small Town Analysis* Bulletin 4, 5 (June). Statistics Canada cat. no. 21–006XIE.

Albas, Daniel, and Cheryl Albas. 1993. 'Disclaimer Mannerisms of Students: How To Avoid Being Labelled as Cheaters', *Canadian Review of Sociology and Anthropology* 31, 4 (Nov.): 422–45.

Altenbaugh, Richard J. 1995. 'The Irony of Gender', in Mark B. Ginsburg, ed., *The Politics of Teachers' Work and Lives*. New York: Garland Publishing, 73–90.

Althusser, Louis. 1971. 'Ideology and Ideological State Apparatuses', in Althusser, ed., *Lenin and Philosophy and Other Essays*. New York: Monthly Review Press, 172–86.

Anderson, James G. 1968. *Bureaucracy in Education*. Baltimore: Johns Hopkins University Press.

Andres Bellamy, Lesley. 1993. 'Life Trajectories, Action, and Negotiating the Transition from High School', in Anisef and Axelrod (1993: 137–57).

———. 1994. 'Capital, Habitus, Field, and Practice: An Introduction to the Work of Pierre Bourdieu', in Erwin and MacLennan (1994: 120–36).

Angus Reid Group. 1999. 'Canadians' Assessment and Views of the Education System', press release, Toronto, 22 June.

Anisef, Paul, and Paul Axelrod, eds. 1993. *Transitions: Schooling and Employment in Canada*. Toronto: Thompson Educational Publishing.

———, ———, Etta Baichman-Anisef, Carl James, and Anton Turritin. 2000. *Opportunity and Uncertainty: Life Course Experiences of the Class of '73*. Toronto: University of Toronto Press.

——— and Norman Okihiro. 1982. *Losers and Winners: The Pursuit of Equality and Social Justice in Higher Education*. Toronto: Butterworths.

Apple, Michael W. 1979. *Ideology and Curriculum*. London: Routledge & Kegan Paul.

———. 1982. *Education and Power*. New York: Routledge & Kegan Paul.

———. 1986. *Teachers and Texts: A Political Economy of Class and Gender Relations in Education*. New York: Routledge & Kegan Paul.

———. 2000. *Official Knowledge: Democratic Education in a Conservative Age*. New York: Routledge.

Arbus, Judith. 1990. 'Grateful to be Working: Women Teachers During the Great Depression', in Frieda Forman, Mary O'Brien, Jane Haddad, Dianne Hallman, and Philinda Masters, eds, *Feminism and Education: A Canadian Perspective*. Toronto: Centre for Women's Studies in Education, 169–90.

Armstrong, Pat, and Hugh Armstrong. 2001. *The Double Ghetto: Canadian Women and Their Segregated Work*, 3rd edn. Toronto: Oxford University Press.

Arnot, Madeleine, and Kathleen Weiler, eds. 1993. *Feminism and Social Justice in Education: International Perspectives*. London: Falmer Press.

Aronowitz, Stanley, and Henry A. Giroux. 1993. *Education Still Under Siege*, 2nd edn. Toronto: OISE Press.

Ashton, David, and Graham Lowe. 1991. 'School-to-work Transitions in Britain and Canada: A Comparative Perspective', in Ashton and Lowe, eds, *Making Their Way: Education, Training and the Labour Market in Canada and Britain*. Toronto: University of Toronto Press, 1–14.

Ashton, David N., and Johnny Sung. 1997. 'Education, Skill Formation, and Economic Development: The Singaporean Approach', in Halsey et al. (1997: 207–18).

Assembly of First Nations. 1988. *Tradition and Education: Towards a Vision of Our Future, National Review of First Nations Education*, vol. 1. Ottawa: Assembly of First Nations.

Axelrod, Paul. 1997. *The Promise of Schooling: Education in Canada, 1800–1914*. Toronto: University of Toronto Press.

———. 2002. *Values in Conflict: The University, the Marketplace and the Trials of Liberal Education*. Montreal and Kingston: McGill-Queen's University Press.

Bacon, Allan. 1995. 'The Teachers' Perspective on Accountability', *Canadian Journal of Education* 20, 1 (Winter): 85–91.

Balcom, Susan, and Mike Crawley. 1996. 'Trying To Pick "Best Schools" a Tricky Business', *Vancouver Sun*, 10 Feb., A14.

Baldhead, Sheila. 1988. 'My Survival School and What It Means to Me', *Our Schools/Our Selves* 1, 1 (Oct.): 42–4.

Barlow, Maude, and Heather-Jane Robertson. 1994. *Class Warfare: The Assault on Canada's Schools*. Toronto: Key Porter Books.

Battiste, Marie. 2000. 'Introduction: Unfolding the Lessons of Colonization', in Marie Battiste, ed., *Reclaiming Indigenous Voice and Vision*. Vancouver: University of British Columbia Press, xvi–xxx.

Bauer, Gabrielle. 2001. 'Why Boys Must Be Boys: Is your son's school giving him what he needs to succeed?', *Canadian Living* (Nov.).

Beach, Charles M., and George A. Slotsve. 1996. *Are We Becoming Two Societies? Income Polarization and the Myth of the Declining Middle Class in Canada*. Toronto: C.D. Howe Institute.

Beattie, Catherine. 1996. 'The Computer in Schools: Visions, Illusions, and Mistakes', in Geoffrey Milburn, ed., *'Ring Some Alarm Bells in Ontario': Reactions to the Report of the Royal Commission on Learning*. London, Ont.: Althouse Press, 95–107.

Beck, Nuala. 1992. *Shifting Gears: Thriving in the New Economy*. Toronto: HarperCollins.

Becker, Howard S. 1952. 'Social Class Variations in the Teacher-Pupil Relationship', *Journal of Educational Sociology* 25 (Apr.): 451–65.

———. 1953. 'The Teacher in the Authority System of the Public School', *Journal of Educational Sociology* 26 (Nov.): 128–41.

———. 1996. 'School is a Lousy Place to Learn Anything In', in Robert G. Burgess, ed., *Howard Becker on Education*. Buckingham, UK: Open University Press, 99-112. Originally published in *American Behavioral Scientist* (1972): 85–105.

Bell, Daniel. 1973. *The Coming of Post-Industrial Society*. New York: Basic Books.

Bernhard, Judith K., and Joyce Nyhof-Young. 1994. 'Towards Increased Participation of Women in Science and Technology: Social Theory and Interventions for Girls in Ontario Elementary Schools', in Erwin and MacLennan (1994: 397–416).

Bernier, Rachel. 1996. 'The Labour Force Survey: 50 years Old in 1996', in Statistics Canada, *Labour Force Annual Averages 1995*. Ottawa: Minister of Industry, Science and Technology, A33–A50.

Bernier, Suzanne. 1995. 'Youth Combining School and Work', *Education Quarterly Review* 2, 4 (Winter): 10–23.

Bernstein, Basil. 1977. 'Class and Pedagogies: Visible and Invisible', in Jerome Karabel and A.H. Halsey, eds, *Power and Ideology in Education*. New York: Oxford University Press, 511–34.

Bibby, Reginald W. 1995. *The Bibby Report: Social Trends Canadian Style*. Toronto: Stoddart.

———. 2001. *Canada's Teens: Today, Yesterday, and Tomorrow*. Toronto: Stoddart.

Birchard, Karen. 2002. 'European report compares student conditions in eight countries', *University Affairs* (Dec.): 24.

Blake, Dan. 1991. 'Should Teachers Have the Right to Strike? Yes', *Vancouver Sun*, 30 Mar.

Blau, Peter M., and Otis Dudley Duncan. 1967. *The American Occupational Structure*. New York: John Wiley and Sons.

Bohatyretz, Sandra, and Garth Lipps. 1999. 'Diversity in the classroom: Characteristics of elementary students receiving special education', *Education Quarterly Review* 6, 2 (Mar.): 7–19.

Bolaria, B. Singh. 1987. 'The Brain Drain to Canada: The Externalization of the Cost of Education', in Terry Wotherspoon, ed., *The Political Economy of Canadian Schooling*. Toronto: Methuen, 301–22.

———. 2000. 'An Introduction to Social Issues and Contradictions: Sociological Perspectives', in Bolaria, ed., *Social Issues and Contradictions in Canadian Society*, 3rd edn. Toronto: Harcourt Brace & Company, 1–19.

———, Harley D. Dickinson, and Terry Wotherspoon. 1995. 'Rural Issues and Problems', in Bolaria, ed., *Social Issues and Contradictions in Canadian Society*, 2nd edn, 419–43.

——— and Peter S. Li. 1988. *Racial Oppression in Canada*, 2nd edn. Toronto: Garamond Press.

Bosetti, Lynn. 2001. 'The Alberta Charter School Experience', in Claudia R. Hepburn, ed., *Can the Market Save Our Schools?* Vancouver: Fraser Institute, 101–20.

Bourdieu, Pierre. 1977. 'Cultural Reproduction and Social Reproduction', in Jerome Karabel and A.H. Halsey, eds, *Power and Ideology in Education*. New York: Oxford University Press, 487–511.

———. 1984 [1979]. *Distinction: A Social Critique of the Judgement of Taste*. Cambridge, Mass.: Harvard University Press.

——— and Jean-Claude Passeron. 1979. *The Inheritors: French Students and Their Relations to Culture*. Chicago: University of Chicago Press.

Bowers, Norman, Anne Sonnet, and Laura Bardone. 1999. 'Background Report: Giving Young People a Good Start: The Experience of OECD Countries', in Organization for Economic Co-operation and Development, *Preparing Youth for the 21st Century: The Transition from Education to the Labour Market*. Proceedings of the Washington, DC, Conference, 23–4 Feb. 1999. Paris: OECD, 7–86.

Bowlby, Geoff. 1996. 'Relationship between Postsecondary Graduates' Education and Employment', *Education Quarterly Review* 3, 2 (Summer): 35–44.

Bowles, Samuel, and Herbert Gintis. 1976. *Schooling in Capitalist America: Educational Reform and the Contradictions of Economic Life*. New York: Basic Books.

Boyd, Monica. 1985. 'Educational and Occupational Attainments of Native-Born Canadian Men and Women', in Boyd, John Goyder, Frank E. Jones, Hugh A. McRoberts, Peter C. Pineo, and John Porter, *Ascription and Achievement: Studies in Mobility and Status Attainment in Canada*. Ottawa: Carleton University Press, 229–95.

Braithwaite, Max. 1979. *Why Shoot the Teacher?* Toronto: McClelland & Stewart.

Braverman, Harry. 1974. *Labor and Monopoly Capital: The Degradation of Work in the Twentieth Century*. New York: Monthly Review Press.

Brink, Satya, and Urvashi Dhawan-Biswal. 2002. 'Investing in our youth for a skilled workforce', *Quarterly Labour Market and Income Review* 3, 1 (Summer): 19. Human Resources Development Canada SP–506–07–02.

British Columbia. 1875. *Annual Report of the Public Schools, 1875*. Victoria: Province of British Columbia.

———. 1904. *Annual Report of the Public Schools, 1904*. Victoria: Province of British Columbia.

———. 1988. *A Legacy for Learners: The Report of the Royal Commission on Education*. Victoria: Province of British Columbia.

British Columbia School Trustees' Association. 1980. 'Rules Required for Teachers in Revelstoke Area, 1915', *BCSTA Reports*, 17 Oct.

British Columbia Teachers' Federation. 2003. 'B.C. Liberals are hurting students' learning conditions, poll shows', news release, 1 May.

Brookes, Anne-Louise. 1992. *Feminist Pedagogy: An Autobiographical Approach*. Halifax: Fernwood Publishing.

Brown, Louise. 2002. 'Two-tier grade schooling feared: Funds crunch warning in report', *Toronto Star*, 31 May, A1, A26.

Brown, Phillip, A.H. Halsey, Hugh Lauder, and Amy Stuart Wells. 1997. 'The Transformation of Education and Society: An Introduction', in Halsey et al. (1997: 1–44).

Bruce, Christopher J., and Arthur M. Schwartz. 1997. 'Education: Meeting the Challenge', in Bruce, R.D. Kneebone, and K.J. McKenzie, eds, *A Government Reinvented: A Study of Alberta's Deficit Elimination Program*. Toronto: Oxford University Press, 383–416.

Bushnik, Tracey. 2003. *Learning, Earning and Leaving: The Relationship between Working While in High School and Dropping Out*. Ottawa: Minister of Industry, Education, Skills and Learning, Research Paper cat. no. 81–595–MIE, No. 004.

Bussière, Patrick, Fernando Cartwright, Robert Crocker, Xin Ma, Jillian Oderkirk, and Yanhong Zhang. 2001. *Measuring Up: The Performance of Canada's Youth in Reading, Mathematics and Science*. Ottawa: Minister of Industry Canada.

Butlin, George. 1999. 'Determinants of postsecondary participation', *Education Quarterly Review* 5, 3 (Mar.): 9–35.

———. 2000. 'Determinants of university and community college leaving', *Education Quarterly Review* 6, 4 (Aug.): 8–23.

Canadian Association of University Teachers. 2002. 'Community Groups Say Universities Should Do More', *CAUT Bulletin* 49, 4 (Apr.): A4.

———. 2003. *CAUT Almanac of Post-Secondary Education in Canada, 2003*. Ottawa: Canadian Association of University Teachers.

———. 2003. Submission of the Canadian Association of University Teachers to the Pay Equity Task Force, Nov. Available at: <http://www.caut.ca/english/issues/equity/payequitysubmission.pdf>.

Canadian Council on Social Development. 2003. Census Analysis: Census Shows Growing Polarization of Income in Canada. Ottawa: Canadian Council on Social Development. Available at: <http://www.ccsd.ca/pr/2003/censusincome.htm>.

Canadian Education Statistics Council. 1996. *A Statistical Portrait of Education at the University Level in Canada*. Ottawa: Statistics Canada and Council of Ministers of Education Canada.

Canadian Institute of Public Opinion. 1976. 'One-In-Three Believe Education has Slipped', *The Gallup Report*, 27 Mar.

Canadian Race Relations Foundation. 2000. *Racism in Our Schools: What to Know about It; How to Fight It*. Ottawa: Canadian Race Relations Foundation.

Canadian School Boards Association. 1999. *Poverty Intervention Profile: Partners in Action*. Ottawa: Canadian School Boards Association.

Canadian Teachers' Federation. 1991. *A Cappella: The Realities, Concerns, Expectations and Barriers Experienced by Adolescent Women in Canada*. Ottawa: Canadian Teachers' Federation.

———. 1993. *Progress Revisited: The Quality of (Work) Life of Women Teachers*. Ottawa: Canadian Teachers' Federation.

———. 2003. *Teaching in Canada*. Ottawa: Canadian Teachers' Federation. Available at: <http://www.ctf-fce.ca/E/teaching.htm>.

Carnoy, Martin. 1974. *Education as Cultural Imperialism*. New York: D. McKay Co.

——— and Henry M. Levin. 1985. *Schooling and Work in the Democratic State*. Stanford, Calif.: Stanford University Press.

Carr-Saunders, A.M. 1966. 'Professionalism in Historical Perspective', in H.M. Vollmer and D.L. Mills, eds, *Professionalization*. Englewood Cliffs, NJ: Prentice-Hall, 2–9.

Castellano, Marlene Brant, Lynne Davis, and Louise Lahache, eds. 2000. *Aboriginal Education: Fulfilling the Promise*. Vancouver: University of British Columbia Press.

Central Advisory Council for Education (The Plowden Report). 1967. *Children and their Primary Schools*, 2 vols. London: Her Majesty's Stationery Office.

Chabbott, Colette, and Francisco O. Ramirez. 2000. 'Development and Education', in Maureen T. Hallinan, ed., *Handbook of the Sociology of Education*. New York: Kluwer Academic/Plenum Publishers, 163–87.

Chafe, J.W. 1969. *Chalk, Sweat, and Cheers: A History of the Manitoba Teachers' Society*. Winnipeg: Manitoba Teachers' Society.

Chalmers, John W. 1968. *Teachers of the Foothills Province: The Story of the Alberta Teachers' Association*. Toronto: University of Toronto Press.

Charland, Jean-Pierre. 2000. *L'entreprise éducative au Québec, 1840–1900*. Québec: Les presses de l'Université Laval.

Chubb, John E., and Terry M. Moe. 1990. *Politics, Markets, and America's Schools*. Washington: Brookings Institution.

Cicourel, Aaron V., and John I. Kitsuse. 1963. *The Educational Decision-Makers*. Indianapolis: Bobbs-Merrill.

Clairmont, Don, and Richard Apostle. 1997. 'Work: A Segmentation Perspective', in Axel Van den Berg and Joseph Smucker, eds, *The Sociology of Labour Markets: Efficiency, Equity, Security*. Scarborough, Ont.: Prentice-Hall Allyn and Bacon, 388–404.

Clark, Burton R. 1962. *Educating the Expert Society*. San Francisco: Chandler.

Clark, Warren. 1991. *The Class of '86: A Compendium of Findings of the 1988 National Graduates Survey of 1986 Graduates with Comparisons to the 1984 National Graduates Survey*. Ottawa: Employment and Immigration Canada.

———. 2000. '100 Years of Education', *Canadian Social Trends* 59 (Winter): 3–7.

Clement, Wallace. 1974. *The Canadian Corporate Elite: An Analysis of Economic Power*. Toronto: McClelland & Stewart.

——— and Glenn Williams. 1989. *The New Canadian Political Economy*. Montreal and Kingston: McGill-Queen's University Press.

Coleman, James S. 1968. 'The Concept of Equality of Educational Opportunity', *Harvard Educational Review* 38, 1 (Winter): 7–22.

——— et al. 1966. *Equality of Educational Opportunity*. Washington: US Government Printing Office.

Collins, Randall. 1971. 'Functional and Conflict Theories of Educational Stratification', *American Sociological Review* 36, 6 (Dec.): 1002–19.

———. 2000. 'Comparative and Historical Patterns of Education', in Maureen T. Hallinan, ed., *Handbook of the Sociology of Education*. New York: Kluwer Academic/Plenum Publishers, 213–39.

Collis, Betty. 1991. 'Adolescent Females and Computers: Real and Perceived Barriers', in Gaskell and McLaren (1991: 147–61).

Connell, R.W. 1985. *Teachers' Work*. Sydney: George Allen & Unwin.

———, D.J. Ashenden, S. Kessler, and G.W. Dowsett. 1982. *Making the Difference: Schools, Families and Social Division*. Sydney: George Allen & Unwin.

Contenta, Sandro. 1993. *Rituals of Failure: What Schools Really Teach*. Toronto: Between the Lines.

Corbett, Bradley A., and J. Douglas Willms. 2002. 'Information and communication technology: Access and use', *Education Quarterly Review* 8, 4 (Oct.): 8–15.

Corporation des Enseignants du Québec (CEQ). 1974. 'Our Schools Serve the Ruling Class', in George Martell, ed., *The Politics of the Canadian Public School*. Toronto: James Lorimer, 172–85.

Corrigan, Philip, Bruce Curtis, and Robert Lanning. 1987. 'The Political Space of Schooling', in Wotherspoon (1987: 21–43).

Cottingham, Mollie E. 1958. 'The Canadian Conference on Education', *The B.C. Teacher* 37, 8 (May–June): 398–9, 407–8.

Coulter, Rebecca Priegert. 1993. 'Schooling, Work and Life: Reflections of the Young in the 1940s', in Coulter and Ivor F. Goodson, eds, *Rethinking Vocationalism: Whose Work/Life Is It?* Toronto: Our Schools/Our Selves, 69–86.

Council of Ministers of Education Canada. 1993. 'Joint Declaration: Future Directions for The Council of Ministers of Education, Canada'. Victoria: 64th Meeting of the Council of Ministers of Education Canada.

———. 1996. *Enhancing the Role of Teachers in a Changing World*. Report of Canada in response to the International Survey in Preparation for the Forty-Fifth Session of the International Conference on Education. Toronto: Council of Ministers of Education Canada.

——. 2001. *The Development of Education in Canada: Report of Canada*. Toronto: Council of Ministers of Education Canada.

Crawley, Mike. 1995. *Schoolyard Bullies: Messing with British Columbia's Education System*. Victoria: Orca Book Publishers.

Creese, Gillian, Neil Guppy, and Martin Meissner. 1991. *Ups and Downs on the Ladder of Success: Social Mobility in Canada*. Ottawa: Minister of Industry, Science and Technology, Statistics Canada cat. no. 11–612.

Crompton, Susan. 1996. 'Employment prospects for high school graduates', *Education Quarterly Review* 3, 1 (Spring): 8–19.

——. 2002. 'I still feel overqualified for my job', *Canadian Social Trends* 67 (Winter): 23–6.

—— and Michael Vickers. 2000. 'One hundred years of labour force', *Canadian Social Trends* 57 (Summer): 7–8.

Crysdale, Stewart, Alan J.C. King, and Nancy Mandell. 1999, *On Their Own? Making the Transition from School to Work in the Information Age*. Montreal and Kingston: McGill-Queen's University Press.

—— and Harry MacKay. 1994. *Youth's Passage Through School to Work: A Comparative Longitudinal Study*. Toronto: Thompson Educational Publishing.

Cuneo, Carl. 2002. 'Globalized and Localized Digital Divides Along the Information Highway: A Fragile Synthesis Across Bridges, Ramps, Cloverleaves, and Ladders'. Saskatoon: University of Saskatchewan, 33rd Annual Sorokin Lecture.

Currie, Jan, and Janice Newson, eds. 1998. *Universities and Globalization: Critical Perspectives*. Thousand Oaks, Calif.: Sage.

Curtis, Bruce. 1988. *Building the Educational State: Canada West, 1836–1871*. Barcombe, Lewes: Falmer Press.

——, D.W. Livingstone, and Harry Smaller. 1992. *Stacking the Deck: The Streaming of Working-Class Kids in Ontario Schools*. Toronto: Our Schools/Our Selves Education Foundation.

Curtis, James, Edward Grabb, and Neil Guppy, eds. 1999. *Social Inequality in Canada: Patterns, Problems, Policies*, 3rd edn. Scarborough, Ont.: Prentice-Hall Allyn and Bacon.

Danylewycz, Marta, Beth Light, and Alison Prentice. 1991. 'The Evolution of the Sexual Division of Labor in Teaching: Nineteenth Century Ontario and Quebec Case Study', in Gaskell and McLaren (1991: 33–60).

—— and Alison Prentice. 1986. 'Teachers' Work: Changing Patterns and Perceptions in the Emerging School Systems of Nineteenth and Early Twentieth Century Central Canada', *Labour/Le Travail* 17 (Spring): 59–80.

Davey, Ian E. 1978. 'The Rhythm of Work and the Rhythm of School', in McDonald and Chaiton (1978: 221–53).

Davies, Scott. 1995. 'Leaps of Faith: Shifting Currents in Critical Sociology of Education', *American Journal of Sociology* 100, 6 (May): 1448–78

——, Janice Aurini, and Linda Quirke. 2002. 'New Markets for Private Education in Canada', *Education Canada* 42, 3 (Fall): 36–8.

de Broucker, Patrice, and Arthur Sweetman. 2002. 'Introduction', in de Broucker and Sweetman, eds, *Towards Evidence-Based Policy for Canadian Education*. Kingston: John Deutsch Institute for the Study of Economic Policy/Statistics Canada, 1–14.

Dei, George J. Sefa. 1996. *Anti-Racism Education: Theory and Practice*. Halifax: Fernwood.

—— and Agnes Calliste, eds. 2000. *Power, Knowledge and Anti-Racism Education: A Critical Reader*. Halifax: Fernwood.

——, Irma Marcia James, Leeno Luke Karumanchery, Sonia James-Wilson, and Jasmin Zine. 2000. *Removing the Margins: The Challenges and Possibilities of Inclusive Schooling*. Toronto: Canadian Scholars' Press.

Denis, Wilfrid B. 1995. 'The Meech Lake Shuffle: French and English Language Rights in Canada', in B. Singh Bolaria, ed., *Social Issues and Contradictions in Canadian Society*, 2nd edn. Toronto: Harcourt Brace & Company, 161–92.

Dennison, John D. 1981. 'The Community College in Canada: An Educational Innovation', in J. Donald Wilson, ed., *Canadian Education in the 1980's*. Calgary: Detselig, 213–30.

Department of Indian Affairs and Northern Development. 1997. *Basic Departmental Data*. Ottawa: Minister of Supply and Services Canada.

Dewey, John. 1966. *Democracy and Education*. New York: Free Press.

Dibski, Dennis. 1995. 'Financing Education', in Ratna Ghosh and Douglas Ray, eds, *Social Change and Education in Canada*, 3rd edn. Toronto: Harcourt Brace & Company, 66–80.

Dominion Bureau of Statistics. 1924. *The Canada Year Book 1922–23*. Ottawa: King's Printer.

———. 1962. *Survey of Vocational Education and Training*. Ottawa: Minister of Trade and Commerce.

———. 1963. *Survey of Higher Education 1954–1961*. Ottawa: Queen's Printer.

Downie, Bryan M. 1978. *Collective Bargaining and Conflict Resolution in Education: The Evolution of Public Policy in Ontario*. Kingston: Queen's University Industrial Relations Centre, Research and Current Issues Series No. 36.

Dreeben, Robert. 1968. *On What is Learned in School*. Reading, Mass.: Addison-Wesley.

Dryburgh, Heather. 2002. 'Learning computer skills', *Education Quarterly Review* 8, 2 (Mar.): 8–18.

Durkheim, Émile. 1933 [1893]. *The Division of Labor in Society*. New York: Free Press.

———. 1956 [1922]. *Education and Society*. Glencoe, Ill.: Free Press.

Easton, Stephen T. 1988. *Education in Canada: An Analysis of Elementary, Secondary and Vocational Schooling*. Vancouver: Fraser Institute.

Economic Council of Canada. 1991. *Employment in the Service Economy*. Ottawa: Minister of Supply and Services Canada.

Edwards, R. Gary, and Josephine Mazzuca. 1999a. 'Armed Forces Top Institutional List for Respect and Confidence', *The Gallup Poll* 59, 31 (20 May).

——— and ———. 1999b. 'Canadians Divided Over Satisfaction with Education Children Receive', *The Gallup Poll* 59, 19 (31 Mar.).

Ellsworth, Elizabeth. 1992. 'Why Doesn't This Feel Empowering? Working Through the Repressive Myths of Critical Pedagogy', in Carmen Luke and Jennifer Gore, eds, *Feminisms and Critical Pedagogy*. New York: Routledge, 90–119.

Erwin, Lorna, and David MacLennan, eds. 1994. *Sociology of Education in Canada: Critical Perspectives on Theory, Research & Practice*. Toronto: Copp Clark Longman.

Eyre, Linda. 1991. 'Gender Relations in the Classroom: A Fresh Look at Coeducation', in Gaskell and McLaren (1991: 193–219).

Fine, Sean. 2001. 'Schools told to fix boys' low grades', *Globe and Mail*, 27 Aug., A1, A7.

Finnie, Ross. 2000. 'Holding their own: Employment and earnings of postsecondary graduates', *Education Quarterly Review* 7, 1 (Nov.): 21–37.

———. 2001. 'Graduates' earnings and the job skills-education match', *Education Quarterly Review* 7, 2 (Feb.): 7–21.

——— and Gaetan Garneau. 1996. 'Student Borrowing for Postsecondary Education', *Education Quarterly Review* 3, 2 (Summer): 10–34.

Finucan, Kerry. 1994. 'The Competitiveness Craze: A Critique of the Recent Vocationalism in Canadian Education, 1984–1992', M.Ed. thesis, University of Saskatchewan.

Fischer, Claude S., Michael Hout, Martin Sanchez Jankowski, Samuel R. Lucas, Ann Swindler, and Kim Voss. 1996. *Inequality by Design: Cracking the Bell Curve Myth*. Princeton: Princeton University Press.

Fleming, Thomas. 1986. '"Our Boys in the Field": School Inspectors, Superintendents and the Changing Character of School Leadership in British Columbia', in Nancy M.

Sheehan, J. Donald Wilson, and David C. Jones, eds, *Schools in the West: Essays in Canadian Educational History*. Calgary: Detselig, 285–303.

Fleras, Augie, and Jean Leonard Elliott. 1992. *Multiculturalism in Canada: The Challenge of Diversity*. Scarborough, Ont.: Nelson Canada.

—— and ——. 2003. *Unequal Relations: An Introduction to Race and Ethnic Dynamics in Canada*, 4th edn. Toronto: Prentice-Hall.

Floud, Jean, A.H. Halsey, and F.M. Martin. 1956. *Social Class and Educational Opportunity*. London: Heinemann.

Forcese, Dennis. 1997. *The Canadian Class Structure*, 4th edn. Toronto: McGraw-Hill Ryerson.

Fournier, Elaine, George Butlin, and Philip Giles. 1995. 'Intergenerational Change in the Education of Canadians', *Education Quarterly Review* 2, 2 (Summer): 22–33.

Fraser, Steven, ed. 1995. *The Bell Curve Wars: Race, Intelligence, and the Future of America*. New York: Basic Books.

Freedman, Joe. 1995. *The Charter School Idea: Breaking Educational Gridlock*. Red Deer, Alta: Society for Advancing Educational Research.

Freire, Paulo. 1970. *Pedagogy of the Oppressed*. New York: Herder and Herder.

——. 1985. *The Politics of Education: Culture, Power and Liberation*. South Hadley, Mass.: Bergin and Garvey.

Frempong, George, and J. Douglas Willms. 2002. 'Can School Quality Compensate for Socioeconomic Disadvantage?', in Willms, ed., *Vulnerable Children: Findings from Canada's National Longitudinal Survey of Children and Youth*. Edmonton: University of Alberta Press and Human Resources Development Canada, 277–303.

Fuller, Bruce. 2000. 'Introduction: Growing Charter Schools, Decentering the State', in Fuller, ed., *Inside Charter Schools: The Paradox of Radical Decentralization*. Cambridge, Mass.: Harvard University Press, 1–11.

Gaffield, Chad. 1982. 'Schooling, the Economy, and Rural Society in Nineteenth-Century Ontario', in Joy Parr, ed., *Childhood and Family in Canadian History*. Toronto: McClelland & Stewart, 69–92.

Galarneau, Diane, Howard Krebs, René Morissette, and Xuelin Zhang. 2001. *The Quest for Workers: A New Portrait of Job Vacancies in Canada*. Ottawa: Minister of Industry, The Evolving Workplace Series, Statistics Canada cat. no. 71–584–MPE No. 2.

Gallen, Verna, Bruce Karlenzig, and Isobel Tamney. 1995. 'Teacher Workload and Work Life in Saskatchewan', *Education Quarterly Review* 2, 4 (Winter): 49–58.

Galt, Virginia. 1997. 'Teachers Buying Own Class Supplies', *Globe and Mail*, 12 Aug., A5.

Gaskell, Jane. 1992. *Gender Matters from School to Work*. Toronto: OISE Press.

—— and Arlene McLaren. 1991. 'Women as Mothers, Women as Teachers', in Gaskell and McLaren (1991: 19–32).

—— and ——, eds. 1991. *Women and Education*, 2nd edn. Calgary: Detselig.

——, ——, and Myra Novogrodsky. 1989. *Claiming an Education: Feminism and Canadian Schools*. Toronto: Our Schools/Our Selves.

Gerth, H.H., and C. Wright Mills. 1946. *From Max Weber: Essays in Sociology*. New York: Oxford University Press.

Ghosh, Ratna. 1995. 'Social Change and Education in Canada', in Ghosh and Ray (1995: 3–15).

—— and Douglas Ray, eds. 1995. *Social Change and Education in Canada*, 3rd edn. Toronto: Harcourt Brace & Company.

Giddens, Anthony. 1987. *Sociology: A Brief but Critical Introduction*, 2nd edn. San Diego: Harcourt Brace Jovanovich.

Gilbert, Sid, Lynn Barr, Warren Clark, Matthew Blue, and Deborah Sunter. 1993. *Leaving School: Results from a National Survey Comparing School Leavers and High School Graduates 18 to 20 years of age*. Ottawa: Minister of Supply and Services.

—— and Jeff Frank. 1998. 'Educational Pathways', in Human Resources Development Canada and Statistics Canada, *High School May Not Be Enough: An Analysis of Results from the School Leavers Follow-up Survey, 1995*. Ottawa: Minister of Public Works and Government Services Canada, cat. no. 81–585–XBE, 9–20.

Gilliss, Geraldine. 1995. 'The Grade is Made if One Looks at the Data Carefully', in Thomas T. Schweitzer, Robert K. Crocker, and Gilliss, *The State of Education in Canada*. Montreal: Institute for Research on Public Policy, 119–26.

Gintis, Herbert. 1980. 'Communication and Politics', *Socialist Review* 10 (Mar./June): 189–232.

———— and Samuel Bowles. 1980. 'Contradiction and Reproduction in Educational Theory', in Len Barton, Roland Meighan, and Stephen Walker, eds, *Schooling, Ideology and the Curriculum*. Barcombe, Lewes: Falmer Press, 51–65.

Giroux, Henry A. 1983. *Theory and Resistance in Education*. South Hadley, Mass.: Bergin and Garvey.

————. 1988. *Teachers as Intellectuals*. Westport, Conn.: Bergin and Garvey.

————. 1989. 'Schooling as a Form of Cultural Politics: Toward a Pedagogy of and for Difference', in Giroux and McLaren (1989: 125–53).

———— and Peter McLaren, eds. 1989. *Critical Pedagogy, the State, and Cultural Struggle*. Albany: State University of New York Press.

Goffman, Erving. 1961. *Asylums*. Garden City, NY: Doubleday.

Gorbutt, David. 1972. 'The New Sociology of Education', *Education for Teaching* 89 (Autumn): 3–11.

Government of Canada. 1991. *Learning Well . . . Living Well*. Ottawa: Minister of Supply and Services Canada.

————. 2001. *Achieving Excellence: Investing in People, Knowledge and Opportunity*. Ottawa: Industry Canada, Catalogue no. C2–596/200i.

————. 2002. *Knowledge Matters: Skills and Learning for Canadians: Canada's Innovation Strategy*. Ottawa: Minister of Industry.

Government of Saskatchewan. 2003. *School Plus: Well-being and Educational Success for ALL Children and Youth*. Regina: Saskatchewan Learning (Spring).

Gramsci, Antonio. 1971. 'The Intellectuals', in Quintin Hoare and Geoffrey Nowell Smith, eds and trans, *Selections from the Prison Notebooks of Antonio Gramsci*. London: Lawrence and Wishart, 13–23.

Grayson, J. Paul. 1997. *Who Gets Jobs? Initial Labour Market Experiences of York Graduates*. Toronto: Institute for Social Research, York University.

Grenier, Sylvie. 1995. 'Survey of Private Training Schools in Canada', *Education Quarterly Review* 2, 3 (Fall): 50–62.

Grieshaber-Otto, Jim, and Matt Sanger. 2002. *Perilous Lessons: The Impact of the WTO Services Agreement (GATS) on Canada's Public Education System*. Ottawa: Canadian Centre for Policy Alternatives.

Guppy, Neil, and Scott Davies. 1998. *Education in Canada: Recent Trends and Future Challenges*. Ottawa: Statistics Canada.

———— and ————. 1999. 'Understanding Canadians' Declining Confidence in Public Education', *Canadian Journal of Education* 24, 3 (Summer): 265–80.

Hall, E.M., and L.A. Dennis. 1968. *Living and Learning: The Report of the Provincial Committee on Aims and Objectives of Education in the Schools of Ontario* (Hall-Dennis Report). Toronto: Ontario Department of Education.

Halsey, A.H., Hugh Lauder, Phillip Brown, and Amy Stuart Wells, eds. 1997. *Education: Culture, Economy, and Society*. Oxford: Oxford University Press

Hargreaves, David H. 1967. *Social Relations in a Secondary School*. London: Routledge & Kegan Paul.

Haughey, M.L., and P.J. Murphy. 1983. 'What Rural Teachers Think of Their Jobs', *Canadian School Executive* 2, 8 (Fall): 12–14.

Health Canada. 1999. *Healthy Development of Children and Youth: The Role of the Determinants of Health*. Ottawa: Minister of Health Canada.

Heisz, A., A. Jackson, and G. Picot. 2002. *Winners and Losers in the Labour Market of the*

1990s. Ottawa: Statistics Canada Analytical Studies Branch Research Paper Series No. 184 (Feb.).

Henchey, Norman. 1977. 'Pressures for Professional Autonomy and Public Controls', in Hugh A. Stevenson and J. Donald Wilson, eds, *Precepts, Policy and Process: Perspectives on Contemporary Canadian Education*. London, Ont.: Alexander, Blake Associates.

Henry, Frances, Carol Tator, Winston Mattis, and Tim Rees. 2000. *The Colour of Democracy: Racism in Canadian Society*, 2nd edn. Toronto: Harcourt Brace & Company.

Hepburn, Claudia Rebanks. 1999. 'The Case for School Choice: Models from the United States, New Zealand, Denmark, and Sweden'. Vancouver: Fraser Institute Critical Issues Bulletin (Sept.).

Herrnstein, Richard J. 1973. *IQ in the Meritocracy*. Boston: Little Brown.

———— and Charles Murray. 1994. *The Bell Curve: Intelligence and Class Structure in American Life*. New York: Free Press.

Hess, Melanie. 1989. *Children, Schools and Poverty*. Ottawa: Canadian Teachers' Federation.

Hoff Sommers, Christina. 2000. *The War Against Boys: How Misguided Feminism Is Harming Our Young Men*. New York: Simon and Schuster.

Holmes, Janelle, and Elaine Leslau Silverman. 1992. *We're Here, Listen to Us! A Survey of Young Women in Canada*. Ottawa: Status of Women Canada.

Holt, John. 1964. *How Children Fail*. New York: Pitman.

Houston, Susan E. 1982. 'The "Waifs and Strays" of a Late Victorian City: Juvenile Delinquents in Toronto', in Joy Parr, ed., *Childhood and Family in Canadian History*. Toronto: McClelland & Stewart, 129–42.

———— and Alison Prentice. 1988. *Schooling and Scholars in Nineteenth-Century Ontario*. Toronto: University of Toronto Press.

Hughes, Graham. 2003. 'Economic advantages add up to better scores', *Ottawa Citizen*, 17 June.

Hughes, Karen D., and Graham S. Lowe. 2000. 'Surveying the "Post-Industrial" Landscape: Information Technologies and Labour Market Polarization in Canada', *Canadian Review of Sociology and Anthropology* 37, 1 (Feb.): 28–53.

Human Resources Development Canada. 1994. *Profile of Post-Secondary Education in Canada*, 1993 edn. Ottawa: Supply and Services Canada.

————. 1996. 'Labour Market Polarization . . . What's Going On?', *Applied Research Bulletin* 2, 2 (Summer–Fall): 5–7.

————. 2000. *Profile of Canadian Youth in the Labour Market*, Second Annual Report to the Forum of Labour Market Ministers. Ottawa: Human Resources Development Canada, cat. no. RH61–1/2000E.

Hunter, Alfred J., and Jean McKenzie Leiper. 1993. 'On Formal Education, Skills and Earnings: The Role of Educational Certificates in Earnings Determination', *Canadian Journal of Sociology* 18, 1 (Winter): 21–42.

Hurst, Charles E. 1992. *Social Inequality: Forms, Causes, and Consequences*. Boston: Allyn and Bacon.

Illich, Ivan. 1970. *Deschooling Society*. New York: Harper and Row.

Industry Canada. 1992. *A Lot to Learn: Education and Training in Canada*. Ottawa: Industry Canada.

Ipsos-Reid. 2003. 'A Good Understanding of the Basics (91%) Tops 7 Goals As To What Parents Say Their Children Need For A Successful Education—But Only Half (51%) Are Satisfied With Their Child's Progress Towards This Goal', press release, Toronto, 23 Feb.

Jackson, Nancy S. 1987. 'Ethnicity and Vocational Choice', in Young (1987: 165–82).

————. 1993. 'Rethinking Vocational Learning', in Rebecca Priegert Coulter and Ivor F. Goodson, eds, *Rethinking Vocationalism: Whose Work/Life Is It?* Toronto: Our Schools/Our Selves Education Foundation, 166–80.

————. 1994. 'Rethinking Vocational Learning: The Case of Clerical Skills', in Erwin and MacLennan (1994: 341–51).

Jackson, Philip W. 1968. *Life in Classrooms*. New York: Holt, Rinehart and Winston.

Jaenen, Cornelius J. 1986. 'Education for Francization: The Case of New France in the Seventeenth Century', in Jean Barman, Yvonne Hébert, and Don McCaskill, eds, *Indian Education in Canada*, vol. 1: *The Legacy*. Vancouver: University of British Columbia Press, 45–63.

Jaine, Linda, ed. 1993. *Residential Schools: The Stolen Years*. Saskatoon: University Extension Press.

James, Carl E. 1993. 'Getting There and Staying There: Blacks' Employment Experience', in Anisef and Axelrod (1993: 3–20).

———. 2000. *Seeing Ourselves: Exploring Race, Ethnicity and Culture*, 3rd edn. Toronto: Thompson Educational Publishing.

Jencks, Christopher, et al. 1972. *Inequality: A Reassessment of the Effect of Family and Schooling in America*. New York: Basic Books.

Jenks, Chris. 1998. 'Introduction', in Jenks, ed., *Core Sociological Dichotomies*. London: Sage, 1–7.

Jenish, D'arcy. 1997. 'Flirting with "Chaos"', *Maclean's* (21 July): 51.

Jensen, Arthur. 1973. *Educability and Group Difference*. New York: Harper and Row.

Johnson, F. Henry. 1968. *A Brief History of Canadian Education*. Toronto: McGraw-Hill.

Johnston, Basil H. 1988. *Indian School Days*. Toronto: Key Porter Books.

Kanpol, Barry. 1992. *Towards a Theory and Practice of Teacher Cultural Politics: Continuing the Postmodern Debate*. Norwood, NJ: Ablex Publishing.

Katz, Joseph. 1969. *Society, Schools and Progress in Canada*. Toronto: Pergamon Press.

Karabel, Jerome, and A.H. Halsey. 1977. 'Educational Research: A Review and an Interpretation', in Karabel and Halsey, eds, *Power and Ideology in Education*. New York: Oxford University Press, 1–85.

Kazemipur, Abdolmohammad, and Shiva S. Halli. 2001. 'The Changing Colour of Poverty in Canada', *Canadian Review of Sociology and Anthropology* 38, 2 (May): 217–38.

Kenway, Jane, and Helen Modra. 1992. 'Feminist Pedagogy and Emancipatory Possibilities', in Luke and Gore (1992: 138–66).

——— and Sue Willis. 1998. *Answering Back: Girls, Boys and Feminism in Schools*. London: Routledge.

Kerckhoff, Alan C. 2000. 'Transition from School to Work in Comparative Perspective', in Maureen T. Hallinan, ed., *Handbook of the Sociology of Education*. New York: Kluwer Academic/Plenum Publishers, 453–74.

Kerr, Kevin. 1997. *Labour Market Developments*, Library of Parliament Research Branch Current Issue Review. Ottawa: Minister of Supply and Services Canada.

King, Alan J.C., William F. Boyce, and Matthew A. King. 1999. *Trends in the Health of Canadian Youth*. Ottawa: Health Canada.

——— and Marjorie J. Peart. 1992. *Teachers in Canada: Their Work and Quality of Life*. Ottawa: Canadian Teachers' Federation.

Kirkness, Verna, and Sheena Selkirk Bowman. 1992. *First Nations and Schools: Triumphs and Struggles*. Toronto: Canadian Education Association.

Knight, Doug. 1993. 'Understanding Change in Education in Rural and Remote Regions of Canada', in Earle Newton and Knight, eds, *Understanding Change in Education: Rural and Remote Regions of Canada*. Calgary: Detselig, 299–310.

Knighton, Tamara, and Sheba Mirza. 2002. 'Postsecondary participation: the effects of parents' education and household income', *Education Quarterly Review* 8, 3 (June): 25–32.

Kozol, Jonathan. 1967. *Death at an Early Age: The Destruction of the Hearts and Minds of Negro Children in Boston Public Schools*. New York: Houghton Mifflin.

Krahn, Harvey, and Graham S. Lowe. 1990. *Young Workers in the Service Economy*. Ottawa: Economic Council of Canada, Working Paper No. 14.

Lacey, Colin. 1970. *Hightown Grammar: The School as a Social System*. Manchester: Manchester University Press.

Lareau, Annette. 1989. *Home Advantage: Social Class and Parental Intervention in Elementary Education*. London: Falmer Press.

—— and Erin McNamara Horvat. 1999. 'Moments of Social Inclusion and Exclusion: Race, Class, and Cultural Capital in Family-School Relationships', *Sociology of Education* 72, 1 (Jan.): 37–53.

Lauwerys, Joseph. 1973. *The Purposes of Education: Results of a CEA Survey*. Toronto: Canadian Education Association.

Lawr, Douglas, and Robert Gidney, eds. 1973. *Educating Canadians: A Documentary History of Public Education*. Toronto: Van Nostrand Reinhold.

Lawson, Robert F., and Roger R. Woock. 1987. 'Policy and Policy Actors in Canadian Education', in Ratna Ghosh and Douglas Ray, eds, *Social Change and Education in Canada*. Toronto: Harcourt Brace Jovanovich, 133–42.

Lawton, Stephen B. 1995. *Busting Bureaucracy to Reclaim Our Schools*. Montreal: Institute for Research on Public Policy.

Leacy, F.H. 1983. *Historical Statistics of Canada*, 2nd edn. Ottawa: Statistics Canada.

LeBlanc, Jules. 1974. 'Becoming Political: The Growth of the Quebec Teachers' Union', in Martell (1974: 151–64).

le Riche, Timothy. 1996. 'A Primer on School Changes', *Edmonton Sun*, 25 Aug., 21.

Lessard, Claude. 1995. 'Equality and Inequality in Canadian Education', in Ghosh and Ray (1995: 178–95).

Lévesque, M. 1979. *L'égalité des chances en éducation, considérations théoriques et approches empiriques*. Québec: Conseil Supérieur de l'Education.

Levin, Benjamin. 1990. 'Tuition Fees and University Accessibility', *Canadian Public Policy* 16, 1 (Mar.): 51–9.

Lewington, Jennifer. 1995. 'Report Cards Get a New Twist', *Globe and Mail*, 13 Nov., A1.

—— and Graham Orpwood. 1993. *Overdue Assignment: Taking Responsibility for Canada's Schools*. Toronto: John Wiley & Sons.

Li, Peter S. 1988. *Ethnic Inequality in a Class Society*. Toronto: Wall and Thompson.

——. 1996. *The Making of Post-War Canada*. Toronto: Oxford University Press.

——. 2003. *Destination Canada: Immigrant Debates and Issues*. Toronto: Oxford University Press.

Livingstone, D.W. 1983. *Class, Ideologies and Educational Futures*. London: Routledge.

——. 1985. *Social Crisis and Schooling*. Toronto: Garamond Press.

——. 1987. 'Crisis, Classes and Educational Reform in Advanced Capitalism', in Wotherspoon (1987: 57–67).

——. 1994. 'Searching for Missing Links: Neo-Marxist Theories of Education', in Erwin and MacLennan (1994: 55–82).

——. 1999. *The Education-Jobs Gap: Underemployment or Economic Democracy*. Toronto: Garamond Press.

——, D. Hart, and L.E. Davie. 1999. *Public Attitudes towards Education in Ontario 1998: The Twelfth OISE/UT Survey*. Toronto: Ontario Institute for Studies in Education/University of Toronto Press.

——, ——, and ——. 2001. *Public Attitudes towards Education in Ontario 2000: The Thirteenth OISE/UT Survey*. Toronto: Ontario Institute for Studies in Education/University of Toronto Orbit Magazine.

Lockhart, Alexander. 1979. 'Educational Opportunities and Economic Opportunities— the "New" Liberal Equality Syndrome', in John A. Fry, ed., *Economy, Class and Social Reality: Issues in Contemporary Canadian Society*. Toronto: Butterworths, 224–37.

——. 1991. *School Teaching in Canada*. Toronto: University of Toronto Press.

Lortie, Dan C. 1975. *Schoolteacher: A Sociological Study*. Chicago: University of Chicago Press.

Love, James. 1978. 'The Professionalization of Teachers in Mid-Nineteenth Century Upper Canada', in McDonald and Chaiton (1978: 109–28).

Lowe, Graham S., and Harvey Krahn. 1994. *Job-Related Education and Training Among Young Workers*. Kingston: Industrial Relations Centre, Queen's University.

Luke, Carmen, and Jennifer Gore, eds. 1992. *Feminisms and Critical Pedagogy*. New York: Routledge.

Lynch, Kathleen. 1989. *The Hidden Curriculum: Reproduction in Education, an Appraisal*. London: Falmer Press.

McAndrew, Marie. 1995. 'Ethnicity, Multiculturalism, and Multicultural Education in Canada', in Ghosh and Ray (1995: 165–77).

McDonald, Neil, and Alf Chaiton, eds. 1978. *Egerton Ryerson and His Times: Essays on the History of Education*. Toronto: Macmillan.

McFate, Katherine, Timothy Smeeding, and Lee Rainwater. 1995. 'Markets and States: Poverty Trends and Transfer System Effectiveness in the 1980s', in McFate, Roger Lawson, and William Julius Wilson, eds, *Poverty, Inequality, and the Future of Social Policy: Western States in the New World Order*. New York: Russell Sage Foundation, 29–66.

McLaren, Arlene, and Jim Gaskell. 1995. 'Now You See It, Now You Don't: Gender as an Issue in School Science', in Jane Gaskell and John Willinsky, eds, *Gender In/forms Curriculum: From Enrichment to Transformation*. New York: Teachers College Press, 136–56.

McLaren, Peter. 1998. *Life in Schools: An Introduction to Critical Pedagogy in the Foundations of Education*, 3rd edn. New York: Addison-Wesley Longman.

McNeil, Linda M. 1986. *Contradictions of Control: School Structure and School Knowledge*. New York: Routledge & Kegan Paul.

McRobbie, Angela. 1978. 'Working Class Girls and the Culture of Femininity', in Women's Studies Group, Centre for Contemporary Cultural Studies, *Women Take Issue*. Birmingham: University of Birmingham, Centre for Contemporary Cultural Studies, 96–108.

Mandell, Nancy, and Stewart Crysdale. 1993. 'Gender Tracks: Male-Female Perceptions of Home-School-Work Transitions', in Anisef and Axelrod (1993: 19–41).

Mangan, J. Marshall. 1994. 'The Politics of Educational Computing in Ontario', in Erwin and MacLennan (1994: 263–77).

Manitoba Association of School Trustees. 2003. 'Real Costs of Amalgamation Becoming Evident; Sunrise School Division Labour Dispute "Tip of the Iceberg"', news release, 8 Apr.

Mann, Jean. 1980. 'G.M. Weir and H.B. King: Progressive Education or Education for the Progressive State', in J. Donald Wilson and David C. Jones, eds, *Schooling and Society in 20th Century British Columbia*. Calgary: Detselig, 91–118.

Mannheim, Karl. 1936. *Ideology and Utopia: An Introduction to the Sociology of Knowledge*. New York: Harcourt, Brace and World.

Manzer, Ronald. 1994. *Public Schools and Political Ideas: Canadian Educational Policy in Historical Perspective*. Toronto: University of Toronto Press.

Martel, Denis, Jocelyn Gagnon, Joanne Pelletier-Murphy, and Johanne Grenier. 1999. 'Pygmalion en éducation physique: un mythe bien réel', *Canadian Journal of Education* 24, 1 (Winter): 42–56.

Martell, George, ed. 1974. *The Politics of the Canadian Public School*. Toronto: James Lorimer.

Martin, Wilfred. 1976. *The Negotiated Order of the School*. Toronto: Macmillan.

———. 1982. *Teachers' Pets and Class Victims*. St John's: Publications Committee, Faculty of Education, Memorial University of Newfoundland.

——— and Allan J. Macdonell. 1982. *Canadian Education: A Sociological Analysis*, 2nd edn. Scarborough, Ont.: Prentice-Hall.

Marx, Karl. 1963 [1869]. *The Eighteenth Brumaire of Louis Bonaparte*. New York: International Publishers.

———. 1977. *Capital: A Critique of Political Economy*, vol. 1. New York: Vintage Books.

——— and Frederick Engels. 1965 [1848]. *Manifesto of the Communist Party*. Peking: Foreign Languages Press.

Miller, James R. 1996. *Shingwauk's Vision: A History of Native Residential Schools*. Toronto: University of Toronto Press.

Mills, C. Wright. 1951. *White Collar: The American Middle Classes*. New York: Oxford University Press.

———. 1956. *The Power Elite*. New York: Oxford University Press.

Ministerial Task Force on Youth. 1996. *Take on the Future: Canadian Youth in the World of Work*. Report—Ministerial Task Force on Youth, 15 June. Ottawa: Human Resources Development Canada.

Monture-Angus, Patricia. 1995. *Thunder in My Soul: A Mohawk Woman Speaks*. Halifax: Fernwood.

Morissett, René, Xuelin Zhang, and Marie Drolet. 2002. 'Are families getting richer?', *Canadian Social Trends* 66 (Autumn): 15–19. Statistics Canada cat. no. 11–008.

Moscovitch, Allan, and Glenn Drover. 1987. 'Social Expenditures and the Welfare State: The Canadian Experience in Historical Perspective', in Allan Moscovitch and Jim Albert, eds, *The 'Benevolent' State: The Growth of Welfare in Canada*. Toronto: Garamond Press, 13–43.

Moss, Gemma and Dena Attar. 1999. 'Boys and Literacy: Gendering the Reading Curriculum', in Jon Prosser, ed., *School Culture*. Thousand Oaks, Calif.: Sage, 133–44.

Muir, J. Douglas. 1968. *Collective Bargaining by Canadian Public School Teachers*. Task Force on Labour Relations Study No. 11. Ottawa: Information Canada.

Mullen, Judy Kwasnica. 1994. *Count Me In: Gender Equity in the Primary Classroom*. Toronto: Green Dragon Press.

Murray, Debbie. 2001. *E-Learning for the Workplace: Creating Canada's Lifelong Learners*. Ottawa: Conference Board of Canada.

Myers, Douglas. 1973. 'Introduction', in Myers, ed., *The Failure of Educational Reform in Canada*. Toronto: McClelland & Stewart, 11–13.

Myles, John, and Gail Fawcett. 1990. *Job Skills and the Service Economy*. Ottawa: Economic Council of Canada, Working Paper No. 4.

Nakhaie, M. Reza. 1996. 'The Reproduction of Class Relations by Gender in Canada', *Canadian Journal of Sociology* 21, 4 (Fall): 523–58.

National Council of Welfare. 1995. *Poverty Profile 1993*. Ottawa: Minister of Supply and Services Canada.

———. 2002. *Poverty Profile 1999*. Ottawa: Minister of Public Works and Government Services Canada.

Naylor, Charlie. 2002. 'Teacher Workload and Stress: An International Perspective on Human Costs and Systemic Failure', *Our Schools/Our Selves* 11, 3 (Spring): 125–50.

——— and Anne C. Schaefer. 2002. 'Teacher workload and stress: A British Columbia Perspective', *Education Quarterly Review* 8, 3 (June): 33–6.

Neatby, Hilda. 1953. *So Little for the Mind*. Toronto: Clarke, Irwin.

Nelsen, Randle W. 1997. 'Reading, Writing and Relationships among the Electronic Zealots: Distance Education and the Traditional University', in Nelsen, ed., *Inside Canadian Universities: Another Day at the Plant*. Kingston, Ont.: Cedarcreek Publications, 184–210.

——— and David Nock, eds. 1978. *Reading, Writing, and Riches: Education and the Socio-Economic Order in North America*. Kitchener, Ont.: Between the Lines.

Ng, Roxanna. 1991. 'Teaching Against the Grain: Contradictions for Minority Teachers', in Gaskell and McLaren (1991: 99–115).

Nikiforuk, Andrew. 1993. *School's Out: The Catastrophe in Public Education and What We Can Do About It*. Toronto: Macfarlane Walter & Ross.

O'Brien, Mary. 1983. *The Politics of Reproduction*. London: Routledge & Kegan Paul.

Oderkirk, Jillian. 1996. 'Computer Literacy—A Growing Requirement', *Education Quarterly Review* 3, 3 (Fall): 9–29.

Ogbu, John. 1994. 'Racial Stratification and Education in the United States: Why Inequality Persists', *Teachers College Record* 96: 264–98.

Olson, Paul. 1995. 'Poverty and Education in Canada', in Ghosh and Ray (1995: 196–208).

Organization for Economic Co-operation and Development (OECD). 2001a. *The New Economy: Beyond the Hype*. The OECD Growth Project. Paris: OECD.

——. 2001b. *OECD Economic Outlook* 70 (Dec.). Paris: OECD.

——. 2002. *Understanding the Brain: Towards a New Learning Science*. Paris: OECD.

Ornstein, Michael, Penni Stewart, and Janice Drakich. 1998. 'The status of women faculty in Canadian universities,' *Education Quarterly Review* 5, 2 (Dec.): 9–29.

Osberg, Lars, Fred Wien, and Jan Grude. 1995. *Vanishing Jobs: Canada's Changing Workplaces*. Toronto: James Lorimer.

Ozga, Jennifer, and Martin Lawn. 1981. *Teachers, Professionalism and Class: A Study of Organized Teachers*. London: Falmer Press.

Pagliarello, Claudio. 1994. 'Private Elementary and Secondary Schools', *Education Quarterly Review* 1, 1 (Spring): 42–50.

Paquette, Jerry. 1989. 'The Quality Conundrum: Assessing What We Cannot Agree On', in Stephen B. Lawton and Rouleen Wignall, eds, *Scrimping or Squandering? Financing Canadian Schools*. Toronto: OISE Press, 11–28.

Parelius, Robert James, and Ann Parker Parelius. 1987. *The Sociology of Education*, 2nd edn. Englewood Cliffs, NJ: Prentice-Hall.

Parsons, Talcott. 1959. 'The School Class as a Social System: Some of its Functions in American Society', *Harvard Educational Review* 29 (Fall): 297–318.

Paton, J.M. 1962. *The Role of Teachers' Organizations in Canadian Education*. Toronto: W.J. Gage.

Pendakur, Ravi. 2000. *Immigrants and the Labour Force: Policy, Regulation, and Impact*. Montreal and Kingston: McGill-Queen's University Press.

Phillips, Charles E. 1957. *The Development of Education in Canada*. Toronto: W.J. Gage.

Piore, Michael J. 1979. *Birds of Passage: Migrant Labour in Industrial Societies*. New York: Cambridge University Press.

Poelzer, Irene. 1990. *Saskatchewan Women Teachers, 1905–1920: Their Contributions*. Saskatoon: Lindenblatt and Hamonic.

Portelli, John P., and R. Patrick Solomon, eds. 2001. *The Erosion of Democracy in Education*. Calgary: Detselig.

Porter, John. 1965. *The Vertical Mosaic: An Analysis of Social Class and Power in Canada*. Toronto: University of Toronto Press.

——, Marion Porter, and Bernard R. Blishen. 1982. *Stations and Callings: Making It Through the School System*. Toronto: Methuen.

Prentice, Alison. 1977. *The School Promoters: Education and Social Class in Mid-Nineteenth Century Upper Canada*. Toronto: McClelland & Stewart.

—— and Susan E. Houston, eds. 1975. *Family, School and Society in Nineteenth Century Canada*. Toronto: Oxford University Press.

—— and Marjorie R. Theobald. 1991. 'The Historiography of Women Teachers: A Retrospect', in Prentice and Theobald, eds, *Women Who Taught: Perspectives on the History of Women and Teaching*. Toronto: University of Toronto Press, 3–33.

Raham, Helen. 1991. 'Should Teachers Have the Right To Strike? No', *Vancouver Sun*, 30 Mar.

——. 1996. 'Revitalizing Public Education in Canada: The Potential of Choice and Charter Schools', *Fraser Forum* (Aug.), special issue.

Randhawa, B.S. 1991. 'Inequities in Educational Opportunities and Life Chances', in Terry Wotherspoon, ed., *Hitting the Books: The Politics of Educational Retrenchment*. Toronto and Saskatoon: Garamond Press and the Social Research Unit, 139–58.

Ray, Brian D. 2001. 'Homeschooling in Canada', *Education Canada* 41, 1 (Spring): 28–31.

Rees, Ruth. 1990. 'Gender Distribution in Canada's Schools: It's Still as Bad as You Think', *Our Schools/Our Selves* 2, 3 (Sept.): 20–2.

Reitz, Jeffrey G. 2001. 'Immigrant Skill Utilization in the Canadian Labour Market: Implications of Human Capital Research', *Journal of International Migration and Integration* 2, 3 (Summer): 347–78.

Regnier, Robert, and Brian D. MacLean. 1987. 'Hegemony in Education: The Nuclear Industry in Northern Schools', in Wotherspoon (1987: 165–79).

Repo, Satu. 1974. 'BC Teachers Turn Political', in Martell (1974: 200–17).

Reynolds, Cecilia. 1990. 'Too Limiting a Liberation: Discourse and Actuality in the Case of Women Teachers', in Frieda Forman, Mary O'Brien, Jane Haddad, Dianne Hallman, and Philinda Masters, eds, *Feminism and Education: A Canadian Perspective*. Toronto: Centre for Women's Studies in Education, 145–68.

Rice, James R. 2002. 'Being Poor in the Best of Times', in G. Bruce Doern, ed., *How Ottawa Spends 2002–2003: The Security Aftermath and National Priorities*. Toronto: Oxford University Press, 102–20.

Rist, Ray C. 1970. 'Student Social Class and Teacher Expectations: The Self-Fulfilling Prophecy in Ghetto Education', *Harvard Educational Review* 40 (Aug.): 411–50.

Ritzer, George. 2000. *Classical Sociological Theory*, 3rd edn. New York: McGraw-Hill.

Roberge, Roger, Jean-Marie Berthelot, and Michael Wolfson. 1995. 'Health and Socio-Economic Inequalities', *Canadian Social Trends* 37 (Summer): 15–19.

Robertson, Susan. 1998. *No More Teachers, No More Books: The Commercialization of Canada's Schools*. Toronto: McClelland & Stewart.

Robertson, Todd. 2003. 'Changing patterns of university finance', *Education Quarterly Review* 9, 2 (June).

Rockhill, Kathleen, and Patricia Tomic. 1995. 'Situating ESL Between Speech and Silence', in Jane Gaskell and John Willinsky, eds, *Gender In/forms Curriculum: From Enrichment to Transformation*. New York: Teachers College Press, 209–29.

Rosenthal, Robert, and Lenore Jacobson. 1968. *Pygmalion in the Classroom: Teacher Expectation and Pupils' Intellectual Development*. New York: Holt, Rinehart and Winston.

Royal Commission of Inquiry into the Delivery of Programs and Services in Primary, Elementary, Secondary Education. 1992. *Our Children, Our Future*. St John's: Government of Newfoundland and Labrador.

Royal Commission on Aboriginal Peoples. 1994. *Toward Recognition: Overview of the Fourth Round*. Ottawa: Minister of Supply and Services Canada.

———. 1996a. *Report of the Royal Commission on Aboriginal Peoples*, vol. 1, *Looking Forward, Looking Back*. Ottawa: Minister of Supply and Services Canada.

———. 1996b. *Report of the Royal Commission on Aboriginal Peoples*, vol. 3, *Gathering Strength*. Ottawa: Minister of Supply and Services Canada.

Royal Commission on Learning. 1994a. *For the Love of Learning*, vol. 1, *Mandate, Context, Issues. Introduction to the Report*. Toronto: Queen's Printer for Ontario.

———. 1994b. *For the Love of Learning*, vol. 2, *Learning: Our Vision for Schools*. Toronto: Queen's Printer for Ontario.

———. 1994c. *For the Love of Learning*, vol. 4, *Making It Happen*. Toronto: Queen's Printer for Ontario.

Royal Commission on the Relations of Capital and Labour in Canada. 1889. *Report of the Royal Commission on the Relations of Capital and Labour in Canada*. Ottawa: Government of Canada.

Runté, Robert. 1998. 'The Impact of Centralized Examinations on Teacher Professionalism', *Canadian Journal of Education* 23, 2 (Spring): 166–81.

Rushton, Philippe, and Anthony Bogaert. 1987. 'Race Differences in Sexual Behavior: Testing an Evolutionary Hypothesis', *Journal of Research on Personality* 21: 529–51.

Samuelson, Les. 1991. 'The Neo-Conservative Sacrifice of Youth: Quality of Youth Employment and Its Consequences', in Terry Wotherspoon, ed., *Hitting the Books: The Politics of Educational Retrenchment*. Toronto and Saskatoon: Garamond Press and the Social Research Unit, 119–38.

Saskatchewan Education. 1996. *Building Communities of Hope: Best Practices for Meeting the Learning Needs of At-Risk and Indian and Métis Students*. Regina: Saskatchewan Education.

Saskatchewan Teachers' Federation. 1995. *The Workload and Worklife of Saskatchewan*

Teachers: Full-Time Teachers 1994–95. Saskatoon: Saskatchewan Teachers' Federation Research Report No. 1.

Satzewich, Vic, and Terry Wotherspoon. 2000. *First Nations: Race, Class, and Gender Relations*. Regina: Canadian Plains Research Centre.

Schecter, Stephen. 1977. 'Capitalism, Class, and Educational Reform in Canada', in Leo Panitch, ed., *The Canadian State: Political Economy and Political Power*. Toronto: University of Toronto Press, 373–416.

Schembari, Patricia. 1994. 'Teacher Workloads in Elementary and Secondary Schools', *Education Quarterly Review* 1, 3 (Fall): 11–16.

Schissel, Bernard. 1997. *Blaming Children: Youth Crime, Moral Panics and the Politics of Hate*. Halifax: Fernwood.

———— and Terry Wotherspoon. 2003. *The Legacy of School for Aboriginal People: Education, Oppression, and Emancipation*. Toronto: Oxford University Press.

Sciadas, George. 2002. *The Digital Divide in Canada*. Ottawa: Statistics Canada Research Paper, 1 Oct., cat. no. 56F0009XIE.

Sears, Alan. 2003. *Retooling the Mind Factory: Education in a Lean State*. Aurora, Ont.: Garamond Press.

Sewid-Smith, Daisy. 1991. 'In Time Immemorial', in Dorothy Jensen and Cheryl Brooks, eds, *In Celebration of Our Survival: The First Nations of British Columbia*. Vancouver: University of British Columbia Press, 16–32.

Shack, Sybil. 1973. *The Two-Thirds Minority: Women in Canadian Education*. Toronto: Guidance Centre, University of Toronto.

Shor, Ira. 1980. *Critical Teaching and Everyday Life*. Boston: South End Press.

Siedule, Tom. 1992. *The Influence of Socioeconomic Background on Education*. Ottawa: Economic Council of Canada, Working Paper No. 34.

Silver, Jim, and Kathy Mallett, with Janice Greene and Freeman Simard. 2002. *Aboriginal Education in Winnipeg Inner-City Schools*. Winnipeg: Canadian Centre for Policy Alternatives and Winnipeg Inner-City Research Alliance.

Skolrood, Arthur Harold. 1967. 'The British Columbia Teachers' Federation: A Study of Its Historical Development, Interests and Activities from 1916 to 1963', Ed.D. thesis, University of Oregon.

Smaller, Harry, Rosemary Clark, Doug Hart, David Livingstone, and Zahra Noormohammed. 2000. 'Teacher Learning, Informal and Formal: Results of a Canadian Teachers' Survey', New Approaches to Lifelong Learning Working Paper 14-2000. Available at: <www.oise.utoronto.ca/depts/sese/csew/nall/res/index.htm>.

Smyth, John. 2001. *Critical Politics of Teachers' Work: An Australian Perspective*. New York: Peter Lang.

———— and Geoffrey Shacklock. 1998. *Re-Making Teaching: Ideology, Policy and Practice*. London: Routledge.

Statistics Canada. 1973. *Education in Canada 1973*. Ottawa: Information Canada.

————. 1984. *Education in Canada 1983*. Ottawa: Minister of Supply and Services Canada.

————. 1993. *Schooling, Work and Related Activities, Income, Expenses and Mobility: 1991 Aboriginal Peoples' Survey*. Ottawa: Minister of Industry, Science and Technology, Catalogue no. 89–534.

————. 1994a. *Education in Canada: A Statistical Review for 1992–93*. Ottawa: Minister of Supply and Services Canada, Catalogue no. 81–229.

————. 1994b. *Profile of Urban and Rural Areas—Part B*. Ottawa: Minister of Industry, Science and Technology.

————. 1995. 'Advance Statistics', *Education Quarterly Review* 2, 3 (Fall): 90, Catalogue no. 81–003.

————. 1996. *Reading the Future: A Portrait of Literacy in Canada*. Ottawa: Minister of Industry, Catalogue no. 89–551.

————. 2000. *Education Indicators in Canada: Report of the Pan-Canadian Education Indicators Program, 1999*. Ottawa: Centre for Education Statistics, Catalogue no. 81–582.

————. 2001a. *Education in Canada, 2000*. Ottawa: Minister of Industry, Catalogue no. 81–229.

————. 2001b. *Historical Labour Force Statistics, 2000*. Ottawa: Minister of Industry, Catalogue no. 71–201.

————. 2001c. 'Trends in the use of private education', *The Daily* (4 July).

————. 2002a. 'Computer access at school and at home', *The Daily* (29 Oct.).

————. 2002b. 'Part-time University faculty', *The Daily* (8 May).

————. 2003a. *Aboriginal Peoples of Canada: A Demographic Profile*, 2001 Census (Analysis Series). Ottawa: Statistics Canada, Catalogue no. 96F0030XIE2001007.

————. 2003b. *Canada's Ethnocultural Portrait: The Changing Mosaic*, 2001 Census (Analysis Series). Ottawa: Statistics Canada, Catalogue no. 96F0030XIE2001008.

————. 2003c. *The Changing Profile of Canada's Labour Force*, 2001 Census (Analysis Series). Ottawa: Statistics Canada, Catalogue no. 96F0030XIE2001009.

————. 2003d. 'Education at a glance', *Education Quarterly Review* 9, 1 (Feb.): 53–8, Catalogue no. 81–003.

————. 2003e. *Education in Canada: Raising the Standard*, 2001 Census (Analysis Series). Ottawa: Statistics Canada, Catalogue no. 96F0030X1E2001012.

————. 2003f. *Labour Force Historical Review*. Ottawa: Statistics Canada, Catalogue no. 71F0004XCB.

————. 2003g. 'Profile of Labour Force Activity, Class of Worker, Occupation, Industry, Place of Work, Mode of Transportation, Language of Work and Unpaid Work for Canada, Provinces, Territories, Census Divisions and Census Subdivisions, 2001 Census'. Ottawa: Statistics Canada, Catalogue no. 95F0490XCB01001 (11 Feb.).

————. 2003h. 'Understanding the Rural-Urban Reading Gap', *Education Quarterly Review* 9, 1 (Feb.): 9–18.

————. 2003i. 'Population 15 years and over by highest level of schooling, 1981–2001 censuses'. Available at: <www.statcan.ca/English/Pgdb/educ45.htm>.

———— and Human Resources Development Canada. 2001. *Learning a Living: A Report on Adult Education and Training in Canada*. Ottawa: Minister of Industry, Catalogue no. 81–586–XPE.

Stebbins, Robert A. 1971. 'The Meaning of Disorderly Behavior: Teacher Definition of a Classroom Situation', *Sociology of Education* 44, 2 (Spring): 217–36.

————. 1975. *Teachers and Meaning: Definitions of Classroom Situations*. Leiden: E.J. Brill.

Steering Group for the Situational Analysis of Canada's Education Sector Human Resources. 2002. *The ABCs of Educational Demographics: Report of the Findings of a Situational Analysis of Canada's Education Sector Human Resources*. Ottawa: Canadian Alliance of Education and Training Organizations, Jan.

Stephens, D. 2000. 'Girls and basic education in Ghana: a cultural enquiry', *International Journal of Educational Development* 20: 29–47.

Sutherland, Neil. 1976. *Children in English-Speaking Canada: Framing the Twentieth-Century Consensus*. Toronto: University of Toronto Press.

Sweet, Robert, and Paul Gallagher. 1999. 'Private Training Institutions in Canada: New Directions for a Public Resource', *Journal of Educational Administration and Foundations* 13, 2: 54–77.

Tanner, Julian, Harvey Krahn, and Timothy F. Hartnagel. 1995. *Fractured Transitions from School to Work: Revisiting the Dropout Problem*. Toronto: Oxford University Press.

Tardif, Maurice, and Claude Lessard. 1999. *Le Travail Enseignant au Quotidien: Contribution à l'étude du travail dans les métiers et les professions d'interactions humaines*. Saint-Nicolas, Que.: Les Presses de L'Université Laval.

Taylor, Alison. 2001. *The Politics of Educational Reform in Alberta*. Toronto: University of Toronto Press.

Titley, E. Brian. 1982. 'Tradition, Change and Education in French Canada', in Titley and Miller (1982: 45–56).

—— and Peter J. Miller, eds. 1982. *Education in Canada: An Interpretation*. Calgary: Detselig.

Tomkins, George S. 1977. 'Canadian Education and the Development of a National Consciousness: Historical and Contemporary Perspectives', in Alf Chaiton and Neil McDonald, eds, *Canadian Schools and Canadian Identity*. Toronto: Gage, 6–28.

——. 1981. 'Stability and Change in the Canadian Curriculum', in J. Donald Wilson, ed., *Canadian Education in the 1980's*. Calgary: Detselig, 135–58.

Torres, Carlos Alberto, and Theodore R. Mitchell. 1998. *Sociology of Education: Emerging Perspectives*. Albany: State University of New York Press.

Tran, Dien. 1995. 'Communication Technology and Education in Canada', in Ghosh and Ray (1995: 45–53).

Tsang, Beryl. 1992. 'Thinking in the Rain', in *Racism and Education: Different Perspectives and Experiences*. Ottawa: Canadian Teachers' Federation, 93–101.

Ungerleider, Charles S. 1994. 'Power, Politics, and the Professionalization of Teachers in British Columbia', in Erwin and MacLennan (1994: 370–9).

United Nations Development Program. 2001. *Human Development Report 2001: Making New Technologies Work for Human Development*. New York: Oxford University Press.

United Nations Educational, Scientific and Cultural Organization (UNESCO). 2002. *Education for All: Is the World on Track?* EFA Global Monitoring Report, 2002. Paris: UNESCO.

UNICEF Innocenti Research Centre. 2002. 'A League Table of Educational Disadvantage in Rich Nations', *Innocenti Report Card* No. 4 (Nov.). Florence: United Nations Children's Fund.

Veltmeyer, Henry. 1986. *The Canadian Class Structure*. Toronto: Garamond Press.

Vollmer, Jamie Robert. 2003. 'The blueberry story: the teacher gives the businessman a lesson', *Our Schools/Our Selves* 12, 3 (Spring): 41–2.

Vosko, Leah. 2003. 'Gender Differentiation and the Standard/Non-Standard Employment Distinction: A Genealogy of Policy Interventions in Canada', in Danielle Juteau, ed., *Social Differentiaton: Patterns and Processes*. Toronto: University of Toronto Press, 25–80.

Walford, Geoffrey, and W.S.F. Pickering, eds. 1998. *Durkheim and Modern Education*. London: Routledge.

Walkerdine, Valerie. 1998. *Counting Girls Out: Girls and Mathematics*, new edn. London: Falmer Press.

Waller, Willard. 1965. *The Sociology of Teaching*. New York: John Wiley & Sons.

Warburton, Rennie. 1986. 'The Class Relations of Public School Teachers in British Columbia', *Canadian Review of Sociology and Anthropology* 23, 2 (May): 210–29.

Weber, Sandra, and Claudia Mitchell. 1999. 'Teacher Identity and Popular Culture', in Jon Prosser, ed., *School Culture*. Thousand Oaks, Calif.: Sage, 145–60.

Weiler, Kathleen. 1988. *Women Teaching for Change: Gender, Class and Power*. New York: Bergin and Garvey.

Weis, Lois. 1990. *Working Class Without Work: High School Students in a De-industrializing Economy*. New York: Routledge.

Whitty, Geoff. 1997. 'Marketization, the State, and the Re-Formation of the Teaching Profession', in Halsey et al. (1997: 299–310).

Wilkinson, Bruce W. 1994. *Educational Choice: Necessary But Not Sufficient*. Montreal: Institute for Research on Public Policy.

Willard, Doug. 2001. 'Keeping Canada's Teaching Profession Alive and Well', *Hill Times*, 8 Oct.

Williams, Tom R., and Holly Millinoff. 1990. *Canada's Schools: A Report Card for the 1990s: A CEA Opinion Poll*. Toronto: Canadian Education Association.

Willis, Paul. 1977. *Learning to Labor: How Working Class Kids Get Working Class Jobs*. New York: Columbia University Press.

Willms, J. Douglas. 1997. *Literacy Skills of Canadian Youth*. Ottawa: Minister of Industry, Statistics Canada cat. no. 89–552–MIE no. 1.

———. 2002. 'The Prevalence of Vulnerability', in Willms, ed., *Vulnerable Children: Findings from Canada's National Longitudinal Survey of Children and Youth*. Edmonton: University of Alberta Press and Human Resources Development Canada, 45–69.

Wilson, J. Donald. 1981. 'Religion and Education: The Other Side of Pluralism', in Wilson, ed., *Canadian Education in the 1980's*. Calgary: Detselig, 97–113.

———. 1991. '"I am ready to be of assistance when I can": Lottie Bowron and Rural Women Teachers in British Columbia', in Alison Prentice and Marjorie R. Theobald, eds, *Women Who Taught: Perspectives on the History of Women and Teaching*. Toronto: University of Toronto Press, 202–29.

———, Robert M. Stamp, and Louis-Philippe Audet, eds. 1970. *Canadian Education: A History*. Scarborough, Ont.: Prentice-Hall.

Wilson, S.J. 1996. *Women, Families, and Work*, 4th edn. Toronto: McGraw-Hill Ryerson.

Wolfe, David A. 2002. 'Innovation Policy for the Knowledge-Based Economy: From the Red Book to the White Paper', in G. Bruce Doern, ed., *How Ottawa Spends 2002–2003: The Security Aftermath and National Priorities*. Toronto: Oxford University Press, 137–56.

Worth, W.H. 1972. *A Future of Choices—A Choice of Futures: A Report of the Commission on Educational Planning* (Worth Report). Edmonton: Queen's Printer.

Wotherspoon, Terry. 1984. 'Ideals and Sausage Factories: Schools in Capitalist Society', in John A. Fry, ed., *Contradictions in Canadian Society: Readings in Introductory Sociology*. Toronto: John Wiley & Sons, 207–18.

———, ed. 1987. *The Political Economy of Canadian Schooling*. Toronto: Methuen.

———. 1989. 'Immigration and the Production of a Teaching Force: Policy Implications for Education and Labour', *International Migration* 27, 4 (Dec.): 543–62.

———. 1993. 'From Subordinate Partners to Dependent Employees: State Regulation of Public School Teachers in Nineteenth Century British Columbia', *Labour/Le Travail* 31 (Spring): 75–110.

———. 1995a. 'The Incorporation of Public School Teachers into the Industrial Order: British Columbia in the First Half of the Twentieth Century', *Studies in Political Economy* 46 (Spring): 119–51.

———. 1995b. 'Multiculturalism and the Management of Race and Ethnic Relations in Canadian Schooling', in Wotherspoon and Paul Jungbluth, eds, *Multicultural Education in a Changing Global Economy: Canada and the Netherlands*. Munster: Waxmann, 41–60.

———. 1998. 'Education, Place, and the Sustainability of Rural Communities in Saskatchewan', *Journal of Research in Rural Education* 14, 3 (Winter): 131–41.

Yamamura, Brian, Saimanaaq Netser, and Nunia Qanatsiuq. 2003. 'Community Elders, Traditional Knowledge, and a Mathematics Curriculum Framework', *Education Canada* 43, 1 (Winter): 44–6.

Young, Jon, ed. 1987. *Breaking the Mosaic: Ethnic Identities in Canadian Schooling*. Toronto: Garamond Press.

——— and Benjamin Levin. 2002. *Understanding Canadian Schools: An Introduction to Educational Administration*, 3rd edn. Scarborough, Ont.: Thompson Nelson.

Young, Michael F.D., ed. 1971. *Knowledge and Control: New Directions for the Sociology of Education*. London: Collier-Macmillan.

Zakreski, Dan. 1996. 'Education Crisis Looming', *Saskatoon Star-Phoenix*, 16 Feb., A1–2.

Zeesman, Alan. 2001. 'HRDC Research on Children', in Pan-Canadian Education Research Agenda, *Children and Youth At-Risk Symposium Report*. Ottawa: Canadian Education Statistics Council, 5.

Index